Latino Mass Mobilization

In the spring of 2006, millions of Latinos across the country participated in the largest civil rights demonstrations in American history. In this timely and highly anticipated book, Chris Zepeda-Millán analyzes the background, course, and impacts of this unprecedented wave of protests, highlighting their unique local, national, and demographic dynamics. He finds that because of the particular ways the issue of immigrant illegality was racialized, federally proposed anti-immigrant legislation (H.R. 4437) helped transform Latinos' sense of latent group membership into the racial group consciousness that incited their engagement in large-scale collective action. Zepeda-Millán shows how nativist policy threats against disenfranchised undocumented immigrants can provoke a political backlash – on the streets and at the ballot box – from not only "people without papers" but also naturalized and U.S.-born citizens. *Latino Mass Mobilization* is an important intervention into contemporary debates regarding immigration policy, social movements, racial politics, and immigrant rights in the United States.

Chris Zepeda-Millán is an Assistant Professor in the Department of Ethnic Studies and Faculty Chair of the Center for Research on Social Change at UC Berkeley. He earned his Ph.D. from the Department of Government at Cornell University and his research on Latino politics, immigration, and social movements has been published in top political science and interdisciplinary academic journals. Professor Zepeda-Millán has been an invited contributor to and interviewed by various local, national, and international media outlets, including PBS, *Univision*, the Los Angeles Times, NBC Latino, and the Huffington Post.

Latino Mass Mobilization

Immigration, Racialization, and Activism

CHRIS ZEPEDA-MILLÁN
University of California, Berkeley

CAMBRIDGE
UNIVERSITY PRESS

CAMBRIDGE
UNIVERSITY PRESS

University Printing House, Cambridge CB2 8BS, United Kingdom

One Liberty Plaza, 20th Floor, New York, NY 10006, USA

477 Williamstown Road, Port Melbourne, VIC 3207, Australia

4843/24, 2nd Floor, Ansari Road, Daryaganj, Delhi - 110002, India

79 Anson Road, #06-04/06, Singapore 079906

Cambridge University Press is part of the University of Cambridge.

It furthers the University's mission by disseminating knowledge in the pursuit of education, learning, and research at the highest international levels of excellence.

www.cambridge.org
Information on this title: www.cambridge.org/9781107076945
DOI: 10.1017/9781139924719

First published 2017

Printed in the United States of America by Sheridan Books, Inc.

A catalogue record for this publication is available from the British Library.

ISBN 978-1-107-07694-5 Hardback
ISBN 978-1-107-43412-7 Paperback

Para mis abuelitos, Julia y Jorge Millán, Lupe y José Zepeda. *Su amor, sacrificio, y orgullo de ser mexicanos han servido como ejemplos que influenciaron mi formación, mis pensamientos,* y este libro. Los amo con todo mi corazón.

Contents

Figures

Tables

Acknowledgments

The first time I met renowned Chicano historian, Rudy Acuña, I had him sign my copy of his classic textbook, *Occupied America*. In his dedication he wrote, *"Una mano no se lava sola."* Much as with washing one's hands, writing a book is in many respects a collective – and often not so clean – endeavor. Accordingly, over the past decade, several people have supported me throughout the process of writing this manuscript. While each of them deserves their own personal dedication page, due to space constraints I am limited to only a brief mention of them to express my gratitude.

The members of my dissertation committee, Sidney Tarrow, Sarah Soule, and Maria Cristina Garcia, merit special recognition. I learned a great deal from you and appreciate all of your thoughtful and rigorous feedback. Thank you for believing in me, for pushing me to think beyond my specific case studies, and for your constant support. I am especially indebted to my dissertation chair, Michael Jones-Correa. I couldn't have asked for a better adviser; thanks for never making me choose among my family, politics, and scholarship. A number of colleagues, mentors, and institutions also helped me develop my research and/or have assisted me in other aspects of my career. They include: Denise Sandoval, Suyapa Portillo, Innael Miranda, Maymangwa Flying Earth, Carly Fox, Simon Velazquez, Deondra Rose, Phil Ayoub, Jamie Bleck, Idrissa Sidibe, Desmond Jagmohan, Igor Logvinenko, Pablo Yanguas, Janice Gallagher, Don Leonard, Simon Gilhooley, Pinar Kemerli, Julie Ajinkya, Ben Brake, David Lobenstine, David Cortez, Aileen Cardona-Arroyo, Jane Junn, Al Tillery, Celia Lacayo, Mark Sawyer, Tehama Lopez, Megan Ming Francis, Geoff Wallace, Alfonso Gonzales, Dan Gillion, Chris Lebron, Vessla

Weaver, Ricardo Ramirez, Stephen Nuño, Cristina Mora, Lisa Garcia Bedolla, Rodney Hero, Taeku Lee, Tianna Paschel, Poulomi Saha, Ron Hayduk, Caitlin Patler, Efren Perez, Paula McClain, Alan Gomez, Haven Perez, David Abalos, Matt Barreto, David Montejano, Silvia Monzano, Cristina Beltran, Claudia Sandoval, Adrian Felix, Denise Gonzales, Teresa Cappiali, Andrew Dilts, Sina Kramer, Lowell Turner, Fernando Guerra, Deena Gonzalez, Graciela Limon, Fernando Moreno, the Ford Foundation, the Departments of Political Science and Chicana/o Studies at Loyola Marymount University, and the Department of Ethnic Studies at UC Berkeley (especially the staff!). Cathy Cohen and Michael Dawson deserve special thanks for allowing me to spend a year at the University of Chicago's Center for the Study of Race, Politics, and Culture, where they provided me with the resources and time to substantially revise this manuscript and incorporate much of their valuable feedback. I also want to give a loud shout-out to my co-author and "academic sister," Sophia Jordán Wallace, for having so much confidence in my work and for reading this book more closely – and more times – than any editor or reviewer; we could finally start our next project!

Friends, comrades, and loved ones in Los Angeles were also integral to the successful completion of this book, and there are several on the "*leva*-list" worth noting. Stephanie, Carlos, Mike, Monika, Victor, Charlie, Veronica, Paco, Yoko, Felipe, Deziree, Jessica, Mixpe, Nancy, Steven Patrick, Elizabeth, Jordan, Cris R., Fr. Jim, Mr. J, Roberto, Xóchitl, Aura, Pasky, Ferndawg, Cati, Luz, Jake, Krista, James, Oriel, Olmeca, Eddie, Pablo, Sirena, and (even) Miguel, thank you for putting up with, helping to ground, and reminding me that there's more to life than books. Through our organizing and (often times literally endless) debates and discussions – from the streets of Los Angeles to the jungles of Chiapas – compañ@s from MEChA, the Human Rights Coalition, the Eastside Café, *Estación Libre, Casa del Pueblo*, and the Autonomous People's Collective, also influenced my thinking and political development (even if the content of this monograph might not always show it).

Other individuals whom I have come to know and highly respect through taking part in immigrant rights activism, and who deserve recognition, include: Xiomara Corpeño, Angelica Salas, Nativo Lopez, Fr. Richard Estrada, Arnoldo Garcia, Cathy Tactaquin, and Colin Rajah. Being able to hang out with, learn from, and interview my heroes (the people who organize for migrant rights on a daily basis), oftentimes made writing this book exciting, while at other times made it all the more difficult. I hope you can understand the constraints of academic standards, anonymous reviewers, and limiting my claims to the evidence I was able to gather in a relatively short period of time. I hope at least some of the findings in this book are relevant and helpful to the movement.

Last, but most importantly, are the members of both sides of my family. Throughout the course of writing this book we have been through tragedies – from illnesses to deaths – and triumphs – such as the births of many new members of our *familias* – which have only served to make us stronger and bring us closer together. Without your love and *apoyo*, I would have never survived graduate school and could not survive academia. Collectively and individually, we have journeyed from rural and urban Mexico, to the agricultural fields of the Southwestern United States, to the garment factories of downtown Los Angeles, to the halls of the most prestigious universities in this country. This book is as much the fruit of your labor as it is of mine. Thus, in no particular order, *les quiero dar las gracias a las familias:* Millán, Zepeda, Chávez, Salinas, López, Chidiac, Hernández, Gallo, Morales, Torres, Hamelius, and Landeros (I hope I didn't forget anyone!). Of course, I am especially grateful to my parents, Debbie Millán and John Zepeda. Mom, your unconditional love, empathy for others, constant reminders of the importance of education, and amazing accomplishments (from buying a home on your own to raising me as a single mother to beating cancer – twice!) continue to inspire and sustain me. Dad, you showed me the value of hard work and instilled in me the drive to prove those who doubt us wrong. I would have never finished school without your support. *Los amo mucho* and strive everyday to make you proud.

Chris Zepeda-Millán
Boyle Heights, East L.A.
January 9, 2017
c/s

Introduction

> Instead of a sleeping giant awakened, it's more likely that the giant immigrant workforce never had time to fall asleep to begin with. The immigrant community has been too busy working double and triple shifts harvesting crops, tending gardens, washing dishes, building homes, and taking care of other people's children ... Sometimes the struggle is quiet at work; sometimes it is loud on the streets; there are relative successes along with relative failures – but it has never been asleep ... It might, instead, be the "experts," politicians, and the media ... that has been awakened to the fact that vast portions of the United States are made up of immigrants who will mobilize when threatened ... Hopefully history will get it right this time.[1]
> – Aura Bogado, immigrant journalist April 18, 2006

The spring of 2006 exploded with a historic wave of protests across the United States. The primarily Latino immigrant rights mobilizations that occurred captured the nation's attention with a series of mass demonstrations coupled with various other forms of dissent – both peaceful and militant – ranging from school walkouts and hunger strikes to boycotts and candlelight prayer vigils. During one action in Dallas, Texas, students, priests, and individuals in wheelchairs rallied alongside Iraqi war veterans, small business owners, and senior citizens walking with canes. As they descended on the city's downtown streets, this "sea of people" – by some estimates, up to half a million large – chanted *"Si se puede!"* and carried homemade signs that read, "Today we march. Tomorrow we vote!"[2] Protests erupted in rural and unexpected places as well. In Siler City, North Carolina, for example, "More than 4,000 people, most donning white shirts and waving US flags, crammed into the streets for a march to the same town hall where former-KKK Grand Wizard, David

Duke, once delivered an anti-immigrant speech."[3] Local organizers had originally planned for a permitted rally of no more than 200 participants, but as one of them later recalled, "We started the march with about 2,000 people, and we had close to twice that many by the time we ended it." She added, "One of the most amazing images" of the action "was going street to street and seeing the invisible become visible, seeing people come out of their homes and basements and waiting on street corners to join the march."[4]

The protests took many forms, individual and collective alike, but they all had a common target: *The Border Protection, Antiterrorism, and Illegal Immigration Control Act of 2005*, more commonly known as H.R. 4437, or the "Sensenbrenner Bill."[5] In addition to severely increasing border control and interior immigration enforcement measures, the proposed law sought to change the penalty for being undocumented from a mere civil violation to a federal felony. The bill also intended to punish individuals who assisted – even in the most basic ways – any of the nation's estimated 11 million "people without papers" (undocumented immigrants), by threatening to impose monetary fines and incarceration, potentially criminalizing everyone from teachers and family members to employers and social service providers.

As the marches spread, their historical significance became more and more apparent. Many asserted that "everyone who participated" would remember them "for the rest of their lives"; indeed, the outbursts, as massive as they were varied, were unprecedented (Shore 2006). Members of labor unions, religious groups, hometown associations, and community organizations joined the national "We Are American Alliance" or one of the many citywide "calendar coalitions" (e.g., Chicago's March 10 Coalition and Boston's May Day Committee) that sprouted across the nation to organize local rallies. But the preponderance of protesters were people who did not belong to any of these groups and had never participated in political activism. The bulk of these actions took place across four months, from February to May, and by the end of the protest wave, up to five million people had partaken in close to 400 demonstrations from coast to coast (Wallace, Zepeda-Millán, and Jones-Correa 2014). In all likelihood, the April 10 "National Day of Action for Immigrant Justice" and May 1 "Great American Boycott/Day Without an Immigrant" were the largest civil rights actions in U.S. history, the biggest immigrant rights protests the world has ever witnessed, and marked the dawn of what we understand as contemporary Latino politics (Fraga et al. 2010: 1; Bloemraad, Voss, and Lee 2011: 4).[6]

Although, like so much of the recent past in our fast-moving world, these momentous events may already feel like a distant memory, they have much to teach us. As a group of leading political scientists recently acknowledged, "almost nothing we 'know' about Latinos from the work of social scientists and humanists would have predicted these events" (Fraga et al. 2010: 1). Bringing together insights from scholarship on racial politics, immigration, and social movements, this book offers the first systematic analysis of the 2006 immigrant rights protest wave. Beginning with an overarching theoretical explanation for its emergence, I then zoom in and focus on the local processes and mechanisms that composed the national series of demonstrations through an examination of key episodes of collective action on the West Coast, East Coast, and in the Southern United States. I investigate what accounts for the wave's sudden rise and abrupt decline, theorize explanations for the different degrees of mobilization across varying geographic locations, and examine what – if any – impacts the mass marches had on immigration policy reform efforts and electoral politics. In the process, I hope to reveal how a specific type of legislative threat politicized the collective identities of millions of Latinos and, to a lesser extent, other minority groups with large immigrant populations, in turn making them receptive to calls for mass mobilization. What we know, in retrospect, is that this wave was both created and then ridden by longtime activists and by people who had never held a banner or marched in a rally. This incredibly varied group of individuals appropriated and activated community resources and institutions that already existed, disseminating their calls for protest through ethnic media outlets and organizing one of the largest cycles of coordinated mass mobilizations ever to occur. But while this basic narrative is now clear, there is much that is not.

The Surprising Emergence of the 2006 Protest Wave

American Political Behavior

Research on political behavior in the United States has traditionally shown that the "resources of time, money, and skills are powerful predictors of political participation" (Verba, Schlozman, and Brady 1995: 285); thus, it is a longstanding truism that "the wealthy, the educated, and the partisan" are most likely to be targeted by politicians and political parties for mobilization in electoral politics (Rosenstone and Hansen 2003: 32). In addition, contrary to common belief, although protests are generally thought of as instigated by a society's socially and economically marginalized members, scholars have found that the poor are actually less likely to participate in political activism (Verba, Schlozman, and Brady 1995: 191; Schussman and Soule 2005). Not surprisingly, given these findings, racial and ethnic minorities have likewise been shown to partake in both electoral politics (e.g., voting) and non-electoral politics (e.g., attending marches or rallies) at lower levels than white Americans (Schlozman and Brady 1995: 234–235; Rosenstone and Hansen 2003: 77; Leighly and Nagler 2013). Since immigrants of color in general, and Latinos (both U.S.- and foreign-born) in particular, were the majority of the 2006 protesters, exploring the factors that influence their political engagement may help us better understand this cycle of contention.

Because citizenship is a prerequisite to vote, many scholars of immigrant politics have traditionally focused on naturalization as a key barrier to immigrant political integration (DeSipio 1996; Jones-Correa 1998; Bloemraad 2006). For example, Jones-Correa (1998) notes that while longer lengths of stay in the U.S. increase the likelihood that an immigrant will embark on this process, both the "myth of return" to their homeland and neglect by local political elites and institutions (e.g., political parties) produce a "politics of in-between" that thwarts, or at least slows, efforts at naturalization. Nonetheless, some studies have shown that with the assistance of "social helpers," such as local community-based organizations, unions, and churches, even if mobilization is small in scale, immigrants can sometimes be marshaled to naturalize (Bloemraad 2006) and take part in forms of both mainstream (de Graauw 2016) and unconventional politics (Wong 2006).

Similarly, research shows that although Latinos have lower levels of political engagement when compared to other racial groups (Leighly and Nagler 2013), they also tend to participate more when recruited to do so, especially when asked by a co-ethnic or someone they know (Michelson 2005: 98; Barreto and Nuño 2009). Voter turnout among Latinos also increases with the size of their population (Barreto, Segura, and Woods 2004), because they become more likely to be targeted by political elites in "get-out-the-vote" (GOTV) efforts (Leighley 2001: 171). Furthermore, studies have shown that Latino registration and voting increases in hostile political contexts, suggesting an electoral response to perceived political threats (Barreto and Woods 2005). When disaggregating the Latino electorate by nativity, research suggests that recent immigrants are less likely to participate in politics than their U.S.-born counterparts (DeSipio 1996; Leal 2002; Highton and Burris 2002; Wong 2006). In general, foreign-born Latinos not only "tend to have the age, education, and income characteristics of the electoral nonparticipants" (De la Garza and DeSipio 1997: 108), they also are less civically engaged in the types of organizations that facilitate participation and that political elites target for mobilization (Garcia 2003: 98, 183). But this is not always the case.

In a notable study examining foreign-born voter turnout, Barreto (2005) found that "with extensive mobilization drives targeting naturalized voters," Latino immigrants were actually "significantly more likely to vote than were ... native-born Latinos" (79). And, in terms of context, Ramakrishnan and Espenshade (2001) have shown that the presence of anti-immigrant legislation has a positive effect on electoral participation among immigrants (870). Other studies find that immigrants who naturalize in a hostile political (i.e., nativist) environment express increased levels of political awareness, are more likely to see race as a salient issue, and participate at higher levels than cohorts who become citizens during relatively apolitical periods (Pantoja, Ramirez, and Segura 2001; Pantoja and Segura 2003). These findings imply that despite lacking some of the traditional resources associated with political participation and often not being targeted for mobilization, Latino electoral engagement can increase in certain political environments – such as in times of serious political threat.

To fully understand the dynamics of the 2006 protest wave and its aftermath, however, it is also essential to examine what we know about Latino – both immigrant and U.S.-born – involvement in political activism prior to 2006. According to Marquez and Jennings (2000), "social movement organizations were often the only outlets for political representation and self-defense in a society where Latinos were outnumbered and barred from effective participation in the institutions of government." They contend, "Latino organizations generated a leadership cadre and served as vehicles through which interests of class, gender, occupation, and ideology were mediated through the lens of race" (541). But, in spite of a rich history of activism (for examples see Muñoz 1989; Torres and Velazquez 1998; Torres and Katsiaficas 1999; Fantasia and Voss 2004; Ruiz and Sanchez Korrol 2005; Blackwell 2011), polling data have traditionally shown that Latinos are less likely to participate in contentious politics compared to other racial and ethnic groups (Verba, Schlozman, and Brady 1995: 234–235; Leighly and Nagler 2013). Moreover, survey research has revealed that Latino immigrants in particular are significantly less likely than U.S.-born Latinos to engage in non-electoral political activities, including protests (Leal 2002: 361; Martinez 2008: 197; Martinez 2005; Bloemraad, Voss, and Lee 2011: 19).

Yet, as mentioned earlier, Latinos – both U.S.- and foreign-born – made up the vast majority of participants in the 2006 rallies. In fact, second and third generation Latinos were just as likely to attend the demonstrations as recently arrived Latino immigrants were (Barreto et al. 2009: 753; see also Pallares and Flores-Gonzales 2010: xvi). Consequently, as informative as previous research on Latino and immigrant political behavior has been in elucidating the political incorporation of these groups, they are nonetheless theoretically limited in their ability to explain the dynamics of the historic series of immigrant rights demonstrations. These studies are insufficient because of two reasons. Either (a) they restrict their investigations to voting and naturalization, in effect neglecting more contentious forms of politics (e.g., protests) as well as the participation of the undocumented and those with little, if any, chance of gaining citizenship (see DeSipio 1996; Jones-Correa 1998; Ramkrishnan and Espenshade 2001; Ramakrishnan 2005; Bloemraad 2006; Fraga et al. 2011). Or (b) when they do focus on overt forms of political activism and do consider people without papers, they fail to adequately integrate the valuable insights of social movement theory into their analyses (see Garcia Bedolla 2005; Wong 2006; Pallares and Flores-Gonzalez 2010; Garcia-Rios and Barreto 2016).[7]

Social Movement Theory

The dominant paradigm in the study of social movements, known as "political process theory," maintains that four major factors help generate insurgency: first, and foremost, the confluences of expanding political opportunity structures; second, the establishment of "indigenous organizational strength" (because of their networks, leadership, and resources); third, the "presence of certain shared cognitions" (a feeling of perceived injustice that is subject to change through collective action) within the insurgent group; and last, but not least, the "shifting control response of other groups to the movement" (from state officials to countermovements) (59). Key dimensions of political opportunity structures include: "1) the opening of access to participation for new actors; 2) the evidence of political realignment within the polity; 3) the appearance of influential allies; 4) emerging splits within the elite; and 5) a decline in the state's capacity or will to repress dissent" (Tarrow 1998: 76). Through their political process approach – and its expanding opportunity thesis – these theorists have gone a long way toward helping us comprehend the social, economic, and historic foundations of social movements; the political contexts in which they emerge, do battle, and decline; the institutional barriers they face; their chances for success; the organizational structures they utilize; and various other aspects of major protest waves and political activism (see Tilly 1978; McAdam 1982; Tarrow 1998; Koopmans 2004; Kriesi 2004).

Yet as much as these theorists have contributed to our understanding of social movements, critics argue that their notions of "political opportunities" are not only too broad but also have structural biases that tend to ignore the role that grievances and emotions play in the emergence of contention (Goodwin and Jasper 2004: 5–9; Klandermans 2004: 362). For instance, while some movements have risen up to take advantage of expanding opportunities, others have emerged when the "window of opportunity" seemed to be contracting if not outright closed (Meyer 1993: 37; Ayoub 2016: 15). These movements thus appear to respond not to opportunities per se, but to some type of contextual danger or threat.

External threats have often been conceptualized as "the other side," or the opposite, of opportunities; the standard argument is that as threats rise, opportunities decline. But according to Goldstone and Tilly (2001), a "group may also decide to risk protest, even if opportunities seem absent, if the costs of not acting seem too great" (181–183; see also Buerchler 2004: 61; Almeida 2012; Piven and Cloward 1977). Consequently, prominent social movement theorists have concluded that, "Threats and opportunities co-occur, and most people engaging in contentious politics combine response to threat with seizing opportunities" (Tilly and Tarrow 2006: 58). They add, however, that "it is only when a threat is accompanied by perceived opportunities for action and seen as potentially irreversible if not stopped that challengers will risk what often turns out to be a heroic defeat" (Tarrow 1998: 72). Thus, research on activism now takes a more "dynamic" approach (McAdam, Tilly, and Tarrow 2001) and acknowledges the significance of organizations, resources, networks, culture, coalitions, and emotions to the development of collective action (Jasper 2014; Van Dyke and McCammon 2010; della Porta and Diani 2006), as well as the importance of understanding the political contexts (e.g., opportunities and threats) in which social movements arise, attempt to bring their goals to fruition, and ultimately wane (Klandermans and Roggeband 2010: Buechler 2011; Tarrow 2011; Paschel 2016). That said, social movement scholars have nonetheless under-theorized how different dimensions of threat can impact collective action in different ways. As I argue below, the immigrant rights demonstrations can help shed light on this lacuna.

The 2006 protest wave is an example of large-scale collective action emerging during a time of great political threat and closed, or constricted, opportunities. There are three primary reasons why this characterization fits: (a) the Republican Party (the more anti-immigrant of the two major U.S. political parties) controlled every branch of the federal government;(b) the post-9/11 nativist context in which the marches arose (Abrejano and Hajnal 2015; Gulasekaram and Ramakrishnan 2015; Sampaio 2016); and, perhaps most importantly, (c) the looming legislative threat (H.R. 4437) that rally organizers and participants responded to (Barreto et al., 2009; Pallares and Flores-Gonzalez 2010).[8] This last point is in line with Okamoto and Ebert's (2010) important study that found a positive correlation between nativist legislation and immigrant rights protests, which they speculate may be related to how the former impacts immigrant identity. Unfortunately, their survey data do not allow these authors to further investigate this possibility. Consequently, Okamoto and Ebert (2010) call for future research to "explore the processes and mechanisms" underlying the relationship between threat, identity, and immigrant activism (552). Bloemraad et al. (2011) agree and assert that "a more nuanced account" of the role that "threat and perceptions of threat" played in the 2006 mobilizations is needed to advance our theoretical understanding of this extraordinary series of events (29).

It is my hope that this book will begin to help answer these important questions, given how little we know about the relationship between immigration, social movements, and racial politics (Menjivar 2010; 18). To do so, *Latino Mass Mobilization: Immigration, Racialization, and Activism*, spotlights the actions and motivations that inspired and shaped the trajectory of the historic 2006 protest wave. We will gain these broad insights via a narrow focus on three specific locations (Fort Myers, FL, Los Angeles, CA, and New York, NY), and on what I see as the key commonalities that enabled the mass marches in these places: the utilization of local community resources, the formation of diverse coalitions, and the use of ethnic media outlets to broadcast calls for protests and electoral mobilization. But before we can understand how these unprecedented actions materialized and what explains their varying levels of success, as the scholars cited above observe, we must first grasp the uniqueness of the threat under which they arose and why it impacted certain group identities, particularly specific Latino identities.

Explaining the Emergence of the 2006 Protest Wave

As we get a handle on the particular dimensions of H.R. 4437, we must acknowledge a confounding reality: the argument that the rallies were simply a response to a legislative threat is insufficient (Barreto et al., 2009; Pallares and Flores-Gonzalez 2010; Bloemraad, Voss, and Lee 2011). Prior to the demonstrations, several other federal anti-immigrant laws, such as the REAL-ID and the Patriot Acts, were not only proposed but also enacted without provoking any mass public opposition, including among Latinos. Furthermore, during and subsequent to the anti-H.R. 4437 marches, increases in the number of deportations, workplace raids, hate crimes, and other anti-immigrant measures and attacks did not prompt large-scale collective action. As such, the notion that the mobilizations were merely a manifestation of solidarity with and among undocumented immigrants and their allies, triggered by a proposed anti-immigrant law, is equally unsatisfactory. People without papers were arguably more threatened and under attack after the mass marches than they were before them, yet the protest wave declined rather than escalated. Thus, the 2006 cycle of contention is a useful case in which to explore the different roles that threats can play in mobilization and demobilization processes.

The work of Snow et al. (1998) helps us begin to conceptualize these dynamics. Specifically, these scholars argue "that the kind of breakdown most likely to be associated with movement emergence is that which penetrates and disrupts, or threatens to disrupt, taken-for-granted, everyday routines and expectancies" (2). The four conditions the authors claim "are especially likely to disrupt the quotidian and heighten prospects of collective action," are: (a) sudden "community disrupting accidents and disasters"; (b) the "actual or threatened intrusion into or violation of culturally defined zones of privacy and control," including people's families, neighborhoods, and sense of safety; (c) an "alteration of taken-for-granted subsistence routines as a result of an emergent disparity between available resources and resource demand"; and (d) "dramatic changes in structures of social control" (1, 6). When movements are *not* based on quotidian disruptions, Snow et al. (1998) believe that they must instead "be rich in the cultural work of framing and identity construction" (18).

According to immigrant rights activists, H.R. 4437 embodied many of these disruptions. That so much of the country – individuals ranging from teachers, doctors, employers, priests and family members, to institutions such as unions, service agencies, businesses, and community-based organizations – could be fined thousands of dollars and/or incarcerated for helping or even just interacting with undocumented immigrants, was a potentially sudden and dramatic change to the normal activities of thousands of organizations and millions of U.S.- and foreign-born people across the nation. Hence, it was not simply a legislative threat that catalyzed the massive immigrant rights mobilizations but – more generally – a threat that would have radically altered the daily lives, relations, and routine functions of several sectors of society that inter- act with immigrant communities, particularly Latino immigrant commu- nities. Because of the Sensenbrenner Bill's severity and reach, immigrant rights activists asserted that immigrants and their allies had no choice but to respond. As a naturalized citizen who helped organize a local march in her city declared, "The law was just made with so much hate ... it was an all or nothing thing."[9]

Snow et al.'s (1998) notion of "disrupting the quotidian" contributes significantly to our understanding of how the *scope* – the level of severity and reach – of a threat can help spark collective action. However, their the- ory has a central limitation: it underestimates the crucial role that identity can simultaneously play in quotidian disruptions and collective responses to these disruptions. Their claim that movements not sparked by threats to "the quotidian" must be rich in identity, suggests that a group's race, for example, is detached from the issues of "safety," "neighborhood," "cul- ture," and "resources" (Snow et al. 1998: 8). Yet nothing could be further from the truth for people of color (e.g., Latinos, Asian-, Arab-, Native-, and African-Americans) in the United States. Research has continuously shown that issues such as segregation, poverty, policing, and public safety are intricately linked and cannot be parceled from their racial identities due to the central role that racism has and continues to play in Ameri- can politics (Bonilla Silva 2001; Lerman and Weaver 2014; McAdam and Kloos 2014) and socioeconomic inequalities (Massey 2007; De Genova 2002; Soss and Fording 2011). Whether resisting settler colonialism, Jim Crow laws, police brutality, housing discrimination, punitive immigra- tion policies, or disenfranchisement, race has often been the primary lens through which people of color in the U.S. recognize and fight against the injustices and "quotidian disruptions" they endure; in fact, their race was often the principal reason why they suffered these persecutions in the first place.

The 2006 immigrant rights protests teach us that threats have multiple dimensions – including not only their *scope* (whether they are broad or narrow) but also their *source, timing,* and *visibility* – whose interactions influence mobilization and demobilization processes. For people of color in the United States, race can be the principal thread that binds these dimensions and the primary lens through which they are understood and acted upon. Therefore, comprehending how the multiple dimensions of a threat influence the identities and actions of individuals is essential and the task I now turn to.

The Multiple Dimensions of Threat

Single-Source Threats, Narrow vs. Broad. Insights gained from my interviews with local and national activists suggest that threats that are narrow and emerge from a single source generate either no or a low degree of collective action. An example of one such single-source and narrow threat is the 2005 REAL-ID Act; despite its anti-immigrant ramifications, the bill failed to produce a significant level of opposition among immigrant rights activists. The bill, which emerged from Congress – a "single source" – was narrow, or limited, in that its primary target was a particular segment of society (undocumented immigrants), and its effects were indirect. The REAL-ID Act did not pass as a stand-alone piece of immigration legislation, but as an attachment to a military spending bill, the 2005 Emergency Supplemental Appropriations Act for Defense, the Global War on Terror, and Tsunami Relief. Furthermore, the law did not explicitly focus on undocumented immigrants but targeted them circuitously by establishing national standards (such as proof of legal residency or a valid social security number) for state identification cards and driver licenses. Yet, considering that most states did not – and still do not – offer undocumented immigrants driver licenses, the bill's effects were narrow, only impacting people without papers living in particular states. Consequently, activists were unable to form the broad coalitions that are often sparked by political threats (McCammon and Campbell 2002; Van Dyke 2003; Tattesall 2010: 155), and which were needed to effectively oppose the bill; thus, the level of mobilization against it was minimal.

The Sensenbrenner Bill (H.R. 4437), by contrast, emerged from the same single source (Congress), but had a potential impact that was far broader. There are three reasons why. For one, it would have equally affected *all* people without papers across the country (regardless of the state in which they resided) by elevating their undocumented status from a civil violation to a felony. Furthermore, H.R. 4437 would have impacted a wide range of individuals beyond undocumented immigrants by punishing them for assisting people without papers. And third, since the vast majority of undocumented immigrants are Latino, and the vast majority of Latinos are either foreign-born themselves or "are children, spouses, in-laws, and neighbors" of immigrants (Pedraza, Segura, and Bowler (2011: 2), the Sensenbrenner Bill could have broadly impacted the largest minority group in the United States. As a local organizer explained, "Whether they [the supporters of the bill] knew it or not ... [H.R.4437] actually criminalized whole sectors of our society."[10] Thus, because the proposed legislation came from a single source, could have significantly impacted several segments of society, and disproportionately threatened millions of Latinos, activists opposing it were able to form large coalitions to mass mobilize against it.

Multiple-Source Threats, Narrow vs. Broad. When threats emerge from multiple sources, discerning responsibility for their consequences becomes more difficult. The time and resources necessary for addressing threats that lack a single focal point also dilute the impact of activists' oppositional efforts. Anti-immigrant measures such as raids, deportations, and nativist local and state legislations are examples of dispersed threats that come from multiple sources and that typically have a narrow impact. For example, raids and deportations are threats that come from what can be a bewildering variety of federal, and sometimes state and local, law enforcement agents who carry them out in different settings – workplaces, homes, and city streets – across the country (Golash-Boza 2012; Macias-Rojas 2016; Escobar 2016). Similarly, there are many state and local ordinances that negatively affect undocumented immigrants; the multiple sources here are the hundreds of towns, cities, and state governments that propose and/or adopt them (Gulsekaram and Ramakrishnan 2015). Although these threats could potentially victimize all people without papers, their effects are narrow in scope in being primarily felt at the individual level and limited to the people who are apprehended (and their families), or to those who live within the jurisdictions of the nativist laws. Therefore, forming broad coalitions to protest these policies is challenging and generally instigates little to no collective action against them.

The scope of these kinds of threats can expand when there is a sudden rise in their occurrence, when the number of people impacted by them is relatively large, or when they are carried out on a national scale. Any combination of these factors creates a multi-source threat that is broad, rather than narrow. Not surprisingly, the difficulties of organizing against this type of threat, whether narrow or broad, remain. As a result, multiple-source threats can hamper an emerging movement and can lead to the suppression of future contention. As we will see, during and after the 2006 marches, the Department of Homeland Security intentionally increased workplace raids and deportations around the country. Simultaneous was a rapid escalation in state and local immigration-related measures, most of which were punitive (Gulsekaram and Ramakrishnan 2015). With their broad geographic scale, dramatic increase, concurrence with other local enforcement measures, and impact beyond undocumented immigrants, my research indicates that these factors notably contributed to the demobilization of the 2006 immigrant rights demonstrations.

Timing and Visibility. Two additional dimensions – *timing* and *visibility* – interact with the *scope* and *source* of a threat to explicate their relationship to mobilization. These features are particularly important to the type of threat that led to the rise and decline of the immigrant rights protest wave. Needless to say, a movement is most effective when it has a clear target and sufficient time to organize its attack. Given the sluggishness of the federal policymaking process, legislative threats, such as bills introduced in Congress, are one such clear target: they represent looming threats, and thus activists have time to organize against them. Having enough time to form coalitions to oppose a single-source threat with far-reaching impacts is imperative because alliances "that unite organizations and pool resources are able to stage events with more participants, finance larger campaigns, and sustain actions for longer periods – increasing the likelihood of success" (Mayer 2009, 13). Conversely, threats such as raids and deportation, are more difficult to fight because organizers become aware of them only after they occur, and can therefore only deal with their consequences. A local activist captured these difficulties best when she described her group's unsuccessful attempts to organize against "decentralized" immigration raids as running around "like a chicken with your head cut off" trying to "put out fires."[11]

However, regardless of the amount of time activists have to organize around an external danger, a threat "is not a sufficient condition for collective action. The perception of threat must be shared," as "must a perception that the source" of that threat is subject to being stopped or alleviated by collective action (Flacks 2004: 148). Fundamental to these perceptions is a threat's visibility. How easily potential victims and activists are able to become aware of a threat, understand the likely effects of it and the need to act against it, determines that threat's visibility.[12] A key mechanism in that awareness and understanding is the mass media (Kriesi 2004: 86; McCarthy, McPhail, and Smith 1996). Radio, television, and print journalism have various abilities: these types of media outlets can bring attention to certain issues and legitimize the groups involved, can signal political elites about citizens' discontents, and can even help inspire, or diffuse, protests (Meyer 2007, 96; McCarthy, McPhail, and Smith 1996, 478; Meyer and Minkoff 2004, 1475).

Narrow threats (whether single-source or multiple-source) are harder to make visible because of the limited number of people they affect. These types of threats fail to draw the media attention needed to make a large number of people aware of the necessity to mobilize against them. Conversely, broad threats are easier to make visible simply because their effects are more pervasive. The greater the scope of the threat – in terms of severity and number of individuals it impacts – the more likely media outlets are to cover it. Therefore, if activists are successful in drawing the attention of major news outlets, they have the potential to broadcast their claims and calls for action across a large geographical area. As detailed in Chapter 3, because of the severity and far-ranging nature of H.R. 4437, immigrant rights activists gained access to ethnic media and promoted their calls for mass protests to millions of people across the country.

Notably, the visibility of a threat can be a double-edged sword. Although fundamental to the rise of contention, visibility can also contribute to demobilization. As documented in Chapter 5, the multiple-source threats of raids, deportations, and local anti-immigrant measures contributed to the decline of the demonstrations because they were extensively covered by Spanish-language news outlets. According to activists interviewed in every city examined in this book, widespread coverage of the escalation of immigration enforcement measures – and their effects on Latino families and communities – frightened and alerted immigrants and allies throughout the nation that there was a price to pay for their continued activism.

Whether impacting the rise or decline of mobilization, the content of this visibility – in terms of what it means to the individuals being targeted by the threat – and who its disseminated to, is vital. As McAdam (1982) keenly notes, the mediating factor between contexts and action "are people and the subjective meanings they attach to their situations" (48). When individuals share a common identity or language, the media can indirectly help to diffuse protests, making contention contagious by promoting solidarity and inspiring others like them in different and unconnected locations to emulate the various tactics and strategies they witness on television, hear on the radio, or read about in newspapers (Spilerman 1976; McAdam and Rucht 1993; Myers 2000; Soule 2004). This is especially true when members of the media themselves share a common identity with their audiences and when that common identity is under attack, as was the case in 2006 with Spanish-language news outlets and Latino immigrant rights activists.

In sum, any meaningful threat has multiple and crosscutting dimensions, which can impact identity and collective action in a variety of ways. The 2006 protest wave was sparked by one such combination of these particularities. The Sensenbrenner Bill was a legislative threat that derived from a *single source* and was *looming, highly visible,* and *generalized in scope.* When these external factors converged, Latino and other immigrant rights activists recognized the need for mass mobilization, formed broad organizational alliances, and clearly framed and diffused their demands and proposed actions to as many potential participants as possible. For this to occur, a sense of group consciousness and linked fate was triggered – to varying degrees – among organizers and participants because of the racialized nature of the proposed legislation and public debate it sparked. As argued below, when individuals can clearly discern that both their material interests and collective identities are being threatened, regular people can be provoked into taking astonishing actions.

The Importance of Identity

Social movement scholars define a collective identity as "an act of the imagination, a trope that stirs people to action by arousing feelings of solidarity with their fellows and by defining moral boundaries against other categories" (Jasper and McGarry 2015: 1). Research has shown that the existence of a collective identity is a necessary precursor to participating in collective action (Friedman and McAdam 1992: 156; Snow and Soule 2010: 125) because it helps people see themselves as "linked by interests, values, [or] common histories" (Della Porta and Diani 1999: 109; Fantasia 1988). Students of contentious politics assert that the more one identifies with a group, the more likely one is to take part in activism on behalf of that group (Hunt and Benford 2004: 437; Klandermans 2003: 687). When people see themselves as sharing a common identity, their "solidarity and motivation to work together" is enhanced (Smith and Bandy 2005: 10; Barvosa-Carter 2001; Mayer 2009). Several studies have shown that hostile environments can increase the salience of collective identities (Bernstein 2003: 244; Klandermans 2003, 682) and foster a willingness to join political coalitions (Van Dyke 2003; Tattesall 2010: 155) and participate in protests (Klandermans and de Weerd 2000: 86). Thus, examining how collective identities develop, are made salient, and are politicized is of the utmost importance when attempting to explain episodes of widespread activism by racialized groups such as Latinos. The concepts of "group consciousness" and "linked fate" are instructive in helping us understand this process.

Political scientists define group consciousness as a form of in-group identification that is politicized "by a set of ideological beliefs about one's group social standing, as well as a view that collective action is the best means by which the group can improve its status and realize its interests" (McClain et al. 2009: 476). The notion of linked fate draws from this concept but differs in that it "explicitly links perceptions of self-interest to perceptions of racial group interests" (Dawson 1994: 76). According to Dawson (1994), linked fate captures a situation in which racial group interests serve as "a useful proxy for self-interest" (77). Because these concepts were largely developed using the case of African-Americans and their shared history of oppression (Dawson 1994; McClain et al. 2009: 479), however, the issues, costs, and incentives that trigger feelings of linked fate and group consciousness are likely to be different for other groups (Junn and Masouka 2008: 729; Sanchez and Masouka 2010; Vargas et al. 2017). For Latinos, this "identity-to-politics link" (Lee 2008) seems to be activated by nativist government policies and public sentiments.

Several studies have shown that Latino group consciousness is more pronounced when they perceive group discrimination, especially when these feelings are related to issues associated with immigration (Zepeda-Millán, Street, and Jones-Correa 2015; Valdez 2011; Sanchez 2006a; Sanchez 2006b; Garcia Bedolla 2005). These results are critical to highlight because the presence of Latino-linked fate and group consciousness is positively correlated with several elements relevant to the 2006 protest wave: higher voting rates (Medina Vidal 2016; Stokes 2003; Sanchez 2006a), Spanish-language media consumption (Kerevel 2011; Medina Vidal 2016; Garcia-Rios and Barreto 2016), support for more liberal immigration policies (Sanchez 2006b), and feelings of commonality with other racial groups (Jones-Correa, Wallace, and Zepeda-Millán 2016). Thus, investigating why Latino identity and immigration policies are so intertwined is fundamental to understanding these findings and their degree of relevance to the historic groundswell of demonstrations.

Researchers have shown that, irrespective of their citizenship status or generation, anti-immigrant sentiments have created and sustained a sense of collective identity among people of Mexican descent (Telles and Ortiz 2009; Jimenez 2010). Given that Mexicans are the largest and oldest Latino national origin group in the U.S., experts believe that, "To the extent that boundary work and framing are carried out within American society to position Mexicans as a racialized 'other,' these processes are bound to have spillover effects on other Latinos" (Massey 2007: 116). Consequently, according to Massey and Sanchez (2010), "rising anti-immigrant sentiment, repressive immigration and border enforcement, and the public portrayal of Latino immigrants as criminals, invaders, and terrorists" has reinforced the emergence of a panethnic Latino identity (212). Because the alleged negative attributes of Latino immigrants are often generalized to U.S.-born Latinos (Bloch 2014: 3; Johnson 2004), a growing body of evidence suggests that this leads to both Latino citizens and non-citizens being viewed as potential "illegal alien threats" (Chavez 2008; Allegro 2010, 174; Ponce 2014; Sampaio 2015). Thus, that "illegal" immigration is negatively racialized as synonymous with people of Latin American descent has played a vital role in shaping the collective identity of Latinos in the United States (Rocco 2014; Abrajano and Lundgren 2014; Zepeda-Millán, Street, and Jones-Correa 2015). As Acuña puts it, "regardless of their actual legal status," racist nativism in America "does not distinguish one Brown person from another, citizen from immigrant, recent immigrant from second generation" (quoted in De Genova 2006: 12).

Although extremely informative in helping us comprehend how immigration policies help cultivate the development of a collective Latino identity, current research fails to explain exactly how or why nativism motivates Latinos to participate in collective action to combat this type of discrimination.[13] In other words, what are the mechanisms that link nativism, Latino identity, and political activism? My contention is that when broadened and racialized, legislative threats against disenfranchised undocumented immigrants can provoke a political backlash – on the streets and at the ballot box – against those deemed responsible for the attacks, not only from people without papers but also electorally armed naturalized- and U.S.-born citizens. Depending on the type of threat and the degree to which they feel under attack, activists can rouse racialized immigrants and their descendants to use nativist actions as a heuristic that prods increased political participation. I find that when anti-immigrant policies threaten Latinos directly as individuals (e.g., their material interests) and indirectly as part of a larger collective (e.g., their identities), their sense of latent group membership can be transformed into a racial group consciousness that incites their engagement in mass mobilizations.

All in all, the 2006 immigrant rights demonstrations remind us that protest waves are neither linear nor static; they are dynamic affairs. Factors both outside and inside of movements can change the environments from which they emerge, as well as the mobilizing structures and individuals who take part in them. All of these elements can impact and alter each other, causing an array of effects ranging from escalated reaction to submission and inaction. In this fashion, many of the same factors (i.e., threats, coalitions, the media, etc.) that contributed to the rise of the historic immigrant rights marches also played a role in their demise and in the redirection of the movement. More specifically, as this book will illustrate, H.R. 4437 triggered feelings of linked fate and racial group consciousness among millions of Latinos in general, but people of Mexican descent in particular – and, to a lesser extent, members of other minority groups with large immigrant populations – in turn making them more responsive to calls for mass mobilization. Both professional organizers and people who had never participated in activism appropriated and activated community resources and institutions that already existed, disseminating their calls for action through ethnic media outlets and organizing what became one of the largest cycles of coordinated protests ever to occur in the U.S. On top of helping stop H.R. 4437 from becoming law, the demonstrations incited a predominately anti-Latino backlash that contributed, along with several intra-movement factors, to the rapid decline of the marches. In response, and utilizing the organizational infrastructure established and solidified during the protest wave, activists redeployed their efforts toward the upcoming 2008 presidential election. As a result, the immigrant rights movement and Latino voters played pivotal roles in helping elect the United States' first African-American president.

Research Approach

Before briefly reviewing my research methods and defining key terms, I want to restate the relationship between the theory just expounded and the substantive content of my chapters. So far we've discussed the *contexts* (a single-source, looming, highly visible, and broad legislative threat) under which immigrant rights activists operated, as well the *motivations* (a nativist attack on their material and ideational interests) behind their participation in the demonstrations, giving only cursory attention to the protest wave itself and the actual *actions* of the people who made it possible. In order to understand why people throughout the nation risked so much and went to such great lengths to stop the Sensenbrenner Bill, it was necessary to first take a step back and explain why H.R. 4437 was so pernicious and why Latinos – who were the vast majority of marchers – disproportionately perceived the bill to be a racist legislative attack against them. As such, up until now much of this chapter has taken a more macro-level approach, explaining why the issue of immigration is so intricately linked to Latino identity and how the multiple dimensions of the Sensenbrenner Bill interacted to provide the optimal environment for this cycle of contention to emerge and spread across the country. National protest waves, however, are ultimately composed of numerous local actions that must be analyzed to fully understand the larger, more general phenomenon (Tilly and Tarrow 2015: 28–30). Accordingly, the remainder of this book takes a more micro- and meso-level approach by investigating and underscoring the specific factors that facilitated different degrees of mobilization in different geographic locations. As the themes spotlighted in my case study chapters will show, of central importance were the *identities and agency of these remarkable individuals* and their *utilization of local community resources*; their *formation of diverse coalitions*; and the *broadcasting of their pleas to protest through ethnic media outlets*. Below I describe why I chose to investigate the locales I studied as well as how I went about examining them. (A more thorough account of my case study selection and data collection processes can be found in Appendix A).

Among the several surprising aspects of the immigrant rights rallies were the unanticipated places where many of them occurred, as well as the relative over- and under-performance of certain cities in terms of the magnitude of the protests they hosted. As such, I chose to study Los Angeles because – due to its large foreign-born population, long history of immigrant organizing, and well-established immigrant rights organizational infrastructure – it is a place where, according to social movement theory, high levels of mobilization would have been expected to, and actually did, occur. New York City was examined because although it also has a long history of immigrant activism, a plethora of immigrant rights groups, and the largest citywide immigrant population in the nation, its level of mobilization was significantly less than that of other major immigrant metropolises (e.g., Chicago, Los Angeles, and Dallas). Lastly, I selected Fort Myers, FL because it was an unexpected location for immigrant mass mobilization, which prompts questions about how a city with practically no immigrant rights organizational infrastructure, a relatively small Latino and immigrant population, and a minimal history of prior activism, achieved such a degree of collective action.

Employing a process-tracing approach (George and Bennett 2005; Beach and Pedersen 2013), I examined how the marches were organized in these three cities by searching through newspapers, protest flyers, and websites for reports and mentions of rally organizers and coalition leaders. As an active participant in the immigrant rights movement for nearly 15 years, I utilized contacts I have developed to identify key people and organizations that played fundamental roles in their local protests. I then applied a "snowball" method of sampling to seek out additional individuals to interview (Tracy 2013: 136; Weiss 1994). Using data gained from 131 interviews conducted with protest organizers – of various racial and ethnic backgrounds – at both the local and national levels, I examined the motivations, experiences, tactics, and strategies that activists used to coordinate and organize the demonstrations. In addition, I utilized survey and census data, as well as statistics from the Department of Homeland Security and in-depth interviews with mostly Washington, D.C.-based immigration reform lobbyists and organization leaders to examine what effects they believed the marches had on the federal immigration policymaking process and national electoral politics.

Here it is important to explain why, unlike almost all other scholars who have studied the 2006 protest wave, I decided to incorporate the voices of non-Latinos in a study primarily about Latinos. Because they comprised the preponderance of protest participants and play a central role in contemporary U.S. immigration politics, individuals of Latin American descent make up the majority of my interviewees and are the empirical and theoretical focus of this book. Nonetheless, despite encompassing a smaller portion of rally attendees, U.S.- and foreign-born activists of Asian, African, European, and Arab ancestry also partook in and were crucial to organizing several demonstrations across the nation. In fact, without their leadership and participation, local mobilizations in certain parts of the country would not have been possible. Therefore, their inclusion in any account of the 2006 immigrant rights cycle of contention is fundamental not only for the purpose of historical accuracy, but – as especially evident in Chapter 4 – because their experiences enrich our analysis of the different ways in which the politics of immigration in the United States is racialized in distinct ways, at different times, and under dissimilar contexts.

It is also imperative to clarify specific terms I use throughout this text. First, the concepts of "protest waves" and "cycles of contention" are used interchangeably to describe phases of heightened political conflict, characterized by a rapid spread of activism from more to less mobilized and organized sectors of societies (Koopmans 2004). These phases include both traditional and innovative forms of dissent, the creation of new identities (or the transformation of existing ones) and collective action frames, and "sequences of intensified information flow and interaction between challengers and authorities" (Tarrow 1994: 142). These periods of widespread activism are rather rare in American history, but as will become apparent throughout my case studies, the unexpected series of mass mobilizations for immigrant rights that transpired in the spring of 2006 qualify as one of these extraordinary political events.

Second, although there is no universally agreed upon definition of what constitutes a "social movement," my understanding draws from how senior scholars of contentious politics conceptualize such efforts. Accordingly, I define a social movement as "a sustained campaign of claim making, using repeated performances that advertise the claim, based on organizations, networks, traditions, and solidarities that sustain these activities" (Tilly and Tarrow 2015: 11), and that "depend, at least in part, on recourse to noninstitutionalized forms of collective action" (McAdam and Kloos 2014: 107). As will become evident in the succeeding chapter, we can say that the 2006 protest wave fits into the longer social movement for immigrant rights that has been fighting for legislative reforms for several decades (see Chapter 1).

Finally, the concepts of "racialization," "illegality," and the "racialization of illegality" have played central roles in my analysis thus far and will continue to do so. By illegality, I mean the "historically specific and socially, politically, and legally produced" condition "of immigrants' legal status and deportability" (Abrego 2014: 7; see also Menjivar and Kanstroom 2014; De Genova 2002). I understand racialization to be the process through which racial meaning is given or extended to relationships, social practices, groups, or public policies that previously were not classified by race (Omi and Winant 2015: 111). For example, there is nothing inherently racial about being an undocumented immigrant in the U.S., since non-citizens of all races can technically be or become "illegal."[14] Yet, as Gonzales et al. (2014) point out, "Despite the fact that most Latinos are not undocumented and that not all of the undocumented are Latino," in many respects, to be Latino has become "synonymous with being undocumented and to be undocumented is synonymous with being Latino" (Gonzales, Heredia, and Negron-Gonzales 2014: 166). Thus, by the racialization of illegality I aim to convey the process through which, despite their actual legal or citizenship statuses, certain groups of people have come to be equated with undocumented immigration and undocumented immigrants, and all the criminal implications thereof, because of their perceived racial and cultural attributes.

Chapter Roadmap

Although *Latino Mass Mobilization* is not a work of history, it is nevertheless imperative that before investigating the specific dynamics and impacts of the 2006 protest wave, we first gain a basic understanding of the origins and evolution of the U.S. immigrant rights movement itself. Thus, in Chapter 1, "Forging an Immigrant Rights Movement, 1965–2005," I draw upon data from original interviews with long-time national immigrant rights activists to briefly review the evolution of the modern movement. Rather than a "sleeping giant" that was "suddenly awakened," I argue that the confluence of neoliberal economic reforms, specific immigration policies, prior social movement activism, state and societal nativism, and changes in Latino – particularly Mexican – migration patterns laid the groundwork for a national immigrant rights movement and set the stage for the explosive series of marches that occurred in 2006.

As stated earlier, the activation of pre-existing community resources, the appropriation and use of ethnic media outlets to diffuse calls to action, the increased salience of certain collective identities, and the building of broad and diverse coalitions, were fundamental to the protest wave at both the local and national levels. It is the exploration of these mechanisms and processes that compose the core of this book. Therefore, to demonstrate how the unprecedented protest wave materialized – while not losing sight of the dynamics of mobilization unique to each location studied – Chapters 2 through 4 are each devoted to one of my selected cities and to key themes best embodied by that particular locale. The ways in which threat and racialized identities implicate and explicate one another serve as a thread throughout the book, particularly as they redound upon acts of mobilization and resistance.

Chapter 2, "Weapons of the Not So Weak," opens with a brief description of the lack of political opportunities that existed for migrant mass mobilization in Southwest Florida. After elucidating how immigrant protests in unlikely locations complicate our understanding of the circumstances under which mass mobilization occurs, this case study accentuates the important roles that identity and agency played in the immigrant rights demonstrations. Specifically, the chapter illustrates why and how latent group identities transformed into the racial group consciousness that led immigrants and their families to participate in mass political activism. I highlight the efforts of individual immigrant community members – from soccer league players to small ethnic business owners – and how they utilized existing community resources, even though this infrastructure was primarily apolitical, to aid mobilization. These themes emerged in each city under examination, but Fort Myers, FL, best exemplifies their significance.

Spanish-language media is often credited as the driving force behind the 2006 protests (Ramirez 2011; Dionne et al. 2015). Yet neither scholars nor political pundits have sufficiently studied the factors that facilitated ethnic media's role in promoting the immigrant rights rallies. Chapter 3, "Promoting Protests Through Ethnic Media," explicates exactly how immigrant rights activists in Los Angeles gained unprecedented access to Spanish-language news and entertainment outlets. This case study shows how and why activists were able to spread and amplify their calls for action and to frame the issue as a grave threat to the Latino community. The chapter also underscores the tactical and framing debates within the movement during the protest wave. Overall, this case study shows how, in the hands of activists, the mass media can help produce an impressive degree of political mobilization among its audience members.

Although broad coalitions were fundamental to the mobilizations in all of the locales I examined, no city had more coalitions and ethnically diverse protests than New York. However, in Chapter 4, "Coalitions and the Racialization of Illegality," interviews with local Muslim, Christian, African, Latin American, European, Pacific Islander, Caribbean, and South and East Asian immigrant rights activists suggest that having a more racially and ethnically diverse immigrant population meant that not all of the city's immigrant groups felt equally threatened by the proposed federal anti-immigrant legislation (H.R. 4437), nor equally invested in the proposed alternatives. This chapter shows that how the issue of immigrant illegality was racialized impacted the degree to which groups participated in local actions. Revealing the importance of different immigrant group identities and experiences, I find that this diversity ultimately diminished New York's capacity to produce the magnitude of mobilization found in other immigrant-rich cities.

The abrupt decline of the demonstrations is as significant as their astonishing rise. Thus, whereas the previous and subsequent chapters describe various ways in which movement fractionalization and institutionalization led to the demise of the series of rallies, Chapter 5, "The Suppression of Immigrant Contention," analyzes how factors such as an increase in raids, deportations, hate crimes, and state- and local anti-immigrant ordinances also contributed to the protest wave's decline. The data presented in this chapter illustrate that while imminent threats can serve as a motivation for pronounced visible political action, active and enacted suppression can provoke terror and the instinct to retreat from political participation.

Chapter 6, "Today We March, Tomorrow We Vote," examines some of the effects of the mass marches. The chapter chronicles how rallies across the country did, in fact, contribute to blocking the Sensenbrenner Bill from becoming law. But in terms of the movement's larger effort to win legalization for undocumented immigrants, the demonstrations arguably did more harm than good by further polarizing an already-divided Congress.

Consequently, if we judge the movement based on its stated objectives of stopping the legislative threat from becoming law and winning legalization, at best, immigrant rights activists could claim a draw. Yet, as this chapter shows, a thorough assessment of the impact of the protest wave cannot be based solely on the movement's stated goals. The marches had major indirect outcomes as well. Through unprecedented and strategically targeted campaigns, the immigrant rights movement dramatically increased the number of Latinos and immigrants who naturalized, registered, and ultimately voted in the 2008 presidential race.

It bears repeating that even though each of the case study chapters focuses on a particular theme – identity and the utilization of pre-existing resources; coalitions and diversity; the role of ethnic media outlets – these themes were integral to all three of the cities examined in this book. Hence, in my final chapter I explain the similarities and differences of the dynamics of mobilization and demobilization in Los Angeles, New York, and Fort Myers. The chapter demonstrates how even as similar mechanisms and processes play out in various instances of collective action, different regional, demographic, and political contexts can impact the degree to which, and exactly how, these factors materialize and matter. In addition, given the central role that immigration and anti-Latino racism played in the 2016 presidential election, the chapter concludes with a discussion concerning what the 2006 protests reveal about contemporary Latino politics, immigration policymaking, and the activism we could expect under a Trump Administration.

Together, the eight chapters in this book provide an analysis and propel an argument that I hope will be useful both to scholars studying the present and to activists shaping the future. My central contention is that for mass mobilizations to emerge, a wide range of institutional and non-institutional supports must coalesce; organizations, networks, the media, and resources all matter. However, what is equally important, though difficult to quantify, is that in response to a grave injustice, people on the margins of society are capable of profound and unexpected revolt. In 2006, this was especially true for Latinos who felt their identities were under attack and their dignity was at stake.

Forging an Immigrant Rights Movement, 1965–2005

As remarkable as the actions of the people who organized and participated in the 2006 protest wave were, it is important to acknowledge that
the historic series of demonstrations did not occur in a vacuum. Major
global, national, and local economic, demographic, and political processes
occurred that laid the groundwork for the unprecedented events. Moreover, decades of organizing by pioneering activists – both immigrant and
U.S.-born – in many respects, created the ideological and tactical template
still used today for organizing around immigrant rights. As such, although
the history of the American immigrant rights movement deserves and
requires its own book length examination, below I provide a brief, and
admittedly incomplete, sketch of some of the key contextual and organizational developments that provided the foundation for the upsurge of
activism we witness in the spring of 2006.

The Contextual Development of Immigrant Insurgency

Immigration has been a contentious political issue throughout American history. But the last half-century of our ongoing tangle about who
belongs in this country has been focused primarily on one particular facet
of this issue: *undocumented* immigration. This focus hasn't always been
the case. As Mae Ngai (2005) meticulously demonstrates, undocumented
immigration as a salient political issue was largely the consequence of
specific changes to U.S. immigration laws, particularly the passage of the
Immigration and Nationality Act of 1965 (also known as the Hart-Celler
Law). Pushed for by the descendants of early twentieth-century Southern
and Eastern European immigrants (with the intention of increasing the

number of immigrants from Europe), the Hart-Celler Law put an end to America's discriminatory "racial quota system." Yet even as it was undoubtedly a step toward greater equality in U.S. immigration law, this legislation for the first time officially put a cap on migration from the Western Hemisphere. As a consequence, "Although the 1965 immigration act was viewed as a landmark achievement by the civil rights movement, it also launched a new trend of restrictive immigration policies toward Mexico in particular and toward Latin America in general" (Massey 2007: 128).

At the same time, the United States terminated its "guest worker" arrangement with Mexico (the infamous *Bracero* Program), even as it simultaneously continued to recruit and use Mexican immigrant labor in numbers far surpassing Hart-Celler's new legal visa limit. The combined effects of these actions were that they dramatically "restricted the possibilities of legal entry and virtually guaranteed a rise in undocumented migration" (Massey 2007: 128). In other words, the American government's own policies manufactured our contemporary "problem" of illegal immigration (De Genova 2004; Ngai 2005). But whereas the 1965 Immigration and Nationality Act now classified many Mexican immigrant workers as "illegal," post-1960s neoliberal economic restructuring in both Mexico and the United States, as well as Cold War geopolitics, dramatically increased undocumented migration, transforming it into the controversial political issue it is today.

Durand et al. (2005) note that although "the U.S. economy faltered during the 1970s, the demand for unskilled labor continued unabated, and Mexicans expanded their presence in economic niches where they had already established themselves during the Bracero era" (9). On top of this unceasing need for Mexican workers in the United States, by the early 1980s, Mexico entered a severe economic crisis due to "excessive debt payment obligations coupled with declining petroleum prices," which produced economic instability across the country. Because the "lion's share of the foreign debt was owed to U.S. banks, and faced with a potential financial catastrophe, the U.S. government pressured Mexico to deregulate its economy, undertake monetary and fiscal reforms, downsize the state, and liberalize trade" (Massey, Durand, and Malone 2002: 48). U.S.-educated Mexican "economic policymakers radically liberalized Mexico's trade and industrial policy regime, rapidly privatized state-owned enterprises, and aggressively deregulated foreign investment flows and domestic economic activities" (Cook, Middlebrook, and Horcasitas 1994: 15–16). This economic restructuring had devastating effects on Mexican workers, leading to a decrease in wages and an increase in income inequality throughout the nation (Cornelius and Labastida Martin del Campo 1994: xiv–xv).[1] In addition, foreign direct investments that entered the country hardly created any employment opportunities because "well over half of the foreign funds" were "invested in stocks and other financial instruments, rather than in job-creating direct investment projects" (Cornelius 1995: 141). Not surprisingly, this period saw a rapid increase in undocumented Mexican immigration to the United States (Massey, Durand, and Malone 2002: 44, 111).

As these neoliberal reforms were taking place in Mexico, Cold War politics were increasing the flow of refugees and people seeking asylum in the U.S., from Southeast Asia, the Caribbean, and especially Central America. Regardless of their similar causes of displacement, people from different regions were treated very differently. Whether these migrants were classified as political exiles or as "an illegal group of economically motivated immigrants" depended heavily on U.S. foreign policy interests (Portes and Rumbaut 2014: 43). For example, despite the fact that the United States was sponsoring the very wars and acts of terror that were causing people to flee various Central American countries (Golden and McConnell 1986; Grandin 2007), these political refugees were officially seen and treated as unwanted "illegal aliens" (Coutin 2000; Hamilton and Chinchilla 2001).

Hence, by the mid-1980s, a stagnant U.S. economy, increases in undocumented Mexican migration, Cold War geopolitics, and U.S. refugee policies all combined to position immigration near the top of the nation's preoccupations (Tichenor 2002). In 1986, these factors aided the passage of the Illegal Immigration Reform and Control Act (IRCA), which sought to deter unauthorized immigrants from coming to the United States by increasing border enforcement and, for the first time, making it illegal for employers to hire undocumented immigrants.

Throughout the 1980s and early 1990s, the U.S. not only continued to promote neoliberal economic policies abroad but also adopted several of these reforms domestically. The "massive restructuring" of the American economy inaugurated by President Reagan led, by one count, to the outsourcing and loss of over 40 million U.S. jobs between 1979 and 1996 (Fine 2006: 31). During this period, "global cities" – such as Los Angeles, Chicago, and New York, where the corporations that benefited most from neoliberal reforms were located – developed increasingly bifurcated economies, with shrinking middle classes, growing well-paid high tech and professional classes, and a rapidly expanding low-waged service

sector (i.e., hotel and restaurant workers, gardeners, janitors, day laborers, and domestic workers) that made the upper-class American lifestyle
possible. Immigrants from the global south, who were often undocumented and willing to work long hours, for little pay, and under poor
conditions (Sassen 1988: Sassen 1999), filled much of these new labor
needs. Many of these immigrants would eventually be part of the millions of demonstrators who took to the streets in 2006 to protest the
same U.S. government that promoted and facilitated their labor through
these economic policies but later came to demonize their presence.

Meanwhile, Mexico reentered a profound economic crisis in 1994,
"when a bungled peso devaluation led to a recession that not only created
a need for greater income among poor families in traditional immigrant-
sending states, but also fostered new needs for capital, credit, and security among middle-class households in states that heretofore had not sent
many migrants" to the U.S. (Massey, Durand, and Malone 2002: 12). In
this vulnerable position, Mexico entered into the North American Free
Trade Agreement (NAFTA) with the belief that it would create more jobs
and reduce the need of its citizens to emigrate. But, as with Mexico's economic policy shifts during the 1980s (because of the inability to compete
with transnational corporations that, just a few years later, would come to
dominate the nation's agricultural industry as a result of NAFTA), many
Mexican farmworkers lost their livelihoods and were "forced to migrate
or be unemployed" (Frazier and Reisinger 2006: 266). Despite higher levels of worker productivity, by 2001 real wages in Mexico were lower than
they had been in 1994 and, by 2003, half of the country's population was
impoverished, with 42 million of its citizens living off less than $2 a day
(Martin 2005: 10). One result should come as no surprise: "by most estimates, the population of unauthorized Mexican immigrants in the United
States more than doubled between 1990 and 2000 (with most of that
growth after 1994)" (Papademetriou 2004: 39–40).

During this same period, U.S. economic reforms spurred an anti-
immigrant backlash from white America (Flores-Gonzalez and Gutierrez 2010; Varsanyi 2010). Starting with California's infamous Proposition 187 in 1994 – which sought to ban undocumented immigrants from
receiving public benefits and "required state and local officials to both
verify a client's immigration status and report suspected undocumented
migrants" to immigration officials (Durand, Massey, and Capoferro 2005:
2) – the restrictionist impulse quickly went national, with the passage
of three major anti-immigrant laws in 1996 that, together, further criminalized and curtailed the rights of both documented and undocumented

immigrants.[2] These nativist sentiments were not limited to immigrants who were already in the country. In the mid-1990s, the United States also started to heavily militarize its southern border (Andreas 2000; Nevins 2001). Ironically, this border militarization helped turn undocumented immigration from a primarily regional phenomenon into a national one, and helps explain why the spring of 2006 protests in defense of people without papers was countrywide.

Traditionally, the major destinations for Mexican migration has been the southwestern United States, especially California, Texas, New Mexico, and Arizona (Frazier and Reisinger 2006: 263). For much of the twentieth century, most of this migration was "both circular and itinerant, with workers moving from state to state following harvests and rail lines" (Zuniga and Hernandez-Leon 2005: xiii–xiv). Because of their high concentration in the southwest, Mexican immigrants were "virtually invisible elsewhere" in the country (Light 2007: 1). This dynamic changed considerably during the 1990s, when immigrants increasingly began to migrate to new destinations and away from global cities and established gateway locations (Millard and Chapa 2004; Massey and Capoferro 2008; 26). Four primary reasons explain why migration grew beyond traditional receiving states: IRCA's amnesty provision, increased border militarization, California becoming a less attractive location for both established and new immigrants, and the restructuring of certain sectors of the American economy.

In addition to creating sanctions for employers who hired undocumented workers, IRCA also legalized over 3 million non-residents. Of these 3 million, about three-fourths (2.3 million) were Mexican, most of whom were living in California at the time (Massey and Capoferro 2008: 28). The "effect of IRCA on Latino migration ... was the increase in domestic migration of Latinos out of the traditional settlement areas especially the southwest" (Frazier and Reisinger 2006: 265). With "documents in hand," Mexican immigrants were now "suddenly free to leave historical Mexican enclaves in search of better opportunities elsewhere" in the U.S. (Zuniga and Hernandez-Leon 2005: 2).

Even as neoliberal reforms of the 1990s encouraged capital and corporations to flow freely across the borders of North America, the United States began to militarize its official state boundary with Mexico to thwart the flow of people attempting to come north – often the very same individuals displaced by the free-trade policies promoted under NAFTA (Andreas 2000; Nevins 2001). One outcome of this increased border enforcement was that many migrants altered their typical entry points into the country from California, to new and more hazardous – and more expensive – routes through Arizona and New Mexico (Zuniga and Hernandez-Leon 2005: 2; Andreas 2000). But the border buildup "did not really stop undocumented migrants from entering the United Sates, it simply channeled them to other, less visible, locations along the two-thousand mile border" (Massey and Capoferro 2008: 31). As a result of being forced to cross through more dangerous paths, thousands of dead migrant bodies have been found along the U.S.-Mexico border since 1995 (Nevins 2007). In addition, these increased costs and risks of border crossings also "prompted migrants to remain in the United States rather than returning home to face the gauntlet at the border on a return trip." Moreover, as migrants stopped circulating and stayed in the U.S. longer, they also sent for their families and, as a result, the composition of the Mexican community started to shift from primarily male workers to women and children as well (Massey, Durand, and Malone 2002: 131; Massey and Capoferro 2008: 32).

Another factor redirecting the flow of Mexican migration to new destinations was that the "Golden State" had become a much less attractive place to locate, because the national recession in the 1990s was sharper, deeper, and longer lasting in California than in other parts of the country (Massey and Capoferro 2008: 32). This "Cold War recession" – sparked by cutbacks in the defense industry – "hit southern California's economy particularly hard raising rates of unemployment among both immigrants and natives and tarnishing the lure of U.S. jobs" (Zuniga and Hernandez-Leon 2005: 2, 12). With this recession, the state's anti-immigrant sentiments grew, as epitomized by the notoriously nativist California ballot measure Proposition 187 (Acuña 2000: 154–158; Davis 2001).

While the "recession was slow to end in California, the rest of the country quickly entered a sustained boom, which by the mid-1990s produced tight labor markets, rising wages, and improving work conditions in other regions" (Duchon and Murphy 2001: 1). In locations with no significant history of Mexican immigration, "unemployment rates fell to record low levels, generating a sustained demand for unskilled and semi-skilled workers" (Zuniga and Hernandez-Leon 2005: 2). This "economic boom" in places such as the U.S. South drew many new immigrants to a wide variety of jobs, from the construction to the service sectors, but primarily to employment in food processing and agriculture.

During the latter half of the twentieth century, many "American industries and employers, facing greater international competition and declining profit margins," moved to the Southern United States "to cut costs through subcontracting, deskilling, and decentralizing production" in rural areas, where they could pay lower wages (Massey and Capoferro 2008: 10). These dynamics were particularly prevalent in the food processing industry. For example, from the 1960s to the early 1990s, poultry, fish, and meat processing plants moved from the Midwest to the Southeast to take advantage of cheap and relatively docile poor black and white "hillbilly" labor. At first, families used to "tenant farming, sharecropping, and other low-income and seasonal economic activities provided abundant reliable labor for the plants" (Griffith 1995: 130; Broadway 1995: 23–33). But by the 1970s, more educational opportunities, the civil rights movement, and expanding social services from the Great Society programs constricted labor supplies and decreased worker tolerance by blacks and whites alike for the "authoritarian labor control" that was the norm in many food processing plants (Griffith 1995: 13; Frazier and Reisinger 2006: 266).

Throughout this same period, the population declined throughout much of the South (Zuniga and Hernandez-Leon 2005: xx; Massey and Capoferro 2008: 8); the little growth that did occur was often due to "groups who were unlikely to provide labor," such as retirees, tourists, and seasonal residents (Griffith 1995: 131). Many new industries – including tourism and construction – began to develop in the South to take advantage of the "business-friendly" environment. The "presence and expansion of poorly paid jobs that are difficult, dirty, and sometimes dangerous in small towns and rural areas," and that were frequently "shunned by native-born workers" who increasingly had employment opportunities in other industries, were often filled by new immigrants (Massey and Capoferro 2008: 8, 16). Those new immigrants became more and more vital for these growing industries. As their value and their numbers rose, however, so too did resentment towards them (Grey and Woodrick 2005; Lattanzi Shutika 2005; Fennelly 2008; Marrow 2008).

The Organizational Development of Immigrant Insurgency

Starting sometime in the broad upheavals of the 1960s, across the country emerged, in fits and starts, with great coordination and also great chance, a national movement in the defense and for the rights of the foreign-born, particularly those *"sin papeles"* [without papers]. Given that California – and the greater Los Angeles area in particular – has been the primary destination of Mexican migrants (both authorized and "illegal"), not surprisingly the genesis of undocumented immigrant rights activism and the ideological roots of the movement can be traced back here.

The founders of the modern struggle for the rights of immigrants without papers are, arguably, the legendary Los Angeles labor and community activists Bert Corona and Soledad "Chole" Alatorre, and the organizations they helped found – *Hermandad Mexicana* and the Center for Autonomous Social Action (CASA).[3] According to historian Rudy Acuña (2011), "Corona correctly assumed" that the passage of the 1965 Immigration and Nationality Act would spark a wave of nativism against Mexican immigrants now criminalized by U.S. law (296). Thus, throughout the 1960s and 1970s, Corona and Alatorre trained cadres of immigrant rights activists across the country,[4] "popularized the protection of the undocumented as a civil and human rights issue," and "set the progressive template for the protection of the foreign-born" (Acuña 2000: 350, 403; Gutierrez 1996; Chavez 2002). According to former CASA member Arnoldo Garcia, "CASA was present in Arizona, California, Colorado, Illinois, Oregon, Texas, Washington State, New York, Mexico, and possibly other regions," with a total membership of undocumented immigrants, legal immigrants, and Chicanos (Mexican-Americans) ranging in the thousands during its peak period of 1968–1973 (Garcia 2002). As such, *Hermandad Mexicana* and CASA chapters served as training grounds for many young organizers and fostered a transnational political consciousness among them that promoted the need to organize Latino workers with and without papers, and on both sides of the U.S. border (Garcia 1994: 309; Chavez 2002; Garcia 2002).[5]

During the 1970s, the nativism that Corona predicted began to emerge. In response, in 1973, CASA called a national meeting in Los Angeles for activists opposed to restrictionist immigration proposals being debated in Washington as a result of the increase in post-1965 "illegal" immigration. This meeting – attended by over 450 people – laid the groundwork for the National Coalition for Fair Immigration Laws and Practices (NCFILP), an umbrella coalition primarily composed of Mexican American labor and community groups, which would help defeat restrictionist legislation in multiple states over the next several years (Gutierrez 1984: 11; Gutierrez 1996: 187). By the decade's end, however, internal disagreements over ideology and strategy led to the demise both of the coalition and of CASA (Chavez 2002; Rodriguez 2006).

The decline of CASA and NCFILP did not mean the end of activism around immigration reform. In fact, according to Rick Swartz, who founded the National Immigration Forum (NIF) in 1982, as nativists and the mainstream media sensationalized the increase in undocumented Mexican immigration, along with the so-called Haitian Boat People and war refugees from Vietnam and Central America, activism actually increased and became more diverse. As the numerous social movements of the 1960s and 1970s declined – from the civil rights and anti-war movements to the various Third World liberation solidarity struggles – many of those activists helped start local groups serving immigrants and refugees, or joined the mainstream American labor movement with a commitment to organizing foreign-born people (Ganz et al. 2004: 150–151; Milkman 2006: 70). Several of these activists – Chicano, Filipino, Arab, Asian, African-American, and white alike – became key organizers for just immigration reform as the 1970s became the 1980s.

Catherine Tactaquin, Executive Director of the National Network for Immigrant and Refugee Rights (NNIRR), remembers that when Congress proposed the employer sanctions provision during the early 1980s, immigrant rights advocates in New York, Illinois, Massachusetts, California, Texas, and Washington state began to independently (and, occasionally, collectively) organize against restrictionist bills. Then, in 1985, the National Council of Churches sponsored a "National Consultation for Immigrant Rights" in Los Angeles, hoping to get local groups from across the country to "share information and develop coordinated plans." Their efforts culminated in a "National Day of Action for Justice for Immigrants and Refugees," on October 18, 1985. On this day, over twenty cities held mobilizations calling for an end to deportations and declaring their opposition to the "Simpson-Rodino-Mazzoli Bill," the main piece of legislation then circulating through Congress.[6] Although, as mentioned earlier, in 1986, restrictionist legislation eventually passed – in the form of the Immigration Reform and Control Act (IRCA) – the ad hoc grassroots alliance opposed to the law was formalized with the founding of NNIRR.[7] While these activists – in conjunction with more mainstream Washington, D.C.-based groups such as the ACLU, MALDEF, NCLR, and the National Immigration Forum – failed to stop IRCA from passing, the law itself actually became a crucial ballast for the organizational development of immigrant activism.

The frightening portent of the law's employer sanctions provision provided a very concrete motivation to continue the struggle to protect immigrant rights, as critics feared that this aspect of the bill would increase discrimination against not only the undocumented but also legal immigrants and U.S.-born Latino citizens – fears that, unfortunately, did in fact come to fruition (Massey 2007: 143–145). However, in addition to its punitive elements, the law's "amnesty" provision, as we have seen, legalized three million recent migrants. In response, Hondagneu-Sotelo and Salas (2008) point out:

As soon as IRCA was signed into effect in November 1986, community centers and churches in undocumented-immigrant neighborhoods were filled with lawyers and service providers explaining the barrage of documents, forms, and fees that successful applicants for legalization would need. Groups such as US Catholic Charities, the International Institute, One Stop Immigration, and *Hermandad Mexicana* used both paid staff and volunteers to help Mexican immigrants navigate the confusing federal instructions required by amnesty-legalization provisions (214).

Just as important, IRCA mandated state resources for new and existing immigrant-serving organizations. For instance, as part of an effort to integrate people who qualified for legalization, the federal government allocated "$1 billion a year for four years to fund English, US history, and government classes … mandatory for all amnesty applicants" (Acuña 2011: 357). Both established and new organizations seized the opportunity to draw from this pool of money, hoping to meet the aforementioned requirements while politicizing qualifying immigrants by teaching them about their rights and their need to defend them.[8]

As a result of the additional resources and the need to help eligible immigrants apply for IRCA's amnesty provision, immigrant rights organizations and coalitions cropped up in major cities across the United States (Hondagneu-Sotelo and Salas 2008: 213–214; Flores-Gonzalez and Gutierrez 2010: 7–8). In addition, as Mexican immigrants spread beyond California and across the nation, they formed hundreds of "hometown associations" (HTAs) that, at first, were dedicated to local development projects in their country of origin but, as anti-immigrant sentiment grew (Sanchez 1999) began to focus on domestic issues as well (Ayon 2006; Rivera-Salgado 2006; Milkman and Terriquez 2012). As these associations and coalitions were strengthening their networks throughout the U.S., international upheaval across the hemisphere only sharpened the urgency of the immigrant struggle.

U.S. foreign policy during the late 1970s and 1980s, shaped almost entirely by the lumbering Cold War with Russia, had the result – sometimes intentional, sometimes accidental – of supporting oppressive and undemocratic regimes in Southeast Asia, Latin America, and the Caribbean. One effect of bolstering these repressive governments was the displacement of many thousands of people, pushing them to seek new homes. The cycle of American intervention in and forced migration from Central America was especially important for the development of the immigrant rights movement. As peasants, students, labor unions, and other political activists resisted American-supported military dictators, civil wars broke out across Central America and displaced tens of thousands of individuals. Many of them sought sanctuary in the United States (Hamilton and Chinchilla 2001; Perla and Bibler Coutin 2009). But because officially considering these people "political refugees" would mean that the U.S. was openly acknowledging the negative effects of its support for despotic regimes, these migrants were instead classified as "illegal aliens." Given the revolutionary environments they were coming from, many of these Central American immigrants were what Pulido (1998) refers to as "migrating militants" – foreign-born individuals who were involved in political activism in their countries of origin (see Lovato 2006; Perla 2017). With the hope of influencing U.S. foreign policy toward their home countries, migrating Central American militants helped start the transnational Central American Peace and Solidarity Movement and its religious offshoot, the U.S. Sanctuary Movement (Golden and McConnell 1986; Perla 2008).[9]

According to Roberto Lovato, longtime Central American community activist and former director of the Central American Resource Center (CARECEN), at first, "immigrant rights" was "a secondary consideration... their primary objective, politically, was peace." But by the 1990s, as conflicts in the region waned and peace accords were signed, immigrant activists and their allies realized that most displaced Central Americans had established families and roots in the United States and were unlikely to return to their homelands. In response, organizers redirected their efforts from "helping" *refugees* and changing U.S. foreign policy, to "incorporating" *immigrants* into American society (Bibler Coutin 2000; Hamilton and Chinchilla 2001). Toward that end, many Americans who were sympathetic to the plights of these migrants became dedicated to helping them integrate into the U.S.[10] Perhaps more importantly, many Central American activists stayed in the United States and redirected their efforts toward immigrant rights issues, infusing the movement with a highly politicized cadre of foreign-born advocates who possessed extensive organizing skills (Nicholls and Uiermark 2017: 98). With other migrating militants who were veterans of social movements from places such as South Korea and the Philippines, these individuals would later prove vital to the divergent forms of immigrant activism that emerged across the country during the 1990s.[11]

More immigrants came to America between 1990 and 2000 than during any previous period in U.S. history. Compared to other major influxes in the nineteenth and twentieth centuries, these immigrants were mostly people of color, and many were undocumented (Fine 2006: 28). In response to these demographic changes, a tide of racist nativism emerged across the country, from the streets to the statehouse (Sanchez 1999; Bloemraad, Voss, and Lee 2011: 15–16; Flores-Gonzalez and Gutierrez 2010: 8–12). A renewed attempt at restrictionist legislation, along with several gory physical attacks, sparked resistance from many immigrants, their children, and allies, many of whom were simultaneously fighting to increase college campus diversity and participating in the rapidly growing global justice movement. As Brodkin (2007) notes, "Immigrant worker initiatives and anti-racist efforts on college campuses, in high schools, and in communities of color shaped the political practice of a large cohort of young activists who came of age in this decade" (3). Despite this activism, during the early 1990s, there was no "national" immigrant rights movement that was organizationally connected and able to launch countrywide campaigns. As Lovato put it, "There were people doing things in different cities, but we weren't integrated . . . There were some national attempts, but they were very sporadic and inconsistent." Moreover, because the immigrant-focused organizations of the 1980s had been primarily dedicated to providing services rather than to mobilizing a constituency that was engaged politically, these groups were unable to respond effectively to and stop the legislative attacks at the local and national levels in the first part of the decade.[12]

Recognizing the need to move, as one activist put it, "from service to organizing," previously established immigrant rights organizations and coalitions began to focus on developing a politically organized base and helped found new organizations and coalitions throughout the nation.[13] Foreshadowing what would later become a key weapon in the movement's arsenal, immigrant rights advocates realized the need to combine political activism with electoral influence. Thus, with hopes of establishing a pro-immigrant electorate, and although small in scale, several regional immigrant citizenship and voter registration drives were organized, the most successful of which were in California (Hondagneu-Sotelo and Salas 2008: 214; Gottlieb et al. 2006; Flores-Gonzalez and Gutierrez 2010: 12).

No factor was more important to increasing the movement's resources, however, than the decision by labor organizations to change their stance on immigration, particularly undocumented immigration. Before 2000, most American unions were stanchly anti-immigrant, as illustrated by their support for stricter immigration laws such as the employer sanctions provision in IRCA. But as veterans of 1960s and 1970s social movements gained positions of power within the AFL-CIO, as activists who came of age in the 1990s became union organizers, and as unions became more desperate for new members, the combination revitalized the American labor movement and gave immigrants a new vehicle of advocacy (Turner and Hurd 2001; Ganz et al. 2004).

The U.S. labor movement's renewed commitment to militant political activism – a phenomenon often referred to as "social movement unionism" – was often successful in union organizing drives, particularly immigrant union organizing drives, because of support from local religious and community groups, including immigrant rights organizations. By the year 2000, these, mostly West Coast, victories gave union organizers committed to immigrant rights the influence they needed to convince the national AFL-CIO to officially support the legalization of people without papers and publically commit to organizing documented and undocumented immigrants (Milkman and Wong 2000; Fantasia and Voss 2004). Moreover, because political parties were no longer attempting to mobilize immigrants as they had during the early 1900s (Wong 2006), and because more and more immigrants were working in the informal economy – as nannies and day laborers and everything in between – community groups, churches, and service organizations started creating "worker centers" to politically organize these informal laborers (most of whom were undocumented) (Gordon 2005; Fine 2006). Thus, by 2000, an organizational infrastructure and new resources dedicated to defending and fighting for the rights of immigrants existed, or was emerging, in many parts of the country. As these factors increased the movement's resources and grassroots mobilizing abilities, another occurrence began to augment its formal political influence – the development of a national Latino electorate.

The black civil rights movement was made possible by the massive migration of African-Americans from rural to urban areas and from the South to the North. That move, in turn, made blacks into a politically significant block of voters. According to Doug McAdam (1982):

What made this mass exodus more than simply a demographic curiosity were the political consequences that flowed from it … The migrants were drawn disproportionately from southern states with the lowest percentage of registered black voters in the nation and, in turn, settled overwhelmingly in seven industrial states – New York, New Jersey, Pennsylvania, Ohio, Illinois and Michigan in the North and California in the West – that were widely regarded as the key to electoral success in presidential contests (xix).

A similar process has occurred with Latinos. As the Latino – especially the Mexican – population grew in the U.S., a national and largely Democratic

Latino electorate slowly began to emerge (Bowler and Segura 2011). One result of this new electoral sway was that the number of Latino elected officials at the local, state, and federal levels started to gradually increase as well (Casellas 2010; Wallace 2010; Rouse 2016). The combined effects of demographic changes, the advent of a national Latino voting bloc, and increases in Latino elected officials enhanced Latino political influence, especially in several key presidential swing states (Ramirez 2013).

These developments are important to note because although racialized minority groups in the U.S. sometimes shun and further marginalize stigmatized members of their communities (Cohen 1999; Gutierrez 1995), by the late-1990s, Latinos in general, and Latino elected officials in particular, tended to be very supportive of immigrants, including the undocumented, and especially compared to the broader American pubic (Wallace 2010; Masuoka and Junn 2013). As we will see in later chapters with regard to the political impacts of the 2006 protest wave and the contemporary politics of immigration, Latino elected officials and Latino voters came to serve as political brokers for people without papers. As a result, despite their inability to vote, and contrary to popular belief, people without papers are not electorally impotent. They can – and do – participate in voter registration and get-out-the-vote (GOTV) campaigns but also wield electoral influence through their U.S.-born family members and electoral representatives.

Thus, by the turn of the twenty-first century, the immigrant rights movement had garnered two important allies – the U.S. labor movement and Latino voters – which indirectly gave them some political influence within in the Democratic Party and, effectively, in national electoral politics. With the 2000 election of George W. Bush – a Republican border-state governor who, at the time, was seen as relatively pro-immigration – to the American presidency, pro-immigrant forces saw an opportunity to make a major push for immigration reform that would include legalizing the millions of undocumented immigrants who lived throughout the nation.[14]

Soon after he took office in January 2001, George W. Bush began discussions with then-President of Mexico Vicente Fox about passing immigration reform that included a new guest worker program (Castañeda 2007). With what seemed like great momentum, immigrant rights groups and union leaders started meeting and strategizing ways to influence these policy negotiations. Their goals were to ensure that any resulting legislation would include a path to citizenship for undocumented immigrants and that the rights of all immigrant workers would be protected.[15]

Unfortunately, the terrorist attacks of September 11, 2001 dashed these hopes. These tragic events, and the wars in Afghanistan and Iraq that followed, ushered in a new wave of anti-immigrant sentiment across the country that, at first, was directed at Muslim and Arab immigrants but quickly spread to other ethnic groups, including Latinos (Nguyen 2005; Chavez 2008; Bloemraad, Voss, and Lee 2011). The terrorist attacks reinvigorated the relatively dormant anti-immigrant movement – led by rightwing groups such as the Federation for American Immigration Reform (FAIR) and the Minutemen – that took advantage of the xenophobic political climate to call for tightened borders and for the deportation of the nation's estimated 11 million undocumented immigrants (Navarro 2008). Rather than instituting immigration reform that included a legalization program, Congress passed the Patriot Act in October 2001, and the Enhanced Border Security and Visa Entry Reform Act and the Homeland Security Act in the following year; all three were detrimental to the rights of foreign-born people in the U.S. (Flores-Gonzalez and Gutierrez 2010: 18; Massey 2007: 148).

Many activists refused to be discouraged by the revived nativism and loss of congressional support for immigration reform. Immigrant advocates slowly began to renew their calls for progressive legislation. In 2002, the labor movement "officially launched a campaign for legalization and family reunification for immigrant workers" (Flores-Gonzalez and Gutierrez 2010: 16). In 2003, union leaders, some of whom were active in various 1960s and 1970s civil rights groups (including CASA), launched the Immigrant Workers Freedom Rides (IWFR). The IWFR was a series of caravans filled with immigrant rights activists that stopped in communities across the country as they made their way to Washington, D.C. and New York, where they held large pro-immigrant rallies. According to Shaw (2011), "A critical aim of the IWFR was to boost working relationships between labor unions and the many community, civil rights, religious, student, and immigrant rights groups that collectively comprised the nation's immigrant rights movement." As the fear that followed the terrorist attacks waned, labor activists "hoped to return immigration issues to the national political agenda" and "to encourage greater civic participation by immigrants" (89–90).

Also in 2003, Catholic bishops from the U.S. and Mexico issued a joint pastoral letter calling for "an overhaul of the U.S. immigration system."[16] Following this bold declaration, in 2004, the United States Conference of Catholic Bishops launched its "Justice for Immigrants Campaign," which was "designed to unite and mobilize a growing network of Catholic institutions, individuals, and other persons of good faith in support of a broad legalization program and comprehensive immigration reform principles" (Heredia 2011: 105; see also Hondagneu-Sotelo and Salas 2008: 218). This same year, a loose affiliation of national service, labor, civil and immigrant rights groups meeting as the "New American Opportunity Campaign" created the Coalition for Comprehensive Immigration Reform (CCIR) to push for the passage of progressive immigration legislation (Hondagneu-Sotelo and Salas 2008: 218). Whereas in the early 2000s, the West Coast–based NNIRR emphasized a radical critique of the global root causes of international migration and were vocal about the limits of merely national reforms, more moderate activists connected to Washington D.C.-based policy groups now felt the need to create a cross-country alliance of local organizations with the aim of gaining a stronger voice in the federal immigration policy debate. Correspondingly, in 2004, the Center for Community Change and several grassroots immigrant rights groups from throughout the nation started a coalition based in Washington D.C. called the Fair Immigration Reform Movement (FIRM).[17]

Allied with major business interests, such as the Essential Worker Immigration Coalition (EWIC) and the Agriculture Coalition for Immigration Reform, CCIR and FIRM lobbied for a bi-partisan compromise legislation that, between 2004 and 2005, became known as the "Kennedy-McCain Bill" (Wong 2006: 178; Hondagneu-Sotelo and Salas 2008: 220).[18] Despite what again seemed like great momentum, immigration policy advocates had their hopes quashed. From mid- to late 2005, two Supreme Court nominations and the devastation of Hurricane Katrina took Congress's attention away, once more, from immigration reform.[19] Even worse, catching local and national immigrant rights leaders by surprise, on December 16, 2005, GOP House member James Sensenbrenner and his Republican colleagues passed what would have been one of the most punitive anti-immigrant laws in the nation's history, the *Border Protection, Anti-Terrorism and Illegal Immigration Control Act of 2005* (H.R. 4437). The bill, as discussed earlier, sought to severely criminalize undocumented immigrants and anyone who assisted or associated with them in the most basic manner. Thus, over the span of just a few weeks, a very pragmatic hope for vast, albeit imperfect, immigration reform turned to collective horror at the draconian world imagined by the Sensenbrenner Bill. In shock and in anger, immigrants and their supporters prepared for the most significant fight for the defense of the foreign-born in decades.

2

Weapons of the Not So Weak

At a Forever 21 warehouse in Los Angeles, Latino workers filled cardboard boxes, as they did every day, with piles of inexpensive, poorly made clothes. But that day, as they sealed the boxes, several of the workers scribbled on them with a black marker:

¡Marcha!
Sábado 25 de marzo, 10AM
Olympic y Broadway

Latino truck drivers then picked up the cargo and distributed it across the county to local retailers. At one of these stores, Latina immigrant employees received the boxes, saw the message, and fervently discussed – first with the drivers and then with their Latina coworkers – the approaching day of protest; they spoke in Spanish so that their non-Latina managers would not understand what they were saying.[1]

In New York City, through their family and neighborhood networks, immigrants of various racial and ethnic backgrounds promoted the upcoming march and rally set to take place on April 10. Days before the event, a group of these individuals (many of who would not personally be able to take part in the action) gathered after work at a local community center to help make posters and pack sandwiches for rally participants. As they made the lunch sacks and placards, they eagerly spoke about the devastating effects H.R. 4437 would have on their families and community.

Central to the theoretical explanation for the protest wave presented in this book is the contention that a multi-dimensional anti-immigrant bill (H.R. 4437) simultaneously posed an individual and collective threat that transformed certain immigrant communities' latent sense of group membership into the racial group consciousness that spurred them into action. Across the country, the proposed legislation motivated unconventional political actors – from local soccer league players and nannies to agricultural workers and ethnic small business owners – to utilize pre-existing neighborhood resources to mass-mobilize their communities. Although the activation of a racial group consciousness – albeit to different degrees – and the use of community resources were fundamental to the large-scale collective action that occurred in each of the cities examined in this book, this chapter uses the case of Fort Myers, FL to illustrate some of the central dynamics of these processes.

Immigrant Mass Mobilization in an Unexpected Location

If demography is destiny, then we should be paying more attention to the changes that have occurred over the past three decades in Southern states. In the American story of immigration, until relatively recently, the South has often been completely ignored. As we have seen, focusing on the U.S. Southwest made sense during much of the latter half of the twentieth century. But, as detailed in Chapter 1, the national portrait of immigration is far more complex today. For example, although the state of Florida has historically not been considered a gateway for Mexican migration (Zuniga and Hernandez-Leon 2005: ixv; Durand, Massey and Capoferro 2005: 5), the "Sunshine State" was certainly part of the rapid growth of Mexican immigration that occurred during the 1990s and early 2000s in the U.S. South. While the state's percentage of immigrants from all of Latin America went from 0.6 percent in 1980 to 6 percent in 2005 (Massey and Capoferro 2008: 39), Mohl and Pozzetta (1996) note that "the number of Mexicans in Florida – about 20,000 in 1970 – grew by over 600 percent to 150,000 in 1990" (411–412). According to a study of "the fastest-growing metropolitan areas" in the nation for Latinos, the Cape Coral–Fort Myers region in Southwest Florida "rose in rank from number eight in the 1990s to number one" between 2000–2004 (Frey 2006: 7). Most of these immigrants were undocumented (Polopolus and Emerson 1994; Greene 2003d) and went into the labor-intensive, low-waged (Roka and Cook 1998: 1, 28; Bowe 2007), agricultural (Hirchman and Massey 2008: 17), construction (Mormino 2005: 66–67), and service industries (Crummett and Schmidt 2003: 2).

According to the Southern Poverty Law Center, during this same period, Florida was also home to some of the most militant nativist activists in the country and even had its own anti-immigrant political party (Beirich et al. 2008). Not surprisingly, in the early 2000s, as the number of Latinos in the state grew, so too did the hostility they felt.[2] For instance, a 2004 opinion poll revealed that 77 percent of Latinos in Florida believed that discrimination against them was a problem – and one in four felt it was a "major problem" (Pew Hispanic 2004: 3). In addition, because many of them were without proper legal documentation, these individuals also lacked a formal political voice. And because Southwest Florida was a relatively new destination for Mexican migration, a second-generation electorate (like the more established Mexican-American electorate in California) and a political infrastructure (e.g. local elected officials and social movement organizations) that could serve as political brokers, shields, and representatives for the community had not – and still has not – formed.[3]

Moreover, in the early 2000s, not only was the state legislature and executive branch controlled by Republicans, but some of the state's local politicians were also the same farm owners who benefitted from a docile and exploitable workforce (Greene, 2003b; Mormino, 2005: 215–218). Republicans, the more anti-immigrant of the two major U.S. political parties, also dominated every branch of the federal government during this period. It is thus not surprising that Mexican immigrants in Southwest Florida remained segregated and were among the least politically active in the state, largely – scholars believed – because many of them lacked the "power of papers" (legal citizenship) that could bring them a political voice (Griffith et al. 2001: 85–89). Researchers contended that a dearth of unity within the community was also partly to blame for the population's social and political invisibility (McDuff 2004).

This political climate is important to note because some social movement theorists contend that a supportive electoral base, influential elite allies, and established social movement organizations are essential to movement-building and mobilization processes (McCarthy and Zald 1977; McAdam 1982; Tarrow 2011; Smith and Wiest 2012). If this is so, then by all accounts, the open "political opportunity structures" that many scholars believe are vital to the rise of large-scale collective action was constricted, if not absent altogether, for Southwest Florida immigrants. And yet, on April 10, 2006, upwards to 100,000 Latino immigrants and their families across the region took to the streets in Fort Meyers, FL to express their opposition against legislation that would have shaken the foundations of their daily lives.

Unexpected Activists

As mentioned in the introductory chapter, given the strong statistical correlation between socioeconomic status and political participation, because immigrants tend to live in poor and seemingly under-resourced communities (Rector 2006; Suro, Wilson, and Singer 2011), it is not surprising that established quantitative research showed that foreign-born people were much less likely to take part in political activism (Martinez 2005; Martinez 2008: 197; Bloemraad, Voss, and Lee 2011: 19; Leighly and Nagler 2013). These findings make the 2006 protest wave, and the case of Fort Myers in particular, all the more fascinating. As the remainder of this chapter illustrates, although scholars have indeed identified the "conventional" kinds of political actors, and the resources and skills they draw on, what Fort Myers and the 2006 protests show us is that there is a wider gamut of skills and resources that immigrant communities possess and can utilize for political purposes. Put another way, basing our understanding of their political behavior solely on quantitative survey data runs the risk of missing the fact that immigrant communities possess their own distinct resources and are home to individuals with unique civic skills who can play central roles in coordinating large-scale collective actions. As such, identifying these people and understanding how they used their individual agency, economic assets, and local social spaces as political resources to mass-mobilize their communities is imperative.

Immigrants are often assisted by family members, organizations, or agencies that liaise between them and their new society (Zuniga and Hernandez-Leon 2005: xix). Examples are numerous: service organizations that help them with the naturalization process (Bloemraad 2006); unions, churches, and advocacy groups that serve as political bridges to electoral politics (Wong 2006; de Graauw 2016); and children of immigrants who translate for their parents (Parke and Buriel 2006; De Ment, Buriel, and Villanueva 2005). However, our typical understanding of this kind of immigrant assistance often overlooks an important category: local individuals who operate as central nodes between different immigrant networks. Many of the key organizers of the Fort Myers march had long served as local, informal community brokers who assisted recent migrants in adapting to their new country of residence. These individuals were often well-regarded and traditionally nonpolitical actors. Immigrant residents respected them because of their professions, because they were bilingual, or because they actively participated in neighborhood activities. These unlikely political activists included nannies and domestic workers, owners of ethnic restaurants, bakeries, and grocery stores, presidents and members of neighborhood soccer leagues, farmworkers and construction site managers, Spanish-language radio DJs, and owners of local weekly ethnic newspapers.

These individuals often wore multiple hats in their communities. For instance, Moises, from South Florida, worked his way up from field-worker to an agricultural labor contractor (also known as a "crew leader") and helped start a local soccer league and a parents-of-migrant-students association; his family also owned a popular local Mexican restaurant.[4] Zebedeo from Central Florida had many skills as well; he not only organized his area's annual *Cinco de Mayo* parade but also owned a small "Mexican store" (that sold everything from groceries and clothes to remittance services and toys) and hosted his own independent radio show called *La realidad en la Florida*. Other local leaders gained status and respect in the immigrant community partly for being one of the few, if not the only, bilingual Latinos in their professions. For example Marcos, a Mexican-American born in Texas who was an attorney and president of a local Chamber of Commerce at the time, was known to Latino immigrants throughout the region because of his ability to speak Spanish and English, and his history of helping local residents with workplace abuse and immigration issues.

Just as Mexico's neoliberal restructuring of its economy during the 1980s and 1990s displaced rural workers, it also pushed many educated, urban, and middle-class Mexicans to migrate (Massey, Durand, and Malone 2002: 12; Hernandez-Leon 2008: 3–8). One such educated urban migrant was Tacho of Southwest Florida. Before emigrating, Tacho attended college in Mexico for three years, pursuing two degrees – one in civil engineering and another in English. In the United States, however, he and his family harvested crops in the fields of Southwest Florida. By 2006, he had "moved up" and become a crew leader. The status he had gained among immigrants in his area was largely due to his bilingual skills, legal residence status, his experience as a farmworker and supervisor of countless fieldworkers, and his role as president of the first Latino soccer league in his community, which his family founded in the late-1980s.[5]

Ana Maria of South Florida was also a college-educated migrant. A schoolteacher in Mexico before immigrating in 1970 without papers to the U.S., she was unable to transfer her credentials to her new country of residence despite learning English and obtaining the equivalent of an American high school degree. Consequently, Ana Maria had few options other than farm work. While living in Texas, she learned about a recruiter looking for people to pick in the fields of Florida. Although, Ana Maria explained, labor contractors during that period preferred to enlist male farmworkers, she convinced the recruiter to take her with him. Days later, when they arrived at the Florida field where she was supposed to work, the grower did not believe she had done farm labor before. After demanding to see Ana Maria's hands as proof of her work experience, he barely glanced at them and signaled to the contractor that he had no use for her. Eventually, the grower and the contractor agreed to a price for the male workers, but because the recruiter "didn't have change," he "made a deal and sold" Ana Maria as payment for the $60 he owed the farmer. Subsequent to witnessing and experiencing several abuses in the agricultural fields of Florida, and after "becoming legal," Ana Maria realized she could use the skills and resources she possessed from having papers and being bilingual to help other immigrants. Consequently, during the late-1980s, she traveled around the state working with the Catholic Church and the Mexican Consulate assisting immigrants in applying for the IRCA amnesty provision. By 2006, Ana Maria had become a secretary for a local immigration attorney.

Ana Maria, Moises, Zebedeo, Marcos, and Tacho are just some of the local Southwest Florida residents who spearheaded the coalition that led the Fort Myers march. These immigrants emigrated with human capital and civic organizing experiences – many of the characteristics that studies have correlated with political participation, but that some scholars have argued most immigrant communities generally lack (De la Garza and DeSipio 1997: 108; Garcia 2003: 98, 183; Rector 2006; Suro, Wilson, and Singer 2011). The roles that these brokers and others played in the daily lives of local immigrants made them central figures in their communities who, when spurred into action, helped get thousands of their fellow residents to protest against proposed federal anti-immigrant legislation.

Motivations for Action

The reasons for taking action given by the people who initiated the Fort Myers demonstration against the Sensenbrenner Bill (H.R. 4437) are of particular interest, given that scholars traditionally consider most of them nonpolitical actors. Southwest Florida protest organizers (most of whom had not considered themselves activists prior to helping coordinate the demonstration) gave a combination of motivations for deciding to participate. They stated the different ways in which H.R. 4437 threatened them as both individuals and as part of a larger group. As an immigrant construction worker and coalition member put it, "It was going to affect us directly and indirectly."[6]

Collective Threat and Group Consciousness

Because the bill "would have been a disaster" for their communities, most of the Florida activists I spoke with asserted that the broad scope and severity of H.R. 4437 was a main motivation for fighting against the passage of the proposed legislation.[7] They continuously cited the "felonization" of people without papers and the criminalization of anyone who assisted them as a primary reason for organizing the Fort Myers march. For example, a founder of a local soccer league remembered that the "community was offended. It was worried that [H.R. 4437] was ... going to criminalize" everyone. "You weren't only an undocumented person anymore," he explained, "now you were an actual criminal. So the whole world reacted and said '*No!* ... We aren't criminals, we're workers.'"[8] Pointing out the potential far-reaching nature of the bill, Rosalinda, an apartment manager and coalition member agreed with this analysis, stating that, if passed, the law would have criminalized "anyone who had anything to do with undocumented people, which could have been a church, a hospital ... You [couldn't even] give your brother a plate of food because that made you a criminal." As a result, she felt "there was no way that we could sit back as human beings and let someone else be treated like the scum on the bottom of your shoes."

An owner of a small Mexican store described the sweeping nature of the Sensenbrenner Bill in the following manner, "The law wasn't giving any space for relationships, for friendship, for compassion, for brotherhood. That law [had to have been] proposed by someone who didn't realize what they were doing because ... people need hope, humanity, compassion, and with that law, all human values would have been taken away."[9] As a result, stated a Southwest Florida labor contractor, "When people saw they could lose all their dignity, their credibility, their rights, their personhood, they had to come out to the streets to say, '*No!* I'm not what you're saying I am.' ... That's why people reacted. It didn't matter anymore because there was nothing left to lose."[10]

The immigrants I interviewed in Florida believed that H.R. 4437 was racially motivated and stated that this attack on their collective identities provoked them into taking action against the looming legislative threat. As Ramona, a Honduran domestic worker and single mother of two in the Tampa area, explained:

More than anything, I think that the law woke up in our people a feeling of not letting ourselves be humiliated, that we were worth something ... It was as if they saw us as less. [The bill caused a] great feeling of racism ... that helped awaken the sleeping giant the people had inside of them. So in reality, it was a good thing, they did us a favor because it united us.

An agricultural contractor in South Florida added that because the rhetoric behind the bill was so racially charged, "I think what happened was that all Latinos, not only the undocumented ... felt the necessity to express ourselves in one way or another. To say ... 'We need to make a change' ... That was my sentiment as a [naturalized] citizen [of the U.S.] and that's how lots of other people felt too that wanted to send that message."[11] Time and time again, the immigrants I spoke with expressed feeling not only that their contributions to the country (both as community members and as workers) were being negated, but also that they were constantly used as scapegoats for the social and economic problems of the U.S. Consequently, the harsh and racialized nature of the proposed legislation helped transform their latent sense of ethnic identity into the Latino group consciousness that motivated them to take action.

The U.S.-born Latinos who participated in the coalition that organized the Fort Myers protest also expressed these types of sentiments. For instance, a Mexican-American mechanic in a small rural town stated, "Our father was illegal when he first got here. Illegals work hard and they need to be respected ... We're all human, we're all created the same." She added, "We [may] have different color skin, but we're all the same, we all came from the same [God] ... Don't put us down because we have Mexican blood and because our skin is brown with black hair and brown eyes. That don't make us bad people."[12] Marcos, the Mexican-American attorney mentioned earlier, said that growing up in Texas, he recalled his parents "always helping" undocumented immigrants in various ways (e.g. clothes, food, loans, etc.) and being upset whenever they heard about raids and undocumented people "being taken advantage of." Thus, when he learned about H.R. 4437, he interpreted the bill as an attack on the entire Latino community and felt the need to help try to stop the bill from becoming law.

These feelings of solidarity were prevalent throughout my interviews with the people who organized the Fort Myers demonstration. A Central American activist with papers, but who was previously undocumented, best captured these sentiments of linked fate (Dawson 1995). Ramona declared, "Thank God that I already had my papers, but everyone around me [without them] was scared to go to work ... Being so close to them, I felt their pain. I would put myself in their situation . . . It made me feel as if I was the one living what they were going through. That's what motivated me to act." The desire to collectively respond to a racialized attack was not limited to expressing unity with people in their local communities or whom they knew personally, the span of their group consciousness was national.

Many immigrants stated that marches they saw or heard about in other cities, prior to the Fort Myers demonstration, inspired them and made them feel part of a larger group. The palpable feeling of belonging to this "imagined community" (Anderson 1991) is important given that immigrants in new immigrant receiving destinations, such as Southwest Florida, are still very much minorities without political influence or the sense of security often found in established ethnic enclaves like those in Los Angeles and New York. Identifying with a bigger group of people, even one that is spread over thousands of miles across the country, helped to minimize their feelings of isolation and reaffirmed their desire to act on behalf of – and in solidarity with – other Mexican and Latino immigrants. These dynamics demonstrate the mental and material power of imagining oneself as part of a larger collective that is geographically separated and dispersed, but cognitively grounded and united by similar experiences of discrimination, a shared racialized identity, and the inspiration that this mental geographic remapping created during the protest wave.[13]

As an example, a soccer league president remembered that the rallies in other places were "a big motivation." He recalled, "When we saw there were protests in big cities, we started thinking about doing one too . . . We identified with them, we even chose to have our march the same day as them."[14] A founder of a different soccer league remembered, "Then there were the big protests in other states . . . so the whole world was wanting to do the same . . . People would come up to me and ask, 'What are we going to do here? . . . Let's do something here, we have to . . . ' People on the streets, soccer players, our clients from the restaurant, the owner of the sports store told me" that they too wanted to take part in a march.[15] In all of the cities examined in this book, protest organizers concurred with these remarks, stating that after seeing Latinos rallying in other places on the news, family and community members would express their desire to also participate in a demonstration. Media images of large protests elsewhere showed Southwest Florida immigrants the strength and security in numbers. According to several of the people I interviewed, in seeing millions of Latinos take to the streets without being harassed by *la migra* [immigration officers] or local police, they learned that it was also safe for

them to demonstrate without fear of repercussions. Moreover, the participation of members of the Catholic Church, Latino elected officials, and
nationally recognized organizations in other cities legitimatized the rallies
and further signaled to immigrants in the Fort Myers region that protesting was safe.

As stated beforehand, most of the people who initiated and organized
the Fort Myers march had never participated in any form of political
activism. Although they had been aware of anti-immigrant laws enacted
prior to 2006, most of these individuals – particularly the businessmen
and soccer league leaders – had not been motivated enough to organize
and publicly protest them. Thus, because some degree of group solidarity existed before 2006 and these unexpected activists had been aware of
previous attacks on undocumented immigrants, investigating what was
so different about the Sensenbrenner Bill and why these individuals felt
the urgency to act at this time is imperative. As I will show below, unlike
past threats against the foreign-born, the broad scope of H.R. 4437 meant
that it would have directly affected not only many of their fellow Latino
community members but also these specific individuals themselves. Put
simply, the Sensenbrenner Bill was potentially more collectively and personally felt than previous legislative attacks.

Individual Threat and Personal Interest

As noted in the preceding chapter, H.R. 4437 proposed to amplify being
undocumented from a civil offense to a federal felony; additionally, it stip-
ulated fines of thousands of dollars, and the possibility of jail time, for
people who aided undocumented immigrants in the most basic ways. As
a result, Latino (especially Mexican) immigrants responded not only to a
broad threat against their communities and collective identities but also
to a direct threat to themselves and their personal interests. For example, Marcos, the Mexican-American lawyer, admitted, "I could have been
charged with multiple felonies. Most of my clients don't have papers ...
At that time I counted ... 65–75 felony counts of aiding and abetting."
A farm labor contractor and protest-coalition member added, "I'm an
American citizen ... but in the area where I work, in agriculture, 99.9%
of the workers are undocumented ... Without those people working for
me, I wouldn't have the opportunity to do my work either."[16] In addition, Susana, a radio disk jockey who hosted activists on the air on several occasions, and consistently announced the protest on her program,
acknowledged that her station had a personal interest in the issue because
it was a primarily "Mexican music station" with a mostly "farmworker

audience" that tended to be undocumented. Listeners apparently shared this sense of urgency. The DJ recalled people constantly calling in to radio programs and saying that if the bill became law, they were going to get fired anyway so they might as well go to the protest and try to stop it from passing.

A law that explicitly targeted their customer base would have especially impacted many local Latino businesses. Studies have shown that immigrant entrepreneurs are highly dependent on other members of their ethnic group – who often are undocumented – both as a source of cheap labor and a primary pool of clients (Teixeira 2001: 2067; Efrat 2008: 697–698; Shinnar and Young 2008: 246). The business owners who helped organize the Fort Myers demonstration were well aware of this dynamic. Immigrant entrepreneurs clearly understood their "financial linked fates" to the undocumented immigrant population in their communities.

Despite these vital personal interests, determining which type of threat – collective or individual – was the more important motivating factor is difficult because they existed simultaneously. For instance, David, an immigrant business owner who previously lacked "papers," explained, "I was illegal before so I couldn't let that happen to our community. Plus, all of my businesses have only been possible because of the community. So if the community does badly, I do badly." But while both identities (businessman and immigrant) already co-existed, they had not been equally or concurrently targeted before. When first asked what motivated them to act, most immigrants said they were responding to the inhumane nature of the Sensenbrenner Bill and what felt like an attack on their collective identity as Latinos. But when pressed about what they felt was different about H.R. 4437 compared to past nativist legislative threats, many cited its far-reaching nature, which would have affected them directly.

Noting these personal interests is not to say that claims of group solidarity as a motivating factor were insincere. Research on the role of collective identity in social movements has found that people possess multiple identities – as in the case of the business owners who themselves had been undocumented – some of which are more salient at different times and under different circumstances (Fantasia 1988; Della Porta and Diani 1999; Cohen 1997; Barvosa-Carter 2001). For the immigrant entrepreneurs I interviewed, the direct and personal threat the bill posed to their financial well-being as businessmen combined with the broader attack on their racialized identities pushed them over the hump from feeling moral outrage to taking concrete political action. In other words, the nativist bill accentuated the links between their self- and group-interests and in the process activated the racial group consciousness that provoked them into taking action.

Tacho, the crew leader and soccer league president, best exemplified the interconnections between personal interests, a collective identity, and having a sense of linked fate. In his interview, he stated that everyone in the Latino community knew him because over the years he had worked with so many people in the agricultural fields or played with them in the soccer leagues. He felt that because he had lived in his town for so long and had "made it" – he had a family, owned a home, worked as a manager – community members always went to him for advice, about everything from personal family issues to the difficulty of adjusting to life in America. Tacho (who when first migrating to the U.S. was also undocumented) unnecessarily risked – and eventually quit – his job of over a decade because of his disgust with the lack of sympathy the farm owners had for their workers during the protest. He acknowledged a simultaneous dependence on and loyalty to the people he worked with – as their manager, fellow immigrant, and community member. These intersecting motivations to act resulted from both the individual and collective threat that H.R. 4437 concurrently posed to his personal and group interests. Tacho recalled that the morning of the demonstration,

[The bosses] called me to the company office and they sat me down with all the other crew leaders … One by one they went down the row asking us what we knew about the march … They sat us in front of the owner of the company and [the supervisors] asked each one of us what we knew about the work stoppage… When they got to me I told them … "Don't even ask me because you already know that I'm part of the movement" … [A supervisor responded saying], "All those people going to the march are ungrateful … because the very people that we [the company] extend our hand to [by giving them jobs], now want to turn around and bite it." So I [Tacho] told them, "You know what? Because of those people you're talking about, you eat, I eat, and all of you eat … In the 10 years [that I've worked here] I've seen that this company isn't anything without the fruit of those workers' labor, *undocumented* [labor]" … [To which a supervisor replied], "Well we don't care, we want them all here [working] … You have to be on the side of the company"… They told me they needed me there [too], but I said, "Don't count on me, I'm going to Fort Myers," and then I walked out … All they cared about was their pockets … We care about money too, but we also have to see those workers as people.

Farm labor crew leaders and ethnic small business owners are an unlikely cadre of organizers who are commonly stereotyped as being not all that concerned with the welfare of their immigrant workers. Yet studies show that immigrant neighborhoods are often composed of dense social networks with a strong sense of community (Brown 2002; Schmidt 2007). Throughout his interview Tacho – like other crew leaders and storeowners – repeatedly spoke about how close he was to his workers' families and how tight-knit his community was. His loyalty to his workers (whom he saw more as coworkers and neighbors) and his identity as a Latino immigrant made him take the personal risk, and eventually pay a personal cost, for participating in a protest in defense of his community. These actions reveal a different way of understanding the identities of some immigrant crew leaders and small business owners with regard to the relationships they have with their immigrant workers. The punitive and far-reaching nature of H.R. 4437 was an unprecedented threat against many of these unexpected activists. It attacked their personal and group interests in a racialized fashion and – in the process – triggered the feelings of linked fate and group consciousness that eventually motivated them to respond to the looming legislative threat of the Sensenbrenner Bill. Their first endeavor was to form the unique coalition that coordinated the mass mobilization.

Coalition Formation

The informal alliance that organized the Fort Myers march was composed of three groups: the *Concilio Mexicano de la Florida* [Mexican Council of Florida], a group representing over 300 mostly Mexican small businesses; the *Coalición de Ligas Hispanas del estado de la Florida* [Florida State Coalition of Hispanic Leagues], a regional association of Latino immigrant soccer leagues with over 10,000 players; and a collective of a handful of individual activists who banded together and called themselves *Inmigrantes Latinos Unidos de la Florida* [United Latino Immigrants of Florida] (ILUF).

The formation of ILUF was an outgrowth of a small rally held in 2005 in Arcadia, FL organized by Eduardo, an undocumented farmworker, and Fidelia, an immigrant radio disk jockey. The demonstration was in response to the 2005 REAL-ID Act, a bill that sought to prevent undocumented immigrants from obtaining a driver's license.[17] Since Mexican and immigrant activism in the area was uncommon, the few independent advocates in the region had over the years heard about each other through word of mouth or ethnic news outlets. For instance, because Marcos, the Mexican-American lawyer, had previously received local media attention after speaking out against the abuse of immigrant workers, Fidelia and Eduardo asked him to give a speech at their rally.[18] In addition, when

Eduardo contacted the Mexican Consulate in Miami to ask for their support, the consulate suggested he contact a woman named Ana Maria (the
teacher turned farmworker described earlier) because of her long history
of helping migrants in the area. After the small Arcadia rally, Eduardo,
Fidelia, and Ana Maria decided to form the informal group they eventually named ILUF.

The soccer leagues and ethnic businesses united in a much different
manner. When word got out about the potential negative impacts of H.R.
4437, several Mexican merchants throughout the region began to individually discuss the need to unite and to do something about the bill. As
we will see, the question of why Mexicans felt acutely threated by this
nativist measure resurfaces in New York City (see Chapter 4), but for
now it will suffice to say that in the case of Southwest Florida, these individuals believed that established Latino groups in the area did not represent their interests and were ignoring the severity of the legislative threat.
As one of the coalition members put it, "Although we might share some
[common] historical past... lets be very honest about it, Cubans and
Puerto Ricans don't give a shit about what happens to Mexicans."[19] Consequently, a Mexican merchants explained, "We realized that the Cubans
and the Puerto Ricans had their own [organizations] and it was time that
Mexicans came out and showed our faces too."[20] Spanish-language print
media outlets played an important role in connecting these small business
owners and in linking them with the region's immigrant soccer league
association.

Local ethnic newspapers report on the results of soccer league games
and thus are extremely prevalent in immigrant communities. Due to their
popularity, immigrant businessmen use these news outlets as their primary
way of advertising to Latino immigrants (Shinnar and Young 2008: 253;
Teixeira 2001: 2069). Since team captains and league presidents are the
ones who report weekly game results to these media, they also have personal relationships with reporters and newspaper owners. These relationships eventually helped unite local immigrant businesses and soccer league
leaders and promote the demonstration. But although several Spanish-
language print media owners assisted by covering coalition meetings and
advertising the protest, Maxo, an undocumented Mexican immigrant and
owner of a now defunct regional magazine, was particularly instrumental. As he went around Southwest Florida dropping off his weekly paper,
Maxo informed immigrant small business owners about the Sensenbrenner Bill and invited them to a meeting in late January that was being
planned to discuss the legislative threat. In addition, as soccer league

representatives called him to report the results of their games, Maxo also explained to them what was going on and invited them to the same meeting.[21] These invitations were reinforced by the fact that many of these immigrant businesses not only sponsored several of the soccer teams but also because they had personal relationships with each other since soccer league players and leaders were often the customers of these same businesses.[22]

The informal coalition that formed as a result of the January meeting was composed of the regional Latino immigrant soccer leagues (which had over 10,000 players at the time) and over 300 Latino small business owners (including several local print media owners) across the state of Florida; the vast majority of whom were Mexican.[23] After discussing it with other *Concilio* leaders, Marcos, who had known ILUF from their small 2005 rally, contacted the group and invited them to join forces. ILUF agreed, and by late February, the *Concilio* was heading the protest coalition and began to organize and promote a one-day march and strike.[7] They chose Fort Myers as the location for their action because it was home to Florida Congressman Connie Mack, a staunch supporter of the Sensenbrenner Bill.

Activating Preexisting Community Resources

Despite being socially and geographically isolated from the broader public (Zuniga and Hernandez-Leon 2005; Massey 2008), the case of the 2006 Fort Myers protest supports the notion that "subordinate communities residing in the most highly segregated places" are often times "the most likely to find the privacy and cultural resources to develop oppositional cultures and oppositional consciousness" that can be incited into taking political action (Morris and Braine 2001: 29). As Morris contends, the "resources that allow marginalized groups to engage in sustained protest are well-developed internal social institutions and organizations" that "provide the community with encompassing communication, networks, organized groups, experienced leaders, and social resources" (1984: 282). Along these lines, I argue that despite high levels of poverty in immigrant neighborhoods (Rector 2006; Suro, Wilson, and Singer 2011), these communities are actually filled with various individual, economic, and social resources and spaces that may not seem overtly political but can become so under certain conditions. More specifically, in the remainder of this chapter I illuminate how immigrant soccer leagues, workplaces and businesses, as well as the agency of individual immigrant community members, should be viewed as valuable pre-existing resources that can be activated for political purposes.

Individual Agency as a Resource

With any mobilization of a massive group of people, it is easy for us to focus on the group – the *mass* – itself. Yet without the personal skills and efforts of individual activists, no mass protests would ever happen, and no social movements would ever develop. Starting in late-January of 2006, immigrant community leaders in Southwest Florida began to drive hours from their homes (as far north as Tallahassee and as far south as Homestead) to speak to crowds (ranging in size from less than a dozen to several hundred) to educate them about the Sensenbrenner Bill and to encourage them to participate in their upcoming action. Ana Maria best described the dynamics of these efforts, thus her *testimonio* is worth quoting at length:

We had different meetings in different places. I was in charge of going from Homestead to Miami, Sarasota, Plant City, Tampa, Wimauma, Sun City, and Ruskin. We would get groups of people together ... to educate [them] about what was going to happen if they didn't come out and speak up ... I would drive and stop [at places] wherever I saw [Latinos] and with a megaphone would just start saying out loud, "Your attention please! Your attention please!" Then I would tell them what was going on. People would come up to me and say, "Hey, where I live there's a lot more people. Why don't you come [speak there]?" ... I would tell them that I'd go if they got me 50 people together. Then I'd try to show them how to talk to others about [H.R. 4437] so that they could then go [and do the same] ... We ended up having meetings in people's houses on Fridays, Saturdays, and Sundays ... People would come up to me and say, "I could get you 20 families to come if you meet with them." And we would go ... We would even go to people's work ... We'd just show up at construction sites and start speaking to the workers through the megaphones. Sometimes they would chase us out ... So what we would do was wait and see if we saw a manager that was Mexican, and if we did, we would talk to him and give him flyers to give to the workers for us during their lunch. They'd even ask us for more because they'd say there were a lot of people where they lived that they could give them to.

At these meetings, Ana Maria would ask, "Are you willing to stop working for a week? Are you willing to invite 50 people to make 250 flyers and give them out?" According to her, "The people themselves would commit to it." She'd also tell them, "Those of you who have family in Texas, New Mexico, Arizona, call them – this law is national." Coalition members would go to various immigrant neighborhoods, churches, flea markets, restaurants, grocery stores, agricultural fields, and – as Ana Maria mentioned – even construction sites to spread the word about the march.

One of the construction foremen she spoke to in Sarasota was Isaías, who "got the message" from various sources, including Spanish-language radio and newspapers. The call for action resonated with him, so he eventually went on to "speak to a lot of people in the construction industry." He explained, "A lot of people know me in construction. I talked to them about the law and how it was going to affect us and about the better bills that we could fight for." According to Isaías, "I'd go talk to them during their lunch and break and we'd agree to a meeting place for later... We frequently had meetings at the park on Sundays. A lot of times we'd meet at soccer fields too. There would be like 300 to 400 people at the meetings."

Up in Tampa, Ramona, the domestic worker introduced earlier – and who before migrating volunteered for a conservative political party in Honduras and participated in the struggle to get Central American immigrants Temporary Protected Status (TPS) when she first arrived to the U.S. – also helped get the word out for the Fort Myers rally. She said that at the *Concilio* meetings, the organizers would distribute stacks of flyers among the attendees and assign each of them a place to pass them out. According to Ramona, "We'd give the flyers out everywhere, laundromats, in the evening at night clubs, on cars ... at restaurants" and other places.

Fort Myers protest organizers also developed clever messaging strategies and gained unprecedented access to ethnic media outlets. Explaining how they promoted the march on the radio for close to two months, one coalition member stated, "We spent a lot of time on what [H.R. 4437] was. In other words, why [immigrants] should be mad ... Then we started to fill them with pride" by reminding them of everything they contribute to this country and how much they sacrificed to come here. When people called into the radio stations expressing fears about potentially losing their jobs if they participated in the protest, organizers would tell them, "'You could get a job by the next day and you guys know it' ... And at that time it was true, there was so much work to go around that nobody was really scared about losing their job." The group's goal was "to let [immigrants] know that they were just as human and had just as much a right to be here as somebody with that piece of paper. They had sacrificed their lives for their children, they came here, they were working in the fields with pesticides, and we were trying to tell them that they should admire their efforts."[24]

As previously mentioned, the respect that many of these coalition members garnered from their communities due to their professions, length of residency in the area, and roles as cultural brokers, also gave legitimacy to their calls to action. According to Zebedeo, a store owner and one of the immigrant DJs who promoted the march:

> To say that the businessman Gustavo, who everyone knows, was not only supporting but was also one of the main organizers – that gave people a lot of confidence. To know that the lawyer Marcos was participating and was one of the main promoters; to see that Ismael and his magazine *Aguascalientes* were promoting; to see that the sports newspaper *Los Caracoles* and its owner Mr. Filemon were supporting; to see that Mr. David, someone with papers and an owner of several restaurants was involved and giving support; Tacho who runs the biggest soccer league in Florida was involved; to see that Javier with the largest Mexican boot store in all of Florida … to see that Zebedeo was on the radio talking about all of this without fear; to know that all the commercials were sponsored by … the same merchants who were part of their community … [All of this] gave people the confidence to participate … because they knew we were all going to be there … and that *la migra* [immigration officials], the police, or whoever [wouldn't be able to] take everyone away.[25]

Individual immigrant community members also contributed to making the demonstration a success in their own ways. For example, it was not uncommon for community residents who read or heard about the planning of the protest through ethnic media outlets to show up at coalition meetings to become more informed about the issue and pick up flyers to distribute on their own. Furthermore, explained Moises, people would show up to meetings or call coalition members and say things like, "I have a lunch truck so I'm going to take it with water, ice, and sodas at this certain spot and donate everything for free." The day of the rally, "someone that sold corn just showed up and started making and giving them out to people" and, independent of the coalition, several neighborhood residents also gathered at a local church (that was not involved in organizing the protest) and voluntarily prepared over 2,000 plates of food to distribute to marchers.[26]

Thus, one of the reasons why the protest in Fort Myers and across the U.S. were characterized by the media as "leaderless" was because they lacked a nationally recognizable head or spokesperson – in contrast to individuals such as Martin Luther King Jr. and Cesar Chavez during the black civil rights and farmworker movements of the 1960s and 1970s.[27] But without Fort Myers coalition and individual immigrant community members putting in the efforts they did – driving hours to inform others about the issue at neighborhood meetings, going to multiple radio stations several times a week to talk about the importance of the march, developing strategies to convince people to leave work, getting ethnic store owners to support, and so forth – the local demonstration and national protest wave would not have been possible. Through the process of organizing and coordinating the Fort Myers action, local civic leaders became local political leaders themselves – leaders who reside in Southwest Florida immigrant neighborhoods and who should be viewed as political resources that can be activated into mass mobilizing their communities when they feel seriously threatened. The resourcefulness of this stereotypically resourceless community manifested itself not only through the individual agency of these unexpected activists but also through their use of preexisting local economic and social assets as well.

Economic Resources

Edwards and McCarthy (2004) contend that the "resources crucial to the initiation or continuation of collective action are unevenly distributed within societies and among them" (118). Consequently, "middle-class groups remain privileged in their access to many kinds of resources" and "the mobilization of ... poor groups [is] quite rare in advanced industrial democracies" (117). When marginalized people do attempt to initiate collective action, resource mobilization theorists have argued that assets from external actors are key (McCarthy and Zald 1977; Buechler 2000: 35–36). Yet movement resources do not only "come from above," they can come "from below" as well. Local communities have often provided key financial support for movement activities in their neighborhoods (for examples see Piven and Cloward 1978: 209; Beifuss 1985: 48; Cameron 1993: 128; Payne 2007). Such economic resources were fundamental to organizing and coordinating the Fort Myers action.

Some major U.S. corporations did support the 2006 protests, albeit in indirect ways. Several large companies, highly dependent on undocumented immigrant labor, closed their factories, receiving centers, and meatpacking plants to allow their workers to attend local marches (Carpenter 2006). Likewise, in Southwest Florida, several major agribusiness companies, revealing their own fear of the bill and their dependence on immigrant labor, not only allowed their employees to skip work but also – in a few instances – provided buses to transport workers to the rally.[28] However, as stated above, it was not major corporations, but small local Latino immigrant merchants who provided the most vital business support for the Fort Myers protest.

After the *Concilio* formed, members used the influence of their networks and standing as respected local ethnic businessmen to help organize and fund the Southwest Florida mobilization. According to one coalition member, "In our community their customers follow them. Their customers go to them for every problem. They are the little mini-leaders
in our community." If an immigrant business owner "says something, it
trickles down [to the rest of the community.] It's powerful ... they're
powerful in their neighborhoods."[29] One of these storeowners agreed,
explaining, "The businessmen are the ones with the most direct contact with people. Here locally, as a merchant I'm the central contact
point for everyone. I know the whole world here."[30] Ethnic entrepreneurs
have been found to use migrant networks to spread information about
their businesses to potential clients and employees (Light and Karageorgis
1997; Teixeira 2001: 2067). According to Light and Karageorgis (1997),
such messages spread along these networks are particularly "credible
because of the relationships of mutual trust that link members" (10; also
see Light et al. 1993: 38). The local immigrant entrepreneurs who led the
Concilio used these business networks to promote the Fort Myers protest.
Yet these ties were not the only economic resources local businesses utilized to support the movement; they used their financial assets as well.

The more than 300 small ethnic-owned businesses involved in the
Concilio invested thousands of dollars in organizing the march. For example, a small Mexican clothing storeowner explained, "We all chipped
in... I spent more than $1,000 on the event. Other ... smaller stores
gave $100, $200, $150 dollars. All my friends around here gave money."[31]
Concilio members drove all across the state to gather support and donations from as many Latino storeowners as they could find. As another
coalition member remembered, "There were lots and lots of small businesses that helped. From Arcadia, Wauchula, Tampa, Clearwater, Fort
Myers, Immokalee, they participated by giving food, trash bags, and
transporting people. Lots of [crew leaders] didn't go to work and gave
their workers the day off."[32]

As in other parts of the country, advertising the march on local
Spanish-language radio stations throughout the region was fundamental
to spreading the word about the rally. Local merchants also played a vital
role in making this happen. One storeowner and radio DJ recalled, "We
bought ads on all the radio stations. Yes they [the radio stations] helped,
but how did we pay for publicity? All the local merchants of each community did. We would go and ask them for money. Not all of them were able
to give, but the majority of them, mostly Mexican, supported." *Concilio*

members convinced the local businesses and radio stations that it was in their best interest to help.[33] Zebedeo remembers "telling them why we wanted to have a march and that because all of their clients were undocumented, if they all got thrown out [of the country], they wouldn't have any more customers." Protest organizers also gave small businesses incentives to support. For instance, the commercial that promoted the march and was played all across the region would end by listing the names of all the ethnic businesses that had sponsored it and that were endorsing the demonstration. In addition, storeowners were told by coalition members, "If you give us $300, we'll also make you 100 t-shirts. If you give us $500, we'll give you 150 t-shirts with the store's logo and the *Concilio's* logo, and then we'll put a nice quote in Spanish and English saying 'We're All Equal Under Gods Eyes' or 'We're Not Terrorists, We're Workers,' or 'I'm Not Your Enemy, We Want to be Your Friends.'"[34]

Although it did pay for some of its advertisements, the *Concilio* also got a lot of free airtime and publicity from local media. Local magazine and newspaper owners donated sections of their papers to cover coalition meetings and to inform the public about what was being discussed, why it was so important to come out and support, what to wear and how to behave at the march. Similar to what happen in Los Angeles (see Chapter 3), Southwest Florida DJs allowed activists to take the airwaves, sometimes for hours at a time, to promote the protest and to answer callers' questions. Yet the free airtime and print publicity were not given solely for altruistic reasons. As business owners, *Concilio* members had considerable influence over local radio and newspapers, because these media outlets were financially dependent on the advertisements of Mexican businesses. For example, a coalition businessman remembered receiving promotions for the protest for "two months and every single publication [was] free in this area." According to him, because he spends thousands of dollars a year on newspaper advertisements, "I didn't ask anybody. It was more like, *you're gonna* put [this flyer promoting the march] in, right?" and the newspaper owners would do it.[35]

Collectively, the immigrant community was an additional economic resource leading up to the mobilization. Not only did non-*Concilio* members of the coalition donate time and money to pay for flyers and for the gas they needed to drive around the state and promote the march,[36] but the economic power of the immigrant population as a whole was also an essential weapon in the local movement's arsenal. As the April 10 national day of action approached, immigrants became more and more confident that they were a driving force behind the economy – a claim activists were

constantly reminding them of at meetings and on the radio. Because agriculture is integral to the Florida economy, growers were threatened by
what an immigrant boycott could mean to productivity. Local farm owners were especially vulnerable to a labor strike because the fields were in
the peak of harvest season (Roka and Cook 1998: 33; Figueroa 2006),
which meant that billions of dollars of crops could rot if not picked. As
a result, several local Chambers of Commerce agreed to tell their members not to penalize workers who participated in the subsequent national
day of action in exchange for coalition leaders agreeing not to call for a
weeklong work stoppage.[37] Hence, in contrast to the stereotypical view
of immigrant communities as financially deprived, the story of Fort Myers
indicates that under certain circumstances, they can, in fact, muster sufficient economic resources for large-scale collective action.

Social Resources

In his seminal book *Domination and the Arts of Resistance*, James
C. Scott notes the importance of autonomous social spaces created by
marginalized groups for developing political action on their own behalves.
He asserts that "the practices and discourses of resistance" cultivated by
the oppressed cannot exist "without tacit or acknowledged coordination
and communication within the subordinate group." To this end, "the subordinate group must carve out for itself social spaces insulated from control and surveillance from above" (Scott 1990: 118). Social movement
scholars likewise note the significance of "free spaces" that are "defined
by their roots in community, the dense, rich networks of daily life; by
their autonomy; and by their public or quasi-public character as partic-
ipatory environments which nurture values associated with citizenship
and a vision of the common good" (Evans and Boyte 1986: 20; Ayoub
2016).

Immigrant communities also possess these types of social spaces, which
"play a vital supporting role" in sustaining immigrant culture and ethnic identity (Frazier and Reisinger 2006: 267, 271). One of the ways in
which they have manifested themselves in Southwest Florida and other
new migration destinations is through the creation of immigrant soccer
leagues (Steigenga and Williams 2008: 114; Souza Alves 2008: 142). As
a Fort Myers coalition member jokingly put it, "Mexicans come to the
US" for three reasons: to "work, send money back, and soccer."[38] These
soccer leagues "create a cultural space that is familiar, entertaining, practical, inexpensive, transnational, and ephemeral, where immigrants gather
to reaffirm their sense of identity and belonging" (Price and Whitworth

2004: 168). Soccer is fundamentally a family and community affair in many immigrant enclaves. Not only do several ethnic businesses sponsor teams and games (Price and Whitworth 2004: 181), but also women in the community regularly sell food on the sidelines or take part in their own all-female teams, children watch the adults play or participate in their own youth leagues, and spectators socialize and share information about jobs, housing, and news from their home countries (Price and Whitworth 2004; Steigenga and Williams 2008: 114).

These leagues can also be used for political means. Indeed, soccer games have served as key recruiting grounds for immigrant rights groups and union-organizing drives (Gordon 2005: 118; Fine 2006: 55–56). In these ways, local soccer leagues have operated as the "social spaces insulated from control and surveillance from above" that Scott (1990) contends subordinate groups "must carve out" for themselves to coordinate and communicate their "practices and discourses of resistance" (118). Understanding how central soccer leagues are to immigrants in Southwest Florida requires awareness that, unlike in traditional immigrant-receiving destinations (such as L.A. or New York), full-fledged Mexican "ethnic enclaves" (Portes and Rumbaut 1996: 21), had yet to fully develop in this region. Consequently, soccer leagues have become central social spaces for immigrants throughout Southwest Florida. As one league president described, "Here we live differently, we don't have complete neighborhoods like in other places. Here we hardly see each other. On weekends the only time we gather, besides church, is the soccer field."[39] Another league founder agreed, adding that soccer "is one of the ways we've been able to unify, bring our people together and organize them."[40]

Because of the sport's importance to community members, league founders and presidents feel a special responsibility for their fellow immigrants. According to one of these league presidents:

The reason why I got involved [with the protest] was because despite my family and me not having any problems with our papers, there are people here who make an honest living working very difficult jobs to earn their bread...I have lived and worked with these people...for 18 years in the soccer league...[These are] people who always come and ask me for advice and about my opinion on things...I don't consider myself a community leader, but because I know these people so well, I feel obligated to them.[41]

Because of these feelings of group consciousness and linked fate, after the ethnic magazine owner mentioned earlier put *Concilio* coalition members in contact with Tacho, he agreed to help them organize a local demonstration and strike for the April 10 national day of action. As described below, given the important roles they played in their communities – as coworkers, bosses, confidants, league leaders, and so forth – once all the soccer league presidents throughout the region joined and supported the march, "the soccer leagues [became] the seedbeds of the movement."

Their ability to mobilize a large number of immigrants in the region is easier to comprehend once one understands how the leagues are structured. Being league president put these people in contact with networks of team captains who were in charge of their distinct teams, which of course consist of all of the players, and by default their friends and family members. In 2006, throughout Southwest Florida several leagues had from a few hundred to over a thousand members, almost all of which were Mexican. Tacho, the president of his local league and of the more than 10,000-member regional soccer association described previously (the *Coalición de Ligas Hispañas del estado de la Florida*), gave an example: "[In my league] we had more than 76 [adult male] teams, 10 for veterans [older players], 12 women's teams and more than 1,500 players in this league alone ... All together we were close to 100 teams."[42] He said that after meeting with all of the region's league presidents and convincing them to support the march – which, according to him, was easy to do given the drastic effects the Sensenbrenner Bill would have had – each of the presidents went back to their respective communities to organize the various teams in their leagues to participate. Daniel, one of these league presidents who, along with all of his family, was undocumented, recalled that weekly meetings with team representatives became opportunities to discuss the need for everyone to participate and to hand out flyers for players to take home and distribute. Whether documented or undocumented, he said the day of the protest it felt as if, "All of the community and all of the players supported" by attending with their families and friends.[43]

These soccer league players, as well as their friends and family members who watched them play every week, were the same people who were hearing on the radio and reading in their local newspapers about the punitive provisions of H.R. 4437 and the need for them to come out and protest against it. Oliver and Myers (2003) argue that "social influences between groups increase and deepen information flows beyond the information presented in the mass media," and that "messages delivered to individuals by their personal contacts and by the media can also reinforce each other during the critical time when the individual is presented with an opportunity to decide whether or not" to participate in collective action (184–185; see also McAdam and Paulsen 1993). In addition, several political scientists have found that Latinos tend to be more responsive to calls for electoral mobilization when asked to participate by co-ethnics and people they know (Michelson 2005: 98; Barreto and Nuño 2009) and that there is a strong and positive correlation between ethnic media consumption and Latino group consciousness (Kerevel 2011; Medina Vidal 2016; Garcia-Rios and Barreto 2016). My research shows that a similar dynamic seems to have occurred with regard to Latinos in Southwest Florida and their engagement in contentious politics. Southwest Florida immigrant soccer league and community members not only heard calls for action from their local Spanish-language radio and print media outlets but also were urged to participate in the Fort Myers protest by highly respected people with whom they had personal relationships. As a result, these individuals helped make Florida and American history by organizing one of the largest demonstrations of the unprecedented 2006 protest wave.

Conclusion

On the morning of their April 10 action, despite all of their efforts, organizers worried about a possible lack of turnout. They feared "looking stupid" in the eyes of the public. But as the start time of the event approached, one of the coalition leaders recalled, "All of a sudden it was like people were multiplying... I was standing on the stage and I just saw people coming, and more people coming, and more people coming... We just looked at each other and thought '*Wow!*'... You couldn't see the end of them... I could see buses still coming in... People were just pouring onto the streets, all you could see were people, people, people" approaching from all directions.[44]

An estimated 75,000 to 100,000 people poured onto the streets of Fort Myers that day to take part in the mass mobilization. Mainly wearing white t-shirts and waving American flags, many of the participants carried homemade placards that read: "I'm Your Friend," "We Support Just and Humane Immigration Reform," "No to Terrorism, Yes to Papers," "Who Works the Fields?," "Amnesty Now!," and "Today We March, Tomorrow We Vote." Local news outlets reported that the "stream of protesters was at least a mile long," and that the presence of the police riot squads patrolling the area was "drowned out by marchers chanting, 'Together we can do it,' in Spanish."[45] A soccer league member recalled that at one point, "There wasn't even anyone directing" the march, it was "like a monster moving on its own." He remembered that once "the stage was set, people would just jump on and talk about the movement. They'd say

'*Ya basta* [Enough] with the abuse! *Ya basta* with them ignoring us! *Ya basta* with them not passing immigration reform!' ... By then there was no agenda, there was no program, everything just happened on its own."[46]

An ILUF member described the significance of the event in the following manner,

Every immigrant who felt that they didn't have a right to be here, who felt they didn't have a right to speak up, who thought they didn't have the right to be on the streets or look someone straight in the eyes, that definitely changed ... Whether they were legal or illegal ... the people who clean shoes, who clean bathrooms, who clean tables, the people who earn a living working, not stealing ... [they] realized that they too have rights and that if they came out to the streets and mobilized ... they could have a major impact.[47]

Legal scholar Michelle Alexander (2011) observes that "the act of embracing one's stigma is never merely a psychological maneuver; it is a political act – an act of resistance and defiance in a society that seeks to demean a group based on an inalterable trait" (166). The case of Fort Myers shows how the "psychological maneuver" of realizing that the fates of U.S.- and foreign-born (documented and undocumented) Latinos are, in many respects, linked can lead to widespread political action when nativist legislation threatens the collective identities and personal interests of key immigrant community members.

Regardless of the stereotypically impoverished locales where many of them reside, this chapter has also made evident that Latino immigrants have pre-existing individual, economic, and social community assets that can be activated for political purposes. As we have seen, the massive Fort Myers protest was not a case in which professional social movement actors (e.g., paid activists, national organizations, or foundations) parachuted in with external resources to organize and convince docile immigrants to participate in a national campaign. Rather, the demonstration is an example of a community in movement using its various local assets for its own self-defense and desire to demonstrate its dignity and discontent. Contrary to what previous studies may have predicted, this episode of contention illustrates how even among unlikely political actors, in unexpected locations, and under a hostile organizing context, large-scale collective action can still emerge among supposedly "resourceless" people.

3

Promoting Protest Through Ethnic Media

We saw in the preceding chapter that throughout Southwest Florida, local activists gained unprecedented access to Spanish-language magazines, newspapers, and radio stations, which they used to frame H.R. 4437 as a severe and looming threat to the Latino community, and to encourage audiences to participate in the Fort Myers demonstration. In New York, a Korean-language radio station "produced one-minute promotional spots that ran 10 times a day informing people of the rally" being held in the Empire City. According to Chung-Wha Hong of the New York Immigration Coalition (NYIC), through conversations with their colleagues in Chicago and Los Angeles, local activists learned that ethnic media could be an indispensable vehicle for promoting protests. Accordingly, New York organizers attempted to saturate and marshal the ethnic media's entire "communications infrastructure with information about [the] rallies" (Miller 2006).

From coast to coast, during the protest wave, ethnic media became an essential tool to broadcast and make visible local activists' calls for action against the Sensenbrenner Bill, which in turn inspired countless new activists to join the cause. But while there is widespread agreement among scholars over the critical part that Spanish-language media outlets in particular played in promoting the historic demonstrations (Barreto et al. 2009; Pallares and Flores-Gonzalez 2010; Voss and Bloemraad 2011), previous research on this topic has several noteworthy limitations. For example, television is by far the most widely consumed form of ethnic media by Latinos (Fraga et al. 2011: 238, 243), and surveys of 2006 protest participants have shown that the majority of marchers heard about the rallies through TV more than any other news source

(Flores-Gonzalez et al. 2006: 3; Felix et al. 2008: 629; Dionne et al. 2014: 9). Yet studies on the role of Spanish-language media in the mobilizations have focused solely on the backing activists received from radio, which has been credited with "leading" the marches (Miller 2006; Ramirez 2011; Dionne 2014), and newspapers (Aparicio 2010), which (along with the Internet) was among the type of media least used by Latinos during the time of the protests (Fraga et al. 2011: 235–241). Furthermore, despite the consensus on the significance of Spanish-language media to the protest wave, we know almost nothing about exactly how activists seemingly appropriated the ethnic media airwaves to advertise their cause, or about their attempts to influence English-language news outlets.

This chapter aims to help fill these lacunae. Drawing on a case study of Los Angeles, CA, the nation's largest Spanish-language media market, I document how H.R. 4437 helped activate the group consciousness of local activists and members of mainstream ethnic news and entertainment outlets, who in turn gave local organizers unprecedented access to multiple channels of mass communication. More specifically, I examine the unique role that Spanish-language television played in promoting the demonstrations in L.A., the tactics and strategies local organizers used to gain access to radio and TV stations, and the internal movement debates activists had regarding how best to frame their demands to both the English- and Spanish-language mass media.

But before examining the results of my analysis, it is important to briefly distinguish between the types of media I investigate and my reasons for doing so. Activists frequently use what is known as "new" (e.g. the Internet, Web sites, blogs, listservs, and other digital technology) or "alternative" (zines, pirate and community-run radio, newsletters, and other activists publications) media to promote their issues (Atton 2001; Coyer, Dowmunt, and Fountain 2008; Lievrouw 2011). These forms of communication are important to social movements because they are often created by activists themselves explicitly for political purposes, and thus give them complete control over their content. Nonetheless, these mediums are usually limited in terms of the resources they have at their disposal and the types and size of audiences they can reach, especially when compared to mainstream mass media outlets. By the mainstream (in terms of their focus on the general pubic) and mass (regarding their ability to reach a large number of people) media, I am specifically referring to English- or Spanish-language, privately or corporate owned, channels of communication – such as newspapers, television and radio stations – whose primary goals are to generate revenue through selling advertisements. The content of these media outlets typically focus on general news (e.g. daily papers and nightly newscasts) or entertainment (e.g. radio disk jockeys) and are rarely overtly political. Unless otherwise stated, throughout this chapter and the remainder of the book, I use the terms mainstream and mass media interchangeably, and refer to ethnic- and Spanish-language media as equivalents.

Although social movement scholars have recently noted the growing importance of new media to political activism (Bennett and Segerberg 2011), and new and alternative forms of media were in fact used by some (usually younger) activists during the 2006 immigrant rights demonstrations (Costanza-Chock 2014), as mentioned above, it was traditional forms of mainstream media – particularly television and radio – that played the most significant roles in mobilizing Latino and immigrant communities throughout the nation (Barreto et al. 2009; Voss and Bloemraad 2011). Again, this makes sense given that during the period of the protest wave, studies on Latino media consumption patterns showed that they primarily used TV and radio and reported very low levels of Internet usage (Fraga et al. 2012). Thus, because of their central roles in the mobilizations, my analysis specifically focuses on television and radio stations. But to comprehend why and how these mass channels of communication exerted the influence that they did during the immigrant rights cycle of contention, we must first understand the functions that mainstream English- and Spanish-language media have traditionally played in American politics.

The Role of the Mass Media in Politics

In their authoritative study *What Americans Know about Politics and Why it Matters*, Delli Carpini and Keeter (1996) find that the reasons "democracy functions best when its citizens are politically informed" is that this knowledge "assists citizens in discerning their individual and group interests, in connecting their interests to broader notions of the public good, and in effectively expressing these views through political participation." Consequently, they argue, "the more equitably information is distributed among citizens, the more likely that the actions of government will reflect the public's interest and, thus, the public will be supportive of those actions" (1).

One of the primary ways Americans learn about politics is through the mass media. Survey research and experimental methods alike have consistently shown that the news profoundly shapes how, what, and the extent to which people in the U.S. think about politics.[1] Given its influence, it is not surprising that activists have long noted the mass media's importance to promoting their causes (Alinsky 1989: xiv; Ryan 1991; Shaw 2001: 150; Bobo, Kendal, and Max 2001: 158). In fact, according to Ferree et al. (2002), "the mass media forum is *the* major site of political contest," because all of the political actors with whom movements engage – including both government and grassroots allies and rivals – "*assume* its pervasive influence (whether justified or not)" on both themselves and their constituents (10; also see Gamson 2004). Indeed, researchers have found that the media can bring attention to matters activists try to promote (McCarthy, Smith, and Zald 1996: 293; Meyer 2007: 96), help mobilize their bases, attract new recruits (Bobo, Kendall, and Max 2001: 158; Sen 2003: 150), and can legitimize certain issues and actors involved in contention (Gamson and Wolfsfeld 1993; Gamson and Meyer 1996: 285).

Yet while they often seek out media attention for its potential influence, activists quickly discover that there is no guarantee that news outlets will report what they would like (Ferree et al. 2002: 13; Klandermans and Goslinga 1996, 324). Consequently, "even when movement organizers succeed at obtaining the attention of mass media coverage," the reports can "represent the protest events in ways that neutralize or even undermine social movement agendas" (Smith et al. 2001: 1398). News coverage, for example, can emphasize divisions within a movement, give standing to more moderate groups, create leaders who have no organized bases, or focus on individuals who have sensational personalities that distort a movement's image to the broader public (Gitlin 2003; Zald 1996: 270; McCarthy, McPhail, and Smith 1996: 478). Despite these risks of misrepresentation, movements nonetheless consistently attempt to draw the media's attention to their issues and to promote their frames (Gamson and Meyer 1996, 287–288; McCarthy, Smith, and Zald 1996: 291; Kriesi 2004: 86).

As related to social movements, Snow (2013) explains that framing "refers to the signifying work or meaning construction engaged in by movement adherents (e.g. leaders, activists, and rank-and-file participants) and other actors (e.g. adversaries, institutional elites, media, social control agents, countermovements) relevant to the interests of movements and the challenges they mount in pursuit of those interests" (470). Key to successfully promoting movement frames is not only how well they become visible to and resonate with their target populations and the general public (Snow and Benford 1992; Tarrow 1998: 109), but also the degree to which activists are able to diffuse or spread their messages. According to Soule (2004), a key mechanism in this process is the mass media because it "can both broadcast the actions of the transmitter to the potential adopters *and* connect otherwise unconnected individuals via a shared response to events covered" (Soule 2004: 295–296). Consequently, scholars have found that increased media attention often correlates with an increase in movement protests (Meyer and Minkoff 2004: 1475). During the 2006 protest wave, immigrant rights activists across the country used Spanish-language news outlets to amplify their calls for action and to mobilize millions of people. Examining the history and development of Spanish-language media in the U.S. may help us begin to understand how and why this impressive achievement was accomplished.

Spanish-Language Media

At least since the 1848 invasion and annexation of half of Mexico, "Spanish-language media has been part of the experiences and struggles" of Latinos in the United States (Ayon 2006: 27). According to media scholar America Rodriguez (1999), in the 1800s, newspapers written in Spanish "exposed atrocities and demanded public services" for Latinos, "all the while urging their readers to fight back against European American mistreatment" (15). Although it has often been proactive – such as helping Latinos register to vote and to win political office – from the Great Depression and Operation Wetback to California's Proposition 187 and the 2005 Sensenbrenner Bill, the Spanish-language media has mostly mobilized its community during times of crisis (Rodriguez 1999; Ayon 2006; Garcia 2008).

The reach of Spanish-language media has grown along with Latino immigration and changes to federal communications policies (Mora 2014; Costanza-Chock 2014). As a result, during the demonstrations against H.R. 4437, estimates put the number of Spanish-language television stations at over 400, more than 600 radio stations, and at least 700 daily and weekly newspapers nationwide (Ayon 2006: 28; Lafayette 2008). In 2006, *Univision* Radio boasted about its "unmatched ability" to reach more than 11 million listeners, from L.A. and Houston to Chicago and Miami (Garcia 2008: 75). During the protest wave, *Piolín* (Tweety Bird) – the radio DJ most credited for helping promote the Los Angeles demonstrations – was heard by more than 3 million people (Felix et al. 2008: 624) in more than 20 cities across the country, including metro areas in California, Nevada, Texas, Arizona, and Arkansas (*Business Wire 2003*; Hernandez 2006; Garcia 2008: 75). *El Cucuy* (The

Boogieman), another L.A.-based DJ who publicized the marches, was also heard each weekend by more than 3 million listeners, from Southern California to Utah (Baum 2006). Los Angeles is not only home to both of these popular disk jockeys and several others, but as previously mentioned, it is also the largest Spanish-language media market in the United States. For example, *La Opinión*, the city's leading Spanish newspaper, claimed in 2007 to have over 500,000 daily readers (Garcia 2008: 39). And on any given day, KMEX, *Univision* television network's Los Angeles affiliate, has a viewing audience of several hundred thousand in five different counties throughout Southern California. Thus, as Latino immigration has expanded throughout the country, so has Spanish-language media's ability to reach this population, as reflected by the fact that, according to one study, on a regular basis, 87 percent of Latino adults consume Spanish-language newspapers, radio, or TV (Poole 2006).

The impressive growth and influence of Latino ethnic media has had important political ramifications. Aside from helping cultivate a national panethnic Latino identity (Mora 2014), studies have shown that Spanish-language media tend to "cover immigration in a more positive and informative manner when compared to English-language news coverage" (Abrajano and Singh 2009: 23), including when it comes to how they report on community activism around immigration issues (Aparicio 2010: 69). Moreover, scholars have found a strong relationship between Spanish-language media usage and increased Latino voter turnout (Panagopoulos and Green 2011), naturalization rates (Felix et al. 2008), feelings of linked-fate (Garcia-Rios and Barreto 2016), and even support for the 2006 rallies (Barreto et al. 2009: 754). But despite these positive political impacts, and Spanish-language news outlets' early history of local grassroots activism, according to Ramirez (2011), it is imperative to note that today Latino ethnic media "is first and foremost a money generating business" that at its core is part of the corporate mass media (76; see also Aparicio 2010: 67 and Davila 2001). Nevertheless, the spring of 2006 demonstrated the extent to which these news outlets had grown not just in their reach, but also their capacity to mobilize audiences for political purposes. The remainder of this chapter explains why and how this process unfolded during the momentous Latino protest wave.

Media Appropriation and Movement Message Amplification

Activists have long expressed the challenges of drawing media attention to their causes (Ryan 1991: 8; Sen 2003: 148). They often spend valuable time and resources organizing demonstrations that they hope will be large enough to generate the interests of major news outlets (McCarthy, Smith, and Zald 1996: 308; Meyer 2007: 96). But in the spring of 2006, rather than staging rallies to draw the media's attention, immigrant rights activists actually used Spanish-language mass media to promote their demonstrations. The two major protests – the March 25 *"Gran Marcha"* and May 1 "Day Without An Immigrant/Great American Boycott" – that together drew over a million people onto the streets of Los Angeles, are remarkable for many reasons, not the least of which because of the extent to which these gatherings were promoted by the city's major Spanish-language mainstream news and entertainment outlets.

To be sure, the two mass demonstrations did not occur in a vacuum. On December 22, 2005, less than a week after the Sensenbrenner Bill had passed in the House of Representatives, organizations such as the National Korean American Service and Education Consortium (NAKASEC), the Coalition for Humane Immigrant Rights of Los Angeles (CHIRLA), and other local immigrant rights groups staged a rally of about 300 people at the Los Angeles office of H.R. 4437–supporter and Republican congressman Gary Miller. They presented him with a "Grinch Who Stole Christmas Award" along with Christmas-themed wrapped "gifts of dignity and respect."[2] In January of 2006, Los Angeles cardinal Roger Mahony announced the launching of the Catholic Church's Justice for Immigrants Campaign, which he hoped would "remind Catholics of the wonderful history of migrants coming to this country from the earliest days and the church's constant outreach to them" (USCCB 2006). On February 1, in the East Los Angeles neighborhood of Boyle Heights, Dolores Mission Church declared that its parishioners would begin a month-long fast and "dared Los Angeles to get by one day without immigration" (Gencer 2006). Also in early February, local immigrant rights groups held actions outside the L.A. offices of both the Democratic National Committee (DNC) and the Republican National Committee (RNC) and sent 15,000 "Valentine's Day" postcards to California senator Dianne Feinstein to signal their opposition to the bill.[3] On February 4, foreshadowing the wave of protests, longtime activist Javier Rodriguez published an article in *La Opinión*, in which he summarized the history of the local immigrant rights movement and called on Los Angeles to galvanize the nation by uniting and staging a mass march in opposition to H.R. 4437 (Rodriguez 2006). During this same month, activists, mostly from Southern California but also a few from the Midwest, met in Riverside, CA, and called for a national day of action to take place on March 10 – though only the Chicago delegates followed through (see Pallares and Flores-Gonzalez 2010).[4]

Yet it was not until March 1, 2006, that the call to oppose the Sensenbrenner Bill began to garner national attention. On that Ash Wednesday, Cardinal Mahony publicly "vowed a campaign of civil disobedience" against H.R. 4437 (Pomfret 2006). In the largest Catholic archdiocese in the country, made up of some 5 million members and close to 300 parishes, "Mahony said he would instruct his priests to defy [the] legislation" if it were approved by Congress (Watanabe 2006). According to Xiomara Corpeño of CHIRLA, the cardinal's statements were "a turning point because he is pretty conservative and doesn't really overtly come out for progressive issues." So when he did, "it really got everyone's attention." Reverend Alexia Salvatiera of Clergy and Laity United for Economic Justice (CLUE), an interfaith group made of over 600 religious leaders throughout L.A. County, agreed, "It reframed the whole debate because it framed immigrants as children of God, brothers and sisters, rather than ... people that were a drain on our society." Thus, although several small anti–H.R. 4437 actions took place between December of 2005 and February of 2006, activists had only minimal success in putting the issue on the Spanish-language – and to an even lesser degree the English-language – media's radar until the cardinal's bold statements.

Also, early in the year, a small group of Latino activists calling itself the "*Placita* Working Group" (named after the Olvera Street church where they held their gatherings), who had begun to meet in response to the shooting death of an immigrant by a border patrol agent, shifted its focus to the Sensenbrenner Bill and decided to organize a protest against it. As they began to concentrate on H.R. 4437, the group quickly grew and became an informal coalition (later called the March 25 Coalition after the day of their historic action) composed of several mostly Latino local organizations and independent activists. Longtime Chicano community organizer Rosalio Muñoz proposed that the group stage its demonstration on March 25, because on the following Monday, March 27, the Senate was to begin debating its own version of an immigration bill. Muñoz recalled hoping, "If we have a big demonstration in L.A., the people in D.C." would hear about it through the media, and it would "have an impact." The campaign for the protest went public on March 3, 2006. According to a "media advisory," the informal coalition declared that "a major mass mobilization against the passage of the Sensenbrenner Bill [was] to be held in downtown Los Angeles ... [demanding] an integral, comprehensive and family oriented immigration reform that will lead to the legalization and eventual citizenship for the 12 million undocumented immigrants in this country."[5] At the press conference, Gloria Saucedo of *Hermandad Mexicana Transnacional* (an early member of the coalition) declared, "People should not be scared" to protest "because the [U.S.] Constitution is on our side, we should be united for this common cause" (Almada 2006).

Similar to what occurred in Fort Myers, through news coverage, L.A. coalition members learned about anti-Sensenbrenner protests erupting in different and unexpected parts of the country. According to Jesse Diaz, a local activist and one of the original *Placita* Working Group participants, these other marches "kind of led us to the idea of having a mobilization here in Los Angeles." What really got their attention, though, was the first major demonstration on March 6, which drew tens of thousands of participants in Washington D.C. According to Latino Movement USA's Juan Jose Gutierrez, "We said, wait a minute – here we are thinking that we're going to be able to mobilize 25 or 50,000 [people in L.A.], but these guys in D.C. already did 30 to 60,000." He remembered asking, "What's gonna happen next?" What happened next was a massive 300,000-person demonstration in Chicago on March 10 that "took everybody by surprise," recalled Gutierrez. "I think it kind of woke everybody up."[6] L.A. organizers saw the success of Chicago activists as a friendly challenge. Claiming that Los Angeles was the epicenter of the immigrant rights movement, activists felt they needed to raise the bar set by Chicago. L.A. organizers took particular notice of the role that local *locutores* (Spanish-language radio disk jockeys) had played in the mobilization. Advertently and inadvertently, immigrant rights activists throughout the country would later replicate this strategy of getting local ethnic radio stations to promote their marches.

According to Diaz, as late as March 10, "We still didn't have all our planning yet for the March 25 *marcha*, but we knew we had to get it together and kick it up a notch," because of what they had witnessed in Chicago and other cities. Coalition member Sarah Knopp of the International Socialist Organization (ISO) remembered thinking that the media coverage of the other demonstrations taking place across the country was showing potential immigrant protesters that there was strength and safety in numbers. For instance, the size of the Chicago demonstration, Knopp recalled, "gave people the confidence" to participate because they witnessed other immigrants like themselves not being "punished" for protesting, because "the police wouldn't be able to arrest so many people."

The week after the huge protest in Chicago, Nativo Lopez of *Herman-dad Mexicana-Latino Americana* had the idea of bringing key Chicago rally organizer Artemio Arreola to Los Angeles. He and Arreola began to talk to Spanish television and radio stations about the significance of what had occurred in Chicago, how and why it was organized, and the need for Los Angeles immigrants to do the same.[7] Independent of the local coalition, other activists, such as Angelica Salas of CHIRLA, had been talking to schools and churches, as well as doing short radio interviews about the dire consequences the Sensenbrenner Bill could have on the immigrant community.[8] Social movement scholars use the concept of "social appropriation" to describe the process through which activists successfully convert or incorporate previously existing non-political institutions, groups, or networks into overt political actors (Tilly and Tarrow 2006: 217; McAdam et al. 2001: 47–48). A March 14 "media breakfast" would in retrospect be the beginning of what would eventually seem like the near-total social appropriation of Spanish-language radio, and later television, stations throughout in the City of Angels.

According to Diaz, holding a "media breakfast" where organizers express their desire for Spanish-language news outlets to become active participants in promoting a demonstration was not a new tactic; they had done the same during the campaign against Proposition 187 in 1994. Gutierrez recalled that the goal of the event was to explain the significance of the March 25 protest and to express the "hope" that the Spanish media would help inform "the public about what we were planning to do." The basic strategy, according to Javier Rodriguez, was to "use the media as a venue to be able to connect with our people." He explained, "It consisted of going after the media and convincing ... media members, the reporters, the camera people, the studio people, everybody" to support the protest. Demonstrating a sense of group consciousness, Rodriguez said that members of the Spanish-language media "identified" with the cause "because many of them are [or have been] undocumented" and because "the majority of them [were] Mexican." In short, he added, "We went after their hearts and minds."[9]

The Social Appropriation of Radio Stations

Given that protests had recently occurred in places like Portland, Philadelphia, Washington, D.C., and Chicago, L.A. activists were not surprised when local Latino news outlets covered the media breakfast.[10] They felt that all eyes were on Los Angeles, the capitol of Latino America. Thus, after what they deemed a successful media breakfast where reporters

seemed to have been genuinely convinced of the Sensenbrenner Bill's punitive and broad scope, Jesse Diaz and Gloria Saucedo were disappointed
and surprised that the popular Spanish–radio DJ *El Cucuy* was absent.
They had hoped to convince him to play the same role as Chicago DJs
in galvanizing the local immigrant population in that city. Because Diaz
had previously appeared on the radio show of one of *El Cucuy's* competitors, *El Piolín*, to discuss his involvement with an anti-Minutemen
campaign, Diaz asked Gloria if he should attempt to contact *El Piolín* to
see if he'd be willing to put them on his show. Before Diaz even had an
opportunity to do so, he noticed that he had several missed calls on his
cell phone from *Piolín's* producer. According to Diaz, "*Univision* Radio
[which owns *Piolín's* program] ... was calling us before we were calling
them."[11] A few members of the coalition immediately drove to the station
to speak with the producer. One of these activists recalled, "We told [the
producer] about the *marcha*, H.R. 4437, and how it was going to affect
the community. We told them that we wanted to call for a march and
that we wanted them to help us [by doing] the outreach." Activists used
"what had been done in Chicago" to convince the producer that his station's participation would not be unprecedented and would actually be in
the best interests of his audience.[12] As a result, *Piolín's* producer agreed
to give them 20 minutes of airtime to discuss the issue later in the week.
But that afternoon, the activists received a call from him. Instead of waiting two days, he wanted them to come back the following morning to do
the interview. Diaz and Saucedo got the sense that, "They didn't want us
going nowhere else. In other words, they wanted exclusivity."[13]

Though activists usually have to work extremely hard to get recognized by the press, on rare occasions, the opposite becomes true. At
times, news outlets can get caught up in what are called "media attention
cycles," in which coverage of an issue or event is minimal at first, but then
rapidly increases and suddenly leads to overexposure when news producers believe these topics capture their audiences' interests (McCarthy,
Smith, and Zald 1996: 298; Oliver and Myers 2003: 184; Meyer 2007:
95). Gitlin (2003: 270) contends that, in these instances, reporters can lose
their objectivity by over-representing one side of an issue. The first interview on *Piolín's* show marked the beginning of one such cycle. According
to Rodriguez, because the show was syndicated across various cities and
states,

The moment we got on *Piolín's* program we began talking to the nation. We began
explaining why we had to demonstrate. We began talking about the history, giving

people perspective of what we did before, of how we gained the amnesty law of 1986. They heard us motivating them. They heard us saying the undocumented community is us, we are them ... we are one people ... They listened to our calls for solidarity, for tenderness, for love, and for hope.

Although they were only supposed to be on the air for 20 minutes, the coalition members received so many calls that they broadcasted live for over four hours. Rodriguez remembered, "From there we kicked off. That was the qualitative leap."

There had been some disagreement within the local movement about whether to have a protest specifically dedicated to H.R. 4437 on Saturday, March 25, or to encourage people to attend the annual Cesar Chavez mass at the Los Angeles Cathedral on Sunday, March 26, and hold a small rally against the bill afterward. During the radio interview, famed United Farm Workers (UFW) cofounder Dolores Huerta called in and spoke critically about staging two actions on the same weekend. With signs of division in the movement, *Piolín* ended the show by stating that although he agreed with their opposition to H.R. 4437, he was not willing to commit to promoting the protest because of the lack of unity among the activists. The following day, Juan Jose Gutierrez gave an interview with another local DJ named *El Mandril* (The Baboon). He invited other coalition members to appear with him. Again, the activists were able to get significant airtime – over two hours – to answer callers' questions and to discuss the need to demonstrate. On *El Mandril's* show, the DJ questioned the activists about the disagreement within the movement regarding whether they should have two actions on the same weekend. Gutierrez responded by saying that if the Spanish media complained about activists being divided and felt justified in demanding that they work out their differences to forge greater unity for their cause, then organizers felt "entitled to demand from [the Spanish-language media] ... to also unite in order to serve as a catalyst" to mobilize the community to attend the protest.[14]

This assertion led to an extraordinary moment later in the show when competing DJs, *El Mandril* and *El Piolín*, spoke live on the air to each other and committed to joining forces. Subsequently, *Piolín* called several other rival DJs and invited them to join in promoting the mobilization. On the air, the DJs asked their listeners to come to the march wearing white and carrying American flags to symbolize peace and unity. They also attempted to ease possible fears of protesting by promising that it would be "a peaceful march, a civilized march, an organized march" (Baum 2006). During this on-air multi-DJ call for action, another disk jockey proclaimed, "This isn't about radio stations and competition, it's about something bigger" (Baum 2006). As the DJs "began to discuss the issue on the air, listeners felt even more inspired to take action because these radio personalities, whom they regarded as personal friends, had turned their attention to an issue that would affect them all" (Felix et al. 2008: 623). From this point, the March 25 demonstration media attention cycle was in full effect.

Starting the week they first appeared on *Piolín's* show through the day of the actual mobilization, activists used several strategies to draw and hold the Spanish media's attention and keep themselves on the air. For instance, organizers held "press conference after press conference ... with different characters, leaders, [and] organizations ... announcing their entrance into the movement." According to Rodriguez, the coalition's media strategist, activists felt that this tactic "was really important and helped us to build the hype from the press conference, to *Piolín*, to the radio stations [uniting], to the TV stations. We built the hype in order to maintain" the media's attention.[15] As a result, one organizer recalled, "Practically every [Spanish] news outfit, every information outlet, every mass communication outlet became accessible."[16] "It was free press, free public announcements over and over again," remembered Mike Garcia, President of the Service Employees International Union (SEIU) Local 1877, the famous L.A. "Justice for Janitors" immigrant union.[17]

Once this media attention cycle started, the activists who had initiated it were unable to completely manage it. News outlets began to interview other immigrant rights groups and activists who had not been part of the coalition coordinating the March 25 demonstration. As one organizer put it, "They started to bring in other people, too. It was kind of convoluting [our] message, but ... we couldn't control it anymore, it was taking [on] a mind of its own."[18] Even organizations that usually didn't focus on activism began to lobby the media to support the rally. One of these was COFEM, a coalition of California Mexican immigrant hometown associations (HTAs) that, at the time, had about 50,000 active members and anywhere from 100,000–150,000 general members. According to Arturo Carmona, executive director of COFEM, various HTAs began to "put a lot of pressure on the media" by beginning to "call them and schedule meetings" where they would ask station managers to "open up the airwaves to promote this historic" event. When *Piolín* interviewed him a few days before the march, then-president of COFEM, Salvador Garcia, pledged that his federation alone would bring "tens of thousands" of people to the march (Garcia 2008: 63).

Despite the diversity of protest supporters getting media attention (from labor unions and immigrant rights groups to hometown associations and local businesses), their opposition to H.R. 4437 was uniform, and the access they obtained was unprecedented. Harking back to the early days of the immigrant rights movement, former CASA member Nativo Lopez, now of *Hermandad Mexicana Nacional*, remembered, "When we were organizing in the '70s there was only one [Spanish-language] television station and not everybody had it – you had to have a special box ... and there were only two Spanish radio stations," which would only make themselves available to activists "on egregious occasions." But in 2006, "for the first time in our history, [Latino activists] had access to Spanish-language media like never before."[19] Another historic event took place on Monday, March 20, when, on the steps of Los Angeles City Hall, "despite long-standing rivalries" (Felix et al. 2008), 10 of the regions most popular Spanish-language DJs officially announced that they were coming together to support the March 25 demonstration. They decided to unite and "promote the cause" because "rally organizers" had convinced them of the negative "ramifications of the legislation," H.R. 4437 (Watanabe and Becerra 2006).

Contrary to the conventional narrative then, the radio DJs do not deserve sole credit for mobilizing millions to march. Activists played a crucial role in convincing Spanish-language disk jockeys to give them free reign on the airwaves to answer callers' questions, to frame the Sensenbrenner Bill as potentially having widespread and horrendous effects on the entire Latino community, and to amplify their calls to protest. Many sympathetic members of the ethnic media identified with those most directly targeted (the undocumented) by H.R. 4437 through their personal experiences, sense of linked fate, and group consciousness. As *Piolín* explained: "It was the first time I had done anything like this, but I remember thinking once, when I was almost deported, that if I had a chance I would try and help someday... When I heard what they were trying to do in Congress, and I heard from people who were afraid their families were going to be torn apart, it touched me. I really wanted people to know about this rally" (Baker-Cristales 2009: 66–67). Once the Spanish-language radio stations made themselves available to protest organizers, audiences joined the cycle by engaging in a flurry of on-air discussions. Listeners from throughout Southern California – and even other states – began to call in, stating that they were planning to fly or drive to Los Angeles to attend the *marcha*. One DJ described the effects of their efforts, "It's incredible, the people's response. Everywhere we go, they are talking about it, even at Disneyland... We have been getting emails, telephone calls, faxes – everything" (Ramirez 2011: 63).

According to coalition member Juan Jose Gutierrez, himself a naturalized citizen, because of the racist rhetoric around the immigration debate, he recalled feeling that even though he and many other Latino immigrants had gained their "papers," they still were not seen as equals in the eyes of most Americans. He claimed that the Spanish-language media audiences activists were trying to mobilize "understood and lived the fact that those new undocumented persons ... were their family members, their brothers, cousins, [or] at the very least their *compadres* [close friends] or *paisanos* [countrymen]." Displaying a sense of racialized illegality, Gutierrez remembered asking himself, "How can I think of myself as a full-fledge American when I'm viewed [by U.S. society] not as the American that I am, but as the 'illegal' that they see in me?"[20] Believing that many in the Latino community felt the same, organizers used an appeal to the group consciousness of DJs and their listeners to encourage them to take collective action against H.R. 4437. Several of these disk jockeys – who usually function as sources of entertainment not actors seeking to create political change – responded by speaking candidly during their programs "about their experiences as undocumented immigrants, validating the sense of injustice felt by many undocumented immigrants, and legitimizing the call" to protest (Baker-Cristales 2009: 67). Activists convinced many members of the ethnic media that the Sensenbrenner Bill was not solely an attack on people without papers, but an assault on the entire Latino community – both immigrants and U.S.-born.

Support from Spanish Television

Studies have shown that television news is an educator "virtually without peer," because it "shapes the American public's conception of political life in pervasive ways" (Iyengar and Kinder 1987: 2). Because of [?] production costs and a "scarcity of time and space," scholars have found that "activists face a steep uphill struggle in trying to get coverage on television news" (Meyer 2007: 94). Nonetheless, since Spanish-language television typically did a good job of covering immigration issues, activists believed that the draconian nature of the Sensenbrenner Bill would draw the attention of local new stations. Their hope was to be interviewed about the issue and in the process have the opportunity to promote their March 25 protest. The coverage they received far surpassed their wildest expectations.

The night before the March 14 media breakfast, Javier Rodriguez received a phone call from an *Univision* reporter asking if he would be willing to do a series of interviews starting at 5am and leading up to the

9am press event. He agreed and, with Gloria Saucedo, did about four interviews. To the activists, it seemed as if "*Univision* had made a political decision to take up the charge before anybody else."[21] By "political decision," activists meant that the station had taken a stance against the Sensenbrenner Bill and, as a result, began to give local protest organizers an unprecedented amount of coverage and promotion for their march. For example, according to Rodriguez, "The first interview was taped and made into a promo right on the spot." Diaz remembers seeing the promotional ad from his home:

I started looking at them on the news and ... at 5 o'clock [am] they started showing [the promo] one time and then at 5:30 showed it again, [at] 6 they showed one, 6:15, 6:30, 6:45, [and] before you know it they were looping it like every commercial break. They're showing them and they're saying "*Vete al Gran Marcha!*" [Go to the Grand March!]. They kept showing them and by 9 o'clock, when the press conference was supposed to start, they were looping that shit every few minutes. It would fade out and show the *Gran Marcha cartelones* [posters] ... It was just like they took it up. I thought, "Damn! Wow!"

These protest promos were the first extensive TV coverage the movement received for the march, but it would not be their last. To maintain the attention and to draw more television coverage, activists attempted to play the various news outlets off against each other by questioning their commitment to the immigrant community in its time of need. According to Nativo Lopez, activists believed they "were successful in getting the media to compete with each other to get our message out." If coalition members went to *Telemundo*, and the station was reluctant to give them airtime to promote the rally, they would call *Azteca America* and try to get an interview there. Once that station committed, they would call *Telemundo* back and say, "What's up with that? *Azteca America* is giving us coverage. Aren't you guys with the people?" To the surprise of the activists, often times the stations seemed not to need much convincing. They speculated that Spanish TV and, in particular, *Univision* – the largest Spanish television network in the country – had made a "corporate decision" to support the march.

According to Angela Sombrano of the Central American Resource Center (CARECEN), "I think there was an agreement, a political agreement by the networks to support the march," because "we had a lot of openings to be on the talk shows." More skeptical coalition members felt that the "corporate owned media" decided to "use the mass movement" when it was "in its interest to defend its market."[22] These activists believed that the media was primarily responding to the threat that the proposed law represented to its audience – or "market." If millions of undocumented immigrants were forced to flee the country, the stations' audience would shrink by that same amount. These hunches were half right. A decision by local Spanish television stations *was* made to promote the march, but it wasn't a "corporate" determination made by top executives; it was a local managerial decision.

Researchers have shown that the willingness of news outlets to adopt movement frames depends on several factors, including the personal life experiences and beliefs of their personnel (Gitlin 2003: 269). In this way, because the vast majority of the Spanish media's employees – from janitors and camera operators to managers and news anchors – were immigrants themselves (Rodriguez 1999), activists believed that it was easier to convince them to support the rally. As one L.A. protest organizer put it, "They're part of the community, they're part of the social group that would have been adversely affected by this legislation [and] ... they obviously have sentiments for the people."[23]

The radio DJ *Piolín* offers a perfect example. Having first come to the U.S. by crossing the desert "illegally," he knew what it was like not to be able to leave the country to see his family because he lacked proper documentation, had previously been fired from a job for not having papers, had once washed cars and recycled aluminum cans for a living, and had even been detained and almost deported. According to *Piolín*, "I went through" being undocumented, "I know the feeling, and you feel terrible [and] I don't want no one to go through that. It's painful" (Fears 2006).

Univision news director Jorge Mettey presents a slightly different case. Mettey was responsible for his station's support of the march and for convincing his competitors to run the same promo for the demonstration. Mettey is not a stereotypical Mexican immigrant; he came from a privileged family that possessed the resources to provide him with an elite education. But since moving to the United States, he explained, "It was obvious that immigrants were treated differently and that bothered me. So when I came to live here, it was already on my map that immigrants were not treated" as equals. According to the news director, the broad scope of the Sensenbrenner Bill and the racist anti-Latino rhetoric in the debate it sparked was a stark reminder of this differential treatment. Consequently, despite being a successful professional and not being undocumented, he decided to take the unusual step of getting *Univision* involved with promoting the mobilization. Expressing his sense of linked fate with other Latino immigrants, Mettey explained, "I felt a part of them and I felt insulted by the way they were [being] treated. I felt compelled to do something precisely because of that."

It is also important to point out that Mettey and *Univision* had a long history of "civic journalism," covering the issues that most directly impacted the Latino community. The station had previously assisted with efforts to get Latinos to fill out the U.S. Census, apply for citizenship, and to register and actually vote during elections (Rodriguez 1999; Ayon 2006). According to an editorial board member, "I don't care what company you are. If you're Fox, ABC, or CNN, if you want to be relevant to your community, you [have to] satisfy the informational needs of your audience to the best of your abilities." When he moved to *Univision*'s Los Angeles station, Mettey already possessed this view of journalism, as evidenced by a news segment he created called *A Su Lado* [On Your Side]. The segment featured various experts on topics relevant to the immigrant community – from interacting with police officers to education – and encouraged viewers to call the station, free of charge, if they had any questions. The first *A Su Lado* was produced in conjunction with the Service Employees International Union (SEIU) at one of its local union halls. According to Eliseo Medina of SEIU, the topic was immigration (from citizenship to deportation issues) and, due to the more than 300,000 phone calls they received from viewers, the union's phone system crashed. Because it was a huge success, especially when addressing immigration issues, the segment became a staple of the newscast.[24]

Immigration was, thus, not a new topic for the station. Indeed, the news department had been following the Sensenbrenner Bill since it was first proposed. A *Univision* representative explained, "It was an issue that was on the editorial room table every single day since it was introduced."[25] Because the station had recently run a series of stories discussing the twentieth anniversary of the 1986 Immigration Reform and Control Act's (IRCA) amnesty provision, the news staff was familiar with the slow pace of the immigration policymaking process. As a result, they were shocked and appalled at not only the content but also how quickly the Republican-led House of Representatives was able to pass such a horrendous bill. To get a sense of the potential ramifications of the legislation, producers and reporters contacted people such as Angelica Salas of CHIRLA and Maria Elena Durazo of the Los Angeles County Federation of Labor (the LA County Fed), both longtime immigrant rights advocates whom the station often turned to for commentary on immigration issues. At an editorial board meeting after the bill had passed the House, a station member recalled saying, "This is terrorizing. This is terrorism at its best. The way it was rammed through Congress ... was totally unbelievable, unheard of. I hadn't seen anything like it in [all of my] experience in covering politics and doing journalism in this country."²⁶ Hence, rather than being solely motivated by a corporate desire to "protect its market," in the case of *Univision*, members of the media also responded because immigration had always been one of the issues that resonated most with their audience and their employees. In contrast to the radio DJs, who activists informed of the punitive nature of H.R. 4437, Spanish-language television knew just how dire the consequences of the bill could be.

Due to the severity of the issue, Jorge Mettey decided to get his news station behind the march. He explained, "In *Univision* we had the privilege of a lot of freedom to do things, mainly because most of those making the decisions [at the corporation's headquarters] didn't have a clue of what we were doing." He claimed that most of the network's executives did not speak Spanish, and those who did "don't feel close to our viewers." Mettey asserted, "It's very unfortunate that the guys in Miami, they are of a very different origin" than their majority-Mexican audience. "Most of them came from Cuban origins with very different challenges in life," so although some of them are fully bilingual, "they don't feel close to [undocumented] immigrants at all." Mettey also had this "freedom from top management" because he had been very successful at his job. Under his leadership, "The numbers were great ... I had great ratings ... The sales were going up and that's what they understood ... I had a lot of leverage because of that." Mettey used this freedom to do something unheard of in American social movement history: He created a promotional ad with rival television stations and convinced them to run it simultaneously in order to mobilize their audiences to take part in the March 25 demonstration. The promo "was not the result of a company vision," Mettey asserted. "What you saw on the air was my very own" creation.

According to the news director, "I decided to call all the other stations to do the campaign together to send a message of unity, being mature, and that we can come together."²⁷ The ad showed the main newscasters from almost every major local Spanish-language television station standing in a line, consecutively saying one of the following statements:

> Demonstrate that you are good.
> That it matters to you.
> That you are big.
> That we could be united.
> Participate with Pride.

With Dignity.
With Order.
With Maturity.
Do it for your people.
Do it for your children.
Do it for our community.
And for what's to come.

Then, putting their arms around each other, in unison they all say, "Unite!
Unite! Unite!" A narrator then titles the march "Standing Firm" and states
the date and location of the Los Angeles protest.[28]

Mettey dedicated himself to making sure *Univision* viewers saw the ad
as much as possible. Audience exposure to the promotion was massive.
The Los Angeles media market, which covers not only all of Los Angeles
County, but also Riverside, San Bernardino, Ventura, and Orange Counties, had a potential viewing audience of 14 million people, about half of
whom were Latinos. *Univision*'s local newscasts were the most watched in
the country (regardless of language), so of those 7 million potential Latino
viewers, hundreds of thousands were likely viewing on any given day.[29]
According to Mettey, "I canceled promotions of our newscast, risking my
ratings ... I said no promos of the newscasts. I wanted [people] to get
sick and tired of this [protest] promo. I wanted the viewers of the *telenovelas* [soap operas], of the newscasts, of the kids programming, everybody
to get sick and tired of this message." *Univision*'s rival television stations
also promoted the demonstration through public service announcements
broadcasted during their newscasts, regularly reported on the prepara-
tions for the march, and conducted interviews with protest organizers
(Baker-Cristales 2009: 61).

Tarrow (1998) contends that television, "with its unique capacity
to encapsulate complex situations in compressed visual images," has
brought about a "revolution in movement tactics" because of its ability to diffuse movement strategies (115). Although survey data shows a
strong correlation between participation in the marches and Spanish TV
and radio consumption (Barretto et al. 2009), we may never know exactly
how much of the Spanish-speaking population that participated in the
protest wave was motivated to act by the media. We do know, however,
that while social movement scholars maintain that television is the most
difficult type of coverage for activists to attract, during the 2006 protest
wave Spanish TV stations not only covered but actually helped promote
the city's immigrant rights marches. Although activists were never able to
socially appropriate television airtime to the degree that they dominated

Spanish-language radio, when their protest received free promotion by all of the major local Spanish TV networks – including the largest Spanish-language television station in the nation – they recognized the amazing boost to their cause. The result of this unprecedented support from the ethnic media was the massive *Gran Marcha* of March 25, 2006 – the largest protest in Los Angeles and California history.

La Gran Marcha de Los Ángeles

According to Victor Narro of the UCLA Downtown Labor Center, the original permit application for the march was approved by the city for a gathering of 3,000–5,000 people. But, after the Chicago protest and as Spanish media coverage of the event grew, he went back on several occasions to amend the permit size. Two days before the protest, coalition members tried to rent 10 more buses to bring people in from other counties but, they claimed, no buses were available to rent in all of Southern California. Buses of protesters came from "all over Arizona, Colorado, and other states," recalled Diaz. He heard of people coming from as far as Chicago, Washington, Alabama, Wisconsin, and even Louisiana. On one of Narro's visits to amend the protest permit, he recalled the police telling him, "Victor you're getting unrealistic with us … In L.A. you could never bring out 50,000. Chicago was an anomaly." The officer expressed concern about overstaffing the rally and having to pay officers for unneeded overtime. In the end, the officer told him, "I'll tell you what we'll do. We'll have enough police officers for 10,000 and then we'll call reinforcements if we need to. But we can't have enough police for 50,000 and then you only bring 2,000."[30]

The day of the action, Saturday, March 25, started like most early spring mornings in L.A., hazy and a bit chilly.[31] The protest was scheduled to begin at 10am at the corner of Olympic and Broadway in the city's Fashion District. Hours before it was set to start, the number of people waiting to protest had already more than tripled Narro's highest permit estimate. Buses throughout the city's Eastside were full and unable to make their regular stops on their way downtown, leaving hundreds of white T-shirt-wearing would-be protesters stranded at bus stops. In response, the masses began to walk across the various bridges that link East Los Angeles to the city's downtown. With no parking for miles in every direction, family members served as shuttles, dropping kin, friends, and neighbors off as close as they could to City Hall.[32] The Associated Press reported speaking to people in attendance who said that for weeks they had "soaked up details about the planned march against the bill

from Hispanic TV and radio" (Flaccus 2006). The fact that almost everyone was wearing white was a sign that they had heard ethnic media's call
to do so.

Despite the expense of using helicopters for a newscast, Mettey
deployed one from the beginning of *Univision*'s live coverage, which
began at around 6am. The news director specifically warned all of his
anchors that activists and even radio DJs would likely exaggerate the
number of people attending the demonstration. He told them, "We have
to be very careful with the way we handle numbers," and instructed his
news desk to call the LAPD every 15 minutes to get an official count.
Hours before the protest was supposed to begin, the people started marching. Organizers were unable to lead the "human river" of demonstrators,
which stretched over two miles long. The official protest route – starting
at the corner of Olympic and Broadway and marching down Broadway
up to City Hall – was so packed that ralliers began to spill on to parallel
streets. According to Narro, "You had marches coming down Los Angeles
[St.], Spring [St.], Main [St.], and Broadway [Blvd.] simultaneously . . . The
people figured it out. The whole experience was pretty cool."

By the time the marchers started, the official police estimate was
already at 150,000. But even then, according to Mettey, this was a "ridicu-
lous" figure "because they kept the number 150,000 for more than an
hour when we saw" from the helicopter coverage "that it was getting
bigger and bigger by the second." The station kept calling the LAPD for
an updated count, but the police stood firm at the 150,000 figure. A little after 10am, *Univision* reporter Norma Roque announced live on the
air, "So far they have a half a million" people. According to Mettey, "I
got so mad. So when we finished that insert I called the helicopter" and
said, "What the hell are you doing? Why did you say half a million? That
was absolutely wrong. I have been telling you to be very careful" with
the numbers. She responded, "I'm sorry Mr. Mettey but we heard that
from the LAPD helicopter that is flying right by us. We are listening to
their conversations and we heard their helicopter telling the LAPD that
they have an expert in the helicopter and they told them that their official number is half a million. That's why we said half a million." Mettey
immediately called the police station explaining what had occurred and
demanding an updated number that was *not* 150,000. About 50 minutes later, the LAPD held a press conference stating that the protest size
was 500,000.

According to the *L.A. Weekly*, the protest "felt entirely organic." The
paper reported that:

Grandmothers, elderly *vaqueros* [cowboys], toddlers in strollers, people in wheelchairs, the blind. Skater kids, dudes with gang tattoos, emo-punks, gays, cha cha chicks, transsexuals, Che Guevara adherents. Gardeners, nannies, construction workers, taco truck guys, contractors, business owners. Guatemalans, Nicaraguans, Venezuelans, Hondurans, Puerto Ricans, [and Mexicans]. It seemed that no subsegment of the region's Latino population was left unrepresented. (Hernandez 2006)

All along the protest routes were "mini-rallies," where radio stations had set up their own stages and were talking to the audiences around them. The mood was festive, with live and recorded celebratory music, and food vendors sprinkled throughout the enormous crowd trying to keep up with orders. Although several sizable contingents of Asian groups and African-Americans were present, Latinos clearly constituted the vast majority and, among them, the multitude appeared heavily Mexican. A few flags from various countries were spotted, but the American flag – without a doubt – predominated.[33] People held handmade signs with such messages as, "AFTER I BUILT YOUR HOME AND GROWED [sic] YOUR FOOD, WHY DO YOU TREAT ME LIKE A CRIMINAL?" (Hernandez 2006). Cardboard placards in various languages called for "Amnesty" and "Immigrant Rights Now!" Still others held posters with messages that revealed their own "illegal" status, while announcing that their children were off "fighting for freedom" in Iraq."[34] Surprised and unprepared for the size of the massive crowd that assembled around them, rally organizers spoke to the people from the steps of City Hall with, as one participant put it, "a sound system for like a backyard *quinceañera* [a Mexican "sweet fifteen" coming of age party]."[35]

Legendary immigrant rights activist Soledad "Chole" Alatore remembered during the late-1960s and early-1970s – in what arguably could not even be called a "movement" at the time – having marched down the same route with a few brave participants terrified of the armed police officers walking beside them. When they arrived on the steps of City Hall, more officers greeted the intrepid immigrant rights activists with dirty looks. In stark contrast, in 2006, the massive and peaceful crowd drowned out the police's presence. Los Angeles Mayor Antonio Villaraigosa, who himself had roots in the immigrant rights movement, welcomed the ralliers by stating, "We are workers, not criminals ... We say to Sensenbrenner that there are no illegals here. The only thing illegal is a proposal that would demonize and criminalize eleven million people."[36] The crowd erupted in cheers as speaker after speaker spoke about the importance of immigrants to this country and the need to stop H.R. 4437 and fight for legalization.

The Latino community had obviously heard activists' calls to action, far surpassing the degree of support organizers had hoped for. In fact, according to a local news outlet, "well after the speaker program ... had ended, marchers were still coming ... unaware that the event was officially over" (Hernandez 2006).

America, Love It or Boycott It: Intramovement Frames Disputes

After the remarkable turnout at their massive March 25 protest, activists in L.A. felt emboldened and quickly began to strategize about how they might parlay this newfound momentum and media attention into getting the Senate to pass a bill with a path to citizenship for undocumented immigrants. Getting a bill that included legalization would likely stop H.R. 4437 in its tracks since there was no way the far-right Republicans in the House who supported the Sensenbrenner Bill would agree to a compromise. This issue is explored in greater detail in Chapter 6, but what is important to note for now is that immigrant rights advocates in Los Angeles and throughout the country had to decide how best to influence the more moderate but still Republican-led Senate.

Because of ideological and tactical disagreements on how best to accomplish their goals, the informal coalition that had originated from the *Placita* Working Group split into two factions: the March 25 Coalition, led by some of the more radical independent activists and organizations (such as the International Socialist Organization and *Hermandad Mexicana*) who had initiated the first protest, and the We Are America Coalition (WAAC), made up of more moderate immigrant rights NGOs, labor unions, and the Catholic Church. Although both groups supported national days of action, reflecting similar rifts that occurred in other major cities, divisions manifested in how each faction framed its claims to the media. The March 25 Coalition wanted to expose how vital immigrants were to the economy, so they called for a national economic strike and mass mobilization on May 1, International Workers Day. The official name of their event was "The Great American Boycott," but it would come to be more popularly known as "The Day Without An Immigrant." Alternatively, the We Are America Coalition – which was part of the national We Are America Alliance – sought to show the Senate and the public that immigrants desired to integrate and contribute their talents to the country. As such, instead of having a protest during the April 10 "National Day of Action for Immigrant Justice," local WAAC organizers decided to have a candlelight vigil and procession in Downtown Los

Angeles. They also organized a demonstration on May 1 but asked supporters not to risk losing their jobs and instead come to their evening
rally after they got off of work. The balance of this chapter takes up how
both local May Day actions unfolded and how the intramovement frame
disputes transpired (Benford 1993).

We Are America!

Given the magnitude of the March 25 mobilization and the emergence of
more and more demonstrations throughout the country, the issue of legalization and the upcoming May Day rallies kept immigrant rights activists
on the media's agenda. "There was a lot of press ... we had nothing to do
with," explained a WAAC member. "It was just feeding off each other and
the press wanted to talk to a lot" of people about the protests.[37] Because
the Senate was still deliberating on a bill and the cycle of media attention continued, the We Are America Coalition believed that how they
framed their demands was essential to whether members of congress and
the general public would support their cause. Maria Elena Durazo of the
L.A. County Federation of Labor confirmed that the split in the local
movement had much to do with how each side felt their claims should
be presented. She explained that "the difference of opinion" was over
"what resonates with the general public." Durazo and her fellow WAAC
members felt that to gain the public's support and "build a true movement for social justice," the immigrant rights movement had to articulate
a rationale for legalization that would resonate beyond the immigrant
community.

As soon as it became obvious that the two factions would not be working together on future actions, through funding from SEIU's national
headquarters, WAAC hired professional media consultants and formed a
media strategy team.[38] Though the media consultants specialized in, and
were originally hired to deal with, Spanish-language news outlets, growing interest in the topic by English-language media led them to incorporate these news outlets as well. Examining polling data and conducting
focus groups, the coalition found that a sizeable portion of the American population sympathized with immigrants' desire to gain citizenship.
WAAC members sought to turn this sympathy into political support. They
felt that to do so, they had to operate under a pro-America "master
frame" (Snow and Benford 1992). According to media team member and
spokesperson for the L.A. Archdiocese, Carolina Guevara, "We wanted
to focus on the positive contributions of immigrants to our community
and our economy and to our society ... This whole idea that they're not

paying taxes, they're burdening the system, overcrowding the schools, those are the misconceptions that we needed to clarify." Rosaline Cardenas of OC Media, the firm hired to do media consulting for WAAC, explained, "Our message was no boycott, come to the march after your job, the economy is important, we want our jobs, we need our jobs. We didn't want to show in any way, shape, or form that we were anti-America or anti the American economy." To demonstrate their patriotism, people were asked again to wear white to symbolize peace and to wave American flags to show the nation their desire to be full-fledged members of it. Although being pro-America was the general image the coalition was hoping to project, to turn sympathy into political support, they developed a two-prong tactical approach – diversify and personalize.

The strategy for personalizing the issue was to use not only local immigrant rights leaders as "talking-heads" but also to make "the actual people who were fighting the struggle every day (actual immigrants)" the spokespeople of the movement.[39] To this end, WAAC conducted several media trainings for immigrants, then attempted to get them in front of the camera and the mic so they could express their plights. As Javier Gonzalez, one of the main leaders of WAAC, explained: "We would say, 'Look, man ... American people don't give a fuck about combatants. They care about the villagers that got killed and had nothing to do with the dispute. So that's what we want you guys to be. You guys are the affected people. Tell your story.'" Another tactic was showing them how to stay on message. Cardenas explained that, although an immigrant might be interviewed for 20 minutes, only about 12 seconds of the footage would actually be used. As such, WACC leaders told interviewees that no matter what questions reporters asked them, "If you keep stating your message and you keep repeating it over and over, then they [the media] are going to" have to use your one consistent message. Because they believed the public did not understand the intricacies of immigration policies, the coalition's motto was, "If it's about people, we win; if it's about policies, we lose."

WAAC wanted to show that foreign-born people contribute to the U.S. in a variety of ways, and to contest the general public's negative image of immigrants. To diversify perceptions of the movement, WAAC hoped to show Americans "a personal story of people: this is your gardener, this is your janitor, this is your maid, this is a guy who worked himself up to own his own small business."[40] Hoping to get coverage for such stories, the media team pitched and funneled different interviews and spokespeople to different media outlets, telling each of them that it was getting an exclusive story. To highlight immigrants' religious values, the coalition got religious figures to discuss how important immigrants were to their congregations. They found a mother who was legally in the U.S. but whose husband had been deported and had her discuss how such enforcement measures impacted her American-born children. They got students to talk about how, despite having lived virtually their entire lives in the U.S., the fact that they had been brought to the country as babies without proper documentation meant they now couldn't go to college or get a job. To show the public that some people had not chosen to migrate, the media team got a war refugee to discuss why she was forced to flee her country and how, although she had obtained temporary legal status, her lack of full citizenship meant she was unable to return home to see her children. WAAC was successful in getting the media to interview all of these individuals as well as pro-immigrant labor and business leaders to demonstrate the importance of immigrants to the American workforce. Immigrant rights advocates and legal experts also gave their perspectives on the legislative proposals. In short, the media strategy team "would pitch a specific story to a certain news director," because it "wanted to do exclusives for everybody, so everybody would have different stories running on different stations." As Cardenas put it, "We wanted to cover all angles."[41]

On top of emphasizing the various ways immigrants contributed to and were part of America, WAAC wanted to demonstrate the racial and ethnic diversity of immigrants in the United States. To show the public that there were "white people affected, too," the coalition highlighted the story of a Polish immigrant janitor whose family was broken apart when his wife was deported and forced to take their child with her back to Poland. In another instance, they got interviews for a white American who owned a small landscaping company that was completely dependent on immigrant labor and would go out of business if all her workers were deported. The small business owner also shared the story of her Russian immigrant grandparents who, "just like immigrants today," worked arduous jobs when they first immigrated in order to provide a better future for their children. To illustrate parallels with African-Americans' history of labor and migration, a black union worker told media outlets how his family was forced to leave the South because it feared the Klu Klux Klan, and how when his parents arrived in California, they started off as janitors and gardeners, too.[42]

Although members of WAAC knew that they could count on support for their efforts from the Latino and immigrant communities, they felt that "nothing happens in America unless you affect white people."[43] As such, they had to have a strategy that spoke to two different audiences – their immigrant base and the general (primarily white) U.S. public. Consequently, Cardenas explained, they "had to do multiple targeting because you have a message that resonates with the immigrant community and a message that resonates with the non-immigrant community." For the "Spanish-language media it was more a message of 'we understand where you're coming from, we're with you, we're going to support you, let's stick together.'"[44] For the "non-immigrant community who might have some misconceptions of what it means to be 'illegal' immigrants," they took a different approach.[45] Surveys had shown them that about 15–20 percent of the public was completely anti-immigrant, whereas 15–20 percent was sympathetic to their cause. Therefore, their goal was to reach the 60–70 percent that they thought "could be swayed either way with compelling stories."[46] According to one professional media consultant, "The message to the English media was ... that legalization of these immigrants was important to our economy, was important to all of us because it would provide better jobs and better pay for everybody." They were attempting to show "the injustices that occurred in all of these [immigrant] communities," and ultimately "trying to get more sympathy."[47]

In sum, to get public opinion to support its quest to win legalization, WAAC felt it had to demonstrate immigrants' love for, contributions to, and desire to be incorporated into the U.S. Its goal was to use the media to show that immigrants were part of American society. They were soldiers in the military willing to die for the nation. They were fellow churchgoers. They were friends. WAAC wanted to convince Americans that the foreign-born were not threats, but peaceful neighbors and hard workers who did not adversely affect (but, in fact, helped) the U.S. economy. Snow (2004) contends that activists often frame events in ways that are meant to mobilize potential supporters (384: see also Bloemraad, Silva, and Voss 2016). Out of "a cultural reservoir of possible symbols, movement entrepreneurs choose those that they hope will mediate among the cultural understandings of the groups they wish to appeal to, their own beliefs and aspirations, and their situations of struggle" (Tarrow 1998: 109). This is exactly what the We Are America Coalition hoped to do during the mass immigrant rights mobilizations of 2006. Rather than focusing on sentiments that immigrants had for their home countries, WAAC's leaders attempted to "wrap themselves in the American flag" and show the rest of the United

States all the different ways immigrants contributed to the nation and were "just like them." The March 25 Coalition, however, took a much different approach.

Boycott America!

According to March 25 Coalition member and boycott supporter Juan Jose Gutierrez, "You have to understand that this is a war. The people that get ... handcuffed, humiliated, and deported or removed from the United States of America, divided from their families and loved ones ... those are real casualties. It's not a joke. Those things are happening every day." Given what they saw as the severity of the issue, Alvaro Maldonado of the ISO asserted that, "Our strategy was to continue more militant street protests" and call for a national boycott. As previously mentioned, whereas WAAC planned its upcoming May Day demonstration for the afternoon, so that people would not miss work and school, the March 25 Coalition told youth not to go to classes and people not to go to work or buy anything on May 1. They aimed for a more dramatic demonstration of how dependent the nation was on immigrant labor. Nativo Lopez postulated, "I believe children have more to learn protesting on the streets with their parents, expressing their rights, than in the classrooms" (Becerra and Blankstein 2006).

Jesse Diaz explained that the idea for the one-day boycott was provoked by the anti-immigrant rhetoric that claimed immigrants were a drain on the economy.[48] To prove nativists wrong, activists wanted to shut the American economy down – at least the sectors most dependent on immigrant labor – to prove just how much immigrants were needed. In addition, the March 25 Coalition wasn't *asking* for just any "pathway to citizenship," as many moderates were. They were *demanding* immediate and unconditional amnesty for undocumented immigrants, no more border militarization, and a stop to workplace raids and deportations (Robinson 2007). Thus, their rhetoric was a lot more militant than WAAC's and their demands were much more radical.

Boycott supporters were also very critical of those sectors of the movement that opposed their tactic. Of the labor movement's unwillingness to support the boycott, one March 25 Coalition member commented, "The last weapon the worker has against the employer is the strike, and the very institutions [unions] that live or die by the strike" came out against it. "I think it's shameful that the supposed leader [the U.S. labor movement] of the working class in America was telling [immigrants] that they should behave" and not boycott.[49] In essence, these radicals' dominant frame was that the U.S. needed and was purposely exploiting immigrants. In order to force the country to recognize this, activists were going to make it suffer by calling on the immigrant masses to strike. They envisioned Americans having to take care of their own children, because immigrant nannies would be at the march; having to feed themselves, because immigrant restaurant workers would be on strike; and having to clean their own office buildings, because immigrant janitors would be protesting.

Boycott supporters also asserted that the anti-immigrant sentiments of the day were not merely expressions of disagreements on policies, but a continuation of America's long history of racism, especially toward immigrants of color. According to coalition member Isabel Rodriguez, WAAC's belief that waving American flags was going to win sympathy from white people was "a superficial analysis of the extent of racism in this country." In her view, the March 25 Coalition felt not only that immigrants should not be ashamed of their home countries, but also that the U.S. public should "know where the immigrants that do their labor come from." Therefore, the coalition did not discourage marchers from bringing and waving foreign flags, and the coalition explicitly declared itself not an American movement, but an "internationalist" one (Robinson 2007). Meanwhile, these activists criticized mainstream immigrant rights groups and labor unions for telling people not to carry Mexican flags and for "scabbing" on the national boycott.[50] Hence, the March 25 Coalition also had a two-prong framing and targeting approach: to further radicalize its immigrant base and to make the American public feel what life would be like without the immigrant labor upon which it so heavily depended.

Given the importance of culturally resonant movement frames, the March 25 Coalition's internationalist "Boycott America" action may seem like a tactical error if it hoped to make the U.S. public more sympathetic to its cause. Yet calls for immigrants to be proud of waving the flags of their home countries, and threats of "teaching Americans a lesson" by showing how vital immigrants are to the U.S. economy, makes sense when we understand that the targets or goals of movement frames are not always to draw sympathy from the general public. As with many groups whose identities are marginalized, immigrant boycott supporters' radical frames may have been "directed more at the affirmation of self than at the genuine conversation with others" (Epstein 1999, 64). The March 25 Coalition's frames in all likelihood did not resonate with the broader public. In fact, they may even have played right into Middle America's fears and the anti-immigrant movement's "immigrants want to hurt America" rhetoric. But as evidenced by the millions of foreign-born people across the nation who boycotted work and school on May 1, the March 25 Coalition's frames did in fact resonate with and – in all likelihood – politicized, at least some of their targeted audience – hundreds of thousands of immigrant workers and their allies.

The May Day Without An Immigrant

On the morning of May 1 the *Los Angeles Times* reported, "Marches in Los Angeles and Chicago, demonstrations in New York and boycotts that forced closures of Midwest and Southern meat-packing plants marked a day when immigrant rights activists again called for a new [immigration] policy" (Muskal and Williams 2006). "Thousands of businesses were shuttered ... as workers and their families, most of them from Mexico, participated in a boycott of work and commerce, rallying to demonstrate their importance to the U.S. economy and to demand changes in immigration law that would give illegal migrants a path to citizenship." Media outlets noted that the Los Angeles Unified School District alone "reported 71,942 absences in grades 6 through 12" (Gorman, Miller, and Landsberg 2006). The California State Senate and Assembly passed resolutions acknowledging the boycott and declared that the state government would not "conduct business" in observance of May 1 (Becerra and Blankstein 2006). In Tijuana, Mexico, activists "succeeded in blocking the busiest international border crossing in the world for two hours" (Hernandez 2006b). Spanish-language radio stations across Los Angeles showed their support "by playing music and prerecorded messages in solidarity" (Felix et al. 2008). A local news outlet reported, "under pale and merciless midday sun ... the May Day marchers were shaking it hard, jubilantly, to a euphoric beat made by guys pounding upon drums, their lips pursed in revelatory fury." As one of the dancing domestic workers explained: "What do you mean why am I so happy? ... We are a united *pueblo*!" She proudly proclaimed, "I clean houses, very honorably," and, "If they fire me, I don't care!" (Hernandez 2006b). Official police estimates put the March 25 Coalition's noon protest at 250,000 and the evening We Are America Coalition rally at 400,000 (Gorman, Miller, and Landsberg 2006).

Whereas the March 25 Coalition's demonstration at City Hall could be described as a great success in terms of turnout, the We Are American Coalition's march – from MacArthur Park, close to the city's downtown, to the affluent Westside neighborhood of La Brea – and rally was nothing less than a spectacular professional production. One of its coordinators described it:

We paid for media risers for the media … We had Anderson Cooper [of CNN] on the roof of a building … The media was like "Wow, it's like we're at a presidential campaign" … We had their names, like ABC here, NBC here, *Telemundo* here. We had pre and post media [interview] opportunities. We had a VIP section. We had a professional stage that *La Raza* radio station donated. We had *Los Tigres del Norte*, we had *Paquita la del Barrio, Cucuy*, we had *Piolín*, we had the Mayor … We hired a professional photographer. We knew this was a production. America was gonna see this rally [so we asked ourselves], "What do we want them to see? … Who do we want to speak to? What's the visual?" … We had lighting … a professional sound system with 18 speakers. We had 3 crews just on media. The laborers [union] gave us 1,000 of those people dividers. The teachers [union] gave us 10,000 water bottles, we bought 50,000 water bottles. We rented 27 toilets … We raised like $160,000. SEIU gave us like $80,000, the [LA County Fed] gave us like $10,000, the Catholic Church put in $10,000. [The message we wanted to convey was] "We want to be a part of America. We want full citizenship."

The meticulous coordination was a response to criticism reported by English-language media outlets about the presence of some foreign flags at other rallies across the country. WAAC wanted to control to the best of its ability exactly what the public was going to see. According to Rosalina Cardenas of the media team, "All around the front of the stage … we made sure that in the whole middle section nobody could get in there if they didn't have an American flag," because that is where the media would be facing.

Notably, despite local protest organizers being divided, the marching masses decided that they would remain united. Demonstrating that they had heard their calls to action, hundreds of thousands of protesters showed up to the March 25 Coalition's noontime event, but then independently continued marching all the way to West Los Angeles, where the We Are America Coalition was holding its rally. As Carolina Guevara recalled,

I was on stage and I was told that our march was still an hour away. All of a sudden I turn around and I see a sea of people coming towards us. All of a sudden when you get that feeling, the world and everything around you stops, time just stops. All I could see was just thousands and thousands of people. It just became real at that point. Before then it's all theoretical. It's all strategy. It's who are you reaching? Are you really reaching anybody? You can create as much strategy and media talking points as you want, but if it's not reaching anyone, if you don't really see it, then how do you know? … All of a sudden there were thousands upon thousands of people coming toward the stage. I just felt completely overwhelmed with really a sense of, "We did it! Our message was heard!" It turned out that it was actually the [March 25 Coalition's] folks from the earlier march that had been marching alongside another street … So in the end, it really wasn't about which side you were on. It was [more like], if you can get out of work and go to the earlier event, go to the earlier event, stick around and then go to the other event. That's what really happened.

Conclusion

According to renowned media scholars John Nichols and Robert McChesney (2000), "access to communications is a nonnegotiable demand in a democratic society." They believe that "real victories" by movements for social justice "will be made all the more possible by opening up and democratizing the media" (25). Nichols and McChesney (2000) envision a time when people "will start to see media not as something that happens to them, but rather as something that they have a right and an ability to shape" (119). In the spring of 2006, Americans witnessed the political capabilities of the ethnic mass media when put in the hands of immigrant rights activists.

Mainstream Spanish-language television news and entertainment radio outlets played vital yet much more complex roles in the historic mobilizations than scholars and activists have recognized. The case study of Los Angeles, CA – the largest Spanish-language media market in the U.S. – offers several key empirical and theoretical insights to our understanding of the relationship between the media and contentious politics. Because American social movement scholars have long ignored activism over immigration issues (Bloemraad et al. 2016: 1647; Menjivar 2010), most research that examines the relationship between social movements and the media focuses exclusively on English-language news outlets. But as the 2006 protest wave shows us, this research is not adequate because it fails to consider the many ways ethnic minorities and ethnic media interact.

As an example, whereas Spanish-language news outlets serve as sources of information and as agents of immigrant incorporation, English-language media are expected to do only the former. Consequently, many immigrant advocates have developed strong working relationships with members of the ethnic media, who are usually immigrants themselves. This latter point is crucial to highlight because, as we have now seen in both Fort Myers and Los Angeles (and as will be compared further in our concluding chapter), a looming and racialized legislative threat can trigger feelings of group consciousness and linked fate among members of the ethnic media and their immigrant audiences. These sentiments can in turn compel these news and entertainment outlets to assist activists with galvanizing their viewers and listeners to take action in defense of their communities.

The 2006 cycle of contention also complicates the now customary finding in the literature that activists attempt to stage large demonstrations in order to draw the media's attention and then hope that the resulting coverage is sympathetic. In the case of the L.A. mass marches, immigrant rights activists instead used the mainstream ethnic media to broadcast and make visible their pro-immigrant frames and calls to action to the Spanish-speaking Latino community. This does not mean that they ignored or were unaware of the influence and importance of English-language news coverage. On the contrary, they worked hard to develop dual frames and clever tactics that they believed would resonate with the specific audiences of the news sources they interacted with. But as we have seen in this chapter and will explore further in the following New York case study, how to frame movement claims and who to target created intramovement disagreements and divisions. As the next chapter will demonstrate, the capacities of local ethnic media outlets, and the degree to which calls to mobilize against nativist threats resonate, vary among different foreign-born populations and are impacted by how immigration policies are racialized.

4

Coalitions and the Racialization of Illegality

At the heart of our explorations thus far is a point so obvious that it can be overlooked: mass mobilization is only possible because of the masses. At the same time, in order to culminate in effective collective action, the many thousands – or in our case millions – of individuals who care about an issue need some kind of direction and organization. It is coalitions of activists that often make this possible, translating the passions of the people into successful political protests. As we have seen, during the 2006 immigrant rights cycle of contention, small ethnic businesses, soccer league players, farmworkers, and local ethnic newspaper owners in Southwest Florida formed an alliance to organize a massive march in the city of Fort Myers. In Los Angeles, Mexican immigrant and Chicano activists united with Filipinos, Central Americans, Chinese, Koreans, and other U.S.- and foreign-born allies to form the coalitions that coordinated the huge demonstrations that took place in the city. Throughout the nation, people of different political leanings, religions, races and ethnicities, not to mention a vast list of different types of organizations, came together to oppose H.R. 4437 and to fight for the legalization of undocumented immigrants. Although diversity (of various types), and the coalitions that emerged from this diversity, were important factors in the multiple protests we have examined so far, this chapter uses the case of New York to explore more deeply how these elements can impact mass mobilization.

Nowhere were the diverse coalitions that came together to organize local demonstrations more apparent than in the Empire City. The rallies that took place there on April 10 and May 1 reflected this multiplicity, as people in every borough – from Irish pub owners and Muslim cab drivers to African restaurant workers and Filipina nannies – united to march for immigrant rights. The city's local actions were made possible, in the words of one organizer, by "coalitions of coalitions that came together."[1] This may not be surprising to some given that New York has possibly the most diverse and certainly one of the most dynamic local immigrant rights movements in the country. Examples are numerous: from campaigns for non-citizen voting rights (Hayduk 2006), to the organizing of taxi drivers, street vendors, restaurant workers, and families affected by immigrant detention (see Jayaraman and Ness 2005; Biju 2005; Kateel and Shahani 2008). Yet, in spite of the long history of immigrant activism in the city, the demonstrations that occurred in New York during the 2006 protest wave present some interesting anomalies. As detailed below, the diversity of the coalitions that spearheaded the demonstrations in this locale did not exactly reflect the demographics of those who participated most in these actions. In addition, compared to other big cities with large immigrant populations and established immigrant rights movements (including funders, coalitions, and numerous organizations with significant membership bases), New York had significantly smaller protests. How can we account for these theoretical and empirical puzzles?

A central contention of this book is that depending on the type of threat and the degree to which they feel under attack, activists can rouse racialized immigrants and their offspring to use nativist actions as a heuristic that prodes their political actions. However, because different groups are racialized in distinct ways (Almaguer 1994; Pulido 2006; Cacho 2012), we should not expect all immigrant communities to respond in the same manner – nor to the same degree – to nativist legislative threats. The types of anti-immigrant attacks that trigger feelings of linked fate and group consciousness among racialized immigrants and their families vary and, as a result, so will their levels of outrage and forms of actions they take in response. Accordingly, my interviews with local Muslim, Christian, African, Latin American, European, Pacific Islander, Caribbean, South and East Asian immigrant rights activists in New York suggest that while external threats can provide the impetus to form broad and diverse organizational coalitions, having a more racially and ethnically diverse immigrant population resulted in not all of the city's immigrant groups feeling – though many arguably were – equally threatened by H.R. 4437, or equally invested in the proposed alternatives to it. Consequently, in order to fully grasp the latitude, and also the limitations, of 2006, we must attend to the variety of immigrant group identities and experiences. In this chapter I show how diversity and the specific way immigrant "illegality" was racialized, diminished Empire City activists' capacity to produce the magnitude of mobilizations found in other major immigrant metropolises.

Social Movements and Multiracial Coalitions

Van Dyke and McCammon (2010) contend that researchers "cannot fully understand the dynamics of movement mobilization and success until we gain a more complete understanding of the factors facilitating organizational collaboration" (xii).[2] Several studies have shown that a "serious or political threat" can serve as one of these factors by encouraging activists to form coalitions (Van Dyke and McCammon 2010: xxii) and present a "united defense" (Zald and McCarthy 1987: 177).[3] But although external threats can impact the timing and likelihood of coalitions emerging, Reese et al. (2010) remind us that environmental conditions do not automatically create alliances – they merely generate the contexts in which activists operate (270; see also Rucht 2004: 203; Smith and Bandy 2005: 8).[4] Ultimately, organizers' recognition of and strategic responses to these circumstances determine whether coalitions manifest (Borland 2010: 241; Smith and Bandy 2005: 8).

Because a common identity can be a key mechanism in the formation of a coalition, issues of group identity and diversity are particularly salient in alliances across ethnicities or races (Barvosa-Carter 2001), such as those that were formed in New York and other cities during the 2006 protest wave. According to Smith and Bandy (2005), when group "members see themselves as sharing a common identity, their solidarity and motivation to work together is enhanced" (10).[5] Not surprisingly, people are more likely to interact and cooperate with members of their own racial group (Fearon and Latin 1996: 730). Nonetheless, for decades, scholars have argued that multiracial coalitions are key to the political incorporation and empowerment of communities of color (Browning, Marshall, and Tabb 1984; Sonenshein 1989; Marable 1994; Jones-Correa 2001; Bystydzienski and Schacht 2001). As Park and Park (2001) write, "One of the most enduring assumptions in the literature on urban politics since the civil rights movement" is that "success in local politics for racial minorities is inextricably linked with their participation" in progressive multiracial coalitions (91). Yet, according to McClain and Tauber (2001), not only do Asians, blacks, and Latinos often harbor negative racial stereotypes about each other (129), but "in many urban areas, conflict and competition among racial-minority groups has been increasing" (112; also

see Hazan 2006: 207). Thus, they argue, "competition rather than coalition building may well be the dominant factor structuring intergroup
relationships" among ethnic and racial minority groups in major cities
(McClain and Tauber 2001: 114; Vaca 2004; see also McClain et al.
2006).

Activists attempting to form alliances among different foreign-born
populations face the additional challenges of navigating various manifestations of intra-group diversity, everything from economic class and
education levels to what region you came from and when you emigrated (Foner 1987; Kwong 2001; Park and Park 2001; Bakalian and
Bozorgmehr 2009; Beltrán 2010). But, while difficult, creating multiracial
immigrant rights alliances is not impossible. Prior research has shown that
in the face of pending anti-immigrant legislation, interracial immigrant
coalitions have formed (Okamoto 2010: 144). To do so, immigrant rights
activists must appeal to the self-interest of the different immigrant groups
they target, create solidarity among them through relationship building
and joint collective action efforts, and frame their claims in ways that will
resonate with the various immigrant populations they hope to unite and
mobilize (Tsao 2008: 131–136). As protests against the Sensenbrenner
Bill began to gain momentum and right-wing Republicans in the senate
threatened to introduce a bill that was just as draconian as H.R. 4437,
organizers working with New York's diverse immigrant populations realized the significance of what they were up against, and the difficult task
of mobilization that lay ahead.

Coalition Formation

On Saturday, March 25, in the borough of Queens, a small and racially
diverse coalition named Immigrant Communities in Action (ICA) –
which had previously worked together on a failed campaign to secure
driver licenses for undocumented immigrants – organized a neighborhood
forum to discuss the potential impact of H.R. 4437 on its community.
Organizers were expecting only a few dozen people to attend, but over
500 local residents appeared. Many of the immigrants in attendance gave
passionate testimonies to the standing-room-only auditorium about the
abuses they endured.[6] On that same day, Families for Freedom (FFF), a
multiethnic local organization that works on detention issues, organized
about 75 people to rally outside of the federal building in lower Manhattan (Confessore 2006). The protest was intended to bring attention to
the negative effects of deportations on children; however, as often occurs

in social movements when new pressing concerns arise, the planned rally incorporated opposition to an additional issue – the Sensenbrenner Bill – into its agenda. As Aarti Shahani of FFF explained, "Everyone was doing their own thing and then suddenly this big 'A-Bomb' [H.R. 4437] got dropped on us ... Everything [then became] reinterpreted to respond to the 'A-Bomb.'"

The first protest in the city to focus explicitly on the Sensenbrenner Bill took place in the northern Manhattan neighborhood of Washington Heights. On Sunday, March 26, a group of Dominican expatriates (many of whom knew each other from activism in their home country during the 1960s) called *Acción Comunitaria La Aurora* (or *La Aurora* for short) held a neighborhood march. Months before, in response to H.R. 4437, these "migrating militants" (Pulido 1998; also see Aparicio 2006) had formed a small and informal coalition of local Dominican community organizations, service groups, businesses, and churches, to coordinate their event.[7] Through flyers, on-the-street conversations, and calls for action on a local Spanish-langauge radio program and cable TV station, the group sought to attract 100–300 people to its protest.[8] According to Rhadames Pérez, one of the organizers of the demonstration, the group was shocked when about 2,000 immigrants showed up, the first of whom were a handful of Mexicans from Long Island who arrived over an hour early holding a banner of their country's patron saint, *La Virgen de Guadalupe*. Six days later, on April Fool's Day, following a call by the evangelical Puerto Rican–born New York State senator, Rubén Díaz, several local Latino religious and secular immigrant-based organizations led a march of over 10,000 people across the Brooklyn Bridge in protest of H.R. 4437 (Montero and Mongelli 2006). Local organizers later recalled that immigrants from the Dominican Republic and Mexico accounted for the majority of marchers in attendance at both of these early demonstrations.

Although not momentous in terms of size, these initial marches foreshadowed many themes that would emerge in the protests that occurred in the city during the April 10 and May 1 national days of actions. New York immigrant rights activists recognized and responded to a far-reaching legislative threat, then utilized preexisting social ties to form the diverse coalitions that coordinated local mobilization efforts. The broad and punitive scope of H.R. 4437, the momentum of the growing national protest wave in opposition to it, and the agency of the immigrant masses and activists combined to produce remarkably diverse acts of resistance throughout the city.

April 10: Social Networks and Organizational Diversity
At the Queens community forum on March 25, Miguel Ramírez of *Centro Hispano Cuzcatlán,* a Central American community-based organization and member of ICA, recalled speaking with Rhadames Rivera, vice president of SEIU's local 1199, whom he had known from their participation in the 1980's Central American Peace and Solidarity Movement. Spurred by the severity of the Sensenbrenner Bill and the mounting number of immigrant rights protests across the country in opposition to it, Ramírez expressed to Rivera what was already on the minds of many New York activists: the need to unite and organize a major citywide demonstration. Rivera invited Ramírez to share his idea at an upcoming meeting of unionists working on Latin American solidarity issues. At this gathering, both men decided to call on local labor, religious, and immigrant rights leaders to meet and discuss possibly organizing a citywide anti-H.R. 4437 action. Ana Maria Archila of Make the Road remembered how, "People had been kind of meeting in their own universes. We had been meeting with the New York Immigration Coalition regularly. The unions had been meeting with each other regularly. The more left[ist] groups had been meeting with each other regularly. It was only around April 10 that there was a call to action for everyone."

Within days of Rivera and Ramírez's invitation to congregate, representatives from about 150 organizations from all five boroughs gathered at Local 1199's Manhattan office. Hector Figueroa of SEIU 32BJ, who would come to play a central role in the citywide coalition, explained, "A meeting was simply called by email and everybody showed up, it was quite impressive. The institutions and networks that we had put in place before – fighting police brutality, fighting for immigration reform, fighting for language access in city services – it was those networks that immediately connected people" (also see Cordero-Guzman et al. 2008). Although there was no consensus on how to frame their message, the gathering concluded with the groups agreeing to join the national protest wave by organizing a march and rally for April 10. While several of these organizations had worked together before, others knew of each other's work but had never collaborated. In the midst of the national protest wave, however, the local coalition-formation process helped foster new organizational ties and strengthened old ones.

May Chen, International Vice President of UNITE-HERE, explained that organizing in New York "is not centralized ... There are a lot of grassroots organizations and the trick is trying to figure out a way ... [to] piece those different groups together." Mae Lee of the Chinese

Progressive Association concurred, "In New York, the way you organize is that you really have to organize within each community. There are these umbrella groups that are important, but you have to go into each community and do something." As a result, many members of the citywide coalition (hereinafter referred to as the April 10 alliance)[9] that formed to coordinate the local April 10 action were themselves either coalitional organizations or part of other previously established neighborhood and borough alliances. For example, the statewide New York Immigration Coalition (NYIC) is an official organization composed of over 200 mostly New York City–based service groups. After the April 10 alliance was established, NYIC went back and promoted the upcoming march to its members through meetings at its office, conference calls, and emails distributed through its listserv. These members then independently promoted the demonstration within their own communities and organizational networks.

According to Margaret Chin of Chinatown's Asian Americans for Equality (AAE), after NYIC informed her organization about the protest, AAE "reached out to other groups in [its] community that are not members [of NYIC] to bring them along." Non-immigrant rights organizations also learned about the upcoming action through their personal and virtual ties to members of the April 10 alliance. For instance, despite not focusing on immigration issues, the leaders of Mothers on the Move, a Bronx-based predominantly African-American and Puerto Rican community group, first heard about the local April 10 march because they were on NYIC's email list. But according to the organization's director, Wanda Salaman, her personal relationship with Raquel Batista of the Northern Manhattan Coalition for Immigrant Rights (NMCIR) – a member of both NYIC and the April 10 alliance – compelled her to join the citywide coalition. Salaman said that her organization decided to support the protest because, "Even if we weren't working on the issue" of immigration, "we had friends that were." Thus, organizational, virtual, and personal ties served as multiple overlapping and mutually reinforcing mechanisms through which activists and community organizations were encouraged to join the coalitional efforts.

As was the case in both our Fort Myers and Los Angeles case studies, the broad scope of the Sensenbrenner Bill also made it easier for organizers in New York to recruit traditionally nonpolitical community members and groups to participate in the April 10 alliance and protest. As Guari Sadhwani, executive director of the New York Civic Participation Project (NYCPP), explained, "Whether they knew it or not … it actually criminalized whole sectors of our society that supported or in any way provided services … to undocumented immigrants … It really challenged not just the people that were here without papers, but in some ways our entire social fabric that allowed for immigrants, regardless of whether they were documented or undocumented, to be part of our society." Javier Valdes of NYIC recalled, "Sensenbrenner was so easy to organize against once we got down how to message it to our communities. It was just so easy to say, 'This is really bad, the effect is going to be devastating, we need to come out and kill it.'" Hence, according to Haeyoung Yoon of the Committee Against Anti-Asian Violence (CAAAV), H.R. 4437 "really brought out people who weren't necessarily connected to [immigrant rights] organizations to participate in the mobilizations." Given the sheer extremity of the bill, local activists were able to get the support of groups and organizations that were not overtly political and sometimes even rather conservative.

After the Young Korean American Service and Education Center (YKASEC), a Korean organization based in Queens and member of NYIC, joined the April 10 alliance, the group hoped to gain the support of sectors of Korean-American society that typically did not participate in political activities. According to Jun Bum Cha, the organization's advocacy director, the group called for a local meeting with leaders of various segments of the Korean community. Heads of local Korean immigrant social services; ethnic associations; and business-, religious-, and community-based organizations met at YKASEC to talk "about the importance of the issue and why we had to step up for this mobilization." As a result of this gathering, local Korean community and business leaders agreed to mobilize their constituents and customers against H.R. 4437. Several Korean-owned businesses also decided to donate money for advertisements promoting the march in local ethnic newspapers and radio stations.

A similar process occurred in the Chinese community. According to Mae Lee of the Chinese Progressive Association, after attending an April 10 alliance meeting, her organization knew that if it "wanted a significant Chinatown mobilization," it would "have to involve everyone, whether or not they're already involved in immigrant rights." She explained, "The way you organize the Chinese community is that you have to have a coalition in Chinatown … so the business and civic associations were contacted" and invited to a meeting where the potential impacts of H.R. 4437 on the Chinese community were discussed. As a result, even "rather conservative" organizations, such as the massive Chinese Consolidated

Benevolent Association – which normally concerns itself with local businesses and social services – supported the April 10 action.

Some groups in the April 10 alliance had overlapping membership
bases throughout the boroughs. Such connections served the citywide
mobilization efforts via local community organizations and networks that
either already existed or were formed in response to the legislative threat.
Organizers asserted that these relationships reinforced the need for members to participate. For instance, the New York Civic Participation Project
(NYCPP) is an organizational collaboration between SEIU Local 32BJ,
AFSCME DC 37, Laborers Local 78 and 79, UNITE-HERE Local 100,
Make the Road, and the National Employment Law Project. The goal of
NYCPP is to organize union members in their own neighborhoods around
local community issues. That many people in NYCPP's membership base
were part of unions and other social service organizations had an echo
chamber effect during the protest wave.

According to Zahida Pirani, a NYCPP organizer in Queens, local residents were not only being encouraged to participate at their places of
employment by union representatives but also getting motivated to partake in the action at local neighborhood assemblies. Pirani explained,
"So you hear from your union and you also hear from NYCPP which is
working in the neighborhood," hosting meetings "with your family and
friends," too. Sadwani, also of NYCPP, added, "Our base of members ...
was connected to other networks. People brought it to their churches.
People brought it to their workplace. The unions posted it. We got the
word out through the radio ... We got the word out through [other]
organizations." Motivation to take part in the national protest wave also
came from the bottom up. Local NYCPP groups in different boroughs
informed April 10 alliance leaders that community residents were ready
to participate in a mass action. "It was interesting because I think the
established institutions knew there was going to be something, but they
didn't know to what extent [people wanted to mobilize]," Pirani remembered. "But because we as an organization are based in the community, we
could really communicate" with union leaders, NYIC, and other groups
"that there was a buzz in the community."

Members of the April 10 alliance met frequently and also recruited
other organizations and community residents to join. As Miguel Ramírez
of ICA and *Centro Hispano Cuzcatlán* recalled, "We formed work
teams ... I would have four or five meetings a week. The organizing
committee ... the programming committee, the logistics one, the publicity committee, outreach ... " All of the organizational members of the

alliance also returned to their local communities to promote the march through a variety of channels. Raquel Batista of the Northern Manhattan Coalition for Immigrant Rights remembered, "We would go to churches, we would go to the stores, we would go to the schools. We reached out to the leadership in the community ... There were always a lot of meetings ... and forums." Ana Maria Archila of Make the Road recalled, "We stopped everything else we were doing for two weeks. We did nothing but [promote the march]. We had never in our organization done that before. It was very clear that everyone [who was part of the coalition] was willing to stop their regular normal activities" to focus on promoting the protest.

In immigrant neighborhoods throughout the city participants in the April 10 alliance distributed flyers, spoke at local church services, put up posters in small immigrant-owned businesses, and also borrowed tactics from immigrants' countries of origin. For instance, reminiscent of a strategy often used in Latin American political campaigns, Sussie Lozada, an organizer with both NYCPP and *La Aurora*, said that the groups organized "a caravan of cars with loud-speakers [sic]" and drove through the streets of Latino neighborhoods playing a prerecorded message promoting the march and encouraging residents to participate. AnaLiza Caballes of Damayan Migrant Worker's Association, a Filipina domestic worker organization, explained that similar to how it had played an important role in ousting former Philippines president Joseph Estrada, text messaging was a key organizing tool used by Filipinos in New York during the 2006 protests. She recalled, "At the time we were cooking a lot in members' houses to plan" our actions and "we would send text messages to people to let them know what was happening."

Just as the broad scope of the Sensenbrenner Bill encouraged a wide swath of usually apolitical organizations to get involved, it also provoked a dramatic reaction from the immigrant masses, especially segments of the Latino community which, organizers claim, led them to "auto-mobilize." Ana Maria Archila of Make the Road explained:

People would just call my cell phone randomly because they saw it on a flyer and would say, "Where do I need to be? At what time? All the people at my job want to go." I remember this one phone call in particular. A woman called me and said, "I heard your phone [number] on the radio. Our boss told us that we would be fired, but we just can't stay. We have to go. Where do we need to meet?" ... It was very, very apparent to us that people were just on a different level of engagement ... Regular people were coming [into our office] and saying, "I know there's something happening, what can I do?" ... There was just an incredible level of self-organization and discipline around demonstrating power publicly for the first time ... [People were saying], "I'm tired of being invisible. This is about my dignity. It's not even about the bill. It's about my family. It's about my dignity. It's about not being less forever." It was a very personal thing for every single person that was involved ... Because these people are undocumented, they understand very clearly the connection between policies and their lives.

Even community members who were not going to participate in Make the Road's rally delegation found ways to contribute. Community residents who feared missing work or were simply unable to endure the financial costs of losing a day's wages went to the organization's office (often taking family members with them) days before the march to help make signs and sandwiches for the group's contingent.

The social ties within families and communities were perhaps even more crucial to the mobilization effort than those of the organizations involved in the April 10 alliance (see also Bloemraad and Trost 2011). In fact, organizers expressed that during the protest wave it often felt as if "the advocates and the organizations followed where the masses were leading."[10] This "auto-mobilization" phenomenon was particularly prevalent among Mexican and Dominican immigrants. As an example, Artemio Guerra of the Fifth Avenue Committee, a housing and education advocacy organization in Brooklyn, recounted, "We were not able to do phone banking" to organize community residents for the march "because it was all happening very fast." A few days before the protest, the organization merely suggested that its small group of members invite and "call their friends and family." Guerra remembered, "We were expecting like 40, 50, or 60 people so we rented a bus." But, on the day of the march, "by the time the bus got there we had about 300 people!" Indigenous migrants from the Mexican state of Puebla, who made up the bulk of this group, used their hometown social networks to mobilize family and friends throughout New York, Connecticut, and New Jersey. "We had people from the Tri-State area show up at our little corner... We had like 100 people on the bus and the other 200 took the subway. It was bizarre because we didn't expect that at all." Moisés Pérez of *Alianza Dominicana*, the largest Dominican social service organization in the country, recalled a similar dynamic occurring in Dominican neighborhoods throughout the city:

Word of mouth! It just spread from family to family ... People found out from their friends. It became, for a while, the major topic of conversation [in the *barrios*]. It was like everyday people were talking about it ... It was like a forest fire. It grew with a spark and then before you knew it you couldn't contain it... Our phones were inundated with calls from community residents. Everyone was

asking, "When are we marching?" . . . We didn't organize shit. This was the outrage that our community felt collectively. We just responded to it by trying to put
some shape and form into it.

On April 10, the day of the actual event, immigrants, their families,
and allies gathered at churches, parks, union halls, service organizations,
and numerous other meeting points. Often carrying American flags and
homemade signs that read "Legalize Don't Criminalize Immigrants!,"
"We Are America!," and "Amnistía: Full Rights for Immigrants!," they
proudly headed to one of the many "feeder marches" originating in different neighborhoods and boroughs. Via rented buses, subway, or on foot,
they all eventually merged into a single demonstration of approximately
100,000 people in lower Manhattan. The *New York Times* reported that
on the historic national day of action, "No rally was more diverse than
New York's, where the thousands who converged at City Hall Park were
greeted in Spanish, Chinese, French and Korean, and heard invocations by
a rabbi and the leader of a Buddhist temple" (Bernstein 2006). Marchers
were met by a large union-funded, concert-like stage and sound speakers with "jumbotrons" displaying speeches by local labor and immigrant
rights leaders from various religious, racial, and ethnic backgrounds.
While many of the organizers later expressed frustration that the event
wasn't better attended, most were amazed at what they had achieved
in just a few short weeks. However, although the "coalition of coalitions" that coordinated New York's first sizeable citywide demonstration
appeared unified on stage, behind the scenes, the fissures that often form
in large, broad, and diverse coalitions were beginning to show. These fault
lines ultimately led to a fracture in the local movement and to the creation
of an alternative citywide coalition.

Coalition Fragmentation

Any mass mobilization is only as effective as the message it disseminates.
The essential effort of "getting the word out" happens through a variety
of media, including signs and banners with carefully crafted claims and
slogans, creative chants, speeches, and live interviews with members of
the media. Given the vital role of communication, not surprisingly, disputes over messaging often occur between and within movements (Benford 1993; McAdam, McCarthy, and Zald 1996: 17). As such, much like
in Los Angeles and other major cities, one of the biggest sources of tension that arose within New York's April 10 alliance was who was going to
speak at the rally and how the coalition was going to frame its demands.

As one of the main protest organizers put it, "There was agreement about the action. There just wasn't agreement about the message."[11]

While some members of the April 10 alliance were part of smaller local coalitions, others were connected to larger national organizations. For example, the more mainstream and better-funded groups, such as some of the labor unions and NYIC,[12] were linked to the nationwide Coalition for Comprehensive Immigration Reform (CCIR) and the We Are America Alliance (WAAA) based in Washington, D.C.[13] During the protest wave, CCIR and WAAA attempted to frame the demonstrations in a patriotic manner under the banner of "We Are America," as we saw in our previous chapter with the We Are America Coalition in L.A. One tactic its foundation-funded campaign employed was distributing thousands of signs to local affiliates, who gave them out at rallies for protest participants to hold.[14]

Monami Maulik of Desis Rising Up and Moving (DRUM), one of the key April 10 alliance members, recalled, "When we showed up [on April 10] it was as if the entire event was hijacked by the policy groups ... We were duped. Everything we had discussed [at coalition meetings] was out the window ... For weeks before, nobody in the planning of [the rally] ever told us anything about the 'We Are America' campaign." She added:

The unions were paying all this money for ... all of the media, the placards, the signs, the stage [etc.] ... So we realized when we showed up that the entire theme and the messaging of the event was basically decided by the unions and the major policy players, and that none of the negotiations that happened before were reflected. It was quite disappointing because our position was that [their messaging] did not reflect the sentiments or the demands of the people.

According to several coalition participants, at the protest event, mainstream groups that were connected with national organizations handed out thousands of "We Are America" signs for marchers to hold, gave people American flags to wave, and urged participants not to display flags from other countries.[15] When the Act Now to Stop War and End Racism (ANSWER) Coalition, which was part of the citywide alliance, attempted to distribute several of its own placards that read, "Amnesty for All," NYIC "had someone ... running around trying to take down ANSWER signs so that they wouldn't be seen by the cameras."[16] As another city coalition member recalled, a NYIC leader "went around ... to the people in the front [of the stage] and took all of their posters away ... because there was a whole debate around" whether to use the term "amnesty" or to "stay away from that" word and instead use the term "legalization" to "kind of appease" the mainstream public "and not create more polarity."[17] The NYIC staffer asserted that whereas "the more radical groups were pushing for things like open borders ... We really did not want that message out there because ... we didn't want to be dismissed as radical lefties. What we wanted was a consistent message, something that presented our view and spoke to the wider scope of equality and justice and opportunity." Nevertheless, how different factions within the coalition understood concepts such as "equality and justice" largely depended on their political ideology, which, in turn, influenced the tactics that activists hoped to put into practice.

Ultimately, "April 10th was probably the moment that the contradictions that had been building in the immigrant rights movement came to a head and blew up."[18] After the rally, the citywide alliance was technically still intact, but ideological differences that had been present from the start (but had been set aside for the protest event) could no longer be ignored. This mood change was especially keen, as the environment in which activists were cooperating began to change with the apparent defeat of H.R. 4437, and as the movement's attention was redirected to the compromise Senate bill and the upcoming 2006 midterm elections.

May 1: Ideological and Strategic Diversity

Following the April 10 National Day of Action for Immigrant Justice, a national protest wave was clearly in full effect. Less clear was whether it had reached its peak. Some movement activists thought it best to harness the amazing momentum they had achieved in the previous few weeks and direct it toward more institutional forms of politics, such as voter registration and citizenship drives. More radical activists wanted to increase the level of contention by calling for a nationwide work stoppage and full-blown boycott of the American economy. Local groups across the country had to decide whether movement escalation or institutionalization was the most prudent strategy.

For weeks, movement radicals from the Los Angeles March 25 Coalition had been calling for a national boycott and were traveling throughout the country attempting to get other citywide alliances to adopt their idea. Chuck Mohan of New York's Guyanese-American Worker's United asserted, "You gotta give that Los Angeles group a whole lot of credit because they kind of initiated the action out there and then it just swelled around the nation." During their stop in New York, L.A. activists were invited to speak at one of the April 10 alliances' post–April 10 meetings. According to Bernadette Ellorin of the Philippine Forum and BAYAN, "I remember distinctly [one of the L.A. activists] saying that the objective [of the boycott] was to halt production by waging a general economic strike – meaning no buying, no selling, just mobilize on that day to prove how immigrants really hold the U.S. economy afloat with their labor contributions." The West Coast activists left New York hoping that the citywide coalition would adopt their proposal and join their campaign to hold a national boycott on May 1, International Worker's Day. Some New York immigrant rights activists embraced the boycott tactic, but at the cost of splitting the alliance into two rival coalitions.

A faction of the April 10 alliance wanted to support the May 1 boycott and hold a rally at Union Square; others proposed a less militant "human chain" action. The local movement fractured along these lines, as the more radical segment of the city's alliance splintered off into what became the "New York May 1 Coalition." The less militant wing of the movement never adopted a formal name but remained aligned with the national We Are America Alliance and the Coalition for Comprehensive Immigration Reform.

Whereas the aim of the work stoppage was to hurt the U.S. economy, the idea behind the human chain was to demonstrate not only the diversity and unity of "immigrant New York" but also how integrated immigrants were into American society. Organizers asked New Yorkers to step outside onto their sidewalks on May 1 at exactly 12:16 pm to lock arms and form massive human chains throughout the city. The time was a reference to September 16, the day the U.S. House of Representatives passed the Sensenbrenner Bill (ironically, also Mexican Independence Day). The human chains would be symbolic of people's unity against the bill. Reflecting a division that was national, labor unions and mainstream immigrant rights groups in New York decided to stick with their "pro-America" message, electing to support the human chain action on May 1, and then shift their mobilization efforts to citizenship and voter registration drives. This faction of the movement felt that because immigrants ultimately wanted to become citizens – and thus part – of the United States, the movement's image, tactics, and strategies should reflect these desires. Because H.R. 4437 seemed to have been defeated, the more moderate segment of the local movement wanted to turn its attention to the upcoming 2006 elections. As a member of this faction explained, "What does it matter if you have a million people on the streets if you can't vote some jackass out of office?"[19]

According to Aarti Shahani of FFF, "the single biggest divide" within the citywide coalition was over the question, "Are we trying to show ourselves to be American or are we celebrating internationalism?" The radical flank of the movement was composed of activists who understood issues of migration and immigrant rights through a militant and internationalist theoretical framework. This sector supported a national work stoppage and wanted to restore May Day's historic meaning as "International Worker's Day." According to Teresa Gutierrez of the International Action Center and May 1 Coalition, while "May Day has a real boogie man connotation" and is "seen as a so-called Communist holiday" in the U.S., the group wanted to recover the day's original intention of celebrating the contributions of workers across the globe, especially because the holiday originated in America in honor of the activism of immigrant workers. Their desire to revive May Day was not the only aspect of their ideology that was internationalist. Organizations within the May 1 Coalition also highlighted the United States' role in creating the very conditions that prompt international migration and were critical of the "We Are America" framing which, they believed, attempted to paint the immigrant rights movement as merely a bunch of patriots eager to assimilate.

As AnaLiza Caballes of the Damayan Migrant Worker's Association explained, "Some of our members that are a little more aware were offended with [the idea of being told to wave U.S. flags] because for us the American flag means invasion, it means occupation, it means the symbol of what has caused poverty in our country." Moisés Pérez of *Alianza Dominicana* expressed a similar sentiment: "We're victims of economic and political circumstances that the United States is very much responsible for." Ironically, he continued, "We end up here because [this country] needs our labor," but then it wants to "try and criminalize us" for it. Trishala Deb of the Audre Lorde Project, a community center that organizes LGBTSTGNC immigrants of color, elaborated that she "felt saddened by the US nationalism" and was critical of the mainstream groups' message that immigrants want legalization because "the U.S. is the best country in the world."[20] She argued, "People that are workers [should] have the right to cross borders [and] access benefits and civil rights regardless of their migration status." Because of how they understood the issues of migration and migrant rights, many May 1 Coalition participants refused to carry the U.S. flag and, instead, planned to attend the Union Square rally waving the flags of their countries of origin.

Activists aligned with the May 1 Coalition's boycott found the mainstream coalition's overall discourse to be very problematic. Deb of the Audre Lorde Project maintained that the rhetoric being used by mainstream groups "played on the whole 'good-immigrant' versus 'bad-immigrant' divide," which her organization felt was inevitably dangerous for LGBTSTGNC immigrants because, "in that situation, we're always the 'bad immigrants.'" Monami Maulik of DRUM and the May 1 Coalition, concurred, "A lot of the messaging at the human chain action was around how basically immigrants are workers and we should pass legalization so they could be better, harder workers. It was like immigrants are just labor to be exploited." The May 1 Coalition also disapproved of the implications of some of the mainstream faction's slogans; it felt that saying things like "*We* are not terrorists" mean "you're saying that those immigrants over there *are*" terrorists. After September 11 this framing, they argued, stigmatized Arab and Muslim immigrants (see also Nguyen 2005; Bakalian and Bozorgmehr 2009; Chacho 2012).

As May 1 approached, divisions between the two citywide coalitions grew in terms of both their messaging and their tactics. But much like in Los Angeles, rival entities ultimately complemented, rather than competed, with each other because many supporters decided to take part in both actions. According to the *New York Daily News*, "[A]t exactly 12:16 p.m., thousands linked hands across all five boroughs and peacefully vented their anger ... Short-order cooks wearing grease-spattered aprons and schoolchildren in uniforms joined hands to form a human chain several blocks long" (Siemaszko 2006). The paper documented, "In Manhattan, human chains formed in Battery Park City, Washington Heights and Chinatown; in Brooklyn, in Sunset Park and Coney Island; in the Bronx, along Fordham Road; in Queens, in Jackson Heights, and at an unspecified location on Staten Island" (Rose 2006). In Jackson Heights, "Mexicans, Dominicans, Peruvians, Bangladeshi, Pakistani, Indian, Irish, Korean and many other immigrants held hands on 37th Avenue, where a vibrant string of locally-owned businesses are located." This turnout was the result of "[l]ocal merchant associations such as the Jackson Heights Merchants Associations, Hispanic Chamber of Commerce and the Bangladeshi Merchants Association" working "together with community activists to make sure May 1 was not only a success, but a grassroots, community organized event that represented the diversity of the area" (Pirani 2006, 2). CNN reported, "In all, 12,000 people turned out to form eight chains: five in Manhattan, one in Queens, one in Brooklyn and one in the Bronx."[21] A different news outlet quoted a local organizer who claimed that "more than 20,000 people took part in the human chains created citywide" (Young, Hart, and Nyback 2006).

As for the Union Square rally later that afternoon, and the daylong boycott, the *New York Post* reported "[d]ozens of stores and restaurants closed or had to curtail part of their business because immigrant employees took the day off with or without permission" and "[p]ublic school attendance dropped more than 6 percent citywide, not counting students who showed up for morning classes but walked out to attend midday rallies" (Mongelli, Mazor, and Winter 2006). At a "feeder march" in the Sunset Park neighborhood of Brooklyn, the *New York Times* reported that an immigrant woman, who was a cashier at a local café, held a homemade sign that read, "I lost my job to be here," which the paper confirmed was true (O'Donnell 2006). Indeed, as the *Daily News* noted, "The huddled masses who toil in kitchens, clean offices, remove asbestos, work in car washes – many living in fear of deportation – took to the streets on May Day to show the city what life would be like without them" (Siemaszko 2006). Although rally participants waved many flags from around world, especially Mexico, just as many ralliers held American flags and "We Are America" signs. In all, the mainstream and alternative media claimed that 50,000 to over 100,000 immigrant New Yorkers and their supporters took part in the May 1 Coalition's afternoon rally (*Democracy Now!* 2006; Mongelli, Mazor, and Winter 2006).

Many local activists contended that, much like the April 10 action, on May 1, immigrant communities self-mobilized, with coalitions playing a secondary role in the demonstrations. As a member of the more moderate faction of the local movement recalled, "Organizations played a minor coordination role. But by far we did not have anything to do with the hundreds of thousands of people that came out ... All these mothers, all these fathers, all these kids, all these grandparents, they were self-directed ... It felt like a very genuine demonstration of dignity and power."[22]

Many people participated in both actions and reported that local businesses and individuals contributed in a variety of ways as well, often without knowing or caring about the split in the movement. According to Rhadames Pérez of *La Aurora*, Dominican-owned neighborhood stores donated what they could to the cause. He recalled that leading up to May 1, "I'd just show up at a local business and say, 'Hey, I need 1,000 copies of these flyers,' and they would make them" for free or charge very little. Many of these small immigrant-owned businesses also distributed flyers and posted handmade signs on store walls and doors to declare their support for the boycott and immigrant rights. During the human chain action on May Day, an immigrant organizer in Brooklyn recounted, "There were like 30 blocks, five people deep on the sidewalk. We shut down traffic ... People just went into Footlocker, Burger King, Dunkin' Donuts, and shut down those places at 12:16." At the few businesses that tried to remain open, random "people went in," blocked the doors, and "wouldn't let anybody else in until the people stopped working."[23] Without direction from coalitional leaders, people seemed to merge both the human chain and the boycott demonstrations.

In sum, whereas cities with similar ideological splits within their local movement also hosted two separate marches on May Day, only New York had both a major rally and several smaller local acts of protest across the city via their human chain action. These displays of dissent reflect the local movement's structure – diverse, fragmented by neighborhood, loosely connected, but with the potential to unite when necessary. The broad coalition that organized the first major rally on April 10 was formed by various organizations whose range of ideological leanings ordinarily compelled these groups to work independently. However, with the threat of a broad and highly visible anti-immigrant bill looming, and in the midst of a growing national protest wave, these organizations put their differences aside to join forces and oppose H.R. 4437. After the bill's defeat, those preexisting ideological differences manifested once again around whether or not to support a national boycott. This issue eventually led the citywide alliance to break into two separate coalitions – a mainstream integrationist wing and a militant internationalist faction. But despite these divisions, while movement organizers were caught up in sharp ideological and tactical debates between them, the actions of their supporters ultimately underscored and exhibited the overall unity of protesters when they participated in both the human chain and boycott rally.

Diverse Identities, Diverse Interests

In the balance of this chapter I focus on two unexpected aspects of the city's protests: disparities in levels of participation by different immigrant groups, and the overall under-performance of New York in relation to the size of its immigrant population and compared to other major immigrant metropolises. Immigrant rights activists in New York faced arduous challenges in mobilizing and forming coalitions across borders of all kinds: cultural, linguistic, racial, ethnic, class, cohort, regional, and national. During the protest wave, different foreign-born groups had different policy interests and priorities. Not all immigrants felt – though many technically were – equally threatened by H.R. 4437. Nor did they all believe that they would benefit equally from the pro-immigrant policies being proposed. As we will see, how the issue of immigrant "illegality" was racialized played a major role in the degree to which different groups' participated and why they did or did not decide to do so.

Degree of Participation

Although politicians and the mainstream media have constructed Latinos (particularly those of Mexican descent) as the "face of illegal immigration" (Chavez 2008; De Genova 2004; Sampaio 2015), other racialized groups are also greatly affected by changes to the nation's immigration laws. Nowhere in the United States is this more the case than in New York City, where more than 800 languages are spoken (the largest number in any city in the world) and, "taken together, foreign-born residents and their offspring account for more than 55 percent of the city's population" (Bernstein 2005; Roberts 2010). According to the U.S. Census, after Dominicans (378,384), in 2006, the second and third largest immigrant groups in New York were Chinese (303,462) and Jamaicans (174,861). Immigrants from Guyana (142,946) and Ecuador (128,623) followed closely behind those from Mexico (169,572). At over 17 percent of the city's foreign-born population, Europeans (520,554) also made up a sizable portion of New York's immigrants. Thus, if judged by diversity alone, New York remains America's biggest "Immigrant City." Nonetheless, not every foreign-born group in the metropolis interpreted the immigration policy debate of 2006 as affecting them in the same manner. Many felt that the legislative disputes primarily affected immigrants from Latin America – and more specifically, from Mexico.

In a study on the mainstream media's framing of immigration issues, Merolla et al. (2013) found that during the 2006 immigration debate, "even though legislative efforts...dealt with various topics such as refugees, asylum claims, family visas, and high skilled workers," much of the congressional "floor debate and related media coverage centered on the issue of illegal immigration" (789). According to activists throughout New York City, the slanted reporting impacted how different immigrant communities perceived the policy debate and protests taking place. Ninaj Raoul, of Haitian Women for Haitian Refugees (HWHR), explained that due to the media's portrayal of the issue, when Haitians discussed the proposed changes to immigration laws, many believed they pertained only to Mexicans. She recalled, "There was a lot of confusion about that at the time." Fallou Gueye, president of the Association of Senegalese in America, also explained that during the 2006 immigration debate, his organization had to constantly explain to its compatriots "that this was not only about them [Latinos], we are also part of this." Mae Lee of the

Chinese Progressive Association (CPA) remembered people in her community asking why her organization was taking part in the protests. They would question, "Why is the Chinese community here? Why should [we] be so concerned?" According to Artemio Guerra, an organizer with the Fifth Avenue Committee, such misconceptions were prevalent because "the immigration debate" was being "framed exclusively around *Mexicanos*," which many New York organizers felt fettered their organizing efforts "because immigration is a much larger phenomenon."

A local activist explained, "the perspectives of the different immigrant communities" in New York "come out in the pieces of legislation" that they believe affect them most.[24] Consequently, one reason non-Latinos felt that the immigration debate was a "Mexican issue" was that the legislative proposals most often highlighted in the media – such as legalization, guest worker programs, deportation, and border militarization – did not reflect their primary policy concerns. For instance, organizers in the Filipino and Chinese communities said that family reunification and clearing the visa backlog, *not* deportation or legalization, were the most pressing issues for their constituents. People in South Asian Muslim neighborhoods also did not believe the debate affected them significantly. As a result, local organizers "had to do a lot of messaging about why the enforcement aspects of the bills," particularly "the language around national security," were going to negatively impact them.[25] According to Ninaj Raoul of HWHR, "Since people were hearing things in the press about guest worker bills and things like that," immigrants in her community questioned whether they could benefit from participating in the protests. Thus, the degree to which specific immigrant groups felt immigration reform was important to them depended on the details of the policies under debate and who the media portrayed as most affected by them.

Perhaps because Latinos are the quintessential "illegals" (Chavez 2008; Ponce 2014) and that nativism at the time felt "very racist ant-Latino," as a European immigrant activists put it, many non-Latino immigrant groups with sizeable undocumented populations and/or who were also vulnerable to provisions in the Sensenbrenner Bill did not feel equally threatened by it.[26] In addition, since the prevailing image of the manner in which illegal immigration occurs is that of someone clandestinely crossing the Mexican border, how one becomes undocumented also seems to influence the ways that some immigrants (often mistakenly) understand their own "illegality" – and the vulnerability that accompanies it. As an example, Mae Lee of the CPA explained that most of her community's clandestine immigrant population "overstayed their visa," but that "it's not like they got on a ship and snuck here ... The way they became undocumented is through circumstances." Consequently, according to Haeyoung Yoon of CAAAV, many Chinatown residents believed "the Sensenbrenner provision doesn't really affect us."[27] An NYIC organizer further supported this differentiation, explaining that, having overstayed their visas, an estimated "50,000 Russians ... are undocumented" in the city. However, "When it comes to being attacked as an immigrant, they don't really feel those attacks apply to them," partly because "they're white." As a result, the organizer recalled that these immigrants "didn't come out" to the demonstrations.[28]

Whereas several of the Latino activists quoted earlier described immigrants in their communities as "self-mobilizing," many non-Latino organizers stated that their communities did not participate in the marches to the same extent as Latinos. For instance, New York had more Jamaican and almost as many Guyanese immigrants in the city than those from Mexico. Yet as Chuck Mohan of New York's Guyanese-American Worker's United admitted, "The Caribbean groups were very disappointing, to be honest with you ... I'm not saying that there might not have been sprinkles, but for me to tell you that there were 5,000, I would be lying to you ... This goes for the English-speaking Caribbean in general. They do not come out when it comes to immigration issues." Monami Maulik of DRUM also recounted,

It [was] much tougher to mobilize in the South Asian community, and I think also in non-Latino immigrant communities ... [because H.R. 4437] was very much seen as a Latino thing ... The media promoted it as a Latino thing ... and even in that, only as a Mexican thing, so people stayed away from it. We spent a lot of time trying to speak at community events, we put out a lot of ads in South Asian papers, we did massive amounts of street flyering and door knocking almost every day to get people out ... But it was a pretty poor turnout from what we wanted. Our leadership was pretty disappointed in our own community for not being more at the forefront of this.

Different levels of involvement were also shaped by the particular experiences of each foreign-born group. For example, Shaid Comrade of the Pakistan USA Freedom Forum believed that there was "less response and visibility" from Muslim immigrants because of the repression they had endured under the Bush Administration, specifically it's "Special Registration Program" (see Nguyen 2005; Bakalian and Bozorgmehr 2009). Many feared being picked up by Homeland Security and getting accused of "being terrorists." Another organizer in the Muslim community explained, "There was already so much fear that mass mobilization is not something that we're ready for. It's taken a couple of years after 9/11 just to get people to join political organizations, let alone get on the streets."[29]

Though many non-Latino immigrant rights activists felt that their communities did not participate in the protests to the extent that they would have liked, both Latino and non-Latino activists consistently pointed out that Dominicans and Mexicans mobilized to larger degrees than other Latino groups. Moisés Pérez of *Alianza Dominicana* recalled, "*Dominicanos* are the largest immigrant group in the New York area" and he believed that they also made up the largest group of protesters. But Pérez quickly added, "There was *a lot* of Mexicans there, it was like, *Whoa!*." A South Asian organizer with NYCPP also remembered that the crowd seemed surprisingly "Mexican, definitely Mexican – a lot of Mexican flags."[30] What explains this over-representation of Dominicans and Mexicans at the protests? Was this degree of involvement merely the result of the size of these two populations in New York City? Although sheer numbers were a major factor, these two immigrant groups also seemed to have more to gain and to lose from the policies being proposed, especially their deportation and legalization features.

Arguably, the most devastating aspect of being undocumented is the vulnerability to deportation (De Genova 2002; Kanstroom 2007). Due to changes in immigration laws made in 1996 that retroactively converted several minor infractions into newly deportable offenses (Golash-Boza 2016: 486), Dominican immigrants have become disproportionately susceptible to expulsion. For example, between 1996 and 2007, 36,000–50,000 Dominican immigrants were deported. According to an analysis of the effects of these laws, "Of the top seven immigrant groups deported from the United States in 2007, Dominicans have the highest proportion of those deported for criminal convictions" (NMCIR 2009). Local activists and community residents were particularly enraged because many of the deported had only minor violations. As a result, thousands of law-abiding Dominican legal residents who were productive members of their communities were torn from their families and repatriated. Consequently, during the 2006 protests, Dominicans may have come out in larger numbers than other immigrant groups not only because they were the biggest foreign-born population in the city but also because they had more to gain from the possible changes to deportation laws that activists were calling for. According to local organizers, the possibility of making changes to the 1996 laws was indeed the primary motivator behind the degree of Dominican participation and why, as Moisés Pérez of *Alianza*

Dominicana put it earlier, the motivation to participate in the protests "spread like a forest fire" among them.

That Mexicans accounted for a disproportionate share of the city's protest participants is supported by Barreto et al.'s (2009) quantitative national study, which revealed that despite widespread support for the 2006 rallies across all Latino subgroups, Mexicans were more likely to partake in them (754). Yet, in addition to the facts (discussed below) that Mexicans are neither the largest immigrant group nor the biggest Latino national origin group in New York, there are several other important reasons why their level of involvement in the city's 2006 protests was unexpected and imperative to examine.

Unlike other major immigrant metropolises, such as L.A. and Chicago, where people of Mexican descent make up the bulk of the foreign-born population, have a long history of activism, and have established several professional social movement organizations – Mexicans in New York are notoriously under-organized (Hazan 2006: 211, 264). Thus, the extent of their turnout is intriguing because of the important role organizations are said to play in social movement mobilizations but that Mexicans in the Empire City lacked, similar to Fort Myers (McCarthy and Zald 1977; Clemens and Minkoff 2004; Meyer 2007: 61; Smith and Wiest 2012). Moreover, given the strong relationship studies have consistently found between individual resources (e.g. income, education, etc.) and political participation (Verba, Schlozman, and Brady 1995; Leighley and Nagler 2013), the degree of Mexican engagement in the New York protests is even more surprising. Mexicans had the highest poverty rate among all New York foreign-born residents (32%), the lowest percent of high school graduates (34.7%), the least electoral influence of any ethnic group (only 0.2 percent of Mexicans in the city were voting-age citizens), and are fairly new immigrants to the city (NYC Department of Planning 2000; Logan and Mollenkopf 2001: 25).

Yet notwithstanding their relative lack of numbers, organization, and resources, the impetus for Mexicans in New York to mass-mobilize was more obvious than for other immigrants. Their link to the issue is unavoidable, as we have seen again and again: people of Mexican descent were at the time, and still remain, "the face of illegal immigration." Tellingly, a national survey of U.S. and foreign-born Latinos taken during the 2006 marches showed that Mexicans not only had a more positive view of undocumented immigrants than other Latino national origin groups but also were more likely to report feeling increasingly discriminated against as a result of the immigration debate taking place (Suro and

Escobar 2006). Furthermore, despite composing only a small fraction of the city's total foreign-born population, not having the security of citizenship was a vastly more significant issue for Mexicans than for other immigrant groups in New York.

For example, U.S. Census data shows that New York's 2006 foreign-born population was 6 percent Mexican, 29 percent Caribbean, 14 percent South American, 4 percent Central American, 26 percent Asian, 4 percent African, and 17 percent European. But in terms of these same groups' citizenship status, about 90 percent of foreign-born Mexicans lacked citizenship, compared with 47 percent of Caribbean, 50 percent of South American, 55 percent of Central American, 47 percent of Asian, 61 percent of African, and 36 percent of European immigrants (Zepeda-Millán 2014). Additionally, according to Jeffrey Passel, a senior demographer at the Pew Hispanic Center, "virtually all" Mexican immigration since 1990 has been undocumented, including in New York (Bernstein 2005). Given that 90 percent of Mexican immigrants in the city were not citizens, and that of these non-citizens, 83 percent of them came after 1990,[31] it is reasonable to believe that almost all foreign-born Mexicans living in New York in 2006 were undocumented. As such, with the most to gain and lose from changes in legalization and deportation laws, it makes sense that more Mexicans (along with Dominicans) would participate in the protests than other foreign-born populations.

Contrary to other immigrants, Mexicans seemed to not have questioned whether the issues being debated were going to have a profound effect on them. Whereas activists in other communities had to make an extra effort to explain to their specific immigrant groups how the laws being proposed would affect them, Mexican immigrants did not need anyone to explain to them that "anti-immigrant," or specifically "anti-illegal immigrant," meant *anti-them*. Consequently, they responded without hesitation. In the same way that the activists quoted earlier described Mexican and Dominican immigrants as "auto-mobilizing" for the April 10 actions, Joel Magallán of the *Asociación Tepeyac*, the primary (and one of the few) community-based organizations to focus on Mexican immigrants in New York, remembered,

May 1st wasn't like one of our regular [attempts at] mobilization. Usually for us to organize a mobilization, we have to set up a meeting, explain to people in each community, in each church, what we're going to do, why we want to do it, where we're going to have it, all of that. But that year the motivation was already there ... We didn't have to mobilize ... [Mexican immigrants] moved on their own.

Magnitude Mobilization

Another anomaly of the New York protest wave was the overall size of the city's demonstrations. As May Chen of UNITE-HERE admitted, "While they were large, they were nothing like Los Angeles" or other major immigrant cities. This observation is interesting to note because New York has the nation's biggest immigrant population, arguably the longest history of immigrant activism, and likely more immigrant rights organizations than any other city in the country – yet, activists in the metropolis arrived late to the protest wave (Foner and Waldinger 2013: 355) and when they finally did produce a large demonstration, they relatively underperformed in terms of the size of their actions (Foner and Waldeinger 2013: 355; Hazan and Hayduk 2011). For example, whereas activists in L.A., Dallas, and Chicago boasted demonstrations of 500,000 to 1 million marchers (McFadden 2006; Watanabe and Becerra 2006; Fox, Selee, and Bada 2006), according to the *New York Times*, New York's largest turnout and first major mobilization put only 100,000 people on the streets for the April 10 "National Day of Action for Immigrant Justice" (Bada, Fox and Selee 2006). For the second nationally coordinated day of protest, the May 1 "Day Without an Immigrant/Great American Boycott," participation in New York's noontime "human chain" action included somewhere between 12,000 and 20,000 participants (CNN 2006; Young, Hart, and Nyback 2006). Estimates of the Union Square rally later that day ranged from "more than 50,000 protesters" by the conservative *New York Post* (Mongelli, Mazor, and Winter 2006) to just "over 100,000" by the liberal New York–based radio program *Democracy Now!*[32]

Again, given the city's massive foreign-born population (over 3 million in 2006), long history of immigrant activism, and well-developed immigrant rights organizational infrastructure, "There is a question to be asked of New York," as a longtime organizer in the city put it, "which is, why wouldn't we have had the largest ... march in the country?"[33] To be sure, the attendance of 12,000 to over 100,000 people at any political event is an amazing accomplishment in itself, and a volume that most U.S. social movements (as well as political parties and politicians, for that matter) could only dream of. Nevertheless, since according to local urban politics experts, "New York evidently promotes immigrant political participation ... to a far greater degree than" cities like Los Angeles (Mollenkopf, Olson, and Ross 2001: 63; also see Mollenkopf 1999), why New York under-performed during the historic protest wave calls for a detailed investigation.

TABLE 4.1. *Characteristics of Undocumented Immigrants by Metro Area*

	Estimated Undocumented Population	% of Foreign-Born Who Are Undocumented	% of Mexicans in Undocumented Population
Dallas	460,000	48	75
Chicago	400,000	28	88
Los Angeles	1,000,000	26	59
New York	520,000	16	20

Source: Fortuny, Capps, and Passel (2007).

The answer to this query is twofold. First, the cities with the biggest demonstrations had more homogeneous foreign-born populations with larger numbers of undocumented Mexican immigrants and people (both U.S.- and foreign-born) of Mexican descent. Second, and closely related, because of New York's heterogeneous foreign-born population, organizers had the more difficult task of organizing across multiple "borders" (e.g., linguistic, racial, ethnic, class, cultural, etc.) both between and within immigrant groups. Activists in cities like L.A., Dallas, and Chicago did not have to overcome these challenges, at least not to the same extent; not surprisingly, all three of these cities had greater turnout than New York at their respective protests.

According to a 2007 report by the Department of Homeland Security's Office of Immigration Statistics, California, Texas, and Illinois all had larger numbers of undocumented immigrants than the state of New York (Hoefer, Rytina, and Campell 2007). Moreover, an analysis of 2003–2004 Current Population Survey (CPS) data found that in terms of the percent of Mexicans that made up these states' undocumented populations, California (with 65%), Texas (with 79%), and Illinois (with 88%) all far exceeded New York, where the Mexican segment of undocumented residents was only 16 percent (Fortuny, Capps, and Passel 2007, 38). Furthermore, as Table 4.1 reveals, within the foreign-born populations of the New York, L.A., Dallas, and Chicago metro areas, the percentage of undocumented immigrants – and the percentage of these undocumented immigrants that were Mexican – was significantly higher in L.A., Dallas, and Chicago than in New York. Hence, compared with New York, there were more Mexican people without papers in the former three locales, and thus, more people with more to gain from acquiring their citizenship and more to lose from an increase in the criminalization of undocumented migration.

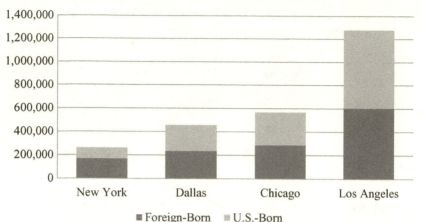

FIGURE 4.1. Size of Mexican Origin Population
Source: U.S. Census 2006 American Community Survey.

Furthermore, not only did Mexican immigrants make up a larger share of the city's entire foreign-born population in L.A. (40%), Chicago (48%), and Dallas (73%) compared with New York (6%), but as Figure 4.1 below makes clear, overall Los Angeles (1,276,870), Chicago (566,801), and Dallas (455,232) also had substantially larger Mexican-origin (U.S.- and foreign-born) populations than New York City (260,622).

These statistics are important to underscore because since individuals of Mexican descent (U.S.- and foreign-born, documented and undocumented) were the primary targets of much of the country's nativism at the time (Chavez 2008), a larger pool of people in the non-New York cities analyzed in this book were motivated to take collective action against H.R. 4437. Thus, these compounding factors help explain why L.A., Dallas, and Chicago all had larger demonstrations than New York.

In light of these demographic contexts, a New York activist, who was originally from Los Angeles, explained that the disparities between the cities' mobilizations were due to activists in L.A. having to reach out to fewer immigrant communities. She said, "In L.A., there's a lot of Mexicans and Salvadorians. So if you get those groups and their leadership on board," you can produce a large demonstration (See also Milkman and Terriquez 2012: 723).[34] A different New York organizer agreed, saying that because the immigrant population in "L.A. is primarily Mexican ... very few methods of outreach are necessary to outreach to that community." On the other hand, "in New York, we're so diverse [that] ... when you're talking about immigrant rights, you're talking about a very different sort of thing."[35] Accordingly, as was illustrated in the previous chapter, once the predominately Mexican Spanish-language media in Los Angeles supported Chicano and Mexican immigrant activists' calls for action, the Mexican masses followed. The process of mass mobilizing immigrants in New York was significantly different. As May Lee of the CPA explained,

One of the characteristics of our city is that our immigrant communities are very diverse and very different so you can't just have one blast announcement for everyone. You actually have to go into each community and have outreach in different languages and different ways that are more culturally appropriate... for different groups in different neighborhoods. Some have a long history of being involved, some may be new immigrants and their whole population is new to the country.

As discussed earlier, organizing across different immigrant groups can be daunting, given their varying experiences in the United States. New York organizers faced the additional challenge of navigating the range of experiences that many immigrant groups brought with them from their countries of origin, which often affected their decision to partake in the protests. For instance, participation in the 2006 actions by immigrants from formerly Communist Eastern European countries was scarce. According to a local organizer in this community, "They didn't support it," their mentality was, "Fuck you. I've done my share of forced marching ... I had to go to demonstrations as a kid ... I'm not dealing with that protest bullshit anymore."[36] Regarding undocumented Filipina domestic workers, AnaLiza Caballes of the Damayan Migrant Workers Association explained, "It was hard for them to come out" because many of them are older women who live with their employers and their "background in the Philippines is also middle class so their thinking is not really to go out and protest" when faced with a problem. Thus, New York organizers had to develop messaging and organizing strategies for immigrants with differing U.S. *and* home country experiences, both of which impacted the degree to which they felt attacked by the Sensenbrenner Bill and their williness to protest it.

To further complicate matters, differences existed *within* the city's foreign-born communities. These multiple layers of diversity also affected New York immigrants' levels of mobilization. May Chen of UNITE-HERE provided an example of this dynamic within one neighborhood. She explained that whereas many immigrants in Chinatown supported the April 10 action, Taiwanese members of the community did not really come out for the May Day march because they viewed "May Day as too radical ... [and] felt that May 1ˢᵗ was kind of like Communist China's Labor Day." Mae Lee of the CPA concurred, pointing out how this divide also surfaced in the support that the local Chinatown coalition received from its ethnic business communities. She recalled that whereas both the long-established Chinese Consolidated Benevolent Association (CCBA) and the relatively newer Fujian Association of Businesses (FAB) (composed of more recent immigrants) supported the April 10 march, only the Fujianese businesses continued to assist with the May 1 actions. Speaking of FAB's members, Lee stated that "a lot of them were very supportive. They printed t-shirts, signs, and those kinds of things – they spent some money on it. They [even] had a big meeting with all of their business members and told them they had to come out." On the other hand, because "China is a socialist country," May Day "is celebrated" there "but not in Taiwan." Consequently, the CCBA was not as supportive because most of its members come from Taiwan.

On top of not all immigrant groups in the city feeling equally threatened by H.R. 4437 and motivated to march against it, New York organizers also faced multiple national, linguistic, racial, ethnic, class, cohort, regional, and other obstacles in their mobilizing efforts. As a result, despite hosting the protest wave's most diverse demonstrations, the city produced much smaller actions than those in other large cities with significant immigrant populations (Bernstein 2006). Nonetheless, that local activists convinced somewhere between 12,000 and 20,000 supporters to participate in their "human chain" action on April 10, and another 50,000 to 100,000 people to take part in their May 1 rally in Union Square, was an impressive achievement once we understand the challenges they faced.

Conclusion

The 2006 immigrant rights protests in New York City help us to better understand both how multiracial mobilizations and alliances work and do not work, their possibilities as well as their limits. Despite claims that competition is more common than coalition building among different racial groups (McClain and Tauber 2001: 114; Hazan 2006: 207), the anti-Sensenbrenner Bill actions in New York show us that in response to a draconian nativist legislative threat, and through the mediation of various types of social ties, large and diverse immigrant rights coalitions are indeed possible. Just as crucial, however, is the role that ideological diversity, and the strategic decision-making practices that result from it, can play in fracturing these same partnerships.

Similar to what transpired during the two May Day protests organized by rival coalitions in L.A., the case of New York also shows the important role that group resources can play when divisions arise over how to best frame movement demands. When coalitions are unable to reach an agreement about what unified message to present at jointly organized public actions, individual groups and activists are left to frame their own claims and grievances. When this occurs, organizations with more assets are able to dominate the frames and the messages disseminated during protest events. After the immediate actions are over, these dynamics can lead to new divisions, the exacerbation of preexisting ones, or even to the fracturing and ultimately disbanding movement coalitions.

The chapter also helps clarify why certain immigrant groups participated in the marches more than others, and why New York immigrant rights activists relatively underperformed in terms of the size of their protests. Although one of the activists quoted earlier stated that immigrants "understand very clearly ... the connection between policies and their lives," we have seen a more complicated and nuanced relationship between immigrants and immigration policies. New York City's 2006 protests illustrate that how the media frames immigration legislation, the political experiences immigrants bring from their countries of origin, and the different ways foreign-born groups and their descendants are racialized in the U.S., can all impact the political engagement of immigrant communities.

Just as the categories of "immigrant" and "illegal immigrant" are socially constructed, these categories were understood and adopted differently by the city's diverse foreign-born populations. These differences of interpretation help explain the disparities in mobilization from one immigrant group to another, as well as the New York demonstrations' relatively modest overall turnout in relation to the city's large immigrant population and numerous immigrant rights organizations. My interviews with African, European, Asian, and Latino immigrant and U.S.-born activists revealed that immigrant "illegality" is racialized as generally Latino, but more precisely as Mexican, not only by the media, politicians and the general American public but also by Latinos and other racialized groups. As a result, the legislative threat posed by the Sensenbrenner Bill seems to have mobilized and triggered feelings of group consciousness and linked fate primarily among Latinos compared to non-Latinos in New York, but especially amongst Mexicans in the city. These findings also help us understand why in smaller locales like Fort Myers, for example, it was primarily Mexicans and not Cubans, Haitians, Columbians, or Puerto Ricans that moblized against H.R. 4437, and why cities with large U.S.- and foreign-born populations of Mexican descent (e.g. Los Angeles, Dallas, and Chicago) had the biggest demonstrations in the nation during the protest wave.

5

The Suppression of Immigrant Contention

More people participated in the May Day demonstrations than in any other action during the roughly three-month cycle of contention (Wallace, Zepeda-Millán, and Jones-Correa 2014: 438). On the heels of this success, some immigrant rights activists vowed to continue calling for more mass marches. A key organizer of the Los Angeles rallies expounded, "After May 1, we tried to keep things going and we wanted to do a national day of action in September," on Labor Day.[1] But rather than serve as a step toward its continued rise, May 1 would come to mark both the pinnacle and the start of the rapid decline of the historic series of protests.

Reporting on the promised September actions, news outlets throughout the nation highlighted the small scale of the marches compared to the size of the movement's previous demonstrations (Marcucci and Sholin 2006; Salles 2006). As the *Associated Press* wrote, "Crowd estimates for Labor Day rallies in cities [across the country] ... ranged from the hundreds to the low thousands, a far cry from the hundreds of thousands who gathered in several cities in the spring" (Wohlsen 2006). Instead of contesting these critical media accounts, organizers conceded their disappointment with the turnout. A member of the New York Immigration Coalition (NYIC) bluntly summarized the results of efforts to mass mobilize immigrant communities subsequent to May 1, "We tried to have a march but nobody fucking came out for it ... We tried a couple of times since then to get people out and failed miserably."[2] How can we explain the abrupt decline of the demonstrations and organizers' inability to continue to get people to take to the streets?

Sometimes sudden and dramatic, other times slow and dull, the ways that protest waves come to an end are as varied as the issues that initially motivate the waves themselves (Koopmans 2004; 36). Social movement scholars have discovered that the decline of mobilization can be attributed to factors ranging from activist burnout and changes in political contexts, to several "mechanisms of demobilization" such as movement factionalization, institutionalization, and repression (Sawyers and Meyer 1999; Hadden and Tarrow 2007; Tilly and Tarrow 2006: 97–98). The results of my research reveal that the 2006 immigrant rights protest wave ended primarily because of three factors: the defeat of H.R. 4437, divisions within the movement, and the shift in mobilization efforts to more mainstream forms of politics.

My New York and Los Angeles case studies highlighted some of the major tactical and ideological disputes that arose between activists throughout the country at the local and national levels. The resulting split among movement leaders was most apparent during the two coordinated days of nationwide protests. More moderate groups, such as those affiliated with the We Are America Alliance, organized the patriotic April 10 "National Day of Action for Immigrant Justice" and encouraged supporters to carry only American flags. Conversely, movement radicals spearheaded the more militant "Great American Boycott/Day Without an Immigrant" on May 1, International Workers Day. Not surprisingly, both factions also differed sharply on policy and on what direction the movement should take. Radicals called for more protests, held firm to their demands for immediate and unconditional amnesty for the nation's millions of undocumented workers and refused to support any compromise federal legislation that included immigration enforcement measures. Many in the more moderate faction of the movement felt limited in their ability to influence the Republican elected officials who controlled Congress and believed that calling for more mass marches might actually do more harm than good. Consequently, these groups cautiously supported the bipartisan Kennedy-McCain Bill (S. 2611) being debated in the Senate because it contained an, admittedly limited, legalization provision. They also eventually shifted their attention to the upcoming midterm and presidential elections.

The defeat of H.R. 4437, divisions within the movement, and how activists attempted to influence electoral politics are each discussed in detail in the next chapter. But while these three reasons may have been the primary causes for the decline of the groundswell of immigrant rights demonstrations, they were not the only contributing factors. According to local and national activists, both during and immediately after the protest wave, the actions of private citizens (e.g. an increase in anti-Latino hate crimes and employers firing workers for participating in the rallies), the state (e.g. immigration raids and anti-immigrant ordinances), and the media (both English- and Spanish-language outlets) all contributed to the creation of a more hostile mobilizing environment for march organizers. Thus, whereas the previous three chapters utilized specific city-level case studies to investigate the principal focus of this book – the rise of the protest wave – the next two chapters zoom out to explore the decline and some of the impacts of the series of national demonstrations. Before I do so, however, some qualifications about the scope of the argument and data presented in this chapter are in order.

As my Fort Myers, Los Angeles, and New York case studies have illustrated, when tracing the organizing processes of protest coalitions, triangulating and verifying the personal accounts of the actions of various coalition members is a valuable source of evidence. Such triangulation is markedly more difficult when examining failed attempts at mass mobilization. When the behaviors of government officials (i.e. politicians and immigration officers) and private citizens (i.e. employers, countermovement activists, or members of the media) are said to be motivated by hate and/or with the goal of stifling legal activities (i.e. participating in permitted protests), demonstrating these intensions with certainty becomes difficult. This is especially true when no systematic data is available on, for example, the number of people who lost their jobs for attending a march, or the exact period in time and location the government conducted workplace immigration raids. Consequently, because the evidence presented this chapter is predominantly reliant on interviews with pro-immigrant activists – supplemented with annual government statistics on immigration enforcement measures as well as newspaper and NGO accounts of these actions – the arguments presented here are more speculative than causal. That said, documenting the various practices of private and state actors that activists claimed hampered their organizing efforts could nonetheless serve as a theory-building exercise. The events presented in this chapter can thus function as signposts for future research to test the multiple explanations organizers identified and examine whether there was a direct relationship between these factors and immigrant rights supporters' unwillingness to continue to publically protest. Hence, while a systematic study of every factor that contributed to the protest wave's abatement is beyond the scope of this book, and although I maintain that the three causes stated above were the primary reasons why the cycle of contention ended, this chapter investigates what I consider to be secondary factors that likely stifled activists' mobilizing efforts.

Theorizing Threat and Demobilization

As we have seen, the mass mobilizations of 2006 were not merely a response by undocumented immigrants and their allies to an external threat (H.R. 4437); though logical, this is an insufficient explanation for the unprecedented level of collective action that occurred in the spring of that year. Indeed, several sources of evidence suggest that both during and after the protest wave there were increases in the number of raids, deportations, anti-immigrant ordinances and hate crimes – indicating that people without papers were arguably more threatened during and after the mass mobilizations than they were before them. Yet the protest wave deteriorated rather than escalated as these threats increased. This conundrum begs for greater attention to the role that threat played in the rise and fall of the mass demonstrations; in particular, why do threats lead to large-scale collective action in some instances, yet in other instances contribute to the decline or suppression of that action?

Recall that in the introductory chapter of this book I asserted that threats that are broad in scope and that derive from multiple sources can lead to the suppression of immigrant contention. I argued that broad, multiple-source threats pose two fundamental problems for activists: they make attributing responsibility for their impacts more difficult, and the amount of time and resources needed to address all (or at least several) of these threats dilutes activists' oppositional efforts. For example, as described later, fighting the thousands of workplace raids that occurred and the hundreds of anti-immigrant ordinances proposed in various states and hundreds of municipalities throughout the nation was extremely difficult, if not impossible, for immigrant rights advocates. Moreover, I maintained that while looming dangers provide activists with at least some time to respond, threats such as being a potential victim of a hate crime or deportation are more difficult to organize against because activists only become aware of them after they have taken place.

When the latter types of threats – anti-immigrant ordinances, deportations, hate crimes, etc. – begin to materialize on a mass-scale and thus affect a greater number of people, I posited that their visibility can also increase because they are more likely to draw media attention, especially from Spanish-language news outlets who consistently cover issues related immigration. When this occurs, ethnic media can function – intentionally and unintentionally – as a demobilizing force by fostering a sense of fear among current and potential participants in immigrant rights activism through frequent broadcasts of anti-immigrant actions. English-language media can also contribute to the suppression of immigrant contention because of the effects that negative or bias coverage of immigrant rights activists and rallies can have on public opinion.

In what follows I elucidate how the massive and primarily Latino protest wave triggered a backlash from nativist citizens, conservative political pundits on mainstream media, and government officials. I argue that while overt state repression (e.g. mass arrests or beatings of protesters) did not occur and cannot explain the decline of the demonstrations, government immigration enforcement measures and the actions of nativist civilians and media outlets (both English- and Spanish-language) contributed to the suppression of immigrant contention because they inhibited the condition under which activists attempted to mass mobilize.[3]

Societal Backlash

When a groundswell of activism occurs by a particular group, other sectors of society sometimes respond if they feel their interests are being threatened (Tarrow 2011: 205). Speaking of the 2006 protest wave, Deepak Pargava of the Center for Community Change (CCC), a key member of the We Are America Alliance, recalled: "I think we all knew a racist backlash was coming, but I don't think any of us were prepared for the level of it. It was like a tidal wave that just swept the whole country at every level." An unwelcomed result of the immigrant rights protest wave was that it sparked a societal backlash that materialized in multiple ways; ranging from the bolstering of anti-immigrant activism, negative media coverage, and a spike in anti-Latino hate crimes, to less dramatic but still distressing actions such as the firing of employees for participating in immigrant rights rallies.

Students of contentious politics have found that "counter-movements" often arise in reaction to the perceived or actual successes of social movements whose goals they oppose (Della Porta, and Diani 1999: 212; Tilly and Tarrow 2006: 133; Snow and Soule 2010: 212). In this fashion, by the end of 2006, the Southern Poverty Law Center (SPLC) – a legal advocacy organization known for its tracking of hate groups in the United States – documented that, "Around the country, an anti-immigration movement is spreading like wildfire" (Mock 2007). According to an investigative report conducted by this organization, in 2005, there were 37 nativist extremist groups in 25 states; by 2007, "there were 255 groups in 42 states." That is to say, between the year before and the year after the immigrant rights marches, the number of nativist extremist groups in the U.S. "increased in number by 600 percent" (BDI 2007).

Not only did the amount of anti-immigrant organizations grow, but so too did the number of people participating in them. Although group membership rosters are not public and thus numbers are unverifiable, the case of the Minuteman Civil Defense Corps (MCDC), one faction of the border militia "Minutemen" movement is illustrative. In early 2006 – before the immigrant rights demonstrations began – MCDC claimed to have 6,000 members. By the end of the protest wave, the group said its membership had jumped to 7,451 (a 24% increase) and that about 60,000 people had made donations to their cause (Navarro 2009: 193). According to the *Miami Herald*, "Membership began to swell for such groups in 2006 – a backlash to massive marches by immigrants in major cities" (Woods 2008). Ira Mehlman of the restrictionist Federation for American Immigration Reform (FAIR) concurred and claimed that the rise in Americans joining anti-immigrant organizations was because, "Most of the public watching [the pro-immigrant protests] saw millions of people on the street demanding rewards for doing something wrong" (2008). SPLC warned that the growth of the anti-immigrant movement was a dangerous development because its "mix of nativist intolerance, armed and untrained civilians, and wild-eyed conspiracy theories could easily explode into violence" (Buchanan and Kim 2006).

Although the sources cited above provide a compelling case for the notion that the immigrant rights marches reinvigorated a nativist social movement, it is worth mentioning that the number of counter protests and oppositional demonstrators at pro-immigrant rallies were relatively minute or nonexistent (Flaccus 2006; Chernoff 2006). As CNN reported on April 10, "Some counter-protests were also held . . . by people who favor stricter immigration laws, but they paled in size and scope next to the pro-immigration rallies."[4] That being said, while the growth in the number of nativist organizations and activists did not serve as demobilizing forces, in and of themselves, I believe the anti-Latino and -immigrant rhetoric spewed by right-wing English-language media outlets and the violence perpetrated by racist individuals likely signaled to organizers and potential participants in pro-immigrant protests that there could be a serious price to pay for partaking in activism.

Evidence exists to substantiate these claims. For instance, the day after the massive March 25 mobilization in Los Angeles, well-known white nationalist radio host and blogger Hal Turner proclaimed, "All of you who think there's a peaceful solution to these invaders [immigrants] are wrong. We're going to have to start killing these people."[5] On April 3, Laine Lawless, a founding member of the Minutemen movement, called for neo-Nazi organizations to start "an anonymous propaganda campaign warning that any further illegal immigrants will be shot, maimed or seriously messed-up upon crossing the border." Her goal was to, "Make every illegal alien feel the heat of being a person without status" (Mock 2007). The day before the April 10 National Day of Action for Immigrant Justice, hundreds of flyers were scattered in front of a predominately Latino apartment complex calling for Americans to burn down the homes of undocumented immigrants (Apocada 2006). Jim Gilchrist, cofounder of the Minuteman Project, another faction of the Minutemen movement, declared, "I will not promote violence... but I will not stop others who might pursue" it (Buchanan and Holthouse 2006). Republican Arnold Schwarzenegger, then-governor of California and a self-professed supporter of the Minutemen, confirmed the gravity of these threats when he publically stated his opposition to acts of hate speech after Latino elected officials – such as then-California lieutenant governor Cruz Bustamante and mayor of Los Angeles Antonio Villaraigosa – received "disturbing and hateful death threats." A postcard mailed to one official read, "All you dirty Mexicans should go back to Mexico. The only good Mexican is a dead Mexican" (Williams 2006).

This animosity went beyond threats and turned into action. An immigrant rights protest organizer recalled, "After the marches the attacks on the community increased. I think it was because they got worried that we were so many and they hadn't really realized that that many of us lived here... They needed in one way or another to stop or control us...so they found those ways to attack us."[6] One such incident occurred on April 10, the day of the countrywide demonstrations. In San Diego, California, a small family-owned Mexican restaurant received an anonymous telephone call that "spewed venom against Mexicans." That night, after the city's immigrant rights rally ended, racist nativists broke into the restaurant, graffitied anti-Mexican slurs on its walls, and set the place on fire (Krueger 2006). Unfortunately, direct attacks were not limited to people's property. On April 22, a 16-year-old U.S.-born Latino boy in Houston, Texas was assaulted by skinheads who screamed "White power!" and called him a "wetback" and "spic" as they beat him unconscious before sodomizing him with a patio umbrella, burning him with cigarettes, and attempting to carve a swastika into his chest. In addition, on April 28, two white men in Salt Lake City, Utah attacked an undocumented Latino high school student as he walked to school. The brutalizers called the boy a "stupid wetback" and told him to, "Go back to your country, you don't belong here." And just two days before the national May 1 day of protest, in East Hampton, New York, three Latino teenagers were "lured into a shed by a neo-Nazi skinhead... and then threatened and terrorized with a chainsaw and machete," while the perpetrator yelled "White power!" and "Heil Hitler!" As the attacker chased the Latino teens around with a chainsaw, he screamed, "This is how you run across the border."[7]

Though graphic, these were not isolated incidents but part of a larger disturbing trend that peaked the year of the protest wave. Even taking into consideration that Latinos notoriously under-report hate crimes (*El Diario* 2011), FBI statistics showed that in 2006, of the 1,305 victims of hate crimes "motivated by the offender's bias toward a particular ethnicity/national origin," 63% (819) were Latino.[8] While the number of anti-Latino hate crime victims was on a rise since 2003 – increasing 8.57 percent (595–646) from 2003–2004 and 11.76 percent (646–722) from 2004–2005 – this growth reached its peak the year of the national demonstrations (2005–2006) jumping 13.43 percent (722–819), before a much smaller increase of 1.34 percent (819–830) from 2006–2007, and then an actual decrease of 11.4 percent (830–735) from 2007–2008.[9] Explaining the reasons behind this rise in anti-Latino hate crimes, SPLC reported, "As anti-immigrant propaganda has increased on both the margins and in the mainstream of society – where pundits and politicians have routinely vilified undocumented Latino immigrants with a series of defamatory falsehoods – hate violence has risen against *perceived* 'illegal aliens'" [emphasis added] (Potok 2008).

Critical race theorist Kevin R. Johnson (2004) maintains that because "direct attacks on minorities with respect to their race is today off-limits, discrimination is displaced to foreign minorities." He argues that, "Hatred for domestic minorities is transferred to a more publicly palatable target for antipathy." Johnson (2004) contends that such "psychological devices help U.S. society reconcile its view of itself as nonracist with its harsh treatment of noncitizens of color. Noncitizens, so the rationalization goes, deserve this treatment because of their immigration status, not because of their race" (15–16). While I concur with Johnson's general argument, the data and illustrations described above indicate that during and subsequent to the 2006 protests, nativists seemed to have had no problem overtly venting their "social frustrations" and "hatred" for American- and foreign-born Latinos.

As Clarissa Martinez De Castro of the National Council of La Raza (NCLR) remembered, "The anti-immigrant backlash" was "really being channeled into an anti-Latino backlash that has had deadly consequences because people go hunting for a Mexican or for an illegal now, and any Latino-looking person they find will do." These insights may explain why, by the end of the protest wave, a majority of "Latinos far removed from the immigrant experience in their family histories" perceived the immigration "debate as a source of greater discrimination every bit as much as" recently arrived immigrants did (Suro and Escobar 2006: 5, 9). The fact that Latinos were increasingly attacked, regardless of their citizenship status, suggests that although the racialization of illegality helps cultivate a collective identity among many people of Latin American descent, merely "looking Latino" in America can make one vulnerable to acts of random violence.

Pro-immigrant activists across the country believed that both actual and threatened attacks against Latinos – U.S.- and foreign-born – fostered a climate of fear in immigrant communities, causing supporters to question the effectiveness of mass marches and whether they were worth the backlash. As one interviewee told me, "We said no more marches because we were scared that there would be some confrontation, that some anti-immigrant group would attack us, or that even some crazy would come and shoot us."[10] Another local activist added, "I think that we woke up the racism in Americans [because] since [the protests], there's been several Latinos attacked ... We believe its racial resentment."[11] Verbal and physical attacks by private citizens were not the only ways this nativist backlash manifested itself. Many mainstream English-language media outlets amplified a general hostility towards Latinos, immigrants, and the protests, which activists believed hurt their ability to continue to mobilize their base and gain support from the general public.

Several studies have shown that the mass media can contribute to the suppression of political activism in a number of ways, including highlighting divisions between activists, publishing false information, creating a sense of fear among organizers' target populations, and by demonizing movements (Marx 1979; Gitlin 2003; Boykoff 2007; Davenport 2010). Immigrant rights activists claimed that, intentionally and unintentionally, the media – especially cable news outlets – subjected them to the latter two forms of suppression. A systematic investigation of media coverage of the 2006 protests is needed to examine the degree to which negative portrayals of the demonstrations occurred but is beyond the scope of this book. What is undeniable, nevertheless, is that instances of this type of coverage did happen and were not limited to networks with conservative political leanings.

One way the mass media's reporting can demonize social movements is when it focuses on individuals in, or aspects of, a movement that may clash with "mainstream values, beliefs and opinions" (Gitlin 2003b: 304; Boykoff 2007: 229). For instance, instead of emphasizing the thousands upon thousands of U.S. flags at the pro-immigrant demonstrations, activists claimed that English-language news outlets continuously highlighted the less-numerous foreign flags being waved. A Washington D.C.–based immigrant rights leader explained,

You had this very interesting way in which the [protests] were being spun [by the English-language media] ... Some of their characteristics were being exaggerated or twisted. For example ... you had marches where the preponderance of symbolism was the American flag, but the thing that the media would zero-in on would be the flags that were not American ... [They'd] then try to use this to interpret that these were anti-American marches, which couldn't be further from the truth.[12]

A study conducted by the progressive media watchdog group Media Matters titled, "'Burn the Mexican flag!': A look back at the hateful anti-immigration rhetoric from 2006," found copious examples of this type of bias news coverage on several networks (Gregory 2010). For instance, on April 10, Fox News correspondent David Asman claimed that the presence of Mexican flags at rallies demonstrated the "antagonistic edge" of protesters, while Neil Cavuto, the host of Fox's *Your World* show, questioned the sincerity of ralliers carrying U.S. flags by saying that they were just using them as a "prop" or "a ploy to win American support." In addition, during his coverage of the May 1 marches, *O'Reilly Factor* host Bill O'Reilly promoted a conspiracy theory claiming that immigrant rights protest "organizers" had a secret "hardcore militant agenda" to "reconquer" the Southwest United States on behalf of Mexico (Gregory 2010).

Examples of negative or bias news coverage are not limited to the notoriously conservative Fox News network. In their April 24 report titled "CNN's Immigration Problem," the organization Fair and Accuracy in Reporting (FAIR) documented several instances in which the network's hosts and guests gave prejudice reporting against immigrants and/or the immigrant rights marches. To illustrate, during the popular show *The Situation Room's* coverage of the April 10 National Day of Action for Immigrant Justice, longtime CNN anchor Jack Cafferty reported that, "Once again, the streets of our country were taken over today by people who don't belong here."[13] Furthermore, on April 24, then-CNN *Headline News* host Glenn Beck claimed, "[I]llegal immigrants are attacking our culture and our way of life." *Lou Dobbs Tonight* host Lou Dobbs also continuously referred to march participants as an "army" of "illegal aliens" and "invaders" who sought to take over the Southwest (Gregory 2006). Examples like these also appeared in some of MSNBC's reporting. On top of the usually liberal network titling its coverage of the May Day rallies, "Immigrant Anger" (Dobbs 2006), suggesting an aggressive nature to the rallies, while guest-hosting *Scarborough Country* on April 10, Michael Smerconish suggested that "law enforcement ought to step in," gather up, and deport the undocumented immigrants attending the demonstrations. On the liberal show *Hardball with Chris Matthews*, conservative Pat Buchanan claimed that immigration was "an invasion of the United States of America." And on April 30, staunch Democrat and *Hardball* host Chris Matthews proclaimed that Republicans had "a right to fear" a "cultural change" if their hometowns became "overwhelmingly Mexican" (Gregory 2006).

John Trasviña of the Mexican American Legal Defense and Education Fund (MALDEF), the nation's leading Latino legal advocacy organization, believed that this type of mainstream media coverage of the protest wave "really poisoned the atmosphere."[14] Javier Valdez of the New York Immigration Coalition (NYIC) agreed, recalling, "We were getting pounded on the airwaves."[15] Angelica Salas of the Coalition for Humane Immigrant Rights of Los Angeles (CHIRLA), a key member of the national We Are American Alliance and one of the most prominent immigrant rights advocates in the country, described the movement's failure to respond to attacks by nativist news outlets in the following manner:

We didn't have a bully pulpit . . . We didn't have the capacity to disarm the Right. They used CNN [and] Fox News. We didn't have [that type of] communications infrastructure . . . Communication from our end was something we did with the ethnic media to tell our community what to do. We never elevated [our capacity] to a place where we needed . . . to play in the big leagues and really counter [the Right] . . . In the absence of that, the loudest people, the people who got the most attention, were the Glenn Becks and Lou Dobbses. They framed every issue from the local to the national level.

Echoing this analysis and describing the impact he believed the negative news coverage had on elected officials, Mike Garcia of SEIU's Local 1877, the famous immigrant Justice for Janitors union, remembered:

We got to a point where we said we're not moving these politicians. If anything, the forces that were moving them were the right-wing DJs that were creating a larger outcry than they really had behind them . . . Their threatening vocabulary . . . really scared Congress into thinking that it was these right-wing DJs – the Lou Dobbes of the world and the radio DJs – that were really moving America, not our marches . . . It got to a point where [the protests] were maybe even hurting because the [non-U.S.] flags and [other] displays of foreign countries . . . created a fear that the right-wing DJs and press were stirring up by saying things like, "You see! You see! They're taking over our country! They're un-American and we have to do something about it!"

Ana Maria Archilla of Make the Road summed up these dynamics as follows: "After May 1 there was a high level backlash" in which the nativists were "very effective at painting May 1 as some communist rebellion . . . The anti-immigrant folks really hit back very hard."

The instances of nativism discussed so far have been perpetrated by pundits on cable news networks or overtly racist private citizens. Moreover, all of the highlighted cases of verbal or physical attacks conducted by private citizens targeted "regular" Latinos that had nothing to do with the demonstrations – none were directed at actual protest participants. Yet several people who joined in the immigrant rights rallies did pay a personal price for their political engagement. According to scholar Jules Boykoff (2007), an expert on the repression of social movements, "Sometimes the silencing of dissent cuts straight to a person's livelihood" and can involve "the deliberate threat of being deprived of one's job or the actual loss of employment because of one's political beliefs" (78). Several examples of this mode of suppression occurred across the country during the immigrant rights protest wave, reminding current and potential participants of one possible consequence of engaging in contentious activities.

In cities and towns from coast to coast, immigrants were fired from their jobs in retribution for their participation in the demonstrations. As a news outlet reported during the peak of the mass marches: "[W]orkers and students have paid a price for attending the immigration rallies that have recently swept the nation. They have lost jobs or been cited for truancy for joining the hundreds of thousands who have protested proposed federal legislation that would crack down" on undocumented immigrants (Johnson 2006). For example, in Tyler, Texas, 22 immigrant welders lost their jobs for attending a local rally, as did asbestos removal workers in Indianapolis, and restaurant and factory workers in Milwaukee, Wisconsin, Bonita Spring, Florida, and Bellwood, Illinois (Davey 2006; Warikoo 2006). In Detroit, Michigan, 15 immigrant women were fired for attending a local demonstration, as were six employees at a seafood restaurant in Houston, Texas (Johnson 2006; Warikoo 2006). Needless to say, these actions by employers had effects both obvious and subtle. The fired men and women lost a vital source of income. But just as pernicious, according to activists, each firing made it harder for them to mobilize others.

A rally organizer in Southwest Florida explained how the dismissals impacted his group's willingness to call for more protests. He remembered members of the Fort Myers coalition thinking, "We can't keep risking our people because . . . if they keep firing people, how are [we] going to justify a family being left without a job and not able to sustain itself?"[16] Another activist in Los Angeles recalled the reactions of people who wanted to take part in the marches, but who were told by her organization that it could not protect them from being fired if they decided to participate. This quandary often led community members to question the usefulness of local immigrant rights groups. The activist recalled people saying, "If they [immigrant rights organizations] can't help us get our jobs back, then what are they good for?"[17]

To better gauge how widespread these events were, one would have to obtain self-reported data from either the employers who did the firing or the employees who lost their jobs. Unfortunately, neither type of evidence is available. Nevertheless, it was not the number of people fired, but the news coverage of these firings that had the most chilling effects. Activists asserted that despite the ratio of protesters to people losing their jobs for participating in the rallies being small, whether merely accurately reporting on specific instances of firings or purposely sensationalizing these cases of punishment, Spanish- and English-language media outlets publicized the potential costs of engaging in activism. Again, a systematic content analysis of media coverage is needed to substantiate these assertions. However, previous research support claims made by activists that "the deterrent effect" of suppression (intentional or unintentional) "is likely to be much more powerful [when it] is highly visible" (Koopmans 2005: 161), such as when the mass media broadcasts it. Hence, from Los Angeles and New York to Fort Myers and Washington, D.C., local and national movement leaders declared that people being fired from their jobs for participating in the rallies made immigrants less amenable to appeals to continue participating in public collective actions.

State Suppression

More so than negative English-language media coverage, the doings of state officials seem to have had the most devastating impact on activist attempts at further mass mobilizations. Local rally organizers across the nation proclaimed that the escalation of immigration enforcement policies occurred specifically "because of the 2006 immigrant marches." They described the rapid increase of government anti-immigrant measures as a "militarization of the interior" and an effort to use "the tools of the state to crack down" on their activism.[18] As the *New York Times* reported on April 29, "[A]dvocates began to suspect a campaign to frighten demonstrators away from the protest rallies planned for Monday. They even worried that vigilantes could be impersonating federal immigration agents" (Bernstein 2006). But minus state officials confessing that they used government resources to halt or thwart perfectly legal activities, such as participating in a permitted public demonstration, the claims of activists are unsubstantiable. It is equally plausible that the images of hundreds of thousands of possibly undocumented immigrants publicly protesting, underscored the federal government's failure to enforce its own immigration laws and motivated officials to take action. My argument in this final section of the chapter is that when studying the suppression of immigrant contention, confirming the intentions of government officials is less important than analyzing the consequences of their actions on activists' strategies, efforts, and the receptiveness of the people they aim to marshal (Della Porta and Fillieule 2004: 218). In 2006, anti-movement state-sponsored suppression was carried out through various federal, state, and local actions; specifically, immigration policing by proxy, deportation, and detention, and worksite immigration raids of potential protest participants.

Immigration Policing by Proxy

So far our attention has been on federal laws, and proposed laws, like H.R. 4437. But just as potent, in shaping the lives of immigrants, are those regulations and decrees passed by city, county, and state officials (Gulasekaram and Ramakrishnan 2015; Armenta 2017). According to Monica Varsanyi (2010), an expert on local immigration policy, although state and municipal governments do not possess the constitutional power to formulate immigration policies:

> [T]hey *do* have explicit power to regulate and police public space within their jurisdictions via local land use and zoning ordinances, ordinances that regulate behavior in public space (for example laws that criminalize loitering), and the enforcement of local and state laws (such as trespassing and traffic ordinances). (139)

A consequence of controlling and criminalizing certain behaviors in public spaces is the policing of people within those spaces (Armenta 2015).

As Varsanyi explains, "[A]n increasing number of cities and states" have been "utilizing [these] tools at their disposal... to constrain the opportunities and/or behavior" of their local undocumented residents, in order to essentially "get these people out of town." She (2010) asserts that by "invoking, formulating, and enforcing" these local laws, "cities are, in effect, doing local immigration policing by proxy" (135–136).

Although no complete list of city or county level immigration-related policies is available, according to Kretsedemas (2008), "In the space of less than six months, in 2006 alone over one hundred municipal governments drafted laws that targeted undocumented immigrants" (335, 354n6; also see Bada 2010). Many of these local laws rely on racial profiling that not only impacts people without papers but also makes legal immigrants and people of color of immigrant descent suspect and vulnerable to the punitive effects of them. In other words, they localize the federal racialization of illegality. Given the history of local anti-immigrant enforcement measures fostering fear in immigrant communities (see Kretsedemas 2008: 339), an actual surge in policies during and after the immigrant marches could have had negative effects on organizers' efforts to mass-mobilize the very people most likely to be impacted by them. Absent of a comprehensive list of local level immigration-related policies, we are unable to confirm whether there was in fact an upsurge of these municipal ordinances during and after the protest wave as activists claimed. That being said, data do exist at the state level for us to test this hypothesis.

As displayed in Figure 5.1, by the end of 2006, a drastic increase had taken place in the number of state laws related to immigrants and immigration, most of which were punitive (Bada 2010: 24; Gulasekaram and Ramakrishnan 2015).[19] The period between 2005 and 2006 saw a 90 percent increase (from 300 to 570) in the introduction of state legislation related to immigration and a 115 percent increase (39 to 84) in the enactment of immigration-related state legislation. The spike from 2006 to 2007 is even more dramatic. The number of immigration-related state legislation introduced increased by 174 percent (570 to 1562), and the number of laws enacted jumped an astounding 186 percent (84 to 240). These new policies were not solely concentrated in a few outlier states either. Although not displayed in Figure 5.1, the number of states that introduced and enacted immigration-related legislation went from 25 in 2005 (the year before the marches) up to 46 out of 50 U.S. states by 2007 (the year after the marches).

Many of these state level laws enhanced the social control of immigrants, ranging from limiting the ability of day laborers to seek

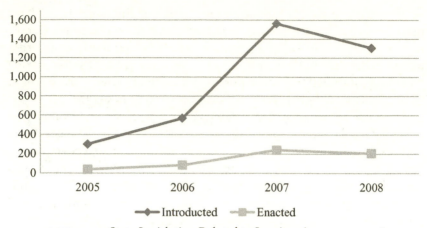

FIGURE 5.1. State Legislation Related to Immigration, 2005–2008
Source: National Conference of State Legislatures.

employment on street corners to restricting undocumented immigrants' capacity to rent housing (Bada 2010: 24). Interviews with immigrant rights organizers revealed that they and their immigrant bases interpreted these state and local legislations as punitive and having suppressive anti-movement effects; they believed they were payback for their protesting.[20]

Another form of increased social control, or "immigration policing by proxy," was the infamous 287(g) agreement – named after a section of the 1996 Illegal Immigration Reform and Immigrant Responsibility Act (IIRIRA) – that city and county law enforcement agencies entered into with federal immigration officials (Gonzales 2013). This measure "allows state, county, and city law enforcement agencies to investigate immigration cases, make immigration arrests, take custody of noncitizens for federal immigration authorities, transport immigration detainees, as well as put together immigration cases for prosecution in the courts" (Coleman 2012: 167). Immigrant advocates claimed that 287(g) agreements increased the racial profiling of all Latinos – both U.S. and foreign-born – by police after the mass demonstrations and severely restricted the mobility of people without papers to travel throughout their communities for fear of getting pulled over and questioned about their legal status (see also Gardner and Kohli 2009; Shahani and Greene 2009; GAO 2009; CLINIC 2009). As geographer Mathew Coleman explains (2012), 287(g) "targets mostly individuals who come into routine contact with police for non-serious reasons, the near majority of which are immigrant

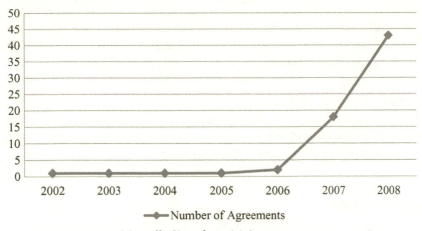

FIGURE 5.2. Mutually Signed 287(g) Agreements, 2002–2008
Source: Department of Homeland Security.

automobile operators." He maintains that this shift in "immigration policing into immigrant populations' everyday spaces" resulted in "driving between spaces of work, leisure, education, shopping, religious practice, and so on" becoming "more dangerous for undocumented immigrants in terms of risking deportation than actually working without papers" (184).

Social control theorists have long established that "[p]olicing is almost always differently targeted on subordinate social groups," such as immigrants and people of color, "and is often one of the tools dominant ethnic groups use to maintain their dominance over" minorities (Oliver 2008: 16). Thus an increase in the 287(g) local-federal policing agreements during the year of the demonstrations would lend credibility to activists' grievances.

Immigrant rights organizers contended that the upsurge in 287(g) agreements displayed in Figure 5.2 contributed to a less hospitable mobilizing environment in immigrant communities that, in effect, helped thwart their attempts at collective action. While I have no doubt that an escalation in these types of mechanisms of social control can spark fear in immigrant communities and discourage them from participating in public protests, I am not convinced that 287(g) agreements contributed specifically to the decline of the 2006 mass marches given that the spike in these measures didn't begin until 2007. That said, while the anti-immigrant state level laws discussed earlier may have contributed more to the demobilization of the 2006 demonstrations than an increase in 287(g) measures did, what is important to take away from this discussion is that local immigration policing by proxy should also be regarded as local immigrant *protest* policing by proxy because of the short- and long-term suppressive effects these policies can have on political activism.

Detention and Deportation

The imprisonment of activists has long been a tool of the state used to squelch contention and to silence political dissent (for examples see Davis 1989; Abu-Jamal 1996; Peltier 2000; Rodriguez 2006). But it is easy to fixate on those headline-catching stories about well-known radicals; on the ways, for example, that key leaders of the American Indian Movement, Black Panther Party, and other social movements were jailed for their political activities. Less noticeable but just as significant is the growth of the prison population as a whole, and its astonishingly disproportionate impact on the poor and people of color (Gilmore 2007; Wacquant 2009; Rios 2011). In an important article subtitled "Why Social Movement Scholars Should Pay Attention to Mass Incarceration as a Form of Repression," Pamela Oliver (2008) asserts that the "acceleration of the mass incarceration of African-Americans in the United States after 1980 suggests the possibility that crime control and especially the drug war have had the consequence of repressing dissent among the poor" (1; see also Camp 2016). Examining the effects of black riots during the 1960s and 1970s on local policing of African-American communities throughout the country, Oliver (2008) concludes:

By 1990, the United States was effectively a police state for its Black citizens, and to a lesser extent for poor Whites as well. The crucial thing to understand is that a repressive strategy initially triggered by massive urban unrest and other social movements was maintained and expanded long after the riots abated. *It was not aimed at preventing unrest by repressing riots; it was preventing unrest by repressing potential rioters.* [emphasis added] (10)

Today, immigrant detention is the fasting growing segment of the prison industrial complex. As immigration enforcement expert Tom Wong (2015) notes, "the annual rate of growth in the number of people held in immigration detention has outpaced the annual rate of growth of the rest of the overall federal prison population" (119: see also Golash-Boza 2012). Criminologist Michael Welch (1996) explains that immigrant detention centers have "emerged as a mechanism of social control for unpopular and powerless persons – namely, undocumented immigrants." He points out that, since the 1980s, "detention has become a

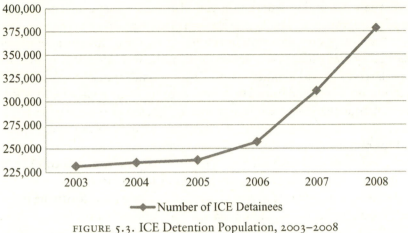

FIGURE 5.3. ICE Detention Population, 2003–2008
Source: Migration Policy Institute.

practice widely used to control and deter" people without papers (178; see also Alexander 2011: 7). If Welch's conceptualization of detention as a mechanism of social control is correct, then similar to Oliver's (2008) argument, I believe immigrant *detention* and *deportation* can be seen as tools for suppression, on a massive scale, of potential immigrant protest participants.

While the trend had been slowly rising the previous two years (increasing 1.6 percent between 2003 and 2004, and 1 percent between 2004 and 2005), Figure 5.3 reveals a major upswing in the number of immigrant detainees starting the year of the protest wave (from 237,667 in 2005 to 256,842 in 2006, an 8 percent increase) and skyrocketing from there, suggesting an expansion of the state's use of this mechanism of social control. Detention expert David Hernandez (2007) contends that throughout U.S. history, when the government has amplified its use of detention, "political expediency and the need to construct a record of security" fuse with public fears during times of perceived national crises, resulting in the targeting and undermining of the rights of racialized noncitizens (63). Along these lines, the sharp rise in the number of immigrant detainees shown in Figure 5.3 suggests that officials in the federal government may have interpreted the millions of immigrants marching on the streets – in almost every state in the union – as just such a "national crisis."[21] As a result, activists claimed that the state responded by "incarcerating the crisis" and used immigrant detention as a form of punishment (Camp 2016; Garcia Hernandez 2014).

Beyond detention, deportation can also be seen as a means to suppress immigrant activism. Legal scholar Daniel Kanstroom (2007) asserts that "contemporary deportation is a living legacy of historical episodes marked by ideas about race, imperialism, and government power that we have largely rejected in other realms." He contends that deportation is "a fulcrum on which majoritarian power is brought to bear against a discrete, marginalized segment of our society" (x; see also Cornelisse 2010: 114; Walter 2010: 85). Indeed, the state has used deportation to repress groups ranging from women, racial minorities, and the poor to lesbians, gays, and "political undesirables" (Johnson 2004). Today, according to Peutz and De Genova (2010), "deportation has achieved a remarkable and renewed prominence as a paramount technique for refortifying political, racial, and class-based boundaries" (4). Consequently, Golash-Boza (2016) argues that the post-9/11 "construction of immigrant men as dangerous criminal aliens and terrorists" has led the U.S. government to use deportation as a tool to repress immigrants of color, particularly Latino immigrants (493). She contends that the deportability of migrants subordinates them "not by actually deporting all those that are deported but by deporting some such that others may remain in a state of enhanced vulnerability" (Golash-Boza 2016: 488). In this manner, it is my opinion that the state sends a symbolic message to potential immigrant activists, warning that the cost of their dissent could be banishment from the country and separation from their families.

In the spring of 2006, immigrant rights protest organizers expressed the belief that immigration officials ramped up deportations in order to suppress any further immigrant activism. As a New York activist recalled, during the height of the protest wave, "there was definitely a need to respond to the direct emergencies and crises" of increases in "deportations, raids, and just outright assaults on immigrants."[22] A protest organizer in Southwest Florida remembered, "People were in panic ... because of the fear that started with the raids and massive deportations."[23]

The data in Figure 5.4 show that a rise in deportations did occur. The Department of Homeland Security (DHS) reported a 14 percent increase (from 246,431 to 280,974) in the deportation of immigrants between 2005 and 2006, compared to only a 2 percent increase (from 240,665 to 246,431) the year before, between 2004 and 2005.[24] Activists asserted that the fear of potentially being detained and/or deported – being picked up either at the rallies or in their homes – caused sufficient panic to prevent many people who had taken part in previous protests – and many who could have taken part in future ones – from heeding calls

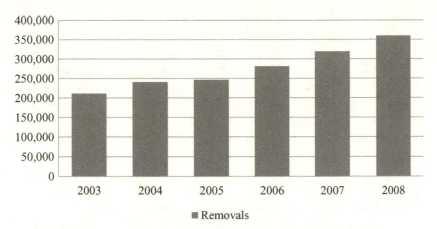

FIGURE 5.4. Deportations, 2003–2008
Source: Department of Homeland Security.

for continued mobilization. Immigrant rights organizers argued that it did not matter that the deportations and detentions were not *explicitly* directed at march participants because they *implicitly* prevented future demonstrations by suppressing potential protesters.

Although the statistics presented above show that there was in fact an increase in deportations, and although quantifying the devastating effects on the families torn apart by these state actions is impossible, the escalation was less abrupt than the activists interviewed would have us believe. The rise seems to be more a continuation of a trend that began in 2003 than a sharp acceleration in reaction to the mass mobilizations against H.R. 4437. Increases in deportations and detention were not the only forces fostering fear in immigrant communities, however. I believe that high profile *workplace raids* – broadcasted across the nation through English- and Spanish-language news outlets – were the forms of suppression that had the most devastating effects on activists' organizing efforts.

Worksite Immigration Raids

According to protest organizers, one of the workplace immigration raids intended to hamper their mobilization efforts came just days before the May 1 Great American Boycott/Day Without an Immigrant. As a major news outlet reported, on April 20, "In raids that set a record for workplace-enforcement arrests in a single day, immigration officials announced...that they had taken 1,187 illegal immigrants into custody at wood products plants in 26 states and had charged seven company managers with crimes that can carry long prison terms." The paper announced that the "raids contained tacit warnings for everyone involved in the debate on immigration." As Homeland Security Secretary Michael Chertoff stated, "The operation marked a new commitment to enforcing immigration laws in the workplace." He further declared that Americans were "rightly concerned about the need to enforce immigration law," proclaiming that his agency was "going to move beyond the current level of activity to a higher level in each month and year to come" (Gaouette 2006). Actual raids, and the threat of future ones, had a chilling impact on the target population immigrant rights organizers were trying to mobilize. As the *New York Times* reported, "[F]alse rumors of federal immigration raids" that were "apparently set off by last week's announcement by Michael Chertoff" sent "panic through immigrant communities around the country . . . emptying classrooms, work sites and shopping areas and sending thousands of people into hiding."

The fact that the raids were sending "people into hiding" is important to note given that mass demonstrations rely on precisely the opposite: people coming out and declaring their presence in public. News outlets around the country reported that rumors of and actual raids had suppressive effects on the movement. As one undocumented immigrant bluntly stated, "They are using intimidation to scare us" into not participating in the rallies. On April 29, the *Los Angeles Times* reported,

> With planned rallies and a boycott for immigrant rights just days away, rumors are spreading throughout California that *la migra* [immigration police] is conducting sweeps at bus stops, schools and work sites . . . The reports of random arrests by immigration agents have caused fear among many illegal immigrants and prompted them to stay close to home. Some said they believe authorities are trying to discourage participation on Monday. (Gorman and Garrison 2006)

Immigrant advocacy and service groups described a continuous stream of calls from people who feared being caught up in a raid. As a representative of an organization in Southern California that provides English-language and parenting classes stated on April 29, "It's panic, [people without papers] don't want to go to the laundromat. They don't want to go to the market. They don't want to do anything" (Gorman and Garrison 2006).

Interviews with local activists across the country corroborate these statements. For example, a New York labor leader involved with organizing the demonstrations stated, "The government took advantage of the environment and began their raids . . . creating an atmosphere of terror in

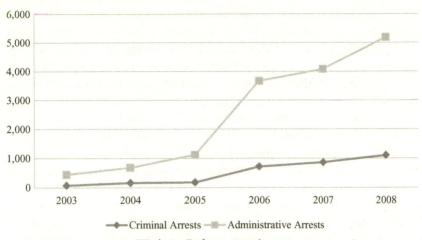

FIGURE 5.5. Worksite Enforcement Arrests, 2003–2008
Source: Department of Homeland Security.

the community."²⁵ A Korean immigrant rights organizer in L.A. recalled that the raids "really just hurt and ravished communities, schools, and so on."²⁶ Another activist explained, "Because the raids had increased and all these other things were happening," immigrants were "more scared to go out" and "continue protesting."²⁷

Although some archival evidence supports the claims made by activists, investigating whether these acts of suppression occurred to the degree organizers felt they did and that the media reported remains important. While I am unaware of data on date and location of neighborhood immigration sweeps, the Department of Homeland Security has released official statistics on worksite raids that indicate that there was, in fact, a major surge in immigration worksite raids in 2006.

Between 2005 and 2006 there was a 229 percent increase (from 1,116 to 3,667) in administrative arrests and a 307 percent increase (from 176 to 716) in criminal arrests of immigrants at their places of work (see Figure 5.5). The distinction between "administrative" and "criminal" arrests is important, because despite the federal government's claim of targeting "criminal aliens," the vast majority of people taken in worksite raids were immigrants with administrative violations, *not* criminal records.²⁸ Furthermore, that the state chose to carry out these raids at potential immigrant protesters' places of employment is important to note because, according to De Genova (2010), "The exquisitely refined legal vulnerability of undocumented migrant labor – above all, materialized in its deportability – plainly serves to radically enhance the preconditions for its routinized subordination within the inherently despotic regime of the workplace" (47). These workplace raids remind other immigrants of their vulnerability to capture and banishment and, as a result, serve as a disciplining mechanism that can suppress their willingness to participate in a march, boycott, or organizing campaign.

Golash-Boza (2012) points out that, "These large scale raids have … the effect of drawing media attention" that broadcasts the "devastation of communities, the tearing apart of families, and the promotion of a culture of fear and terror" (62). Thus, although reporting on current events is the lifeblood of any news outlet, sometimes that reporting has unintentional consequences. For instance, whether or not they occurred in a particular locale, these anti-immigrant actions created a hostile organizing environment for activists. A Southwest Florida farmworker described how these dynamics manifested: "For immigrants and undocumented people that worked in the fields … there were no immigration [agents] after them … We had never been impacted by raids until the media started scaring people."[29] A radio DJ in this same region confirmed these fears, stating that after the protests, when they saw some type of government-looking officials in their neighborhoods, immigrants started to call her radio station to report what they thought (inaccurately) were raids occurring or about to happen. The calls became so frequent that eventually the station realized the effects its coverage of them was having and stopped reporting the claims until they were able to confirm them, because the mistaken information was fostering fear within the immigrant community.[30]

While access to mass channels of communication were vital to disseminating activists' calls for action, a protest organizer in Los Angeles asserted that the raids caused many radio DJs to begin to pull back their support for the demonstrations.[31] As another activist explained, "Some of the DJs began cautioning against [the marches] because of the backlash. So if Spanish media helped to turn people out in the first place, they also later kind of played a role in holding people back."[32] Moreover, protest organizers had not called for another countrywide day of action until Labor Day in early September, leaving about a four-month gap between national mobilization efforts. Without these media-attracting actions, it seems that news outlets shifted their attention to reporting on the policy debate happening in the Senate (discussed in our next chapter), immigration enforcement measures, and abuses against immigrants by private citizens. As government anti-immigrant measures increased, many immigrant rights activists attempted to scale down their organizing efforts from calling for national demonstrations to trying to stop local raids and deportations. Unfortunately, their actions were futile.

Responding to Anti-Immigrant State Suppression

The widespread and decentralized threats described in this chapter (e.g. hate crimes, anti-immigrant ordinances, raids, and deportations) derived from multiple sources (state and city governments, federal and local law enforcement agencies, countermovement activists and employers), making it difficult for activists to discern responsibility and concentrate their efforts on a specific target. Attempting to respond to these concurrent attacks, many of which organizers became aware of only during or after they had occurred, was challenging. Even when they did attempt to respond, more often than not their efforts were to no avail because reacting to decentralized anti-immigrant enforcement measures can easily burn out organizers and usually produces minimal results. Not surprisingly, activists were unable to successfully respond to these forms of government actions during and after the protest wave, especially because the fear of potential raids often had more damaging impacts on their efforts than the raids themselves.

As an example, a local Dominican immigrant rights organizer asserted that although raids "didn't necessarily happen in the city [of New York]," that they *did* occur in different locations throughout his state and others had a ripple effect that "absolutely" hampered the local movement's collective action efforts.[33] Another local New York activist agreed, and illustrated how these dynamics played out:

I would get a call saying, "Oh *mi hermana* [my sister] called me and said that *la migra* [immigration agents] was picking people up on 42nd." So I would drive over there and there would be nobody... All these rumors [were going around.] One time I got a call saying that at the subway station in Sunset Park *la migra* was picking up people. I was like, "Well how do you know it was *la migra*?" and they would say, "Oh, they were wearing green and they were in uniforms and stopping and talking to people." So I went over there and there were all these repairmen fixing one of the streets wearing green and people were totally freaked out. As I got one phone call, I got another, and another, and another.... It was real fear. It was the first time I can say there was widespread paranoia and panic. But in the case of New York, not well-founded because... I don't think that, in general, undocumented immigrants were targeted here the way that they were targeted in other parts of the country.[34]

In the days, weeks, and months after May 1, one discussion recurred again and again within immigrant communities nationwide: did the marches

cause the backlash? The question was divisive. As an activist in Los Angeles (a place where raids did happen) recalled, "The big debate inside the
movement was whether the big protests created the raids and deportations that came afterward. That was the big thing that people were
talking about... We'd be out tabling in different neighborhoods on the
weekends and people would say to us that by us protesting it caused
the raids and deportations."[35] The fact that some immigrants blamed
the protests for the escalation in immigration enforcement measures is
important to note because the point of the marches was to stop the
Sensenbrenner Bill, which would have criminalized undocumented immigrants and led to widespread deportations. Yet for many immigrants,
these fears were becoming a reality on a mass scale as a result of the drastic
increases in raids and deportations that began to occur during and after
the protest wave. Thus, it is no wonder activists interpreted these government actions as forms of anti-movement state suppression, especially
since their attempts to stop them were not successful.

A Los Angeles protest organizer described how the local movement
responded to these immigration enforcement measures – and the ineffec-
tiveness of their efforts. She stated,

We helped start an emergency response network where we tried to organize
protests in response to raids and deportations... We established networks using
phone-trees and text message-trees so that if a raid was going on in a certain place
we could try to show up. Or if there was [an immigration checkpoint] anywhere
we would show up and then people would try to call into [Spanish-language]
radio stations to [announce], "Hey, there's an immigration roadblock at this certain place." It worked out in a couple of instances, in times when we had people
who lived in the neighborhood where the raid was going on.[36]

However, the activist further explained,

What we were trying to do was like putting out fires... The obstacle we came
up against was that the raids were happening in such a small and decentralized
way, like a little raid here in this neighborhood and then a little raid there in that
neighborhood... People would just call-in saying, "We gotta go to this neighborhood or we gotta go to that neighborhood," but half the time you'd go there and
it was either false or there was no one even there. So it was very, very hard to do
that sort of super grassroots response... You could easily burn yourself out just
trying to drive to all of them because every day it was some other neighborhood.
You could just be driving around the city like a chicken with your head cut off
and still it wouldn't really be that effective. So the big problem we had was how
decentralized they were... We didn't have an adequate response on our side so I
think it actually played into some of the fears that people had.[37]

Although organizers said that the vast majority of these rumors were false, they nonetheless contributed to a growing sense of uneasiness within immigrant neighborhoods. For some immigrants, this uneasiness turned into fear and for others it turned into animosity towards the activists who called for and organized the demonstrations. According to my interviewees, the combination of the state and societal backlash, along with activists' inability to respond effectively to these attacks, led to immigrant communities becoming unwilling to continue to participate in public protests.

Conclusion

Throughout this chapter I have traced various factors that impeded immigrant rights organizers' large-scale collective action efforts. Some of these are more obvious (like threats by nativist activists); some of these are less obvious (like the various local immigration policing by proxy measures discussed). Some of these are intentional (like employers firing their workers for participating in the May 1 actions); some are unintentional (like the fear Spanish-language media caused through their coverage of immigration raids). Some are easy to gauge; some are more ambiguous. But what is just as important is also perhaps the least obvious, and the hardest to measure: the cumulative effect that all of these elements had on the thinking and the decision-making of immigrants and immigrant rights supporters themselves.

As a result of the multiple forms of suppression discussed in this chapter, the interview and archival data presented indicate that immigrant communities felt under attack for their collective actions. Cheryl Little, the Executive Director of the Florida Immigrant Advocacy Center, illustrated the impacts of these anti-immigrant measures in the following manner:

The community is paralyzed...I haven't seen this kind of fear in the immigrant community ever. Immigrants are afraid of going to work, of taking their kids to school, of leaving their home. People are not going to important medical appointments. There are pregnant women canceling their prenatal care appointments because they feel immigration will be waiting for them there. (Bernstein 2006)

Little is describing one of the most damaging aspects of the pushback against the protest wave, the cultivation of what can be called a "mental-*migra* mindset" – a paralysis and fear that emerged among both U.S.- and foreign-born supporters of immigrants, those potential participants whose involvement is essential to immigrant rights mobilizations. This cognitive phenomenon was reported in every city examined in this book. Both longtime activists and immigrants who had never participated in a protest until 2006 contended that, as a result of the fear fostered by nativist civilian and state actions, immigrant communities began to self-police and felt pushed "back into the shadows." Consequently, they became less receptive to calls for more public protests, causing organizers to question whether their demonstrations were making immigrants less safe.

Both the suppressive actions of private and state agents, and the negative effects of the mass media's reporting, are important to highlight because several social movement scholars contend that increased media attention to anti-movement government actions tends to reduce the level of state repression against activists (Wisler and Giugni 1999; Earl 2003). But this reaction is not always so. The case of the 2006 cycle of contention suggests that the "spotlight of the media" can also indirectly increase the suppressive impacts of what amount to anti-movement government measures. Similar to Ferree's (2005) concept of "soft repression" (141), the combination of societal and state backlash – and the media attention they attracted – seem to have produced the mental-*migra* mindset that served as a cognitive disciplining mechanism that contributed to the suppression of immigrant contention.

Whereas other scholars have found that the withdrawal of a threat (e.g. HR 4437) can lead to the decline of political activism (Heaney and Rojas 2011), I am suggesting that the fostering of a mental-*migra* among the foreign-born and their supporters reveals that looming threats also have demobilizing consequences. Put another way, the amplification of immigration enforcement measures during and after the protest wave could be understood not as directly repressing actual immigrant rights protests, but as indirectly suppressing the continued and future activism of potential immigrant rights protesters.

6

Today We March, Tomorrow We Vote

In 1920, building off the momentum gained from several decades of protest, the women's suffrage movement finally won the right to vote. Similarly, the persistent bravery of the black civil rights movement, embodied in the historic 1963 March on Washington, led to the passage of the landmark 1964 Civil Rights Act. A decade later, the large demonstrations held by youth across the country during the antiwar movement of the 1970s contributed to the United States pulling its military out of Vietnam. Indeed, American history is full of episodes of collective action in which marginalized groups were a catalyst to widespread social change.

Yet at first glance, perhaps the largest coordinated mass mobilizations in U.S. history – the 2006 immigrant rights protest wave – seem to have produced little, if any, tangible results. Because ultimately comprehensive immigration reform was not passed, many commentators deemed "the protests a failure," despite their remarkable turnout figures (Engler and Engler 2016). Charges of the movement's lack of impact extended to the electoral arena as well. For instance, on Labor Day, September 4, 2006, the *Washington Post* reported:

Immigration protests that drew hundreds of thousands of flag-waving demonstrators to the nation's streets last spring promised a potent political legacy – a surge of new Hispanic voters. "Today We March, Tomorrow We Vote," they proclaimed. But an Associated Press review of voter registration figures from . . . [several] major urban areas that had large rallies found no sign of a new voter boom that could sway elections.

The paper proclaimed that the number of new Latino voters was "more of a trickle than a torrent" (Blood and Prengaman 2006). In fact, just a few years after the historic mobilizations, *Fortune* magazine used them as an example of how social movements "can peter out without achieving meaningful change."[1]

As this chapter chronicles, however, activists did attain their immediate objective of thwarting the passage of the Sensenbrenner Bill, a major accomplishment in and of itself. But if the motivation for protesting the proposed legislation was to defend people without papers, undocumented immigrants were arguably *more* under attack after the historic marches than they were before them. As we saw in the previous chapter, subsequent to the defeat of H.R. 4437, the social costs of lacking papers increased due to an upsurge in raids, deportations, hate crimes, local and statewide anti-immigrant ordinances. Furthermore, the movement's ambition of legalizing the nation's millions of undocumented immigrants – an objective of activists prior to the protest wave that would have guaranteed more rights, constitutional protections, and possibly the eventual enfranchisement of this subordinate group – did not even come close to fruition. Thus, in terms of the legislative ramifications of the immigrant rights demonstrations, the movement failed to achieve its goal of legalization and likely contributed to the increased subjugation of the vulnerable population it professed to defend.

To be sure, falling short of bringing about the social change they seek is not an uncommon experience for activists. In fact, if we measure the success of social movements solely by whether they realize their stated objectives, then arguably most movements fail most of the time. However, while activists may be disappointed with the results of their efforts because they did not live up to all of their own expectations – which are often times improbable to begin with – outside actors and benefactors may, in fact, deem what they *were* able to accomplish a success (Della Porta and Diani 1999: 230; Amenta and Young 1999: 25; Amenta and Caren 2004: 463). Thus, despite the avowed goals and immediate demands of protest organizers, the effects of social movements are often indirect and become apparent only well after the thrill of massive collective action has diminished (Tarrow 1998:164). Now, over ten years later, we are better able to assess the 2006 immigrant rights protest wave's value amidst its consequences. From our more distant perspective we can examine not only the immediate, direct, and stated aims of the movement but also some of its long-term, indirect, and unintended outcomes.

In the introductory chapter of this book I argued that racialized legislative threats – such as H.R. 4437 – against undocumented immigrants can trigger a political backlash, on the streets and at the ballot box, from not only people without papers but also electorally armed naturalized immigrants and U.S.-born citizens of immigrant descent. Accordingly, this chapter continues our focus on the national consequences of the demonstrations and illustrates how in addition to impacting the federal immigration policymaking process, the momentum and organizational infrastructure built across the country in the campaign to defeat the Sensenbrenner Bill enabled strands of the movement to institutionalize their efforts. This shift towards more formal political engagement, as we will see, altered the nation's electoral landscape, rendering Latino and immigrant voters a political force to be reckoned with during the 2008 presidential election and, I believe, for years to come. But before we examine how this process materialized, because the local demonstrations were seeking to influence national legislation it is important to briefly revisit the relationship between local and national immigrant rights organizations.

Intramovement Relations

Because social movements are not homogenous and static entities – they are made up of multiple and often-changing actors – within a given movement it is not uncommon for different activists to have different goals or different priorities (Tilly 1999: 256; Goodwin and Jasper 2003: 347). In this fashion, our Los Angeles and New York case studies revealed that the radical flank – often composed of local, independent leftist groups and activists – and moderate segments – usually including larger, more mainstream and better funded NGOs, unions, service and religious organizations – of the immigrant rights movement had major ideological and policy differences that boiled over leading up to May 1. These divergent hopes and emerging frustrations also had parallel manifestations at the national level.

Since laws are ultimately made by actors within government institutions and by the lobbyists who interact with them, having influential allies can contribute to a movement's ability to affect public policy (Walker 1991; Baumgartner and Jones 1993; Baumgartner and Leech 1998). Correspondingly, students of contentious politics have found that movements "without allies working in mainstream politics will be hard-pressed to make inroads in the policy process" (Meyer 2005: 3; see also Giugni 2004: 5 and Soule and Olzak 2004: 492). During the 2006 protest wave, intramovement tensions were exacerbated by the fact that while the radical flank of the movement usually lacked access to – and frequently balked at working with – federal legislators, many moderate national organizations – commonly referred to as "the D.C. groups" – had long-standing relationships with members of Congress and their staffs. Consequently, the former groups often perceived the latter ones as having a seat at the legislative table and as speaking on behalf of the movement as a whole.

Because they are located inside the beltway and had been lobbying for comprehensive immigration reform prior to the start of the protest wave, national organizations such as the Coalition for Comprehensive Immigration Reform (CCIR), the Center for Community Change, the National Immigration Form, the National Council of La Raza, the AFL-CIO, the SEIU, the U.S. Conference of Catholic Bishops, the Fair Immigration Reform Movement (FIRM) coalition and others, were in the best position to take advantage of any positive legislative momentum the protests created. This frustrated radical activists who often claimed sole credit for the countrywide demonstrations and thus wanted more of a say in the federal policy debate that many of them believed national immigrant rights groups were controlling. The reality, though, was more complicated.

The D.C. groups did not have the uniform power to shape federal policy that many local and radical immigrant rights activists perceived them to have. For instance, a virtual truism in the immigration policy-making literature is that a "left-right" coalition between political parties, labor unions, civil rights groups, and business interests is almost always needed to pass major legislative reforms (Sierra 1999; Tichenor 2002; Wong 2006; Wong 2017).[2] Any chance at both stopping H.R. 4437 and gaining a path to citizenship for undocumented immigrants would require a similar type of alliance. Consequently, national immigrant rights advocates had to converse, compromise, and compete with major business interests – such as the Essential Immigrant Workers Coalition (EWIC), the U.S. Chamber of Commerce, and the Agriculture Coalition for Immigration Reform – who also supported and were trying to shape a bipartisan comprehensive immigration reform bill. In addition, not only was Congress controlled by an increasingly ideologically conservative Republican Party (McAdam and Kloos 2014) – making major business interests even more vital to, and influential in, any left-right coalition – but 2006 was also a midterm election year, which made it much more difficult for members of Congress (including moderate and conservative Democrats) up for reelection to take the risk of supporting an issue as controversial as immigration (see Wong 2017). Hence, far from controlling the federal immigration policy proposals being debated, at best many national immigrant rights organizations – the "D.C. groups" – were struggling to even have a say, let alone a seat, at the legislative table.

The claim that local radical flank groups sparked the national protest wave while moderate national organizations received credit for it – from both the media and liberal Democratic legislators – has more weight to it. In the West Coast, East Coast, and Southern U.S. cities examined in this book, it was local independent activists – not connected with the D.C. groups – who initiated the first successful mass mobilizations against H.R. 4437. That being said, several of the mainstream national immigrant rights organizations mentioned above spearheaded the countrywide We Are American Alliance (WAAA), which largely funded and organized the massive April 10 National Day of Action for Immigrant Justice. Furthermore, WAAA's local affiliates – such as the Los Angeles We Are American Coalition and the New York Immigration Coalition – also helped organize actions in cities across the country during the May 1 "Day Without An Immigrant." Nonetheless, as this chapter will show, there was definitely a disconnect and tension between national Washington D.C.-based immigrant rights organizations and many of the local activists who organized the protests throughout the nation.[3]

Adding to this strain was the fact that on the one hand, numerous radical activists felt the D.C. groups conceded too easily to both Republicans and Democrats and were not concerned with how their compromises would impact future local organizing efforts. On the other hand, several national organizations believed that many local groups and radical activists did not understand the federal policymaking process or the need to pass legislation that included even an limited path to citizenship that would protect at least some undocumented immigrants; they feared Republicans would try to pass a more nativist bill if a bipartisan one failed. Thus, while D.C. groups saw the marches through the prism of achieving moderate policy reform and were acutely aware of the draconian alternatives that Republicans were ready to propose if no bipartisan bill was passed, many local organizations and activists believed that it was they who would have to directly deal with the long-term consequences of any putative legislative concessions. A leader of a national immigrant rights organization explained these dynamics in the following manner:

The people in D.C. were focused on trying to get a bill across the finish line. They had invested years of their lives in the Kennedy-McCain Bill and so everything was viewed by them as a means to the end of passing comprehensive immigration reform [CIR]...Whereas people who were on the ground, local migrant rights advocates outside of the beltway, tended to view the more big picture issues and how [CIR] would impact the movement.[4]

With these local-national intramovement rifts and the increasing levels of anti-immigrant suppression detailed in the preceding chapter as the backdrop, in what follows I assess how the protest wave impacted the policymaking process and electoral politics from 2006 to 2008.

The 2006 Protest Wave: Strong Enough to Kill a Bill, But Not Pass One

Stopping Sensenbrenner

The party that holds power in each chamber of Congress wields disproportionate influence over the immigration policymaking process because it controls key committees, what legislation gets introduced, and when it is debated (Gimpel and Edwards 1999; Tichenor 2002). Accordingly, efforts to pass comprehensive immigration reform had been off the table since the terrorist attacks of September 11, 2001 because Republicans – who controlled the White House and both chambers of Congress at the time – were focused on their war in Iraq and had shown little interest in passing immigration legislation that was not restrictionist (Schmitt 2001; Castaneda 2007). Although on May 12, 2005 Senators Ted Kennedy and John McCain publically announced their intentions to introduce a bipartisan bill, it was not until October of that same year that Republican Senate leaders announced they planned to take up the issue in 2006 (Sandler 2006a).[5] However, on December 16, 2005, Republican Congressman James Sensenbrenner and other House conservatives (including a few Democrats) passed the extremely punitive *The Border Protection, Antiterrorism, and Illegal Immigration Control Act of 2005* (H.R. 4437), preempting the Senate from setting the tone of the legislative debate. As restrictive as the Sensenbrenner Bill was, some GOP members felt it didn't go far enough. One of its chief architects, Congressman Tom Tancredo of Colorado, who at the time headed the close to 100-member House Immigration Reform Caucus, was upset that the final legislation that passed the House did not include an amendment to end birth-right citizenship (Wayne 2005).

Although some of the more conservative senate Republicans welcomed Sensenbrenner's intervention and sought to push for a similar bill in their chamber of Congress, in early 2006 Kennedy and McCain continued working on legislation they believed could win bipartisan approval if they got it through the powerful Senate Judiciary Committee, of which

Kennedy was a part. Passing any bill that had the support of senators from both parties would be an uphill battle. Republicans in the Senate were divided over what to do about the future flow of labor needs and on how to deal with the nation's 11 million undocumented immigrants. The far right of the party supported legislation introduced by Republican Senators Jon Kyle and John Cornyn that "would require illegal immigrants to return to their home countries before applying for a new temporary guest worker program." The more moderate – and much smaller – wing of the GOP, including President Bush, supported the bipartisan Kennedy-McCain approach, which would have allowed undocumented immigrants "to stay in the country, apply for a new H-5B work visa and possibly earn permanent legal status eventually" (Wayne 2006). Democrats were, for the most part, "keeping a low profile" perhaps because of the upcoming midterm elections and the fact that some polls were showing that up to 62 percent of voters felt that "undocumented workers should not be allowed to progress towards citizenship" (Sandler 2006a).

In early 2006 the Senate Judiciary Committee, chaired by Republican Arlen Spector, officially took up the issue of immigration reform (Leal 2009: 4). The committee discussed what was essentially the Kennedy-McCain Bill for weeks but could not come to an agreement on it. Then on March 16, 2006, Senate Majority Leader Bill Frist, who had presidential ambitions and knew that Senator McCain was the GOP's frontrunner to lead his party's ticket, threatened to act on his own bill if the Judiciary Committee did not pass legislation by the end of the month. Frist was "on the far right of this debate, insisting that illegal immigration must be criminalized and the penalties enforced, not just on immigrants but on anyone (employers, doctors, welfare workers) who help them avoid the law" (Rapp 2006). In other words, he was ready to propose a Senate version of H.R. 4437. By doing so, Frist would be able to build support among social conservatives, the same group of Republicans that John McCain was thought to have the most problems with in winning his party's nomination for president (Sandler 2006a). According to one D.C. insider, Senator Frist's proposal "was basically a harsh crackdown bill and if he had introduced that bill it would have passed." A joint chamber congressional committee would then have had to negotiate between "the Sensenbrenner Bill and the Frist Bill" and "split the difference" – a scenario that would have been the worst of both worlds for pro-immigrant advocates.[6] Hence, by early 2006 the immigrant rights movement was in panic: a punitive immigration bill (H.R. 4437) had been passed in the House, and in the Senate not only was an already-compromised bill not able to get through the Judiciary Committee because many Republicans felt it was still too liberal, but Republican leaders were also threatening to take up an even-worse "Sensenbrenner-like" bill if a bipartisan approach failed. The challenge of preventing a draconian "enforcement only" bill – meaning purely restrictive and not including any path to citizenship or legalization – from becoming law seemed overwhelming. As Chris Newman of the National Day Laborer Organizing Network (NDLON) put it, "There was a view in D.C. that the sky was caving in, that Sensenbrenner or something akin to it was going to pass and that they weren't going to be able to get the Kennedy-McCain Bill passed."

Given this grim predicament, immigrant advocates' only hope was that the Senate would pass legislation that included some type of limited legalization program, which they believed would kill any efforts by GOP nativists to ratify a completely restrictionist bill.[7] According to Xiomara Corpeño, whose organization was actively involved with the D.C.-based Fair Immigration Reform Movement (FIRM), a national coalition of local immigrant rights groups, "We knew that legalization of any kind would be a poison pill to Sensenbrenner in the Senate and so that was the strategy. The strategy was to defeat Sensenbrenner by making sure that some kind of legalization passed in the Senate."

Unfortunately for immigrant rights advocates, not only was Senate Majority Leader Frist threatening to push his own anti-immigrant bill (that did not include any legalization program), but as Angela Kelley of the Center for American Progress explained, "We were having lots of trouble just getting [Democrats] to even show up" to the committee mark-up meetings. The more conservative "Republicans were there in force" trying to convince moderate GOP committee members to pull the bill to the right. But on the other side of the aisle, she recalled, "you had just an anemic response by the senate Democrats" who seemed to be avoiding the issue altogether. *Congressional Quarterly Weekly* described the situation in the following manner: "The immigration debate in Congress presented Democrats with a political choice of keeping quiet and hoping that Republicans would shred each other on the issue, or speak up and risk the same sort of divisions in their own party" (Sandler 2006a). As a result, the feeling of D.C.-based immigrant rights groups was, "We're screwed . . . Unless there is some sort of huge response from the immigrant community, we can't stop" a restrictionist bill from passing in the Senate and H.R. 4437 from becoming law.[8] That "huge response," of course, did occur, and it took both immigrant advocates and policymakers by surprise.

Although a few small anti-Sensenbrenner protests had occurred earlier
in the year, on March 10, 2006 over 300,000 people in Chicago demonstrated against H.R. 4437 and in favor of legalization. But as impressive as
the Chicago mobilization was, it was the events of March 25 that finally
forced the issue. When somewhere between 500,000 to over a million people protested in the City of Los Angeles, Democrats seem to have realized
that they had no choice but to "speak up."[9] Rosalio Muñoz, a member
of the coalition that organized the L.A. demonstration, remembered convincing the group to stage its protest on Saturday, March 25 because the
deadline Senator Frist had given the Judiciary Committee was the following week. He hoped, "If we have a big demonstration in L.A., the people
in D.C. are going to notice and it's gonna have an impact on what happens" when they meet.

The massive march in Los Angeles and the hundreds of others that
followed across the nation seem to have accomplished this goal. Frank
Sharry of the National Immigration Forum, who had been attending the
Senate Judiciary Committee meetings, recalled:

The rally in L.A. on the 25th was so mind-blowing that when these Senators
met at the Senate Judiciary Committee, and I was in the room on March 27th,
the atmosphere in the room was completely different. The Republicans were
sort of stunned at the rally. The Democrats were kind of leaning forward and
more aggressive, and [moderate Republican Senator] Specter went from, "I'm not
sure whether we're going to complete the process or not," to "Let's go for it."
[Moderate Democratic Senator] Dianne Feinstein, who had always been someone who was going to vote against McCain-Kennedy, voted for it. So at the end
of the day, on Monday the 27th, it was the McCain-Kennedy Bill that passed
the Senate Judiciary Committee by 12 to 6 on a bipartisan basis...There was a
direct causal relationship between the L.A. rally...and the Senate Judiciary vote
that led to – instead of an enforcement only bill – a comprehensive immigration
reform bill.

Angela Kelley, who worked closely on the bipartisan bill with Senator
Kennedy's office, concurred and elaborated on the protest wave's overall
impact on the legislative process:

The energy that these marches gave to the Senate Judiciary Committee, and to
the Senate generally paying attention to this issue, cannot be overstated. It was
a brilliant demonstration of the confluence of an inside game on the hill with
two champions from both parties [Kennedy and McCain], and then this outside,
unprecedented grassroots pressure that was literally sweeping the country with
marches popping up in so many different cities...The interaction of the two was
really something to behold... People wore white t-shirts, they waved American
flags and they respectively marched and said, "We belong to this country" and

"We are not criminals." It was a message that definitely resonated through the halls of Congress and into that mark-up room, and it resulted in [the Kennedy-McCain Bill] moving forward.

Several national organizations that had been lobbying for immigration reform prior to the demonstrations agreed that the protests "absolutely," as Eliseo Medina of SEIU put it, helped kill the Sensenbrenner Bill and a similar type of legislation from passing in the Senate. Clarissa Martínez De Castro of the National Council of La Raza, the nation's largest Latino civil rights organization, concurred and added that "the marches played a very important role in stopping the forward movement of the Sensenbrenner Bill." D.C.-based advocates contended that the series of demonstrations helped put the issue of immigration reform on the national agenda, helped build support among some key senate Democrats and moderate Republicans for Kennedy and McCain's bipartisan bill, and in the process helped stop H.R. 4437. As John Trasviña of the Mexican American Legal Defense and Education Fund (MALDEF) remembered, the historic mass mobilizations "demonstrated to members of Congress, and really to the country as a whole, that for the first time the people that were most affected by immigration legislation would demand to be part of the discussion – that hadn't happened before."

Although the immigrant rights movement could claim some credit for helping stop a Sensenbrenner-type bill from passing in the Senate, the efforts of national business interests also deserve recognition. According to Craig Regelbrugge, of the Agriculture Coalition for Immigration Reform (a coalition of over 300 national, regional, and state organizations and associations), "Business was passionately against" both the Sensenbrenner Bill and any legislation similar to it in the Senate. Their opposition "was vigorous," he asserted. "You had the U.S. Chamber [of Commerce], the homebuilders, the roofers, the landscapers, all the different construction and contracting organizations. You had all these different business interests working in unison" against H.R. 4437 and in favor of Kennedy-McCain. Major national business lobbying groups (from the Chamber of Commerce to EWIC) "key voted" the bill, sending a message to members of Congress who were planning on seeking their support in the upcoming midterm elections.[10] Thus, while the protests may have pushed some Democrats to the left of the policy debate, given that the GOP was in control of every branch of the federal government at the time, big business' lobbying efforts likely had more sway on Republican lawmakers than the mass marches did.

In sum, if immigrant rights advocates hoped that their protests would help pass the Kennedy-McCain Bill in the Senate and, as a result, prevent an "enforcement only" bill like H.R. 4437 from becoming law, then they seem to have accomplished their goal. But if they thought that the demonstrations would also contribute to winning legalization under a Republican-dominated Congress, then they were mistaken. According to national business, labor, and immigrant rights leaders, the millions of immigrants that took to the streets during the subsequent weeks probably hurt their chance of gaining legalization more than they helped it.

Stopping Kennedy-McCain

As noted earlier, when passing major immigration policy, the strategy of forming a left-right coalition between political parties, major business interests, labor and civil rights groups has been more the rule than the exception (Tichenor 2002). The year 2006 was no different. According to Deepak Pargava of the Center for Community Change, for supporters of the Kennedy-McCain Bill "the strategy was basically a left-right strategy," which meant to "cobble together some business support, with a piece of labor and a piece of the immigrant rights community." John Gray of EWIC (the Essential Worker Immigration Coalition), a group of over forty major national business associations that supported immigration reform, explained the rationale behind the left-right policy coalition:

On the left you're okay with legalization but you're not okay with guest worker programs. On the right you're okay with guest worker programs, but you're not okay with legalization. So what you need to make this work is . . . a grand bargain, a compromise. But it's got to be comprehensive immigration reform so that everyone's holding their nose about one part of it and everyone is getting something [in another part of it] . . . Politically and policy-wise, that's what had the best chance of success.

The strategy was that business groups were in charge of garnering Republican support for a bill that included both a guest worker program and some type of broad legalization. Supportive labor unions, specifically SEIU and UNITE-HERE, and civil and immigrant rights organizations were in charge of mustering Democratic support for similar legislation. D.C.-based advocates had high hopes for their national and bipartisan efforts. As Cecilia Muñoz, Senior Vice President of the National Council of La Raza, declared at the time, "Never before have we brought together under one banner such a formidable political coalition to fight for passage of comprehensive immigration reform. We now have the money, the people and the political will to punch this vital issue over the goal line in Congress and make America a better place to live and work."[11]

But while the marches and intense lobbying from both factions of the left-right coalition helped thwart an anti-immigrant bill from coming out of the Senate, the mass protests seem to have all but guaranteed that there would be no legalization program passed during the 2006 Congressional session. According to several liberal and conservative pro-immigration reform lobbyists, the protest wave had a polarizing affect on Congress. As EWIC's John Gray described,

They [the marches] hurt on the Republican and the conservative Democratic side. When you're waving the Colombian or Mexican flag and demanding *"Amnistia Ahora!"* [Amnesty Now] or whatever, that doesn't sit well because if you're sitting there in Iowa you're thinking, "Wait a minute. They broke the law to come here, they continue to break the law being here, and I owe them what? If they want to be American, why are they waving the flag of the country they came from?"...Also, "How is it that...more than a million people...can actually get across [the border] undetected?"...Well the marches rubbed that fact right in their nose. It rubbed their nose in the lawlessness.

Craig Regelbrugge concurred and remembered that during one of his visits with a supportive Republican member of Congress, the legislator lamented, "For God's sake could you tell them to put away the freaking Mexican flag!" As a consequence, Regelbrugge empathically stated, "I think the net effect [of the protest wave] was quite negative before it was all over" because "it polarized things more."

A national immigrant rights leader who spoke on the condition of anonymity recalled that while the marches did help stop H.R. 4437, some D.C. groups felt they "were gonna disrupt their carefully tailored legislative strategy" to win comprehensive immigration reform. "They thought it was bad messaging and they feared that seeing so many non-white people" on the streets would backfire "because they contributed to the fear of an invasion by immigrants." Rich Stolz of FIRM added that "most of the national groups" especially "didn't like the idea of a boycott because it reinforced the image of immigrants being separate and distinct and wanting to punish America," which made it much more difficult to gain the support of the Democrats and Republicans who were on the fence about whether or not to support the Kennedy-McCain Bill. Ana Avendaño of the AFL-CIO best summed up the overall impact of the protest wave on the legislative process: "It strengthened the belief of those who were already in support of immigration reform. It gave them a new big talking point" and the ability to say, "Look, we also have political power." On the other hand, "To the extreme right, the ones that were rabidly anti-immigrant, it also gave them the power to raise money" and say, "Look at all these people that are invading our country."

This schism went beyond Congress and was reflected among average Americans. According to Frank Sharry of the National Immigration Forum, "There is no question that the rallies had a backlash effect with people who leaned negative but weren't really concerned. When they saw all these people in the streets [they] got kind of angry about it . . . You can see it in the public opinion research. It did have a polarizing effect . . . More of them got angry, so it intensified their negative attitudes." Thus, both factions of the left-right policy coalition contended that although the protests pulled liberal and moderate Democrats to the left of the debate, they also pushed conservative Republicans and conservative Democrats to the right, especially in the House of Representatives.

After being watered down with more restrictive amendments, what was essentially the Kennedy-McCain Bill eventually passed the Senate Judiciary Committee on March 27 and passed the entire chamber on May 25. Senate Majority Leader Frist immediately criticized the proposed legislation proclaiming that it went too far "in granting illegal immigrants what most Americans will see as amnesty." In reality, the bill's "path to citizenship" was extremely stringent. Undocumented immigrants would have had to first "apply for a six-year, conditional non-immigrant visa." After six years, "they could then apply for legal permanent residence . . . on the condition that they pay $2,000 in fines, pay all back taxes, pass a criminal background check, stay employed and demonstrate an effort to learn English and civics." All in all, the Kennedy-McCain Bill would have made undocumented immigrants who qualified merely eligible for citizenship over a decade after having applied for their visas (Sandler 2006).

Despite these limitations, Senator Jon Kyle of Arizona attacked the Senate bill as still too liberal, saying, "You may have the votes [to pass it in the Senate], but it will never become law. I'll vote against that. The House won't even go to conference on that" (Sandler and Crowley 2006). The Republicans kept true to this promise. House GOP members, who had passed H.R. 4437 in their chamber the previous December, effectively stopped any effort to pass major immigration reform when "[t]hey refused to convene a conference to negotiate a final bill, and instead held two dozen field hearings around the country during the August recess." When House Republicans "returned to Washington, it was to proclaim what was for all intents and purposes already known – that they would not accept elements of the Senate bill" (Sandler 2006b). A D.C. group leader summarized the legislative session in the following manner: "The anti-immigrant folks were strong enough to stop McCain-Kennedy, but not strong enough to pass Sensenbrenner. We were strong enough to collectively stop Sensenbrenner, but not strong enough to pass comprehensive immigration reform."[12] Once the legislative reform efforts failed, the battle shifted to the electoral arena.

The 2006 Midterm Elections

A social movement's arsenal contains many weapons. Its power does not derive solely from taking to the streets. One of the main strengths of mass mobilization is the potential electoral threat it poses to politicians who have the power to enact the legislative changes activists often seek. As a local immigrant rights organizer put it, "The lesson learned from 2006 was that you could mobilize millions onto the streets, but if those people don't actually exercise political power" through their votes, immigration reform is "not gonna happen."[13] Exhibiting power at the ballot box, however, would be easier said than done for a movement perceived to be composed of individuals – undocumented immigrants – who are restricted from voting because of their legal status.

A Hollow Victory

It is well established that the passage of California's infamous anti-immigrant Proposition 187 in 1994 led to a surge in both naturalization and voting by Latino immigrants in the Golden State (Pantoja, Ramirez, and Segura 2001; Pantoja and Segura 2003). With this historical precedent in mind, during the 2006 marches some immigrant rights activists proclaimed that the same would happen across the country in response to H.R. 4437 and Congress's failure to pass immigration reform. One such individual was Jesse Diaz of L.A.'s radical March 25 Coalition, who during the protest wave announced to the media, "You're going to see voter registration like never before." But as Diaz later explained, he didn't mean that he or his fellow radicals in the movement would lead these efforts. "I knew we didn't want to do voter registration... All the leftists in the group were against the electoral process." He later admitted, "I went a little overboard," acknowledging, "I shouldn't have said it...I made a mistake. I got caught up in the moment."

At the national level, the movement did not possess the breadth or infrastructure to carry out the type of massive on-the-ground and public awareness campaign needed to significantly increase voter registration and turnout rates. Many in the movement feared that making and then not being able to live up to such ambitious claims could be extremely damaging to the movement's political leverage and credibility. According to Efrain Escobedo of the National Association of Latina/o Elected Officials (NALEO), when they first heard activists tell the media that there would be a dramatic rise in immigrant voter registration and turnout, "We were a little upset and we voiced our concerns internally [among] advocates about saying that." Given that it was an off-year election, NALEO did not believe it was possible to get the million new Latino (U.S. and foreign-born) voters that activists promised, because get-out-the-vote (GOTV) work "is not something that is organic, it's something that is very tactical and very technical" and, at the time, "there was no infrastructure for mobilizing that many Latinos."

The 2006 midterm elections turned out to be a hollow victory for the immigrant rights movement. Although Democrats reclaimed control of both branches of Congress, many of those who won office were politically moderate or conservative on the issue of immigration. On top of this, the promised power of the Latino vote seemed nowhere to be found. Despite not having made the call for massive Latino voter registration drives, mainstream local and national affiliates of the We Are America Alliance (WAAA) attempted to take on the challenge through campaigns such as a "Democracy Summer" and other efforts. But lack of funding and the short time span between the spring protest wave and the November elections resulted in the movement's inability to achieve its publically stated goal. Looking at the raw numbers, Latino voter registration actually decreased from 9,308,000 in 2004 to 9,304,000 in 2006, and Latino voter turnout plummeted from close to 7.6 million in 2004 to less than 5 million in 2006 (U.S. Census Bureau). The movement's efforts appeared to be "more of a trickle than a torrent," as the *Washington Post* article quoted previously put it (Blood and Prengaman 2006). NALEO's fears were thus confirmed. After the elections, the organization received "a flood of calls from the media" asking, "So was it all a hoax? You guys said a million [new Latinos] . . . were going to vote and from what we're looking at, it's only a few hundred thousand that voted. What happened? Why did people not respond? Do people not believe in this?"[14]

Despite the media and the immigrant rights movement itself perceiving the 2006 voter mobilization efforts as a failure, closer analysis of the data reveals more nuanced results. First, midterm elections always have lower turnout rates than presidential elections. Because of this, in order

TABLE 6.1. *Latino Rate of Increase in Midterm Elections, 2002 & 2006*

	2002	2006
Citizen Voting Age Population	25.8%	10.9%
Registered Voters	19.7%	13.5%
Voter Turnout	16.6%	17.8%

Source: U.S. Census Bureau.

to examine whether there was an increase in Latino voter registration and turnout, the 2006 results should have been contrasted with those of the analogous 2002 midterm elections. Furthermore, rather than simply assessing the actual numerical changes in voter registration and turnout between elections, a proper evaluation should have compared voter registration and turnout rates with that of the Latino citizen voting age population (CVAP), the number of potential Latino voters.

Once we conduct this analysis we see that the 2006 Latino GOTV efforts were far from disastrous. Table 6.1 shows the rates of growth in 2002 and 2006, compared to the previous midterm election (1998 and 2002, respectively). Thus, between 1998 and 2002 the natural growth rate of Latinos who were eligible to vote showed an increase of 25.8 percent, outpacing the growth of both Latino registration (19.7%) and voter turnout (16.6%). Comparing the 2006 midterm elections to the 2002 results, however, Latino voter registration and turnout actually surpassed the natural growth rate of the Latino CVAP. Whereas the Latino CVAP grew from 2002 to 2006 at a rate of only 10.9 percent, Latino voter registration and turnout increased by about 13.5 percent and 17.8 percent, respectively. In short, in 2002 Latino voter registration and turnout increased more slowly than did the eligible voting population of Latinos; conversely, in 2006 registration and turnout increased more rapidly than did the size of this same population. This means that even though the movement did not accomplish its stated goal of getting a million new Latinos registered and out to vote during the 2006 midterm elections, its efforts were not completely in vain. Despite its limited resources, the movement arguably did, in fact, have some degree of success in its Latino electoral mobilization efforts (see also Leal at al. 2008). Nonetheless, politics is often more about the perception of political actions rather than their tangible outcomes.

The movement's apparent lack of electoral success in 2006 perpetuated the notion that the millions of people who had marched in support of immigrant rights were all "non-voting illegals." Accordingly, members of Congress could believe that the protests posed no electoral threat to them, and those who sympathized with the immigrant cause could think that immigrants would not be an electoral benefit. As the Coalition for Comprehensive Immigration Reform's (CCIR) Maria Echaveste put it, "Our underperformance as a voting bloc made it easier for members of Congress to ignore people on the streets." Consequently, after the midterm elections Congress ended its session not, as immigrant rights advocates had hoped, by passing comprehensive immigration reform, but by passing the Secure Fence Act of 2006, a bill that sought to add 700 miles of fencing along the U.S.-Mexico border.

The 2007 Push for Comprehensive Immigration Reform

Explaining the importance of allies in immigration policymaking, one national organization leader bluntly stated, "Immigrant rights advocates in D.C. have no power – period. It's always derivative. It's power that we get lent to us by the Chamber of Commerce, or power that is lent to us by SEIU, or power that is lent to us by foundations and other people."[15] In terms of being an electoral threat to politicians, a national advocate explained, "To get immigration reform done you need U.S. citizens who vote to push it. That's who Congressmen are going to look at and listen to . . . You're not going to get it by yourself being non-citizen immigrant voices."[16] Implicit in this logic is the understanding that a movement whose primary base is undocumented immigrants is by its very nature electorally impotent and thus limited in its ability to influence elected officials. This line of thinking posed a significant challenge for the immigrant rights movement, especially given the perceived failure of their 2006 voter mobilization efforts.

It is common knowledge that one of the main priorities of members of Congress is to get reelected and remain in office (Mayhew 1975). As such, because people without papers are unable to vote, not only did nativist members of both the House and Senate not feel electorally threatened by the mass demonstrations – especially because most of them had few, if any, immigrants who voted in their districts (Wong 2017) – but even those who did support pro-immigrant policies had no incentive to do so publicly; in fact, it made more political sense for them not to show support. A national immigrant rights leader recalled that when members of Congress saw millions of immigrants protesting, they believed that the people marching had "nothing to say about whether I stay in office or not."[17] Therefore, despite the Democratic Party winning control of the

House and a slim majority in the Senate after the 2006 midterm elections, the immigrant rights movement was still unable to wield enough political leverage to pass bipartisan immigration legislation in 2007. With no widespread and imminent threat to organize around, and with the fear of raids and backlash still pervasive, activists were unable to mobilize the same number of people in support of a bill as they were when trying to defeat one. As Chris Newman of NDLON put it, "Nothing unifies people like a common threat and a common enemy," so "we were one hundred percent unified against [H.R. 4437]. But when we had to turn the corner and march in favor of something," the movement was unable to do so.

The legislative strategy of national immigrant rights advocates in 2007 was the same as in 2006: start from a centrist position by forming a coalition with big business and hope that they could bring enough Republicans on board to pass bipartisan legislation. According to an AFL-CIO official and critic of the movement's strategy, "The process started from a compromise," so the only way the coalition was "going to keep Republicans on board" was by "caving into the needs of business."[18] The radical flank of the movement was highly critical of the D.C. groups' left-right strategy in both 2006 and 2007. This faction felt that it made more sense to start from an extremely progressive position – namely, immediate and unconditional amnesty, and no increases in immigrant enforcement efforts – and negotiate from there. Responding to this line of argument, Frank Sharry of the National Immigration Forum stated that, in terms of the 2006 debate:

Their instincts probably weren't all wrong. In retrospect, our self-criticism of those of us operating in D.C. is that we didn't understand that starting with a bipartisan compromise would then only move us to the right; that wasn't so clear to us. So that critique in retrospect was right. But if we had started from the left, there wouldn't have been a game either. So in 2006 I am much more confident what we did before Sensenbrenner and after worked.

The following year's policy debate, however, was a different story:

Where it didn't work and where the critique is better founded was in 2007 when there was an immigration bill [the bipartisan Comprehensive Immigration Reform Act of 2007] negotiated in the back room. It was designed to lean right to get Republican votes. Then it went further right during the Senate floor process through amendments to the point where it was hard for any progressive to support it, and *still* it didn't get the Republican votes we needed . . . This was Kennedy in the back room saying we had to follow him because he knew how this was going to work. For groups like us who said, "Well we don't really like the bill, but it will get better in the House," that was our best argument. At that point, starting really center-right and then moving further Right and losing, it's hard to argue that that was a good strategy.

Maria Echaveste, the lead strategist for the national Coalition for Comprehensive Immigration Reform (CCIR), responded to criticism from movement radicals by saying that their arguments were "all very nice," but then asked, "Can you tell me how you're supposed to do that when you have Republicans controlling the White House and you've got Republicans until 2006 controlling Congress, [plus] you have the 60 vote rule in the Senate?" She conceded, "It's a valid criticism that it started in the center," but asserted that CCIR's legislative strategy "started in the center because there was no viable left." As another D.C. group leader put it, "the idea that we were going to get a bill" that included "legalization, family reunification . . . and no enforcement" was completely unrealistic, "I don't know what world they're living in."[19]

The left-right coalition strategy failed again in 2007. Even starting from a position of compromise, the immigrant rights movement did not have the political leverage to get a bill passed. Under a Republican White House and centrist Democratic Congress – in which anti-immigrant Republicans still carried considerable influence given their ability to filibuster any bill in the Senate – chances of passing progressive immigration reform were slim to none. On the right, nativists opposed any bill that included a guest worker program and even a limited path to citizenship for undocumented immigrants. On the left, many local activists around the country disagreed once more with D.C. advocates' support for the bipartisan 2007 bill because it included too many enforcement measures and its legalization program was too limited. Many in the movement's radical flank either did not understand the strategy of supporting a bad bill in the Senate with the hope that it would be improved in the House, or simply did not believe the D.C. groups had the power to "fix it later."

The response the compromised bill elicited from anti-immigrant activists across the country also warrants attention. Whereas immigrant rights activists mobilized millions of people to protest in favor of legalization, they were unable to organize even a small fraction of that amount to call and lobby Congress in support of a bill they favored. Meanwhile, the anti-immigrant movement did a formidable job of mobilizing its base to flood Congress with electoral threats and calls in opposition of legislation that included any form of "amnesty." Unlike the millions of Latinos who marched in 2006, these were individuals whose ability to vote was never in question. As Kevin Appleby of the U.S. Conference of Catholic Bishops explained, "If I'm a Congressman and I'm sort of with CIR [comprehensive immigration reform], but then I'm getting ten-to-one phone calls saying that they're going to vote against me if I vote for this . . . I get scared."

Ira Mehlman of the Federation for American Immigration Reform (FAIR), the nation's leading immigration restriction organization, described exactly how, despite the large pro-immigrant demonstrations, nativist forces were able to put enough pressure on Congress to not pass legislation that included legalization:

I'm very impressed that they could get 500,000 people out on the streets. We can't get 500 people out on the streets . . . But rather than going out to the streets [we] called our members of Congress . . . It wasn't 500,000 calls, but having worked on Capitol Hill, I can tell you that each call that they get on something, they believe that there's probably 20, or 100, or 500 people who share that point of view. So it wasn't that there was no demonstration of public opposition [by anti-immigration activists], it's just that it was demonstrated in a different way.

The anti-immigrant movement was well aware of its electoral threat to elected officials. Despite being unable to get masses of people out to protest, according to FAIR, "What we *can* do . . . working through our direct communication" (especially their email listserv and phone banking efforts) and "working with people in the media," is "get our message out, and that translates into some kind of political action."[20]

While scholars have found Latinos, and Latino immigrants in particular, to be extremely unlikely to contact public officials (Fraga et al. 2011: 229), immigrant rights activists acknowledged the effectiveness of the anti-immigrant movement's media strategy and ability to get its supporters to inundate Congress with phone calls. According to Eliseo Media of SEIU, "The Lou Dobbses of the world manufactured a response" from the right by "having them make phone calls to Congress to make it appear" as if "everybody in the country was mad about the issue," and "we couldn't overcome that." Clarissa Martínez De Castro of NCLR agreed and added that through actions such as phone calls, faxes, and letters, "members of Congress and many elected officials measure the level of risk" that supporting a bill or not poses to them. Appleby of the Catholic Bishops Conference explained that, unlike the nativist forces,

We didn't have people calling in and writing letters. I mean, the other side has a very vocal and passionate group of people who feel strongly that immigration threatens their way of life. We don't have a corresponding vocal group that says the opposite. . . . [Consequently,] in 2007 we just really got beat in the trenches. I think the other side was just more galvanized, more organized, more well funded, had a simpler message and was able to convey that and won the day.

As a result, the immigrant rights movement was defeated again in its efforts to win legalization. The millions of people on the streets only a year before were less of a political threat to Congress than the few thousand phone calls and letters House and Senate members received from anti-immigrant voters.

In fact, the movement actually fared worse in 2007 than it did in 2006. Not only was the Comprehensive Immigration Reform of Act 2007 less appealing to activists than the 2006 Kennedy-McCain Bill, but, unlike the latter, it was not even able to pass the Senate. After trying for months, neither part of the left-right coalition was happy with the bipartisan legislation being proposed. As the *Washington Examiner* later reported: "The bill failed a series of cloture votes in June of 2007. A final effort on June 28 received only 46 votes, 14 short of the votes needed to invoke cloture. Twelve Republicans voted with most Democrats to end cloture. Sixteen Democrats voted with most Republicans to kill the reform" (Higgins 2012).

The disappointing results reinforced the previous year's lesson that in Washington votes matter more than protests when marchers are thought to pose no electoral threat. As a WAAA member put it, "Part of our assessment was that these Congressional members don't fear us, they just don't fear us." A local New York activist added, "We learned that until we changed the current political balance of force in Congress, it [was] going to be very hard" to win legalization. "We felt that we had to gain political power. There was no other way."[21] In response, while continuing to push for comprehensive immigration reform in Washington, the movement also began working behind the scenes across the country with eyes set on the 2008 presidential election.

The 2008 Presidential Election: *Ya Es Hora!* – Now Is The Time!

According to one D.C. immigrant rights advocate, "Politics, I've come to realize, runs on fear. So ultimately Congress was afraid to pass Sensenbrenner and they were afraid to pass comprehensive immigration reform. Only when they are afraid not to will they get it done."[22] Consequently, the movement decided to "speak the language" of elected officials.[23] Whereas some of them had previously worked on GOTV campaigns, immediately preceding the protest wave several of the more established immigrant rights groups were primarily focused on lobbying to stop H.R. 4437 from becoming law – not on protesting or electoral mobilization. But as discussed earlier, by the end of the summer, many of the more mainstream immigrant rights groups deliberately decided to change their tactics from telling people to take to the streets to encouraging them to become citizens and register to vote. They believed the power of mass protest had reached its limits. What was needed was more institutional influence.

In mid-August of 2006, prior to the midterm elections, various local, statewide, and national immigrant rights coalitions – which consisted of everything from unions to community-based organizations – met in Chicago in an effort to find common cause. Their goal was to form one national coalition that encompassed both the moderate and radical factions of the movement. According to Rich Stolz of FIRM, that effort completely failed. "It wound up blowing up because nobody could agree on anything" in terms of policy positions. At this meeting, though, several of the organizations that had done voter registration work in the past decided to continue to work together under the banner of the "We Are America Alliance" (WAAA), which had previously been formed to coordinate demonstrations during the spring protest wave. The various local and statewide immigrant rights coalitions affiliated with FIRM, along with SEIU, decided to collaborate and design a strategy to mobilize the Latino and immigrant vote at the national level. However, as discussed above, the 2006 "election was only four or five months later. It was too soon for us to be able to make a political impact."[24] Nonetheless, the infrastructure being built by WAAA would later prove essential.

As 2006 came to an end, both immigrant rights activists and Latino political leaders were disheartened by the lack of impact the protests had on national policy and by their inability to translate street power into electoral influence. During a lunch meeting between Marcelo Gaete, then-senior director of programs for the National Association of Latino Elected Officials (NALEO), and *Univision*'s Los Angeles station news director, Jorge Mettey, the two men spoke about both of these issues. Gaete explained to Mettey that, despite their actual numbers, Latino immigrants lacked political strength because of their low citizenship and voting rates. Mettey had a simple suggestion: naturalize and register a million new voters. Gaete explained that, given the previous years' failed efforts and the traditionally low naturalization and voter registration rates of Latinos, meeting such a goal would be "impossible." But the following day, Gaete called Mettey and said, "I think you're nuts, but we need to talk."[25]

At this second meeting Gaete presented Mettey with data on exactly how many Latinos in the U.S. were eligible to naturalize and to register to vote but who, for whatever reason, had not done so. Mettey was shocked to learn that 8 million Latino immigrants across the country were qualified to become citizens, and thus to vote, but instead were living as legal permanent residents.[26] He admitted, "I did it too. I got married with an American...and I didn't become a citizen until ten years later because, what for? I was very comfortable with being a legal resident. I didn't need it [citizenship]." As a result of the second conversation and subsequent meetings, NALEO and *Univision* joined forces to create what at first was just a local Los Angeles initiative but quickly became a national campaign to naturalize, then register, and ultimately get as many Latinos as possible to vote in the 2008 presidential election. Thus, even as they realized that the 2006 protest wave symbolized "a pivot point in Latino political history," these Latino political elites knew that for the unprecedented events to become a "transformative point," more institutional follow-up needed to happen and that institutional follow-up needed to come from electorally armed naturalized and U.S.-born Latino citizens.

National Latino political organizations (from NCLR to NALEO) that had nothing to do with sparking the mass rallies nonetheless heard the chants from the crowds: "Today We March, Tomorrow We Vote." The three-pronged campaign that would attempt to realize this declaration was named "*Ya Es Hora*" [Now Is The Time].[27] In 2005, NALEO had commissioned a study to analyze why Latinos who were eligible to become citizens were not doing so. Because NALEO was getting only "trickles of people coming in" to seek help with their citizenship process, and no philanthropies were interested in funding these types of services, the organization was getting ready to cut its naturalization program.[28] The internal NALEO study had shown that Latinos who qualified to be citizens had become comfortable with their lives in the U.S. and that, while they expressed a desire to eventually start the naturalization process, they felt no sense of urgency to do so. Ironically, the racist and nativist rhetoric that surrounded the immigration debate would supply this vital link and motivation. As a Latina who participated in the campaign after being a legal permanent resident for 20 years explained to the *Wall Street Journal*, "We're not illegal, but we have family members who are." Spurred "by the heated debate" over undocumented immigrants, she declared that once she received her citizenship she planned to vote: "We want to have a say in these matters" (Jordan 2007).

NALEO's research of voter data had also shown that as Latinos assimilated, a gap formed in their opinions on immigration, with third and later generations not identifying as much with the issue.[29] This distance had traditionally posed a problem for immigrant advocates because undocumented immigrants were electorally dependent on the voting muscle of naturalized and U.S.-born Latinos. According to Maria Echaveste of CCIR, anti-immigrant activists' racist rhetoric helped the movement bridge this divide. "The great thing was the stupidity of the right wing and the Republican Party because their rhetoric just inevitably went from being anti-immigrant to anti-[Latino] . . . [Which] made it easier for us to talk to second and third generation" Latinos and say, "This is about you!" Eliseo Media of SEIU concurred:

When the debate began in Congress it all crystallized around Sensenbrenner. But then it became not an issue about undocumented workers, it became an issue about Latinos. People started talking about the changing face of America, about the diversity and their fear of it. They [Republicans] started talking about English-only laws and changing the constitution to take away citizenship from children born [to undocumented immigrants] in this country. So the [Latino] community basically perceived that this was about the color of our skin and the language we speak, this wasn't about public policy . . . It was terribly misplayed by the Republicans.

In short, the racist nativism of H.R. 4437 and the hostile public sentiments the bill sparked also activated a sense of group consciousness among U.S.- and foreign-born Latinos who in turn responded politically in naturalization halls and ballot boxes across the nation.

Several conservative business lobbyists tried to explain to Republican leaders that their anti-immigrant strategy was detrimental to the party's future. According to Regelbrugge of the Agriculture Coalition for Immigration Reform, he told GOP leaders, "You're sowing the seeds of your own destruction . . . by alienating . . . Latinos and business all at once," because "by and large we're talking about a population of people [Latinos] that has a work ethic, a family values ethic, and a rather conservative outlook on life." On social issues they're "often pro-life" and have "religious Christian heritage." He wondered, "Why is the Republican Party not seeing an opportunity to be attractive to these people?" John Gray of EWIC remembered thinking, "Republicans have gone with the 'White Guy' thing as far as they're going to get. They've lost the Black vote," and "Latinos are already the biggest and fastest growing minority. They're probably still in play, but maybe not for long." Gray explained, "National Republican leaders got it. Karl Rove got it . . . I think those paid to think nationally got it. The people who were trying to win their next election understood, but they also understood [the politics of] their own district and they went with that."

These anti-immigrant sentiments provided the urgency that the NALEO study had shown Latinos needed to motivate them to become citizens and register to vote. That many immigrant households are of mixed status (i.e. immigrants – both legal and undocumented – and citizens – both U.S. and foreign-born), and that the racist rhetoric spread from fear of undocumented immigrants to the degrading of U.S.-born Latino citizens, increased the pool of people that immigrant rights activists could mobilize for the upcoming 2008 election. The growing We Are America Alliance eventually provided much of the local infrastructure, whereas NALEO and *Univision*'s *Ya Es Hora!* campaign supplied the capacity and breadth for the type of organized and targeted campaign that would be needed to mobilize immigrants and their families to naturalize, register, and ultimately go out and vote. The effort was unprecedented in American history.

The *Ya Es Hora!* campaign came to include Spanish print, radio, and television outlets all across the country. It partnered with SEIU, NCLR, and the We Are America Alliance (WAAA), which by then included hundreds of local, statewide, and national organizations, such as the Center for Community Change, ACORN, *Democracia USA*, the National Korean American Service and Education Consortium, the New York Immigration Coalition, the National Capital Immigration Coalition, *Mi Familia Vota* Education Fund, the Massachusetts Immigrant and Refugee Advocacy Coalition, the Gamaliel Foundation, the Illinois Coalition for Immigrant and Refugee Rights, and other groups. According to a WAAA steering committee leader, the immigrant rights movement decided "to invest in civic engagement . . . in places that matter," meaning swing states and local elections where the Latino and immigrant vote could make a difference.[30] Through their mass communication capacities, *Univision* and its media partners, such as *Entrevision* and ImpreMeda (the nation's largest Spanish newspaper publisher, with outlets in nine states), provided the means to promote the campaign and disseminate information to Latinos all over the country. The first phase of their three-prong effort was a massive naturalization drive, "*Ya Es Hora, Ciudadanía!*" [Now is the Time, Citizenship!].

The *Ya Es Hora!*'s citizenship campaign was launched in early January of 2007. Organizations could be part of the campaign in two ways. They could serve as "information centers," where people could stop by and pick up citizenship applications, or as full *Ya Es Hora!* "service centers" that helped individuals with the naturalization process. *Ya Es Hora!* leaders conducted several training sessions across the country to show community-based groups exactly how to assist people with filling out their applications. Meanwhile, Spanish language media was reinforcing the exigency to naturalize. For instance, ethnic news outlets used the fact that immigration officials were planning to raise the fees for becoming a citizen as fodder for the campaign's fire (Gamboa 2007). Spanish language media provided the motivation and information, while grassroots groups provided access to and assistance with naturalization. As one of the key NALEO strategists explained:

Univision defined its role as saying, "We're going to be the catalyst for this thing. We're going to be the people sounding the horn every day reminding people that they have to become citizens. NALEO is going to become the infrastructure because you guys have your hotline, you have websites, you have all the expertise on naturalization and everything that we could need to make this happen." And *Univision* basically said, "In our news segments, it's going to be about citizenship. There's no way that someone will tune in to KMEX [*Univision's* largest station] and not hear the message that, "You need to become a citizen!"[31]

Univision began to air 30-minute public service announcements (PSAs). The first one explained what one needed to qualify to become a citizen. A second PSA detailed how to fill out a naturalization application without a lawyer or notary. The final one gave advice on "preparing for your interview to make sure that people passed."[32] *Univision* was also promoting the campaign during its main daily newscasts. "We were pursuing it very aggressively on all fronts: promotions, anchors mentioned it, editorial pieces trying to find new angles," said an editorial board member.[33] Print media synergized with these efforts, running articles about the benefits of naturalization, fact sheets, Q&As about qualifying for citizenship, and editorial columns about *Ya Es Hora!*. Furthermore, the most popular Spanish language radio DJ in the nation – Los Angeles-based *Piolín* – added to the media frenzy by going on a national campaign, broadcasting shows in different cities across the country, to get Latinos to become citizens and register to vote. Hence, the media partners helped build the hype and provided the information, while grassroots immigrant rights groups and service organizations made the process accessible to people at the community level. As a result, a 60-year-old Latina who attended one of the citizenship drives declared that the campaign was "waking us up... We kept saying 'mañana, mañana' about our citizenship" but now, she added, "It's time for Latinos to have a voice" (Jordan 2007). A close-to-forty-year veteran of the U.S. Citizenship and Immigration Services described the remarkable impact of the campaign in the following

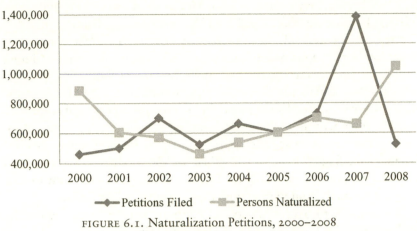

FIGURE 6.1. Naturalization Petitions, 2000–2008
Source: Department of Homeland Security.

manner, "I have never seen anything like it in my career. It's big" (Jordan 2007).

In all, more than 400 organizations joined the *Ya Es Hora!* campaign across the country in states like Massachusetts, Connecticut, Florida, New Mexico, Texas, Arizona, Nevada, California, New York, Colorado, Virginia, Illinois, and others – states that had large Latino populations and/or were presidential election swing states. The results were phenomenal. As Figure 6.1 shows, the number of petitions for naturalization filed spiked from 730,642 in 2006 to 1,383,275 in 2007, an almost 90 percent increase. In addition, in terms of the number of individuals whose petitions were accepted and who actually became citizens before the end of the 2008 election year, the data reveal an almost 60 percent increase (660,477 to 1,046,539) from 2007 to 2008. As striking as these figures were, however, getting people to become citizens is one thing; getting this same group to register and actually vote is quite another. Thus, the next step for the movement was to make sure this voting potential turned into voting power. The subsequent two phases of the campaign were *"Ya Es Hora, Regístrate!" [Now Is the Time, Register!]* and *"Ya Es Hora, Ve y Vota!"* [Now Is the Time, Go and Vote!].

The 2008 presidential election provided an ideal opportunity for the immigrant rights movement to launch voter registration and get-out-the-vote (GOTV) drives. On the Republican side, the one GOP candidate who was pro-compressive immigration reform, Senator John

McCain, led his party's ticket. Senator McCain had name recognition with Latinos because he had helped lead the push for legalization in 2006. On the Democratic side, Senator Barack Obama, a former community organizer with the Gamaliel Foundation (an organization that had long supported immigrant rights), had made history by becoming the first African-American to win the presidential nomination. Liberals across the nation were energized by the possibility of electing a person of color who was a former activist. Both parties launched massive and energetic grassroots campaigns with specific efforts to target Latinos through Spanish-language media (Miller 2008). The historic mobilization efforts by both political parties, but especially the Democrats, to get Latinos out to vote both intentionally and unintentionally supplemented *Ya Es Hora!*.

Interestingly, the recent Mexican elections influenced *Univision's* media strategy for the U.S. presidential elections. The network's Los Angeles news director, Jorge Mettey, had covered Mexico's presidential election and was extremely impressed by MTV's "Rock the Vote" efforts there:

It's like the *telenovelas*. We just bring the *telenovela* that was successful in Mexico to the USA. ... You're just putting proven stuff for the same viewers. Those who watch TV in Mexico, they come across the border and they watch TV here. They have the same habits. They have the same tastes. It was the same with this campaign. It's a proven campaign that had an amazing impact.

Mettey decided to model *Ya Es Hora!*'s media strategy on "Rock the Vote" in Mexico, and flew the two young men who ran the MTV effort in Mexico to Los Angeles to discuss their approach. As a result, much like "Rock the Vote," *Univision* constantly went to live coverage of their voter registration drives and interviewed people about why they felt it was important to register to vote. The campaign helped promote the issue from various angles.

Other non-*Ya Es Hora!* affiliated Latino and immigrant rights groups also launched united and independent campaigns, targeting segments of the Latino electorate who weren't traditionally mobilized to vote. These organizations saw a key role for "electorally impotent" undocumented immigrants and stereotypically apathetic Latino youth. Despite being blocked from voting because of their legal status, people without papers participated in GOTV efforts by "knocking on doors in ethnic neighborhoods, manning the phones in myriad languages and distributing political flyers" to help get those who were eligible in their communities out to vote (Barbassa 2008). In this fashion, undocumented immigrants demonstrated that they could back up their street protests with electoral power as well.

In terms of Latino youth, in July of 2008, organizations such as the Southwest Voter Registration Education Project (SVREP), the League of United Latin American Citizens (LULAC), the National Alliance of Latin American and Caribbean Communities, *Hermandad Mexicana*, and others announced a $5 million non-partisan voter registration effort that mostly targeted "younger voters through 125 organizing committees" (Watanabe 2008). SVREP and its partners concentrated their campaigns in states such as California, Texas, Florida, Arizona, Colorado, Washington, New Mexico, Virginia, Nevada, Oregon, North Carolina, Georgia, Maryland, Illinois, Connecticut, Massachusetts, New York, and New Jersey.[34] On top of these efforts, through the Internet, email lists, social networking Web sites like MySpace, text messages, radio and television PSAs, concerts and media events featuring Latino celebrities such as Jennifer Lopez, Enrique Iglesias, Rosario Dawson, Jessica Alba, and Ozomatli, the organization *Voto Latino* was able to reach millions of Latino youth and households in key swing states. According to the organization itself:

Voto Latino conservatively estimates that it leveraged more than $6,000,000 in *gratis* [free] airtime for its radio and television PSA's via partnerships with major networks like Comcast, Time Warner Cable, *Univision* Radio, *Entravision*, SBS, MTV, Tr3s, and LATV... We were able to negotiate pro bono voter registration and "get out the vote" airtime that would have cost partisan organizations like the Obama and McCain campaigns millions of dollars. In 2008, *Voto Latino* generated more than 275 million television impressions for its PSA's and initiatives, 100 million radio impressions, 80 million print media impressions and 75 million online impressions.[35]

Knowing that the major political parties were going to spend most of their time trying to mobilize frequent voters, which often results in Latino and Asian American voters being disproportionately neglected (Ramirez and Wong 2006), immigrant rights activists made an additional effort to target Asian and Latino new citizens and registered voters who hadn't regularly showed up to the polls. According to its internal numbers, WAAA registered over half a million new voters – including close to 130,000 new voters in battle ground states.[36] WAAA member groups "also organized and implemented 686,411 get out the vote (GOTV) contacts."[37] NALEO focused on 170,000 voters and, "as far as phone calls being generated," made about "a quarter of a million" in "7 different states."

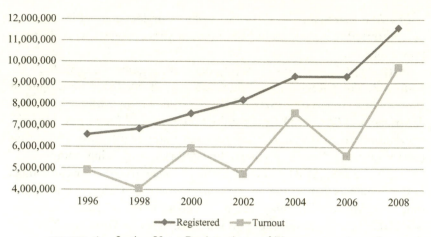

FIGURE 6.2. Latino Voter Registration and Turnout, 1996–2008
Source: U.S. Census Bureau.

Their Web site alone registered about 26,000 new voters.[38] On top of these actions, ImpreMedia inserted a million voter registration cards in its Spanish newspapers in Colorado, Florida, California, Arizona, New York, Illinois, and Texas (Barbassa 2008).

Many immigrant rights activists also took time off from their organizations to do partisan work for the Obama campaign. A WAAA member explained, "There was also direct engagement with Barack Obama as a candidate when he said, 'If this is going to move forward, this is where I need your help.'"[39] Many in the movement believed that despite McCain's attempt to help pass legalization in 2006, his party was the cause of much of the nation's anti-immigrant sentiments. A lot of activists felt that Obama's history as a community organizer and his relationship with one of the movement's biggest advocates, Chicago Congressman Luis Gutierrez, was enough reason to favor him in the presidential race.

So what were the results of these historic electoral mobilization efforts? Again, the data demonstrate impressive outcomes (Figure 6.2). Compared to the 2004 presidential election, in 2008 the number of Latino voters jumped from 7.6 million to over 9.7 million, an increase of more than 2 million voters. Moreover, when we look at the improvement from their "failed" 2006 voter mobilization attempt, the results appear even more remarkable. The increase in Latino voter turnout between the 2006 and 2008 elections was a whopping 4.1 million. But again, examining the change in rates is in order to more thoroughly assess the impact of the voter mobilization efforts. If voter registration and turnout rates

TABLE 6.2. *Latino Rate of Increase in Presidential Elections, 2004 & 2008*

	2004	2008
Citizen Voting Age Population	22.2%	21.4%
Registered Voters	23.3%	24.7%
Voter Turnout	27.8%	28.4%

Source: U.S. Census Bureau.

rose more than the growth of their potential voting age population, then activists' claims of conducting a successful campaign would be strengthened.

As Table 6.2 shows, in 2004 the Latino citizen voting age population (CVAP) rate increased by 22 percent, compared to 2000. That same year, during the contentious Bush versus Kerry election, Latino voter registration surpassed that figure by about one percentage point (22.2% to 23.3%), and Latino voter turnout exceeded it by almost six percentage points (22.2% to 27.8%).

In terms of rate increases during the 2008 presidential race, Latino voter registration outpaced the growth of the Latino citizen voting age population 24.7 percent to 21.4 percent, and Latino voter turnout exceeded it by seven percentage points (28.4% to 21.4%). Hence, the data indicate that in both 2004 and 2008 the Latino citizen voting age population, voter registration, and voter turnout rates all rose. But during the historic 2008 presidential election, the Latino CVAP growth rate slightly slowed (from 22.2% to 21.4%), whereas Latino voter registration and turnout increased at faster rates, thus signifying an additional degree of success in electoral mobilization.

It is of course impossible to prove that immigrant rights advocate's unprecedented GOTV campaigns were directly responsible for the dramatic increase in the number of Latino voters, surely the multiple factors stated throughout this chapter (e.g. the candidates, increases in naturalization fees, etc.) contributed to the success. However, the likelihood that activists' efforts did have a major impact is bolstered by the fact that a substantial body of evidence shows that U.S.- and foreign-born (Michelson and Garcia Bedolla 2014; Baretto 2005) Latino voter turnout can be significantly amplified when the same type of Spanish- and English-language media mobilization efforts (Abrajano and Panagopoulos 2011), identity appeals (Valenzuela and Michelson 2016), phone banking (Ramirez 2005; Ramirez and Wong 2006; Nunoz 2007), and door-to-door canvassing (Michelson 2005) that *Ya Es Hora!* and immigrant rights advocates engaged in across the country are implemented.

Overall, if we look solely at the increase of the actual number of Latinos who registered and voted in 2008 compared to 2004 (and especially compared to 2006), the figures are noteworthy given that, as previously stated, politics is often more about perception than substantive results. Comparing 2008 Latino voter registration and turnout rate increases to the previous presidential election (2004), the results are more modest but still positive. If Latinos voted as a bloc, however, given the competitive nature of the 2008 race, increases in the actual number of voters could have impacted the results of close elections in key swing states.

According to an analysis of election results conducted by the Pew Hispanic Center, Latinos voted for the Democratic presidential ticket "by a margin of more than two-to-one." Moreover:

Nationally, all Latino demographic sub-groups voted for Obama by heavy margins. According to the national exit poll, 64% of Hispanic males and 69% of Hispanic females supported Obama. Latino youth . . . supported Obama over McCain by a lopsided margin – 76% versus 19% . . . Obama carried the Latino vote by sizeable margins in all states with large Latino populations. His biggest breakthrough came in Florida, where he won 57% of the Latino vote in a state where Latinos have historically supported Republican presidential candidates . . . Obama's margins were much larger in other states with big Latino populations. He carried 78% of the Latino vote in New Jersey, 76% in Nevada, 74% in California, and 73% in Colorado . . . The largest increases in the share of voters who are Hispanic occurred in the states of Colorado . . . New Mexico . . . and Nevada . . . all three battleground states in this year's election.[40]

In addition, in an even more detailed analysis, political scientists Matt Barreto, Loren Callingwood, and Sylvia Manzano (2010) concluded that in the 2008 election, "Latinos were very influential in seven swing states: Florida, Nevada, New Mexico, Colorado, Virginia, North Carolina, and Indiana." Their results also indicate "evidence of extensive Latino mobilization, though a lesser overall impact, in additional states including Arizona, Ohio, California, Texas, Missouri and Minnesota, perhaps foreshadowing a greater degree of influence in 2012 and beyond" (2; also see IPC 2008).

Given the apparent impact of the Latino vote, one must also ask whether the issue of immigration was related to these results in any manner and to what degree Latino immigrants went to the polls. According to a survey conducted by the Immigration Policy Center, in 2008, 75 percent of Latino registered voters saw immigration as an "extremely" or "very important" issue leading up to the election. Perhaps more importantly, in 2008 Latino immigrants made up a significant portion of the Latino electorate. As evidenced by a post-election poll of Latino voters conducted by NALEO, in 2008 almost half (46%) of Latino voters were immigrants. Furthermore, whereas the survey found that a majority (62%) of third-generation Latinos (Latinos whose grandparents were immigrants) supported the Democratic presidential candidate, second-generation (the children of immigrants) Latinos and Latino immigrants demonstrated the strongest support for Obama, at nearly 80 percent (NALEO 2008; IPC 2008). Thus, in 2008 not only was the issue of immigration a key motivator for Latino voters, but Latino immigrants in particular also proved to be an electoral force to be reckoned with.

In sum, a longtime D.C. immigration policy insider best captured the electoral effects of the 2006 protest wave when he stated:

> In 2004, Bush and Rove were on the precipice of winning the majority of Latino immigrant voters and maybe wrapping them up for a lifetime if Republicans had played it smart. But the Sensenbrenner Bill and the rallies that led to the 2008 election have completely changed the political calculus for the Latino community and therefore for the country. The Republican Party had an opportunity to become a majority party and has now become a minority party...John McCain would be president today if they hadn't passed the Sensenbrenner Bill...So whatever the effects were in the short term on the legislative stuff...the biggest impact of the rallies was to set the stage for the historic election of 2008 that I think has changed the face of American politics, it's redrawn the electoral map. The "Today We March, Tomorrow We Vote" slogan became true. So if you step back from what happened in Congress in 2006 and 2007 and ask, "What are the long term effects [of the 2006 protests]?" – well, it was a silent march to the polls.[41]

Conclusion

The 2006 protest wave illustrates that the impacts of mass mobilization can reverberate throughout the policymaking process and electoral politics. It shows us that widespread political activism can have positive and negative, as well as short and long-term institutional consequences. As we have seen in this chapter, when the passage of anti-immigrant legislation in Congress seemed eminent, the series of demonstrations helped halt the Sensenbrenner Bill from becoming law. Conversely, the mass marches also further polarized federal legislators by emboldening liberals while pushing conservatives in Congress further to the right. This dynamic reinforced the latter group's desire to close the nation's immigration gates and guaranteed that no legislation with a legalization program for undocumented immigrants would be become law; a political deadlock we still find ourselves in today and that is deeply divided along partisan lines that have only intensified (McAdam and Kloos 2014; Wong 2017).

The unprecedented protests also have implications for how we understand the roles of race and threat in contentious politics. They show us that an assault in one political arena (e.g. Congress) can lead to a response in another (e.g. elections), as well as that attacking a segment (undocumented immigrants) of a racialized group can lead to a political backlash from other members of their community (U.S.-born and naturalized Latino citizens). The racist policy threat – H.R. 4437 – that catalyzed the countrywide rallies resonated with the racialized group it targeted – U.S.- and foreign-born Latinos – long after the legislative assault subsided (Zepeda-Millán and Wallace 2013). Activists realized that undocumented immigrants would continue to come under attack by nativists in Congress until they demonstrated some type of electoral clout. As a local organizer recalled, "Part of our analysis was that we needed to change hearts and minds" through mass mobilizations, "but we [also] needed to be able to back it up with political power" at the ballot box.[42] Accordingly, the Sensenbrenner Bill, and the subsequent state and societal backlash it sparked, created an opportunity for immigrant rights activists to organize a politically complacent segment of their constituency – legal permanent residents. As one longtime green-card holder who decided to become a citizen in response to H.R. 4437 explained, "You never know what law could change and make it harder for us to stay here" (Jordan 2007).

Demonstrating the blurred line between nativism and anti-Latino racism, anti-immigrant sentiments also quickly turned into anti-Latino discrimination, which had the result of triggering a sense of racial group consciousness and linked fate between U.S.-born and immigrant Latinos (Zepeda-Millán and Wallace 2013; Zepeda-Millán, Street, and Jones-Correa 2016). The shared collective attack on their identities and material interests motivated Latinos to become citizens, register, and turn out to vote during the 2008 election. The results of this civic engagement proved to be politically powerful as Latino and immigrant voters helped swing key battleground states in favor of Democrats, contributing to the election of the nation's first black president.

The ability of immigrant rights activists to mobilize their base and its allies in a variety of contexts shows that a movement should not be assessed solely by its ability to organize mass demonstrations. The dissent and mobilization at the core of social movements can manifest in many forms, from the streets to the ballot box, and from radical anger to gaining government concessions. Consequently, the power of political activism resides not only in its ability to conduct large-scale protests but also in its capacity to build a movement whose arsenal contains a variety of weapons, informal and institutional alike, capable of being deployed in multiple political arenas.

Conclusion

The mass marches that swept the country in 2006 are of great significance not only because of their magnitude, unprecedented nature, and national scope but also because of what they tell us about the relationship between immigration, social movements, and racial politics in the United States. Up until the protest wave, both anecdotal examples and academic evidence had shown that Latinos, and especially Latino immigrants, were among the least likely people to take part in contentious politics. Yet in the spring of 2006, scholars were stumped, reporters were stunned, and even long-time activists were taken by surprise when millions of U.S.- and foreign-born people of Latin American descent took to the streets in almost every state in the union.

The primary goal of this book has been to explore and explain why this sudden eruption of widespread Latino political activism occurred, what factors accounted for its abrupt decline, and what impacts the historic events had. As we have seen, I found that when broadened and racialized, legislative threats against undocumented immigrants can provoke a political backlash from people without papers as well as naturalized- and U.S.-born citizens. My case studies revealed that depending on the type of threat and the degree to which they feel under attack, activists could incite racialized immigrants and their descendants to engage in both formal and informal types of politics. More specifically, the chapters in this book showed us that the Sensenbrenner Bill triggered feelings of linked fate and racial group consciousness amongst millions of Latinos in general, but people of Mexican descent in particular – and, to a lesser extent, members of other minority groups with large immigrant populations – in turn making them more receptive to calls for large-scale collective action.

Both professional organizers and people who had never participated in activism, utilized preexisting community resources, created diverse coalitions and publicized their calls for action through ethnic media outlets, leading to what became one of the largest series of mass protests in U.S. history. Although the marches helped stop H.R. 4437 from becoming law, they also prompted an anti-Latino backlash that contributed, along with several intra-movement factors, to the rapid decline of the demonstrations. In response, and utilizing the infrastructure established and solidified during the protest wave, activists regrouped and redeployed their energies toward the 2008 presidential race. As a result of these efforts, the immigrant rights movement and the Latino electorate played pivotal roles in helping to elect the United States' first African-American president.

Today, over a decade after the protest wave, we can better assess its legacy and what it could teach us about our contemporary moment. The 2016 election cemented the fact that while you cannot understand American politics without understanding the central role of race, you also cannot understand the politics of race in America without understanding the central role of Latinos and their relationship to the contentious issue of immigration. From the day Donald Trump declared his candidacy and claimed that Mexicans were rapists and criminals, to his campaign promise to build a wall along our southern border (Reilly 2016), never has a major party's presidential nominee – now the U.S.'s commander-in-chief – been so blatantly and publically anti-Latino before even taking office. Thus, with Republicans now firmly in control of the federal government for the first time since the 2006 demonstrations, it is an opportune moment to look back and take stock of what we can learn from the historic nationwide rallies. As the remainder of this concluding chapter will show, the mass marches have much to teach us about the contextual dynamics of social movements, immigration policymaking, and the role of Latinos in American racial politics.

Comparing Collective Action Across Different Contexts

Because the dynamics of each city analyzed in this book varied, it is fundamental that we pay attention to the unique ways immigrant activism manifested itself in different places and among different groups. We have investigated episodes of collective action in Fort Myers, Los Angeles, and New York for their different levels of mobilization and varying organizational, demographic, and regional settings. These examinations were organized via place, and then for each place I highlighted key themes that were particularly relevant to that manifestation of the movement. In this section I would like to flip that focus and instead explore the varying ways these themes emerged across different parts of the country. With this shift in perspective I hope to illuminate how although resources, coalitions, and ethnic media outlets were crucial to the mobilization processes in each of my case studies, the roles these factors played before, during, and after the protest wave were contingent upon how the issue of "illegal" immigration was racialized and the distinct dynamics of the locales under investigation.

The Role of Resources

As we observed how local protests were organized in New York City, Fort Myers, and Los Angeles, it became clear that poor and marginalized immigrant communities possess individual (e.g. personal skills and agency), social (e.g. workplace and soccer league networks) and economic (e.g. personal and collective finances) resources that community residents can put to political use. In my fieldwork I heard again and again about how regular people utilized the various assets already present in their neighborhoods to facilitate major episodes of collective action – sometimes, even without professional social movement organizations or financial assistance from external actors, such as private foundations or national organizations. From Filipina domestic workers' use of text messaging to organize their march contingent, to Dominican immigrants strapping a loudspeaker onto the back of a pickup truck then driving it around their neighborhood blasting a prerecorded announcement promoting their coming protest, throughout the nation immigrants used their unique skills and experiences – that they either migrated with or acquired while living in the U.S. – to mobilize their communities in ways that would culturally resonate with them. Thus, from a small rural city in the U.S. South like Fort Myers, to major coastal metropolises like L.A. and New York, my research spotlights the political capacities of different immigrant communities and the fact that political resources come in various forms and from a variety of places, including unexpected ones.

Relative differences in resources also help explain differences in how the demonstrations declined in each city studied. My findings show that the resources vital to the emergence of mass protests aren't necessarily the same ones needed to institutionalize or sustain large-scale collective action. For example, while New York and Los Angeles saw different levels of mobilization in 2006, the local movements in these cities were better able to channel the declining momentum into more formal and institutionalized politics – such as the 2007–2008 *Ya Es Hora!* campaign – because of their organizational infrastructures and previous experiences with electoral mobilization. On the other hand, organizers of the Fort Myers rally were, for the most part, political novices in both rabble-rousing and getting out the vote (GOTV). Because most of the Southwest Florida movement leaders were agricultural laborers, ethnic small business owners, and soccer league players – *not* professional activists working for formal organizations – they were not connected to the foundations and national coalitions that facilitated the massive naturalization, voter registration, and GOTV drives discussed in the previous chapter.

Related to the latter issue is the fact that having "papers" or citizenship was also an individual and collective political resource that varied across immigrant communities. The number of green card holders and U.S.-born members of immigrant families in each city was another factor vital to the ability of local movements to institutionalize their activism. Los Angeles and New York both had larger pools of second-generation and legal permanent residents who were eligible for naturalization and voter registration. Consequently, activists in these cities joined the national campaigns to target these populations in GOTV drives in hopes of demonstrating the electoral power of immigrants in their communities. As a local New York immigrant rights organizer explained, "There was this whole push to get people to understand that we're not just undocumented, a lot of us are citizens and we're going to come out and vote."[1]

This institutionalization of movement actions was less possible in places like Southwest Florida because, according to local activists, most of the people whom they had mobilized for their march were undocumented and thus ineligible to naturalize and vote. As a consequence, the decision to shift the national movement's focus to more formal forms of politics excluded many of the very people on whose behalf they were fighting. This finding indicates that while the demographic composition (especially with regard to generation and citizenship status) of a community can impact how a protest wave swells and how it declines, it can also determine the degree to which different segments of a movement can participate as the movement's strategies and priorities change. Nonetheless, in some cities, organizers showed that people without papers could also play important roles in electoral politics. Undocumented janitors in Los Angeles, for example, not only phone-banked and knocked on doors in order to get naturalized and U.S.-born members of their neighborhoods to vote for Barack Obama, but they also traveled to several battleground states to do the same. In fact, one of these janitors was picked up by immigration officials in New Mexico and spent several months in an immigration detention center as a result of her efforts.[2] Despite risking deportation, undocumented immigrants who participate in these types of GOTV drives help dispel the myth that people without papers are politically powerless during elections. As discussed further later, investment in the types of electoral mobilization campaigns that include undocumented, documented, and U.S.-born members of immigrant communities will be vital for their future political empowerment.

The Role of Coalitions

Immigration is perpetually changing the demographic makeup of the United States. As the populations of people from around the world, and especially from Africa, Asia, the Middle East, and Latin America, continue to shift, we must consider how these immigrant groups and their offspring will interact in the political sphere, both with one another and with native-born segments of U.S. society. Will their interests combine or collide? As noted in Chapter 4, some research gloomily suggests that the latter scenario is the more common of the two outcomes. However, for those of us interested in uniting these racial and ethnic minority groups, understanding when and how broad and diverse coalitions can be formed is crucial.

The cities studied in this book reveal how a specific type of external threat, combined with various types of social ties, can spur large coalitions composed of an assortment of religious, racial, and ethnic groups. Yet, as we also learned, these coalitions can be a double-edged sword. Although diversity can increase the number of groups that participate in movement mobilizations – in effect enhancing the potential for large-scale collective action – that same diversity can also pose significant challenges for organizers because attempting to represent diverse groups means attempting to coalesce diverse interests.

This burden, as we have seen, helps explains New York's underperformance during the protest wave. Not every foreign-born group in the city felt equally threatened by H.R. 4437; thus they were not equally invested in the legislative proposals being debated in Washington. For instance, Muslim legal permanent residents more interested in preventing another "special registration program" that categorized them as potential terrorists were not as enthusiastic as were, say, undocumented Central American immigrants to take to the streets and call for changes in the nation's deportation laws. With groups responding so differently to the issues at stake, their levels of mobilization varied. Activists in Los Angeles and Fort Myers did not face these same demographic challenges, at least to the same degree. As a result, relative to their populations, their mobilization efforts were more successful.

How the issue of immigrant "illegality" was racialized is also central to understanding why different immigrant communities mobilized to different degrees. Because Mexicans have been socially and politically constructed as the quintessential "illegals," my case studies with large Mexican descent populations – such as Los Angeles – or homogenous Mexican immigrant populations – such as Fort Myers – produced relatively larger protests because Mexicans (in terms of total numbers and policy interests) had more to gain and lose from both the legislative threat of H.R. 4437 and the policy alternatives called for by activists. Conversely, my case study with a more diverse foreign-born population (in terms of size, ethnicity, policy interests, and the like) hosted relatively smaller rallies. More precisely, my fieldwork indicates that while New York may have held smaller protests than other major immigrant metropolises, the groups that participated the most were Mexicans and Dominicans – the foreign-born populations acutely impacted by the proposed laws.

Finding common ground among the threats that different groups face, and the policy interests different groups are willing to mobilize around, are not the only challenge to coalition building across race and ethnicity. We have seen that ideological diversity in alliances can also impact decisions about which tactics and strategies a coalition (and factions within that coalition) decide to employ. At first, movement radicals and movement moderates were willing to put their political differences aside to unite against the Sensenbrenner Bill. But, as the threat of the nativist proposal diminished, strategic alliances began to crumble and prior ideological differences resurfaced; as a consequence, alternative or rival coalitions formed in several cities across the country. Thus, whereas a severe threat can bring together a variety of groups (and indeed, is essential for this initial unity), once this external grievance is gone, ideological diversity within coalitions becomes more salient and can fragment the alliance. Therefore, for both practical and theoretical purposes, recognizing that diversity can contribute to both the degree of mobilization and to the splintering of coalitions is imperative when developing future organizing strategies.

Regardless of the demographic makeup of their communities and the outcomes of their efforts, the three cities examined in this book also tell us a lot about the different paths alliance building can take: the three types identified in my case studies being the transformation of existing coalitions into new ones; the activation of previously established but dormant alliances; and the brokerage of new organizational connections. For example, in Los Angeles, *La Placita* Working Group, which was originally created in response to the shooting and killing of a young migrant by border patrol agents, transformed into what became the March 25 Coalition, whose primary focus was to organize a mass demonstration to help defeat H.R. 4437. In New York, the process started a bit differently; networks and coalitions that had been formed over years of organizing around other issues – such as police brutality, bilingual city services, and labor rights – were activated and reunited to form a broad alliance against the Sensenbrenner Bill. Lastly, in Southwest Florida, the coalition that organized the Fort Myers march was brokered by informal immigrant community leaders – not professional activists, as in the latter two cities – who served as central nodes within the social fabric of their communities. Owners of local Spanish-language newspapers and magazines convened the small ethnic businesses that advertised in their papers and the league presidents of the soccer teams they covered. The coalition between these two vital immigrant social networks was fundamental to the successful mass mobilization that occurred in Fort Myers. Hence, although a blend of transformation, activation, and brokerage was – to varying degrees – key to the coalition formation processes in Los Angeles, New York, and Southwest Florida, these cases highlight the unique ways that alliances can be initiated and develop.

The Role of the Media

Fundamental to large-scale collective action is the ability to make a significant number of people aware of the need to mobilize. During the immigrant rights protest wave, this information was diffused through various personal, community, and organizational networks. However, the mass media can and did also play an important role in this process, particularly because of its ability to broadcast across large geographical areas. Unfortunately, most of what we know about the role of the media in U.S. social movements focuses solely on English-language news sources. My research shows that many of the results of previous studies may not apply (in the same way or to the same degree) to how movements composed of foreign-born people interact with ethnic media outlets.[3] For instance, much of the established research contends that activists usually attempt to stage large demonstrations to draw the attention of news sources in the hope of gaining sympathetic coverage. Yet, organizers of the 2006 immigrant rights protests actually *used* mainstream Spanish-language media to amplify their calls for action. As a result, via local newspaper, radio, and television coverage, Latino immigrants witnessed people 'just like them' participating in marches across the country, and were inspired to do the same. As a local East Coast activist described the phenomenon: "I think a lot of Latinos here listen to radio coming out of L.A. so they heard a lot of the DJs" and got "all excited" about participating in the rallies. It also "definitely drove a lot of people that were kind of on the fence about coming out" when "they saw in the news that a million people marched in L.A." They said, "Holy shit, I better get out there!" Clearly, ethnic media was crucial in helping the series of demonstrations emerge and multiply. But how and why were protest organizers able to get this unprecedented support from and access to mainstream Spanish-language news and entertainment outlets?

My data show that whereas the English-language media is expected to serve only as a source of information, ethnic news outlets also assist immigrants in politically integrating into their host country. Consequently, immigrant advocates dedicated to helping incorporate the foreign-born into U.S. society have developed strong working relationships with members of Spanish-language media. These social ties helped activists access the airwaves. Additionally, as mostly Latino immigrants themselves (Rodriguez 1999; Mora 2014), members of the Spanish-language media often possess the same collective identities as their audiences and thus can be motivated to support movement mobilization efforts against nativist actions. Put another way, their sense of racial group consciousness and linked-fate can also be activated by anti-immigrant attacks.

That being said, the ethnic composition of a city's immigrant population also greatly impacts the influence that ethnic media can have on immigrant mobilization drives. For example, as the largest Spanish-language media market in the nation, the L.A. area has long had a number of well-established and far-reaching Spanish-language newspapers, radio and television stations. In Southwest Florida, though relatively young – and small, in terms of the size of their individual audiences – Spanish-language radio and print media outlets are also central to the spread of information in Latino immigrant communities. Because Mexicans compose not only most of the audience but also most of the staff of the news outlets in both Los Angeles and Fort Myers, the Spanish-language media in these locations identified more with the cause and had more at stake during the immigration debate.

These dynamics played out somewhat differently in New York, which has more heterogeneous immigrant and Latino populations. Because various foreign-born groups have different histories and tenures in the city, each community's media infrastructure also differs in terms of size, reach, and format. Some immigrant groups may not be large enough to have daily newspapers or television stations that cater to them. Others may have only a radio program (*not* station) that airs once a week or twice a month. As such, not all immigrant groups have the same capability to mass-mobilize through their ethnic media. Moreover, places like New York have large Latino populations as well as high degrees of subgroup diversity. Whereas in Los Angeles, Mexicans have several radio stations catering to their musical preferences, most of New York's major Spanish-language radio stations target the larger Caribbean Latino community. Because of this, its likely that not all staff members at these media outlets were impacted in the same ways by H.R. 4437, and thus did not identify equally with the threat. As a result, the *New York Times* noted at the time, "While many of the [Latino] radio stations in New York are involved in promoting the rally, they have not joined forces the way those in Los Angeles did."[4]

To recap, although many of the same factors – such as the formation of diverse coalitions, the use of ethnic media outlets, and the activation of preexisting local community resources – helped facilitate the three episodes of collective action investigated in this book, the roles they played and how they materialized depended largely on the distinct local dynamics of each city studied. What did not vary across the country, however, was the disappointment immigrant rights activists felt during President Obama's eight years in office. In the remainder of this chapter, I look back to reflect upon how the movement fared under the Obama Administration and then look forward to speculate about the potential Latinos have to transform the politics of race and immigration in the United States.

Immigrant Rights Under the Obama Administration

Whereas the previous chapter showed us how activists channeled the momentum of the 2006 demonstrations into the 2008 election, their experiences under the Obama Administration teach us that while protest is not enough, neither is helping elect a politician into office. In other words, if protest has its limits, so does voting. Immigrant rights activists learned that helping people win an election is one thing, but holding them accountable and shaping their legislative priorities after they have taken office is another. With Obama as the most pro-immigrant candidate in the 2008 presidential race, immigrant advocates across the country had high hopes for his election, especially after Democrats seemed poised take power in both chambers of Congress. Unfortunately, several key factors outside of the movement's control, and later decisions made by the new administration, quickly dashed these hopes.

Despite having a bulletproof majority in the House, the sixty votes in the Senate that would have made the Democratic Party's legislative agenda filibuster-proof were not so solid. Obama claimed on the campaign trail that immigration would be a top legislative priority his first year in office, but three key factors intervened. Even if no Republican and all of the Democratic Senators supported the new president's preferred immigration policy reforms, two senate elections and a tragic death thwarted his party from possessing the sixty votes it needed to pass his first-year legislative priorities.

In the 2008 Minnesota Senate race between incumbent Republican Norm Coleman and Democratic challenger Al Franken, the results were so close that a recount was necessary and several appeals were filed. Franken eventually won, but it took over eight months for him to be sworn into office. On top of this, after losing in the Connecticut Democratic primary, conservative Democratic senator Joe Lieberman ran and won his state's general election as an Independent. Due to tension between him and his former party, whether the controversial senator – who often sided with Republicans on important issues – would caucus with Democrats or the GOP remained unclear during the president's first year in office. Lastly, Obama's key ally in the Senate and the legislative leader in the fight for immigration reform, Senator Ted Kennedy, spent the first few months of the new administration in a battle with brain cancer, which he lost in August 2009. To make matters worse, his seat was eventually taken over by a Republican, Scott Brown.

These three events prevented any liberal policy proposals from becoming law without the support of Republicans in the Senate – who, after losing power, were in no mood to help political rivals push a progressive legislative agenda; in fact, they did everything possible to block Obama's policy proposals (McAdam and Kloos 2014; Wong 2017). Moreover, the main legislative battle Democrats chose to undertake in this political environment was healthcare reform, which took much longer and required more political capital than they had expected. Furthermore, soon after getting elected, the economic recession that Obama inherited hit rock bottom, rendering any argument to legalize 11 million undocumented workers a hard sell to an increasingly unemployed U.S. public. Hence, again, factors beyond the control of both the movement and the new administration prevented the legalization that activists had hoped for and that Obama had promised.

Even more disheartening to immigrant advocates, perhaps to deflect the pervasive conservative criticism that Democrats were unwilling to "protect" or "regain control" of the country's borders, the federal government decided to employ an "enforcement first" approach to immigration reform (Gonzales 2013). Although never proposing anything nearly as punitive as the Republican-sponsored Sensenbrenner Bill – and continuing to state its support for legalization and immigration reform – the Obama Administration out-enforced Republicans by drastically increasing deportations. Even moderate Washington, D.C. advocates, who once supported this legislative approach, eventually came to admit that acquiescing to conservative demands to reduce undocumented migration by increasing enforcement measures – in exchange for later support for legalization – proved to be a failed strategy for liberals (Wessler 2010). Throughout President Obama's eight years in office, people were deported at a higher rate than under George W. Bush's Administration, while Republicans continuously prevented the passing of even minimal legalization programs, such as the Dream Act, which proposes to grant legal residency to undocumented children who were raised and successfully completed high school in the U.S., and who want to go on to college or join the military. The main lesson here for activists is that having the public support of a president they help elect does not guarantee that the commander-in-chief will prioritize (or be able to enact) a movement's policy goals. Having said that, the electoral influence the immigrant rights movement deployed during the 2008 election was not expended in vain; it just was not enough. More was and is needed.

On a more positive note, the radical flank of the movement has shown us that despite advocates' lack of success in winning major policy reform, smaller victories can still be won. For instance, as described in Chapters 5 and 6, right-wing media played a central role in the demonization of the 2006 demonstrations. In response, grassroots organizations launched new and innovative on-line campaigns, such as Presente.org's "*Basta* Dobbs" and Race Forward's "Drop the I-Word" campaigns. In reaction to CNN anchor Lou Dobbs' consistent attacks on immigrants and promotion of racist anti-Latino conspiracy theories, activists launched the former campaign to pressure the news network to oust the controversial television host.[5] While neither CNN nor Dobbs have admitted that the campaign was the reason why the rabid nativist anchor left the network, activists claim this as a major victory given that his 2009 departure coincided with the peak of their national pressure.[6] In a similar fashion, aiming to get the mainstream media to stop using the dehumanizing label of "illegal" to describe people who are undocumented, the "Drop the I-Word" campaign convinced the *Associated Press, Los Angeles Times, USA Today,* and several other major news outlets to stop using the derogatory term.[7]

In addition, reminiscent of the role that the Student Nonviolent Coordinating Committee (SNCC) and other student-led groups played during the black civil rights movement, today undocumented youth (known as "Dreamers") have been the shock-troops of the immigrant rights movement. Fed up with the national movement's failure to win comprehensive policy reform through their electoral and lobbying efforts, these young activists turned to militant civil disobedience and won a key administrative victory when in 2012 President Obama announced the establishment of a new program called Deferred Action for Childhood Arrivals (DACA), which allowed hundreds of thousands of undocumented youth to legally remain and work in the country on a temporary basis (Nicholls 2013: 153; Zimmerman 2016: 1900; Patler and Gonzales 2015: 1458). While important, this policy did not help the vast majority of people without papers in the U.S. and can be undone by the Trump Administration or future presidents.[8] Nonetheless, given the GOP's continued blocking of federal comprehensive immigration reform, many activists welcomed these and several other types of minor but significant victories under the Obama Administration.[9]

Another disappointing development for activists was the degree to which the politics of immigration went local after the 2006 protest wave (Gulasekaram and Ramakrishnan 2015). As the data presented in Chapter 5 revealed, following the mass marches there was a large spike in the introduction and passage of state-level immigration laws across the country, most of which were punitive. Several quantitative studies have since shown that locations where Republicans compose the majority of residents (Ramakrishnan and Wong 2010) and where Republicans control state legislatures (Wallace 2014) were more likely to pass nativist immigration legislation. In other words, local and state anti-immigrant laws are largely Republican actions. Nevertheless, pro-immigrant forces

have also won important local victories (Gulasekaram and Ramakrishnan 2015). States such as California, Hawaii, New York, Illinois, Connecticut, Oregon, and Massachusetts have all passed "Domestic Worker
Bill of Rights" laws, which have gained important protections for some
of the most vulnerable immigrant workers in the country.[10] I point to
these examples not only to highlight the devolution of immigration policies but also to state that both pro- and anti-local immigration legislations can serve as important testing grounds for what the impacts of federal immigration reforms might be, either restrictive or integrative. For
instance, if, as some studies suggest, anti-immigrant ordinances have negative effects on local economies, this might serve as a warning to both
local and federal elected officials as they contemplate similar nativist legislation.[11] Likewise, if, for example, granting undocumented immigrants
access to driver's licenses or allowing undocumented youth to legally
work or attend college is shown to have positive effects on states, these
results can serve as evidence to bolster immigrant advocates' cases for
passing similar legislation at the national level. With that said, one important implication of this book's findings, and of Donald Trump's rise to
power, is that the politics of immigration is, more often than not, not
primarily about material outcomes. The politics of immigration, like so
many of the most divisive elements of American life, is, at bottom, about
race.

Race, Immigration, and the Future of Latino Politics

If the problem of the twentieth century was the problem of the "color-
line," then the problem of the twenty-first century is the problem of the
"border-line," albeit a colored one. Few issues ignite more passion, con-
troversy, and debate than what has come to be known as "the third rail of
American politics" – immigration.[12] From their economic to their social
and cultural contributions at the local and national levels, the foreign-
born are changing the United States to a degree never before seen in the
nation's history. Among their most significant impacts is how the demographic changes that have resulted from post-1965 immigration demand
a more nuanced account of race and racism, one that draws on the past
but updates it to confront the unique challenges of the present.

The passage of the Immigration and Nationality Act of 1965 ended
the United State's infamously discriminatory "racial quotas" immigration
system, which gave preference to white western and northern European
nations (Ngai 2005; Zolberg 2006). Since the enactment of this law, the

share of the total U.S. immigrant population from Africa, Asia, and the Americas (primarily Latin America) has gone from less than 25 percent in 1960 to over 88 percent in 2015, dramatically changing the country's racial composition.[13] How these groups have been received in the United States illustrates how historical time, context, and geographic location differently imbue social markers beyond solely skin color – such as accents, body types, legal status, and religion – with racial meanings that are all too frequently used to marginalize certain segments of society.[14] Immigrants from the global south have thus complicated the conventional and historically inaccurate black/white U.S. racial paradigm[15] and continue to transform our understanding of race and democracy in America. Therefore, it is of the utmost importance that we understand the relationship between their racialization and political incorporation processes.

Some citizenship theorists contend that the specific "patterns and forms of political, cultural, and economic" integration of immigrants today is best described as "exclusionary inclusion," a "type of belonging that regulates and restricts the degree and nature of participation in the primary institutions of society" (Rocco 2014: 152). Immigrant rights activists go even further, contending that America's current "incorporation" of foreign-born people of color should be understood as a system of "immigrant apartheid," a "set of institutional and political processes leading to the creation of separate social, political, and economic spaces for citizens and noncitizens, derived from distinctions based" on one's legal status (Kateel and Shahani 2008). Other critics add that while the civil rights movement has made blatant forms of legal and societal racism unacceptable, these forms of discrimination are still sanctioned under the pretext of someone's perceived national origin or citizenship status (Johnson 2004: 15–16). Recent anti-immigrant legislation, such as Arizona's "papers please law" (SB 1070), that have the effect of using the suspicion of lack of legal documentation as the impetus to racially profile and target an entire population – in this case, Latinos – serve as additional evidence to support the latter arguments. Yet, it is important to note that today's immigrants and people of color of immigrant descent are not passive bystanders to these practices – as this book has made evident, they sometimes resist, revolt, and radically challenge these conditions.

Across the history of the United States, the struggles for democratic inclusion through political engagement and processes of racial identity formation have gone hand in hand (Omni and Winant 1994). As such, understanding how contemporary immigrant communities respond to political attacks through political participation, and how their identities both impact and are impacted by these actions, is fundamental to comprehending contemporary racial politics in America. The 2006 immigrant rights protest wave – arguably one of the most pivital moments in Latino political history – showed us that racially charged legislative threats against undocumented immigrants also impact and will be contested by U.S.-born and naturalized members of their communities. This finding buttresses a vital element of immigrant politics – the dependence of people without papers on political brokers – and has important implications for what I contend is the coalescing of Latino politics and the issue of immigrant rights.

Although the growth of the Latino electorate is, in many respects, contingent on the continuation of high levels of immigration (Bowler and Segura 2011; Ramirez 2013), the political influence of immigrants today, especially the undocumented, is likewise largely dependent on Latino voters. Because people without papers cannot vote, and policymakers are most receptive to their electorates, to win the legislative outcomes they desire undocumented immigrants must gain the support of allies who can exert electoral influence. In other words, noncitizens need political brokers, and naturalized and U.S.-born citizens of recent immigrant descent are best suited to, and have a common interest in, playing this role. The 2006 protest wave and its aftermath underscore that racialized nativism is, and will continue to be, the key element that fuses and maintains this mutually reinforcing political dynamic. Consequently, as long as nativist activists and politicians continue to "alienize" (Sandoval 2014) citizen members of immigrant communities as "perpetual foreigners," we can expect this phenomenon to endure. Because of how the issue of immigration is currently racialized, and because Latinos are the largest minority group with the largest number of foreign-born members, they are crucial to any political influence the immigrant rights movement hopes to exert.

A major implication of my argument is that the immigrant rights movement is significantly dependent on the political power of Latino voters and Latino elected officials. This can make it difficult for non-Latino immigrant groups to put their distinct policy concerns on the movement's political agenda. That said, America's current forms of racialized nativism provide some opportunities for organizing across differences. For example, Donald Trump's attacks on both Mexicans and Muslims during his presidential campaign were not unprecedented. As Lisa Cacho (2012) has keenly pointed out, just as the rhetoric of immigrant "illegality" (usually deployed solely against Latinos) was used to demonize Middle Eastern immigrants immediately after 9/11, "anti-terrorist" rhetoric (typically reserved for Arabs and Muslims) was also used to push through policies and proposals (including H.R. 4437) that adversely targeted and impacted U.S.- and foreign-born Latinos (29–30). Moreover, the fact that attacks against Latino immigrants, African-Americans, Muslims, and the LGBT community – all groups disparaged by the Trump/Pence campaign – increased immediately after the 2016 presidential election, suggests that opportunities to form diverse coalitions against a hostile administration will not only be possible, but needed.[16]

Uniting over crosscutting issues will undoubtedly be a difficult task, given that "the most vulnerable populations in the United States are often represented as if they are the primary sources" of the social denigration of other maringalized groups (Cacho 2012: 27). But by identifying the intersections of multiple, overlapping oppressions, activists can attempt to develop unifying agendas, narratives, and actions; undertakings that are undoubtedly easier said than done but that are demanded in order to build a movement that is fully inclusive and representative of the various struggles and forms of subjugation endured by America's diverse foreign-born populations. Fortunately, the organizing strategies of queer Latino and non-Latino immigrant activists have proven that taking an intersectional approach is both feasible and fundamental to the future of the immigrant rights movement (Rodriguez 2003; Das Gupta 2006; Chavez 2013; Quesada et al. 2015; Terriquez 2015).

To maximize its effectiveness, however, immigrant activism must be accompanied by the ability to pose an electoral threat to legislators. Too many elected officials – on the left and the right – easily dismissed the 2006 marchers as "nonvoting illegals" who, because they lacked the franchise, posed no political threat. Ultimately, for local and national pro-immigrant policies to be enacted, both political parties have to feel that the costs of not passing these types of laws are greater than the possible consequences of doing so. Accordingly, if immigrants and their allies cannot impact the chances of a politician (Democrat or Republican) winning their next election, activists should not expect the representative to pay attention to their demands.

A multi-year, three-prong approach – like the one documented in the previous chapter – with widely publicized and geographically targeted naturalization, voter registration, and GOTV drives, could help lay the groundwork for the type of pro-immigrant electoral influence needed to pressure politicians to pass progressive immigration policies. A major obstacle to enacting this proposal is the fact that a significant amount of post-2000 Latino immigration has been undocumented and has gone to "new immigrant receiving destinations" – such as the rural Midwest and U.S. South – that lack large numbers U.S.-born Latinos and legal permanent residents who could become citizens and voters. Nonetheless, many of the American-born children of immigrants in these locations may be becoming politicized by the attacks on their undocumented parents, family members, friends, and neighbors that have occurred since 2006 and that are likely to continue under the Trump Administration.[17] This suggests that these potential pro-immigrant voters and new generation of immigrant rights activists may eventually play important roles in Midwestern and Southern politics. If this scenario were to materialize in the coming decades, it could alter the American electoral landscape for years to come. The 2016 election provides some valuable insights as to where developments such as these may already be occurring.

Although Donald Trump's 2016 electoral victory was a devastating blow to immigrant rights advocates, it also overshadowed some important implications about the future role that Latino voters could play at all levels of U.S. politics. Locally, grassroots protests in conjunction with door knocking, voter registration, and GOTV drives – similar to the *Ya Es Hora!* campaign – helped oust the notoriously nativist and anti-Latino Arizona Sheriff Joe Arpaio after over-20 years in office (Lazare 2016; Itkowitz 2016). At the state level, similar immigrant voter mobilization drives in Nevada helped elect the first Latina U.S. Senator, Mexican-American Catherine Castro Masto, who during her victory speech promised to be "one hell of a check and balance" on Donald Trump.[18] In terms of the presidential election, the Democratic Party and the Hilary Clinton campaign were criticized for failing to invest in targeting Latino voters the same way, and to the same degree, President Obama successfully did during his two victorious campaigns.[19] Yet, despite what a former DNC employee characterized as "pitiful" Latino mobilization efforts by the Democratic Party, Donald Trump's nativist rhetoric drove an unprecedented proportion of Latino voters (79%) to cast ballots for the Democratic ticket.[20] Moreover, Latinos helped Democrats win the key swing states of Colorado, New Mexico, and Nevada. In fact, despite Clinton ultimately losing the battleground state of Florida and the traditionally solid red state of Arizona, Latino voters came out at record rates and helped put these states in play for Democrats.[21]

The level of Latino voter turnout in 2016 is all the more fascinating when one considers the facts that not only did Republicans enact several voter suppression techniques – from new voter ID laws to reducing the number of polling places – that disproportionately negatively affect communities of color,[22] but there was also no large-scale effort to mobilize Latinos to the same degree as the 2007–2008 *Ya Es Hora!* campaign. Again, if immigrant rights advocates hope to ever win progressive immigration reform and to prevent another overtly nativist candidate like Donald Trump from winning the presidency, activists, foundations, and the Democratic Party must invest in the types of time-consuming, expensive, and tedious Latino naturalization, voter registration, and voter turnout drives documented in this book.

In fact, given that immigration was once again the top issue for Latino voters during the 2016 election,[23] and similar to what occurred after the passage of H.R. 4437, the anti-Latino rhetoric and actions likely to come during a Trump presidency may provide the exact type of fodder needed to make a multi-year campaign like the one proposed above effective. Doing so could eventually convert Colorado, Nevada, and New Mexico into solidly Democratic states and allow the DNC to focus on turning Florida blue again and making Arizona into an actual swing state. Furthermore, the fact that millennials made up almost half (44%) of the over 27 million Latinos eligible to vote in 2016 (Krogstad et al. 2016), and that the vast majority of Latino millennials overwhelmingly supported an openly socialist candidate – Bernie Sanders – during the Democratic primaries, suggests that we could expect the Latino electorate to become increasingly progressive and even more supportive of immigrant rights in the coming years.[24] Indeed, that 93 percent of Latino youth are born in the United States and over 800,000 (one every 30 seconds, or over 66,000 a month) turn 18 each year and become eligible to vote, means that the Latino voting bloc will continue to grow both in size and importance.[25]

In conclusion, on top of continuing to invest in the development of local grassroots immigrant rights organizations, if the five-state strategy laid out above were to be successfully implemented, it could engender an epic political shift that permanently keeps anti-immigrant presidential candidates out of the White House. Whether the foundations that fund, and the Latino and immigrant rights leaders who devise and drive future strategies are committed to building a social movement with this kind of long-term political power remains to be seen. What we can say with confidence is that people from Latin America will continue migrating, transforming, and staking their rightful claim as part of the social, cultural, economic, and political fabric of the United States. We can also anticipate that as anti-Latino nativism continues to grow in reaction to these demographic changes, immigration will remain the defining issue in Latino politics and will continue to demonstrate that the fates of U.S.- and foreign-born Latinos are not only linked but also sealed due to American racism. However, as this book has shown, when met with xenophobic attacks, we can also expect Latinos (with and without papers) to fight back – on the streets and at the ballot box – in defense of their families and communities. No president, bill, or wall – no matter how high – will stop us from doing so.

Appendix A

Research Design

The primary data used in this study come from 131 semi-structured, in-depth interviews conducted in four cities, between 2006–2009, with a wide range of actors. These people included both foreign- and U.S.-born local immigrant rights protest organizers (from paid activists who work for formal organizations to neighborhood residents who before 2006 had never participated in activism before), as well as national labor, business, civil rights, pro- and anti-immigration policy reform lobbyists. When necessary and possible, I triangulated my qualitative evidence with statistics from the U.S. Census and the Department of Homeland Security, and survey research from various think tanks and polling firms. These data sources were also supplemented with information collected from newspaper archives, protest flyers, activist Web sites, secondary scholarly sources, and over a decade of participation in the U.S. immigrant rights movement.

In this methodological appendix, I discuss the details of my case study selection process, why interview data was best suited to answer my main research queries, how I identified interviewees and the types of questions I asked them, as well as the implications of my findings for other locations where immigrant rights mobilizations have and may occur. Furthermore, when discussing research designs and methodologies, political scientists rarely ever mention the roles that their identities and personal politics play in the questions they choose to investigate and in the collection and analysis of their data. Breaking from this tradition, I close with some brief remarks about the objectivity and benefits of research produced by scholar-activists (such as myself) who have personal and political investments in, and commitments to, the communities and movements we study.

Case Studies of Immigrant Mass Mobilization

Gerring (2007) asserts that while a *case* "connotes a spatially delimited phenomenon (a unit) observed at a single point in time or over some period of time" (19), a *case study* "may be understood as the intensive study of a single case where the purpose of that study is – at least in part – to shed light on the larger class of cases" (20).[1] Accordingly, in this book I utilize case studies of large-scale collective action in Los Angeles, New York, and Fort Myers to help both empirically and theoretically enhance our understanding of the 2006 immigrant rights protest wave that swept across the United States. I chose this research strategy because case studies are the most appropriate methodological approach for studying "why" and "how" questions (Yin 201: 4; Small 2009: 25) that, to be answered, require the reconstruction of social processes through the use of detailed descriptions and multiple data sources (Flick 2009: 134; Berg 2004: 251). This type of research is usually "open-ended and flexible in terms of both the design and execution," and is able to adapt to the exigencies of the field with regard to incorporating "new data sources and data-gathering opportunities as they arise" (Snow and Trom 200: 153; Creswell 2003: 181). Investigating social phenomena in this fashion enables us to better ground our observations and concepts, and can offer scholars empirical and theoretical gains in understanding the broader contexts of where the behaviors of actors take place (Orum et al. 1991: 7, 8). At its best, case study research helps produce a holistic understanding of reality that captures the nuances, complexities, and contradictions of people's actions (Flyvbjerg 201: 303; Sjoberg et al. 1991: 39). These core characteristics and benefits of case studies are especially useful when researchers are interested in discovering and analyzing the causal forces behind specific processes and outcomes (Ragin 2004: 133; Bennett and Elman 2006), such as the mobilization of a particular population around a particular issue, and then the effects of that mobilization. Thus, because the main goals of my study were to investigate why and how the 2006 demonstrations emerged and declined, as well as what, if any, impacts they had, a case study approach was best equipped to answer my specific research questions.

Given the dynamic nature of both political activism and case study research, it is not surprising that most social movement scholarship has been based on case studies of individual movements (Snow and Trom 2002: 146). Over the last decade, students of contentious politics continue to use case studies but have begun to focus more on analyzing the inner workings of the numerous mechanisms – independent, stable factors that, under specific conditions, link causes to effects (George and Bennett 2005: 8) – that influence the major processes (e.g. framing, coalition building, mobilization, etc.) of social movements that scholars have identified (McAdam, Tarrow, and Tilly 2001; Tilly and Tarrow 2006). Such a methodological approach is akin to what is commonly known as *process tracing* (George and Bennett 2005: 6; Gerring 2007: 173; Vennesson 2008: 231). According to Beach and Pedersen (2013), process tracing as a mode of analysis is analogous to classic detective work, where researchers work backward "from the outcome by sifting through the evidence in an attempt to uncover" the (often eclectic) combination of causal mechanisms that produce the specific consequences or processes being studied (3, 19–20, 29; see also George and Bennett 2005: 6). Here I have investigated the motivations, resources, networks, tactics, and strategies that activists utilized to coordinate and organize local and national protests, and that national lobbyists used in their attempts to influence the policymaking process. In this manner, as is illustrated throughout the book, I explored the main mechanisms, the resulting processes, and some of the direct and indirect outcomes of the unprecedented 2006 immigrant protest wave.

Selection of Case Studies: Los Angeles, New York, and . . . Fort Myers?

Scholars have numerous options when it comes to how they select their cases, as well as how they categorize those cases and justify their selections (Eckstein 1975; Seawright and Gerring 2008; Vennesson 2008; Flyvbjerg 2011). For example, whereas a "representative" case "exemplifies what is considered to be a typical set of values, given some general understanding of a phenomenon" (Gerring 2007: 91), a "deviant" case is one that for empirical or theoretical reasons is unusual (Seawright and Gerring 2008: 302) and thus especially useful for developing new concepts and comprehending the limits of existing theories (Flyvbjerg 2011: 307). In addition, case studies can be selected and conceptualized at different stages of the research process, and for different reasons. For instance, while some scholars classify and select specific cases at the start of their research process, it is not uncommon for researchers to not be aware of what their study is a "case of" until after they've collected and analyzed their evidence (Ragin 1994: 90). Moreover, during their investigations, social scientists often change or drop cases (Ragin 2004: 125) and even "mix and match," when they realize that their cases can fit multiple classifications or types (Gerring 2007: 147).

Overall, according to Flick (2009), the basic principle should be "to select cases or case groups according to concrete criteria concerning" their relevance and "their content instead of using abstract methodological" principles (121). Thus, what is important for qualitative researchers is not that they randomly select representative cases, but that they clearly explain their theoretical justifications for their selections based on their particular research questions and the literatures they're engaging with (Warren and Karner 2010: 141; Levy 2008: 7). The 2006 immigrant rights demonstrations provide several valuable instances of collective action that are both politically significant and theoretically interesting, and that meet the aforementioned criteria.

As stated at the start of this book, among the several surprising aspects of the immigrant rights rallies are some of the unexpected locations where many of them took place, as well as the over- and underperformance of certain cities in terms of the magnitudes of the protests they hosted. For example, the surprising success of marches held in locales with no real history of immigrant activism and no professional social movement groups complicates our understanding of the significance of organizations, because both traditional resource mobilization and political process theories tell us that they are vital to the emergence of mass mobilization (McCarthy and Zald 1977; Clemens and Minkoff 2004). In addition, some places that did possess organizational resources and histories of immigrant activism arguably did not mobilize to the degree that one would have expected them to. These cases challenge what social movement theory has taught us, in that some of the cities where the movement had relatively more resources and had more open political opportunity structures were "out-mobilized" by places without these assets and favorable local political contexts.

In order to better comprehend these and other theoretical anomalies of the historic protests, I followed the well-established tradition of social movement scholars studying "synecdochical or revelatory" cases. Snow and Trom (2002) explain that these are cases in which "a detailed, holistic study of a specific case is used as a springboard, in almost a synecdochical fashion, for gaining insight into and understanding of the larger movement of which it is a part" (158–163). Following this chain of reasoning, and as I explain below, I sought out cases that could be labeled as *negative*, *critical*, and *extreme*. My belief was that these qualities would best enrich our theoretical understanding of the dynamics of immigrant mass mobilization in general, and the 2006 demonstrations in particular. Consequently, and due to resource and time constraints, I chose not to focus on anywhere in which we would expect little-to-no mobilization, and where relatively little-to-no mobilization actually took place. Furthermore, while studying the absence of mobilization can be an important and theoretically rich endeavor, all books have their limits and foci. My goal was not to analyze *any* level of immigrant protest, but to investigate the dynamics of immigrant large-scale collective action. With that said, in Chapter 4, the issue of why certain immigrant groups participated more than others is analyzed and discussed at length.

I chose to investigate the City of Los Angeles because – due to its long history of immigrant organizing and its vibrant and well established local immigrant rights movement – it is a place where high levels of mobilization would have been expected to and actually did occur: L.A. hosted the largest immigrant rights protest in U.S. history on March 25, 2006, when between 500,000 and a million people descended on City Hall. Los Angeles is also home to the largest Spanish-language media market in the country. Given the important role ethnic media outlets played in the marches (Ramirez 2013; Dionne et al. 2014), this makes L.A. an exceptionally important locale to examine. For these reasons, this case is theoretically intriguing because it is a successful instance of migrant mass mobilization where we are able to examine how well established social movement theories and research on the role of the media in contentious politics hold up. As such, the City of Angels is an example of a *critical case*. In these cases, "the issue of the typicality or representativeness of the case is essentially irrelevant, since it is particular features or characteristics of the case that make it an ideal or critical one for the set of issues or concerns in question" (Snow and Trom 2002: 158–159).

New York City, by contrast, is theoretically valuable for very different reasons. Case selection "can also be justified methodologically on the grounds that they are" *negative* "or 'deviant' in relation to other cases of the same genre or some set of principles" (Snow and Trom 2002: 159; Levy 2008: 13). Accordingly, New York is of interest because although it also has a long history of immigrant activism, a highly developed immigrant rights organizational infrastructure, and the largest citywide immigrant population in the nation, its level of mobilization was nowhere close to the size of protests held in other major immigrant metropolises. Estimates of the Empire City's largest actions ranged from 50,000 to 100,000, as opposed to 500,000 to over a million in places such as Dallas, Chicago, and L.A. Because of this discrepancy, I explored possible reasons for this relative underperformance. Moreover, unlike the aforementioned cities whose immigrant populations are more homogenous and primarily

Mexican, New York has perhaps the most diverse metropolitan immigrant population in the nation, with several groups larger than those of Mexican descent. These demographics make New York an interesting case to investigate because it allows us to examine how immigrant collective action plays out in heterogeneous settings, and why different immigrant groups may mobilize to different degrees.

Researching *extreme cases* can also be theoretically informative. These cases are chosen "on the grounds that they ... stand outside of or beyond the genre of cases with which they are typically associated" (Snow and Trom 2002: 159; Seawright and Gerring 2008: 301). As such, my third case study city is Fort Myers, FL, a locale where little to no mobilization was expected, yet where one of the largest marches in the national protest wave took place. The city's total population was only about 50,000, of which less than 15 percent were Latinos at the time.[2] Yet despite its small size and its relatively new history of Mexican immigration, local police and activists estimated that 80,000 to over 100,000 people – the vast majority of whom were Latino – marched for immigrant rights in this southern city. Thus, we cannot help but wonder how a place with practically no immigrant rights organizational infrastructure, a relatively small Latino and immigrant population, and no long history of prior activism, reached such a degree of collective action. Investigating why and how immigrant mass mobilization occurred in an unlikely location is of the utmost importance for both scholars and activists, given that the former seek in part to predict future social unrest, while a common goal of the latter is to create that unrest.

Finally, because of the unprecedented nature and scope of the nationwide marches, investigating whether or not they had any effects is essential. Many observers of the protest wave have contended that the rallies produced little if any positive results. Others have argued that the rallies may have even had a negative effect on the population that activists claimed to be fighting for – undocumented immigrants – given the increases in state and societal anti-immigrant actions that followed the groundswell of marches (see Chapter 5). I believe the real answer is more complicated and have sought to explore a variety of effects that the protest wave contributed to. Because the rallies were sparked in response to a proposed federal anti-immigrant law and during a congressional election year, I used survey and census data as well as in-depth interviews with mostly Washington, D.C.-based immigration reform lobbyists and national leaders, to investigate what effects the marches had on the immigration policymaking process and national electoral politics. Leaders of a range of national organizations, focused on business, labor, civil rights, and immigration, helped reveal the impacts of the mass mobilizations, both direct and indirect, positive and negative. Using the insights gained from both the local and national data I collected between 2006 and 2009, I was able to reconstruct the inner workings and the external factors that help explain the historic protest wave and some of its impacts.

Face-to-Face Interviews: Who and Why

Qualitative interviews are a vital source of evidence for investigating and developing a holistic account of behaviors and events, as well as the meanings that participants attribute to those same behaviors and events (Warren and Karner 2010: 129; Weiss 1994: 10). Consequently, interview data are acutely valuable to researchers utilizing a process-tracing approach in their studies. As Van Evera (1997) explains, "Evidence that a given stimulus created a given response can be sought in the sequence and structure of events and/or in the testimony of actors explaining why they acted as they did" (65). When studying collective action in particular, interviewing respondents who "were close to the decision-making process or to some other development that set events in motion" is imperative (Weiss 1994: 181). Thus, because my primary research questions focused on how and why the mass mobilizations came to be, interviewing the individuals who actually coordinated the 2006 protests was essential; an interviewee selection strategy called "purposive sampling." Schutt (212) explains that, "In purposive sampling, each sample element is selected for a purpose, usually because of the unique position of the sample elements" (157). When using this sampling technique, decisions about who to interview are based on the study's primary research questions, informants' distinct knowledge of the issue or experience being examined, and with the goal of obtaining a range of points of view (Hesse-Biber 2013: 192; Schutt 2012: 157). Given my research questions and the important mobilizing roles these individuals played in the protest wave, my case study interviews focused on participants and leaders of local and national coalitions, including members of rival movement factions.

Although most participants in and organizers of the nationwide marches were Latino – and, as a result, so were most of my informants – I also conducted interviews with a variety of other local activists, both

U.S.-born and foreign-born, who were of African, Latin American, European, Pacific Islander, Caribbean, and South and East Asian descent. I first identified individuals and organizations that played vital roles in the mobilizations by searching through local newspapers, protest flyers, and Web sites for reports and mentions both of groups and coalitions, and then individual organizers and leaders. As an active participant in the immigrant rights movement myself for over a decade, I also used contacts I had developed across the country to help me gain access to activists who played fundamental roles in local and national actions. I then applied a "snowball" method of sampling to seek out additional key informants to interview (Small 2009: 14; Warren and Karner 2010: 143). In total, I conducted 131 interviews between 2006 and 2009 with individuals of various citizenship statuses (U.S.-born and naturalized citizens, legal permanent residents and undocumented immigrants), racial, ethnic, and religious backgrounds. Overall, I interviewed sixty women and seventy-one men, with a city-level gender breakdown as follows: in Los Angeles, twenty women and twenty-four men; in New York, twenty-three women and twenty-one men; in Fort Myers, eight women and eleven men; and in Washington, D.C. and elsewhere in the country, nine women and fifteen men.

My forty-four interviews in Los Angeles were conducted between 2006 and 2008. The length of these interviews ranged from thirty-one minutes to three hours and fifty-five minutes, with an average time of one hour and twenty-three minutes. In New York City, my forty-four interviews were conducted throughout February and March of 2009 and ranged from twenty-five minutes to two hours and thirteen minutes, with an average length of fifty-seven minutes. I conducted my nineteen Florida interviews throughout two weeks of intensive fieldwork, during which I drove all across the southwest portion of the state; these interviews ranged from thirty-four minutes to two hours and twenty-three minutes with an average length of one hour and four minutes. The remaining twenty-four interviews ranged from fifteen minutes to three hours and thirty-three minutes, averaging an hour and seventeen minutes, and were conducted in Washington D.C. during one week in May of 2009.

The types of questions I asked local coalition members and protest organizers centered around the following categories: why they decided to participate, who contributed to the mobilization process and how, what their various tactics and strategies were, how they disseminated their calls to action, and what they believed the effects of the mass marches were. The questions with people based in D.C. and elsewhere primarily focused on how the rallies impacted their federal lobbying efforts, but depending on the interviewee's organization or affiliation, I also inquired about the role these groups played in helping coordinate the countrywide actions. Lastly, although I never asked, during several of my interviews it became clear that some of the individuals included in this study were undocumented. This fact highlights the serious risks many of the activists I spoke to took in organizing their local demonstrations and empirically demonstrates the extent to which people without papers often exert their political agency. Most of these individuals gave me permission to use their real names, however, instead I chose to use pseudonyms when quoting them or describing their actions. Here it is important to acknowledge that my decision contributes to the erasure of the identities of these individuals from the historical record and sacrifices some of the theoretical richness of my findings. While I understand that my judgment is problematic and take full responsibility for it, security and ethical reasons ultimately determined my final decision on this matter.

Transferability of Findings

Given that there were close to 400 documented demonstrations during the 2006 protest wave (Zepeda-Millán and Wallace 2013: 514), an important question is whether, and to what degree, the results of the case studies analyzed in this book can be extrapolated to other episodes of immigrant mass mobilization. Here it is important to point out that qualitative and quantitative scholars have very different ideas about how to extend the implications of their findings beyond their specific samples. For example, according to Yin (2014), qualitative case studies "are generalizable to theoretical propositions and not to populations or universes." He contends that while in qualitative research the goal is "to expand and generalize theories (analytic generalizations)," the aim of quantitative research is to "extrapolate probabilities (statistical generalizations)" (21). Other qualitative scholars, whose camp I situate myself in, have completely jettisoned the language of "generalization," finding the notion of "transferability" more useful and appropriate for interview- and ethnographic-based research. As Flyvbjerg (2011) explains, just because "knowledge cannot be formally generalizable does not mean that it cannot enter into the collective process of knowledge accumulation in a given field or in a society. Knowledge may be transferable even where it is not formally generalizable" (305).

According to Jensen (2008), whereas quantitative *generalizability* "suggests that the results of a given study can be applied across all environments related to the context being studied," qualitative *transferability* "implies that the results of the research can be transferred to other contexts and situations beyond the scope of the study context" (2; see also Guba 1981; Lincoln and Guba 1985). With transferability, it is ultimately up to readers to decide if, and to what degree, "the setting of the study is sufficiently similar for its results to be transferable to their own contexts" (Kuper et al. 2008: 688; Jensen 2008: 2–3). For readers to make these assessments, investigators must provide sufficient contextual information about their cases, select their research participants due to their unique positions or roles in the process or issue being studied, and give detailed, or "thick," descriptions of the phenomena they are analyzing (Shenton 2004: 69; Scholfied 1990: 207–208; Jensen 2008: 3).

Adhering to the aforementioned guidelines, in this book I have tried to provide enough background information about local contexts (both in my earlier discussion of the case study locations I selected and at the start of my individual case study chapters) and detailed descriptions of local actions, so that readers and activists can judge for themselves how transferable the findings presented in this book are to their own and other contexts. Moreover, because one of the main arguments of this book is that comprehending how "illegality" is racialized in the U.S. is fundamental to understanding why, who, and to what degree certain immigrant groups mass mobilized, in Chapter 4 I also provide national origin and citizenship data by state and metro area, so that readers can assess how the demographics of my case studies compare to each other and to other places where immigrant rights mobilizations have occurred and might occur in the future.

A Note on Objectivity and Identity

Distinguished indigenous methodologist Linda Tuiwai Smith (2012) contends that scholars from marginalized communities are often "concerned with having a more critical understanding of the underlying assumptions, motivations, and values which inform research practices." She asserts that we must center "our concerns and world views" and come "to know and understand theory and research from our own perspectives and for our own purposes" (21). Yet, as mentioned in the introduction to this methodological appendix, scholars (such as myself) who were formally trained in mainstream disciplines (e.g. political science) are rarely ever taught or encouraged to acknowledge, reflect upon, or write about the roles that our own identities and personal politics play in the questions we choose to research or in the data we collect and analyze. Our positivist epistemological tradition and predominately quantitative methodological training teach us that "interview biases" can, and should be, avoided and "controlled" for. While important research can, has been, and should continue to be produced in this manner, I believe that we also have a lot to learn from feminist, queer, and critical ethnic studies scholars who believe that our personal biographies and politics often do and should influence the questions we ask and the processes we utilize to analyze the answers we find (Haraway 1988; Hill Collins 1999; Twine and Warren 2000; Fong 2008; Smith 2012). In fact, especially for scholars of color who study the communities we come from, and movements we consider ourselves to be a part of, my contention is that rather than limit or harm the quality and accuracy of our studies, these "biases" can actually be assets that help us produce more rigorous, reliable, and relevant research. To be sure, my identity and political opinions undoubtedly blinded me from important insights that may otherwise have benefited my analysis. However, I believe these factors also gave me several privileges that allowed me to navigate and aided in my research endeavors. To illustrate this argument, below I discuss how and why I came to select my specific research topic and my experiences in collecting the evidence presented in this book.

Prior to beginning graduate school in the Department of Government at Cornell University, I was involved in activism on a range of issues, from the global justice and anti-Iraq war movements, to local labor organizing drives and transnational solidarity work with an armed indigenous rights movement in southern Mexico (the EZLN). Not surprisingly, when I decided to pursue a Ph.D. in political science, my research interests focused on social movements. For personal reasons, I chose to study the U.S. immigrant rights movement. Not only had I been raised by an immigrant grandmother in the Boyle Heights neighborhood of East Los Angeles, one of the largest Mexican immigrant *barrios* in the United States – and had many immigrant family members and friends who had endured several forms of abuses because of their race and citizenship status – but I had also been an active participant in the movement itself. Thus, I began my graduate studies with both a personal interest in, and commitment to, issues related to the rights of the foreign-born. In other words, my research agenda was sparked not by a desire to "fill a gap in the literature," but by a motivation to acquire as much intellectual ammunition as possible to help defend my community and advance my political beliefs.

The fact that I am a Chicano scholar whose research focuses on a social movement that I have been (and continue to be) an active participant in, and whose primary data sources are interviews with other immigrant rights activists (many of whom I know personally), might cause suspicion. Am I able to produce "unbiased knowledge?" Can my research be objective, neutral, and reliable? By now it should be clear that my political loyalties lie with immigrants; as Acuña (1998) once put it, "Sometimes there's no other side" to take than that of the oppressed. But as I maintain below, these "biases" actually not only served as fundamental resources in helping me gain access to key movement leaders and participants but also obliged me to produce empirically accurate research.

Two experiences during my fieldwork exemplify how my identity and previous political activism were advantages rather than problems; they helped me gain access to, and the trust of, hesitant interviewees who likely wouldn't have spoken to other scholars. For example, during the development of my research design, and again prior to carrying out my initial fieldwork, my dissertation committee suggested that my project focus only on Los Angeles (because it was the city I was from and had the most movement contacts in) and use my two other case study locations (New York and Fort Myers) as "shadow cases." With regard to New York, their reasoning was that activists in the city were infamous for being suspicious of, and closed off to, academic researchers. Fort Myers posed a different problem. The local protest was organized not by professional activists, but by local immigrant community residents, such as farmworkers, ethnic small business owners, nannies, and soccer league members. Moreover, given the high concentration of undocumented immigrants in the region, they believed that many of the local protest organizers likely did not have "papers" and – because they were vulnerable to deportation – would fear sharing their political organizing strategies and experiences with a stranger. Hence, whereas in Los Angeles my committee was confident I could reach my goal of interviewing twenty to forty key protest organizers, they estimated that, at best, I would return from my New York and Fort Myers fieldwork with only a handful of interviews.

In New York, my fieldwork began as my committee predicted. When I tried to arrange meetings with local movement leaders, several of them – often rudely – refused to speak with me and told me that they did not do interviews with academics, because information they shared previously was "used against them," or because the analysis produced was of "no use to the movement." Despite these initial challenges, by the end of my two months of fieldwork in the city, I had conducted over forty interviews with almost all of the key protest organizers, including members of rival local movement factions. How was I able to achieve this?

During the course of my New York fieldwork, many of the central organizations and local protest coalition participants began to agree to meet with me only after I told them that I too was an immigrant rights activist, knew several of the same people in the national movement that they did, and shared similar political beliefs as theirs. For others, my "activist credentials" were not enough. It took my having immigrant rights organizers I knew in Los Angeles contact activists they knew in New York – to let them know that I "could be trusted" – for them to agree to be interviewed by me. In fact, one interviewee, who later connected me with other individuals to speak with, even confessed to me that she was "only speaking to me because *several* people from the movement" in California had called or emailed her and "vouched for me." Hence, my political experience as an immigrant rights activist and my personal networks that I had developed through previous participation in the movement played central roles in helping me gain access in New York. In fact, according to a local professor and expert in New York immigrant politics, I later found out that my access was a major accomplishment: although it had by that point been over two years since the largest immigrant demonstrations in the city's history had taken place – and despite the interest of several universities and immigration researchers in the city and surrounding areas in studying the 2006 protest wave – no other scholar had gained access to all of the protest organizers that I had.

In Florida it was my identity and family history that allowed me to speak with and gain the trust of local organizers. Scholars who study political activism often do so by contacting established social movement organizations and leaders who have Web sites or some other official presence. Furthermore, notwithstanding my experience in New York, professional organizers often feel that speaking to researchers is beneficial because we might bring attention to their causes or demonstrate the importance of their work. But as mentioned above, no such organizations existed in Fort Myers or led the rally there; it was not professional activists, but regular immigrants who organized the local action. Nonetheless, despite these challenges, I exceeded my dissertation committee's expectations. In only a couple of weeks, I interviewed over a dozen (nineteen) of the most important march organizers, some of who were undocumented. How and why was I able to do so?

Having been born and raised in an immigrant neighborhood myself, I knew the importance of local Catholic churches, ethnic businesses, and public parks as central gathering places for immigrants. Through my examination of local newspaper articles about the protest and contacting the aforementioned types cultural spaces, I eventually figured out who had organized the Fort Myers action. Although identifying these individuals was important, it was just the first step; I then needed to gain their trust. This is where I believe my race, the languages I speak, and my life experiences played a major role in helping me get access to the central actors of the local demonstration I was examining. When contacting these individuals, I immediately: spoke to them in Spanish; let them know that I was of Mexican descent, was raised by Mexican immigrants, and had several family members who at one point in their lives were undocumented; and because agricultural work is a primary area of employment for the region's immigrants, I mentioned that my father and my grandparents had been migrant farmworkers. As a result, word quickly spread through local immigrant community social networks that "someone like them" wanted to write a book about their protest and "why they deserved rights." In fact, during my fieldwork in the region, I was even interviewed by a local Spanish-language radio program to, as the disk jockey put it, "show the community" that not all American university professors are white and "that even the children of Mexican farmworkers could succeed in this country." Thus, in part due to my "situated knowledges" (Haraway 1988), informed by my race, language skills, and life experiences, I was able to obtain the trust of the local residents who were at the heart of the story I wanted to tell.

In sum, who we are and what we believe greatly impact our research endeavors and the quality of the work we produce. Given my participation in and political commitment to the immigrant rights movement, many scholars might question the objectivity of my study. While I do believe there is an important place and purpose for political propaganda in social movements, my decision to examine the historic 2006 immigrant rights protest wave stemmed from my desire to understand, as meticulously as possible, why and how these unprecedented demonstrations occurred (so that, if needed, we could attempt to repeat them) and what led to their decline (to prevent that decline from happening in the future). Consequently, because of my personal investment in the issue, it is of the utmost importance to both me and my fellow immigrant rights activists that my analysis be as precise as possible so that it is of practical use to all of us, scholars and activists alike. Moreover, unlike other academics who study political activism but are not activists, in many respects, I remain both personally and politically accountable to the immigrant rights movement; though I completed my research for this book several years ago,

I continue to work with several of the individuals I interviewed in our ongoing efforts to protect and advance the rights of the foreign-born.

For all these reasons, my research findings *must be* as reliable as possible for them to be beneficial not only to scholars of Latino politics, activism, and immigration but also to the immigrant rights movement itself. In other words, rather than hindering or thwarting my ability to produce an "objective" and "trustworthy" study, my personal identity and political "biases" demand that my research be as accurate as can be. For those of us who strive to produce movement-relevant research, the stakes are too high, and erroneous research is too costly – to both the communities and movements we study and are a part of – when our findings can potentially shape our political strategies, tactics, and goals. I hope this book and research approach inspire future scholars who study and come from marginalized communities to take these factors into consideration and embrace, rather than reject, the unique life experiences, identities, and political commitments we bring to the academy.

Appendix B

List of Organizations

Acción Comunitaria La Aurora (La Aurora) La Aurora is a Dominican immigrant grassroots community group based in the northern Manhattan neighborhood of Washington Heights.

Agriculture Coalition for Immigration Reform (ACIR) ACIR is a Washington, D.C.–based national coalition that lobbies for immigration reform that favors the interests of U.S. agribusiness.

Alianza Dominicana (Alianza) Alianza is a New York City–based Dominican community development agency. The organization describes itself as "the leading authority on Dominican-Americans."

American Federation of Labor – Congress of Industrial Organizations (AFL-CIO) The AFL-CIO is the United States' largest labor union federation.

Asian Americans for Equality (AAE) AAE is a New York City-based nonprofit civil rights and social service organization that works on issues ranging from affordable housing and economic development to immigration and environmental health.

Asociación Tepeyac (Tepeyac) Tepeyac is a New York City-based nonprofit organization that focuses on community and immigrant rights issues related to Latino immigrants, primarily undocumented Mexican immigrants.

Association of Senegalese in American (ASA) ASA is a nonprofit organization based in New York City whose mission is to contribute to the political, economic and socio-cultural life of Senegalese immigrants living in the U.S.

Audre Lorde Project (ALP) ALP is a New York-based Lesbian, Gay, Bisexual, Two Spirit, Trans and Gender Non-Conforming People of Color community organization.

Bagong Alyansang Makabayan – United States of America (**BAYAN-USA**) BAYAN-USA is a coalition of progressive Filipino organizations representing students, academics, women, and workers. The New York City affiliate interviewed was the Filipino Forum (described below).

Center for Community Change (CCC) CCC is based in Washington, D.C. and works with hundreds of local community organisations across the country.

Central American Resource Center – Los Angeles (CARECEN) CARECEN is an L.A.-based cultural, economic, and political community organization that works to promote and defend the human and civil rights of Central Americans.

Centro Hispano Cuzcatlan (CHC) The CHC is a Queens, New York-based local community organization that works to empower local Central American and Latino residents.

Chinese Progressive Association (CPA) The CPA is a nonprofit community-based organization in New York City. It works on a wide range of issues – from immigration to housing – related to the city's Chinese community.

Clergy and Laity United for Economic Justice – Los Angeles (CLUE-LA) CLUE-LA is an interfaith worker justice organization that brings together clergy and lay leaders of various faiths to work on worker justice issues.

Coalición de Ligas Hispanas del estado de la Florida (Florida State Coalition of Hispanic Leagues) The Florida State Coalition of Hispanic Leagues is a predominately Mexican, statewide coalition of Latino immigrant soccer leagues.

Coalition for Comprehensive Immigration Reform (CCIR) CCIR was a Washington, D.C.–based umbrella organization for several national immigration, civil rights, labor, and community organizations. During the 2006 and 2007 legislative debate it was the leading lobbying group for comprehensive immigration reform.

Coalition for Humane Immigrant Rights of Los Angeles (CHIRLA) CHIRLA is a Los Angeles-based immigrant rights coalition that works to advance the rights of immigrants and refugees.

Committee Against Anti-Asian Violence (CAAAV) CAAAV is a New York-based grassroots community group that works to build power in poor and working class Asian refugee and immigrant communities.

Concilio Mexicano de la Florida (the *Concilio*) The *Concilio* was a coalition of primarily Mexican immigrant small businesses.

Consejo de Federaciones Mexicanas en Norteamérica (COFEM) COFEM is a Los Angeles-based non-profit organization that serves as an umbrella organization for Mexican hometown associations across the state of California.

Damayan **Migrant Workers Association (Damayan)** *Damayan* is a grassroots non-profit organization based in New York and New Jersey that works to promote and uphold the rights of Filipino immigrant workers, including domestic workers.

Desis **Rising Up and Moving (DRUM)** DRUM is a grassroots, multigenerational, member-led working class South Asian immigrant rights organization based in New York City.

Essential Worker Immigration Coalition (EWIC) EWIC is a national coalition of trade associations, businesses, and other organizations that works on issues related to skilled and unskilled labor shortages.

Fair Immigration Reform Movement (FIRM) Based out of the Center for Community Change, FIRM is a national coalition of grassroots organizations that work on immigrant rights issues at the local, state, and national levels.

Families for Freedom (FFF) Families for Freedom is a multi-ethnic New York-based defense network that works on issues related to deportation and detention.

Federation for American Immigration Reform (FAIR) FAIR is a national, non-profit organization and is considered the U.S.'s leading immigration restrictionist organization.

Fifth Avenue Committee (FAC) FAC is a community organization based in South Brooklyn, New York. It works on local social and economic justice issues.

Guyanese-American Worker's United (GAWU) GAWU is a New York City-based grassroots community organization composed of Guyanese Americans and Guyanese immigrants. It works on various social justice issues ranging from war to labor rights.

Haitian Women for Haitian Refugees (HWHR) HWHR is a Haitian-American and Haitian immigrant grassroots community organization in New York City that works on issues from education and social services to community organizing and democracy in Haiti.

Hermandad Mexicana-Latino Americana Led by legendary activist Bert Corona until his death in 2001, *Hermandad Mexicana* was likely the nation's first undocumented immigrant rights organization. The group split into several factions after Corona's death. The *Latino Americana* faction of *Hermandad* is led by Nativo Lopez.

Hermandad Mexicana Transnacional This faction of *Hermandad Mexicana* is led by Gloria Saucedo.

Immigrant Communities in Action (ICA) ICA is a Queens, New York–based immigrant rights coalition.

***Inmigrantes Latinos Unidos de la Florida* (ILUF)** ILUF was a small and short-lived collective of primarily Mexican immigrants in Southwest Florida.

International Action Center (IAC) IAC is an activist organization with several chapters throughout the country. Issues it focuses on include those related to war, race, and economic justice.

International Socialist Organization (ISO) With branches across the country, including Los Angeles, the ISO is one of the leading American socialist organizations.

***La Placita* Working Group** The *Placita* Working Group was a small, informal collective of local immigrant rights activists that initially called for an anti-H.R. 4437 protest on March 25, 2006 in downtown Los Angeles.

Latino Movement USA Latino Movement USA is a national Latino pan-ethnic coalition of different types of organizations that advocate for immigrant rights and comprehensive immigration reform.

Los Angeles County Federation of Labor (LA County Fed) The LA County Fed is the chartered Central Labor Council (CLC) of the AFL-CIO in Los Angeles County.

Make the Road New York (Make the Road) Make the Road is the largest Latino immigrant-based grassroots organization in New York City.

March 25 Coalition The March 25 Coalition was the radical flank of the Los Angeles immigrant rights movement in 2006. The group was instrumental in initiating and promoting the national May 1 "Great American Boycott/Day Without An Immigrant."

Mexican American Legal Defense and Education Fund (MALDEF) MALDEF is the country's leading Latino legal civil rights organization.

Mothers on the Move (MOM) Mother's on the Move is a primarily Puerto Rican and African-American–based social justice community organization located in the Bronx, New York. The group works on issues such as environmental justice, tenants' rights, youth, and education.

National Association of Latino Elected and Appointed Officials (NALEO) NALEO is the official association for local, statewide, and national Latina/o elected officials.

National Council of La Raza (NCLR) NCLR is the largest national Latino civil rights and advocacy organization in the United States.

National Immigration Forum (NIF) Based in Washington, D.C., NIF is one of the leading pro-immigrant advocacy organizations in the country.

National Korean American Service and Education Consortium (NAKASEC) NAKASEC is a national Korean American organization based in Los Angeles and Washington, D.C.

National Network for Immigrant and Refugee Rights (NNIRR) NNIRR is a national organization based in Oakland, CA, and is composed of local coalitions and immigrant, refugee, community, religious, civil rights and labor organizations and activists.

New York Civic Participation Project (NYCPP) NYCPP works with labor and community members in various New York neighborhoods on immigrant and worker justice issues.

New York Immigration Coalition (NYIC) NYIC is New York's leading statewide immigrant rights coalition.

New York May 1st Coalition (May 1st Coalition) The May Coalition is an alliance of several progressive local New York City political organizations and independent activists that supported the 2006 May 1 boycott.

Northern Manhattan Coalition for Immigrant Rights (NMCIR) NMCIR is a non-profit organization that focuses on educating, defending, and protecting the rights of local immigrants.

Pakistan USA Freedom Forum (PFF) The PFF is an New York-based grassroots organization that works to defend the rights of Pakistani immigrants.

Philippine Forum Philippine Forum is a nonprofit grassroots community organization that offers direct services to Filipino and other immigrants in New York.

Service Employees International Union (SEIU) SEIU is the nation's largest healthcare and property services union, and the second largest public services union.

SEIU 32BJ SEIU's Local 32BJ is labor union in New York City that organizes property service workers (e.g. janitors, security workers, doormen, etc.).

SEIU 1199 SEIU's Local 1199 is a labor union in New York City that organizes healthcare workers.

SEIU 1877 SEIU Local 1877 is a labor union in Los Angeles most famous for its "Justice for Janitors" campaign.

University of California Los Angeles's Downtown Labor Center (Labor Center) Part of the UCLA Center for Labor Research and Education, the Labor Center works to build links between the university and the Los Angeles labor community.

UNITE-HERE UNITE-HERE is a labor union that was formed as a result of the merger of two unions, UNITE (the Union of Needletrades, Industrial, and Textile Employees) and HERE (the Hotel Employees and Restaurant Employees International Union).

United Farm Workers (UFW) Founded by Cesar Chavez and Dolores Huerta, the UFW is a labor union dedicated to organizing agricultural workers.

United States Chamber of Commerce (USCC) The U.S. Chamber of Commerce is a business federation that represents corporations, business associations, and state and local chambers of commerce.

United States Conference of Catholic Bishops (USCCB) USCCB is an assembly of the hierarchy of the U.S. Catholic Church that works to "promote the greater good," including issues related to immigrant and refugee rights.

We Are America Alliance (WAAA) WAAA is a national coalition of immigrant rights organizations, church groups, and labor unions. The alliance was formed during the 2006 protest wave and helped organize massive immigrant naturalization and voter registration drives leading up to the 2008 election.

We Are American Coalition (WAAC) WAAC was an alliance composed of labor unions, the Catholic Church, and local immigrant rights organizations in Los Angeles.

Young Korean American Service and Education Center (YKASEC) YKASEC is a New York City-based organization that works on various social, economic, and political issues related to the Korean American community.

Endnotes

Introduction

1 https://zcomm.org/znetarticle/on-the-myth-of-sleeping-giants-by-aura-bogado/

2 http://www.nytimes.com/2006/04/09/us/09cnd-protest.html?_r=0.

3 http://www.indyweek.com/indyweek/we-are-here-and-we-are-human-and-we-have-rights/Content?oid=1197083.

4 Interview with Ilana Dubester, *El Vinculo Hispano*.

5 https://www.congress.gov/bill/109th-congress/house-bill/4437.

6 Although Latinos in the United States have a long history of participation in social movements, their civil rights activism has traditionally been regionally based (e.g., the Chicano Movement in the Southwest and the Young Lords in the East Coast) and has focused on specific national origins groups (e.g., Mexican-Americans in California and Puerto Ricans in New York). Consequently, while still heavily Mexican in most places, the 2006 protest wave also constitutes the largest national and panethnic Latino social movement in U.S. history.

7 While Bloemraad, Voss, and Lee (2011) review some of the social movement literature in the introduction to their excellent edited volume on the 2006 demonstrations, they do not offer a theoretical explanation for the rise and decline of the protest wave. However, they do note the need for scholars studying the marches to better theorize the role that threat played in the immigrant mobilizations (19), which is what I attempt to do in this book.

8 There is also a growing body of quantitative evidence that shows a strong relationship between the Republican Party and the passage of local and statewide anti-immigrant policies (see Ramakrishnan and Wong 2010; Wallace 2014; Gulasekaram and Ramakrishnan 2015).

9 Interview with Ana Maria Archila, Make the Road New York.

10 Interview with Guari Sadhwani, NYCPP.

11 Interview with Sarah Knopp, ISO and March 25 Coalition.

12 Social movement scholars assert that the success of movements often depend on how well activists frame their grievances and how best to deal with them (Snow and Benford 1992; McCarthy, Smith, and Zald 1996: 291; Tarrow 1998: 88).

13 For a critique of Latino panethnicity see Beltran 2010. For an account of the construction of the panethnic label "Hispanic," see Mora 2014.

14 Throughout this book I follow De Genova's (2002) lead and use quotes around the term "illegal" in order to "denaturalize the reification" of this historically, socially, and legally produced concept (420).

Chapter 1

1 According to Smith and Wiest (2012), neoliberalism is "a form of globalized capitalism that limits government's role to the regulation of monetary policy and the protection of private property, and that promotes economic growth through the expansion of international trade, the privatization of public entities and services, deregulation of business practices, and strict limits on government spending" (27). See also Harvey 2005, 2–3.

2 The three laws being the Illegal Immigration Reform and Responsibility Act, the Personal Responsibility and Work Opportunity Act, and the Antiterrorism and Effective Death Penalty Act. For specifics on these legislations see Arnold 2011; Hondagneu-Sotelo 2008; and Bloemraad, Voss, and Lee 2011: 15–16.

3 Mexican Americans and Mexican immigrants have a long history of cross-border organizing against injustices. For examples of activism related to issues of Mexicans and citizenship, see Rudy Acuña's (2011) discussions of *El Congreso de Pueblos que Hablan Espanol* (the Spanish-Speaking People's Congress).

4 Interview with Soledad "Chole" Alatorre, *Hermandad Mexicana*.

5 Corona called for the political unity of all Mexican Americans, Mexicans, Central, and South American immigrants with and without papers (see Gutierrez 1996: 189).

6 See "NNIRR's first 25 years: A chronology of activities, issues and struggles in the human rights of all migrants" at http://www.nnirr.org/%7Ennirrorg/drupal/sites/default/files/nnirr_25_year_chronology.pdf.

7 Interview with Catherine Tactaquin, NNIRR.

8 Interviews with Nativo Lopez (*Hermandad Mexicana*) and Juan Jose Gutiérrez (Latino Movement U.S.A.).

9 Migrating militants from other countries have also helped start immigrant rights organizations in the U.S. For an example of this phenomenon within the Korean immigrant community, see Omatsu 2008.

10 Interview with Roberto Lovato, CARECEN.

11 Interviews with Danny Park (KIWA) and Aquilina Soriano Versoza (PWC).

12 Interview with Angelica Salas, CHIRLA, CCIR, and FIRM.

13 Interview with Angelica Salas (CHIRLA, CCIR, and FIRM) and Rich Stolz (FIRM). See also Jimenez 2009.

14 Interview with Frank Sherry, NIF. See also Castañeda 2007.

15 Interview with Frank Sherry, NIF.
16 http://www.justiceforimmigrants.org/learn-about-justice.shtml (accessed March 20, 2012).
17 According to an interview with Rich Stolz of FIRM, these groups first began meeting collectively during the mid-1990s as the "Immigrant Organizing Committee" of the broader national anti-welfare reform movement.
18 The bill was also sometimes referred to as the "McCain-Kennedy Bill."
19 Interview with Angelcia Salas, CHIRLA, CCIR, and FIRM.

Chapter 2

1 Interview with anonymous Forever 21 retail store employee.
2 For a historical analysis of how the immigration of people of color can spark anti-racial minority conflict see Shanahan and Olzak 1999.
3 An internationally recognized social movement organization with a history of organizing around farmworker issues, the Coalition of Immokalee Workers (CIW), is based 35 miles outside of Fort Myers. Although the *Sarasota/Manatee Farmworker Supporters* reported that the CIW was a key organizer of the Fort Myers rally (see http://www.smfws.com/articles2006/2006aprilmayjune/arto4162006e.htm), my interviews with the protest organizers revealed that this was not the case. However, in an interview I conducted with lead CIW organizer Lucas Benitez, he stated that while his group "didn't organize" for the march (it was focused on its own national campaign for fair wages at the time) and was not part of the coalition that did organize it, his group did attend the protest, spoke about it on their low-powered radio station, and helped transport participants to the event. Moreover, despite its lack of involvement in organizing the demonstration, the CIW was the only group in the area that continued to successfully organize immigrants in the region, as noted by their national victory over McDonalds. See their campaign's highlights at http://www.ciw-online.org/McDonald%27s_campaign_archive.html.
4 Though I never asked directly, some of my interviewees revealed that they or other individuals interviewed in this study were undocumented. Consequently, for confidentiality and security reasons the names of interviewees in this chapter have been replaced with pseudonyms.
5 Tacho benefited from the amnesty provisions in the 1986 Immigration Reform and Control Act (IRCA).
6 Interview with Isaías, Fort Myers coalition general member.
7 Interview with Omar, *El Concilio.*
8 Interview with Moises, *Coalición de Ligas Hispañas del estado de la Florida.*
9 Interview with Zebedeo, *El Concilio.*
10 Interview with Moises, *Coalición de Ligas Hispañas del estado de la Florida.*
11 Interview with Moises, *Coalición de Ligas Hispañas del estado de la Florida.*
12 Interview with Hortensia, Fort Myers coalition general member.
13 For more on how watershed immigration policies, including H.R. 4437, impacted Latino identity and public opinion, see Abrajano and Lundgen 2012. Their quantitative analysis found that "the discrimination that

Latinos faced during" this period "when immigration rose to national salience also caused an increase in group pride and solidarity, thereby increasing their affinity for their own ethnic groups" (87).

14 Interview with Tacho, *Coalición de Ligas Hispañas del estado de la Florida.*

15 Interview with Moises, *Coalición de Ligas Hispañas del estado de la Florida.*

16 Interview with Moises, *Coalición de Ligas Hispañas del estado de la Florida.*

17 Interview with Fidelia, ILUF.

18 Interview with Marcos, *El Concilio.*

19 Interview with Marcos, *El Concilio.*

20 Interview with Moises, *Coalición de Ligas Hispañas del estado de la Florida.*

21 Interviews with Omar (*El Concilio*), Tacho (*Coalición de Ligas Hispañas del estado de la Florida*), and Marcos (*Coalición de Ligas Hispañas del estado de la Florida*).

22 Interview with Zebedeo, *El Concilio.*

23 Interviews with David (*El Concilio*), Tacho (*Coalición de Ligas Hispañas del estado de la Florida*), and Marcos (*El Concilio*).

24 Interview with Marcos, *El Concilio.*

25 Interview with Zebedeo, *El Concilio.*

26 Interview with Fr. Samuel (Fort Myers Catholic priest) and Moises (*Coalición de Ligas Hispañas del estado de la Florida.*).

27 See New American Media 2006.

28 Interview with Lucas, CIW.

29 Interview with Marcos, *El Concilio.*

30 Interview with Omar, *El Concilio.*

31 Interview with Omar, *El Concilio.*

32 Interview with Zebedeo, *El Conclio.*

33 According to Zebedeo, many stations would give them a "50 percent discount" on advertisements. For example, if they bought ten slots from a station, the station would give them ten more for free.

34 Interview with Zebedeo, *El Concilio.*

35 Interview with Marcos, *El Concilio.*

36 Interviews with Isaías (Fort Myers coalition general member), Ana Maria (ILUF), Ramona (Fort Myers coalition general member).

37 Interview with Marcos, *El Concilio.*

38 Interview with Zebedeo, *El Concilio.*

39 Interview with Tacho, *Coalición de Ligas Hispañas del estado de la Florida.* Interestingly, unlike in Los Angeles, the Catholic Church did not play a major role in the Fort Myers or New York City protests.

40 Interview with Moises, *Coalición de Ligas Hispañas del estado de la Florida.*

41 Interview with Tacho, *Coalición de Ligas Hispañas del estado de la Florida.*

42 Interview with Tacho, *Coalición de Ligas Hispañas del estado de la Florida.*

43 Interview with Daniel, *Coalición de Ligas Hispañas del estado de la Florida.*

44 Interview with Marcos, *El Concilio.*

45 http://www.nbc-2.com/articles/readarticle.asp?articleid=6617

46 Interview with Moises, *Coalición de Ligas Hispañas del estado de la Florida.*

47 Interview with Fidelia, ILUF.

Chapter 3

1 These influences include subtly triggering racial attitudes via political advertisements (Valentino, Hutchings, and White 2002), steering views on foreign policy (Baum 2002), diverting attention away from topics of greater relevance and more immediate concern (Sabato 1991), rendering the public "less likely to hold public officials accountable" for social problems (Iyengar 1991: 3), serving as a channel through which elites can influence popular opinion about public policies (Zaller 1992: 113), or dictating "how political alternatives are evaluated" (Iyengar and Kinder 1987, 4; Kinder 2003, 364).

2 The congressman was not in his office at the time of the protest so activists presented the "award" (a certificate with his name and a picture of the Grinch on it) to his staff along with Christmas-themed wrapped empty boxes meant to symbolize the gifts of dignity and respect. Interviews with Eun Sook Lee (NAKASEC) and Xiomara Corpeno (CHIRLA).

3 Interview with Xiomara Corpeno, CHIRLA.

4 Interview with Jesse Diaz, March 25 Coalition. For other smaller Anti-H.R. 4437 meetings and actions previous to the Riverside Conference, see Navarro 2009.

5 Email from the "Southern California Human Rights Network," February 26, 2006. Subject: "MARCH 25 MASS MARCH AGAINST SENSENBRENNER HR4437 -Media Advisory."

6 Interview with Juan Jose Gutierrez, Latino Movement USA.

7 Interview with Nativo Lopez, *Hermandad Mexicana* and Mexican American Political Association (MAPA).

8 Interview with Angelica Salas. Salas is the executive direct of CHIRLA and one of the most prominant immigrant rights leaders in the nation. She was a key member of various local and national coalitions and organizations, including the L.A. We Are America Coalition, and the national We Are America Alliance, FIRM, Coalition for Comprehensive Immigration Reform, and Center for Community Change.

9 Interview with Javier Rodriguez, March 25 Coalition.

10 Interview with Javier Rodriguez, March 25 Coalition.

11 *Univision* Radio and *Univision* Television are the radio and television divisions of the media conglomerate *Univision* Communications, Inc.

12 Interview with Jesse Diaz, March 25 Coalition.

13 Interview with Jesse Diaz, March 25 Coalition.

14 Interview with Juan Jose Gutierrez, Latino Movement USA. For a slightly different account see Gonzlaes 2013: 59.

15 Interview with Javier Rodriguez, March 25 Coalition.

16 Interviw with Juan Jose Gutierrez, Latino Movement USA.

17 For accounts of the significance of the Justice for Janitors union see Fantasia and Voss 2004 and Milkman 2006.

18 Interview with Jesse Diaz, March 25 Coalition.

19 Interview with Nativo Lopez, *Hermandad Mexicana Nacional.*

20 Interview with Juan Jose Gutierrez, Latino Movement USA.

21 Interview with Jesse Diaz, March 25 Coalition.
22 Interview with Nativo Lopez, *Hermandad Mexicana Nacional.*
23 Interview with Nativo Lopez, *Hermandad Mexicana Nacional.*
24 Interview with Jorge Mettey, *Univison.*
25 Interview with anonymous *Univision* Editorial Board member.
26 Interview with anonymous *Univision* Editorial Board member.
27 Interview with Jorge Mettey, *Univison.*
28 Author's translation from personal copy of promotional ad.
29 Interviews with Jorge Mettey (*Univision*) and anonymous *Univision* Editorial Board member.
30 Interview with Victor Narro, UCLA Labor Center.
31 Weather Underground weather history for Los Angeles, March 25, 2006. Accessed July 22, 2016. https://www.wunderground.com/history/airport/KCQT/2006/3/25/DailyHistory.html?req_city=&req_state=&req_statename=&reqdb.zip=&reqdb.magic=&reqdb.wmo=
32 Author's ethnographic fieldnotes.
33 Author's ethnographic fieldnotes.
34 Author's ethnographic fieldnotes.
35 Interview with Javier Gonzalez, SOL and SEIU 1877.
36 http://www.csulb.edu/~d49er/archives/2006/spring/news/v12n95-rally.shtml.
37 Interview with Rosalina Cardenas, OC Media.
38 The media strategy team of the coalition was composed of several women, including: Rosaline Cardenas and Alina Ossen from OC Media, a private media consulting firm; Maria Elena Jauregui, a former news director for *Univision* who knew several other news directors across the country; Carolina Guevara, the media person for the Archdiocese of Los Angeles; and Mary Gutierrez of the LA County Federation of Labor, who also worked closely with Hilda Delgado formerly of *La Opinion.*
39 Interview with Rosaline Cardenas, OC Media.
40 Interview with Mike Garcia, SEIU 1877.
41 Interview with Rosalina Cardenas, OC Media.
42 Interview with Mike Garcia, SEIU 1877.
43 Interview with Javier Gonzalez, SOL and SEIU 1877.
44 Interview with Rosalina Cardenas, OC Media.
45 Interview with Carolina Guevara, Archdiocese of Los Angeles.
46 Interview with Rosalina Cardenas, OC Media.
47 Interview with Rosalina Cardenas, OC Media.
48 Interview with Jesse Diaz, March 25 Coalition.
49 Interview with Juan Jose Gutierrez, Latino Movement USA.
50 Interivew with Javier Rodriguez, March 25 Coalition.

Chapter 4

1   Interview with Aarti Shahani, Families for Freedom.
2   Social movement researchers define coalitions as "a collection of distinct ... and often unaffiliated groups whose members cooperate on some issues in

order to have" or increase their "political influence" (Meyer 2007: 61; also see Gamson 1961: 374). Although these alliances are hard to create and difficult to maintain (Staggenborg 1986: 388), particularly for grassroots and voluntary organizations (Smith and Bandy 2005: 9), they play a vital role in the production of large-scale protests (Rose 2000; Gilmore 2008; Mayer 2009) and can increase the likelihood of activist groups achieving their goals (Mayer 2009; Roth 2010: 101).

3 Changes in external contexts can also eventually contribute to the decline or prevention of coalitional mobilization efforts (Meyer and Corrigall-Brown 2005: 339). Once "the exceptional environmental conditions which make coalition work attractive return to normal," argues Staggenborg (1986), "[c]ompetition for resources and ideological disputes among organizations make it difficult to maintain" alliances (375). Moreover, "When the political context changes and the threat seems less proximate, less changeable, or less important," individual organizations are "more likely to abandon coalition work, either formally or by focusing their efforts elsewhere" (Meyer and Corrigall-Brown 2005: 342; see also Meyer 2007: 79; McCammon and Campbell 2002: 233).

4 Factors *internal* to social movements that have been found to impact the dynamics of coalitions include ideological congruency (Cornfield and McCammon 2010: 92; Van Dyke and McCammon 2010: xix), shared goals (Staggenborg 1986: 375; Rucht 2004: 202; Mayer 2009: 7; but see Rose 2000: 31), and prior social ties (Meyer 2007: 76; Rose 2000: 11, 24; Corrigall-Brown and Meyer 2010). In terms of *external* factors, scholars of contentious politics have shown that both political opportunities (Staggenborg 1986; Meyer and Corrigall-Brown 2005) and environmental threats (McCammon and Campbell 2002; Van Dyke 2003) can foster the formation of alliances and influence their strategies and successes (Tattesall 2010: 155).

5 Lacking a common identity not only makes alliances between groups less likely to form (Okamoto 2010: 146) but also can prevent coalitions from developing (Bell and Delaney 2001; Mayer 2009: 13).

6 Interview with AnaLiza Caballes, Damayan Migrant Workers Association.

7 Interview with Sussie Losada, *La Aurora* and NYCPP.

8 Interview with Rhadames Pérez, *La Aurora*.

9 Although the coalition that organized the city's April 10 protest never adopted an official name, I refer to it as the April 10 alliance to avoid confusion with and to draw a clear distinction between it and the New York May 1 Coalition.

10 Interview with Monami Maulik, DRUM.

11 Interview with Ana Maria Archilla, Make the Road New York.

12 Interview with Hector Figueroa (SEIU 32BJ) and anonymous NYIC organizer.

13 Although CCIR focused on policy, and WAAA dedicated itself to voter mobilization efforts, both national groups were composed of several of the same regional and national organizations (see Chapter 6).

14 Interview with anonymous NYIC organizer.

15 See Chapter 3 for an example of how this same phenomenon played out in Los Angeles.

16 Interview with anonymous NYIC organizer.

17 Interiew with Raquel Batista, NMCIR.

18 Interview with Monami Maulik, DRUM.

19 Interview with anonymous NYIC organizer.

20 LGBTSTGNC is the acronym for Lesbian, Gay, Bisexual, Two-Spirit, Trans and Gender Non Conforming.

21 "Thousands March for Immigrant Rights." May 1, 2006. http://articles. cnn.com/2006–05–01/us/immigrant.day_1_thousands-march-largest-protests-immigration-laws?_s=PM:US.

22 Interview with Ana Maria Archila, Make the Road New York.

23 Interview with Artemio Guerra, Fifth Avenue Committee.

24 Interview with Monami Maulik, DRUM.

25 Interview with Monami Maulik, DRUM.

26 Interview with anonymous local Eastern European activists.

27 She contended that their primary policy interest was family reunification.

28 Interview with anonymous NYIC organizer.

29 Interview with Monami Maulik, DRUM.

30 Interview with Zahida Pirani, NYCPP. Other Latino and non-Latino activists also stated that Latinos made up the largest group of protesters and that within this panethnic group, Dominicans and Mexicans had the highest turn out.

31 New York City, "Selected Characteristics of the Foreign-Born Population by Region of Birth: Latin America." 2006 American Community Survey (ACS).

32 See the radio program's May 2, 2006 transcripts at http://www.demo cracynow.org/2006/5/2/over_1_5_million_march_for.

33 Interview with Aarti Shahani, Families for Freedom.

34 Interview with Zahida Pirani, NYCPP.

35 Interview with anonymous NYCPP organizer.

36 Interview with anonymous local Eastern European activist.

Chapter 5

1 Interview with Jesse Diaz, March 25 Coalition.

2 Interview with anonymous NYIC organizer.

3 According to Boykoff (2007), "Repression is violent, while suppression, a broader term, also encompasses other, more subtle modes of silencing opposition." He contends that suppression "is less drastic or dramatic and lets us see beyond more spectacular instances of governmental coercion" (11).

4 http://www.cnn.com/2006/POLITICS/04/10/immigration/

5 https://www.splcenter.org/news/2006/03/30/extremists-advocate-murder-immigrants-politicians.

6 Interview with Moises, *Coalición de Ligas Hispanas del estado de la Florida*.

7 For more on these and other incidents of hate crimes that occurred between 2005 and 2006 see https://www.splcenter.org/fighting-hate/intelligence-report/2007/hate-crimes-against-latinos-rising-nationwide.

8 Federal Bureau of Investigation (FBI) 2006 Hate Crimes Statistics. http://www2.fbi.gov/ucr/hc2006/victims.html.

9 Not including the year between 2001–2002, where after the 9/11 terrorist attacks there was a spike in all hate crimes motivated by bias against one's ethnicity or national origin, 2006 saw the largest increase in percentages of hate crimes against Latinos. See FBI hate crime statistics between 2000–2008.

10 Moises, *Coalición de Ligas Hispañas del estado de la Florida.*

11 Omar, *El Concilio.*

12 Interview with Clarissa Martinez De Castro, NCLR.

13 See "CNN's Immigration Problem: Is Dobbs the exception – or the rule?" http://fair.org/take-action/action-alerts/cnns-immigration-problem/. Accessed August 16, 2016.

14 Interview with John Trasviña, MALDEF.

15 Interview with Javier Valdes, NYIC.

16 Interview with Moises, *Coalición de Ligas Hispañas del estado de la Florida.*

17 Interview with Xiomara Corpeño, CHIRLA.

18 Interview with Aarti Shahani, Families for Freedom.

19 The National Conference of State Legislatures released its first report on state legislation related to immigration in 2005.

20 Recent survey research suggests that Latino immigrants are extremely aware and vigilant of local anti-immigrant legislation (Ybarra, Juarez, and Sanchez 2016).

21 For more on the development of the immigration detention system and current abuses of immigrants in these prisons, see Welch 2002; Fernandes 2007; Tumlin, Joaquin, and Natarajan 2009; Amnesty International 2009.

22 Interview with Guari Sadwani, NYCPP.

23 Interview with Ramona, Fort Myers coalition general member.

24 The data in Figure 5.4 only show the number of people deported from within the United States (what DHS refers to as "removals"), not those apprehended by Border Patrol agents as they try to enter the country (what DHS refers to as "returns"). According to DHS statistics, although the general trend for "removals" has been on the rise since 2003, the number of those "returned" has been on the decline since 2004. See DHS "2010 Yearbook of Immigration Statistics."

25 Interview with Hector Figueroa, SEIU 32BJ.

26 Interview with Eun Sook Lee, NAKASEC.

27 Interview with Javier Valdes, NYIC.

28 For more information on ICE's "Fugitive Operations Program," see Mendelson, Strom, and Wishnie 2009.

29 Interview with Tacho, *Coalición de Ligas Hispañas del estado de la Florida.*

30 Interview with Susana, local radio DJ.

31 Interview with Xiomara Corpeño, CHIRLA.

32 Interview with Sarah Knopp, March 25 Coalition.

33 Interview with Raquel Batista, NMCIR.

34 Interview with Artemio Guerra, Fifth Avenue Committee.

35 Interview with Sarah Knopp, March 25 Coalition.
36 Interview with Sarah Knopp, March 25 Coalition.
37 Interview with Sarah Knopp, March 25 Coalition.

Chapter 6

1 http://fortune.com/2011/10/14/where-will-occupy-wall-street-take-us/
2 However, according to Tom Wong (2017), since the passage of the 2005 Sensenbrenner Bill immigration policymaking has been characterized by three features: "the entrenchment of partisan divides among legislators when it comes to the issue of immigration, the political implications of the demographic changes that are continuing to reshape the electorate, and how these changes are creating new opportunities to define what it means to be an American in a period of unprecedented national origins, racial and ethnic, and cultural diversity" (4).
3 Several local and national organizations mentioned the tension between D.C.-based groups who primarily focus on policy change and local organizations who directly organize and provide services for immigrants across the country.
4 Interview with anonymous leader of a national organization with local affiliates.
5 For an excellent account of the efforts to pass bipartisan immigration reform from 2001–2007, see the 2010 Frontline documentary "How Democracy Works."
6 Interview with Frank Sharry, National Immigration Forum.
7 Interview with Angela Kelley, Center for American Progress.
8 Interview with Frank Sharry, National Immigration Forum.
9 Although organizers claimed that the protest was attended by more than 1.5 million people, media outlets contended that between 500,000 and 1 million demonstrators marched in Los Angeles on that day.
10 When a lobbyist or organization "key votes" a bill they are signaling to legislators that their vote on that particular piece of legislation may impact the future support the legislator receives from the constituency the lobbyist or organization represents.
11 See League of United Latin American Citizens (LULAC) March 13, 2007 press release, "Historic Nationwide Campaign Launched for Comprehensive Immigration Reform," at http://www.lulac.net/advocacy/press/2007/ccir.html.
12 Interview with Frank Sharry, National Immigration Forum.
13 Intervie with Xiomara Corpeno, CHIRLA.
14 Interview with Efrain Escobedo, NALEO.
15 Interview with anonymous leader of a national immigrant rights organization.
16 Interview with Maria Echaveste, Coalition for Comprehensive Immigration Reform.
17 Interview with Angelica Salas, CHIRLA, FIRM, and CCIR.

18 Interview with Ana Avendano, AFL-CIO.
19 Interview with Frank Sharry, National Immigration Forum.
20 Interview with Ira Mehlman, FAIR.
21 Interview with Hector Figueroa, SEIU 32BJ.
22 Interview with Frank Sharry, National Immigration Forum.
23 Interview with Angelica Salas, CHIRLA and FIRM.
24 Interview with Rich Stoltz, FIRM.
25 Interview with Jorge Mettey, *Univision*.
26 Interview with Jorge Mettey, *Univision*.
27 For other accounts of this campaign see Ayon 2008 and Felix, Gonzalez, and Ramirez 2008.
28 Interview with Efrain Escobedo, NALEO.
29 Interview with Efrain Escobedo, NALEO.
30 Interview with Angelica Salas, FIRM, CCIR, WAAA, and CHIRLA.
31 Interview with Efrain Escobedo, NALEO.
32 Interview with anonymous *Univision* Editorial Board member and Efrain Escobedo (NALEO).
33 Interview with anonymous *Univision* Editorial Board member.
34 National Latino Congreso Press Release, July 13 2008. http://latinocongreso.org/news.php?id=88
35 Voto Latino, "Voto Latino in the 2008 Election Season." According to the website whatis.techtarget.com, "In Web advertising, the term *impression* is sometimes used as a synonym for *view*, as in *ad view*. Online publishers offer, and their customers purchase, advertising measured in terms of ad views or impressions." See http://whatis.techtarget.com/definition/0,,sid9_gci212334,00.html
36 http://americasvoice.org/blog/alliance_registers_half_million_new_immigrant_voters_128000_in_battleground/
37 http://weareamericaalliance.com/about
38 Interview with Efrain Escobedo, NALEO.
39 Interview with Angelica Salas, WAAA, FIRM, CCIR, and CHIRLA.
40 Pew Hispanic Center. "The Hispanic Voter in the 2008 Election." November 5, 2008.
41 Interview with Frank Sharry, National Immigration Forum.
42 Interview with Xiomara Corpeno, CHIRLA and FIRM.

Conclusion

1 Interview with Alan Kaplan, NYIC.
2 Interview with Mario Chavez, SEIU Local 1877.
3 For an excellent example of the different types of coverage black power activists received from black versus non-black sources see Davenport's (2010) rigorous study.
4 http://www.nytimes.com/2006/04/10/business/media/to-marshal-immigrant-forces-start-at-ethnic-radio-stations.html.
5 http://bastadobbs.com/facts/

6 Interview with Roberto Lovato, CARECEN and Presente.org. See also http://bastadobbs.com/blog/2009/nov/11/bastadobbscom-announces-victory-lou-dobbs-leave-cn/ and http://www.mediaite.com/tv/meet-the-prensa-robert-lovatos-post-dobbs-victory-lap/.

7 http://www.huffingtonpost.com/2013/04/02/ap-drops-term-illegal-immigrant_n_3001432.html.

8 For my critique of these limited administrative reforms see http://www.huffingtonpost.com/chris-zepedamillan/immigration-2012-election_b_1601436.html.

9 Other examples include the Obama Administration's attempt to implement a Deferred Action for Parents of Americans and Lawful Permanent Residents (DAPA) policy, his dismantling of the National Security Entry-Exit Registration System (NSEERS), his ending of the controversial "287(g)" program, which allowed local law enforcement agents to inquire about and arrest people based on their immigration status, and several other administrative actions he took to help make it easier for eligible undocumented immigrants to legalize their status (on the last point see Wernick 2014).

10 https://www.domesticworkers.org/initiatives/labor-protections.

11 http://cdn.americanprogress.org/wp-content/uploads/issues/2011/07/pdf/state_immigration.pdf.

12 http://articles.latimes.com/2010/may/21/nation/la-na-immigration-20100521.

13 http://www.migrationpolicy.org/programs/data-hub/charts/regions-immigrant-birth-1960-present?width=1000&height=850&iframe=true.

14 For an in-depth analysis of the ways in which legal status has come to serve as a central axis of the American stratification system see Massey (2007) and Lee and Fiske (2006). On how language and accents are racialized social markers see Alim et al. (2016).

15 For historical examples of how the "race question" in the U.S. has never been purely "black and white," see Almaguer 1994, Takaki 1994, and Chapter 10 of de Tocqueville [1840] 2011. For a global example of this argument see Quijano 2000.

16 https://www.splcenter.org/hatewatch/2016/11/18/update-incidents-hateful-harassment-election-day-now-number-701.

17 According to Abrajano and Lundgren (2014), "the discrimination that Latinos" face during periods when the issue of immigration rises to national salience causes an increase in their sense of "group pride and solidarity, thereby increasing the affinity for their own ethnic groups" (77).

18 http://nymag.com/thecut/2016/11/catherine-cortez-mastro-wont-let-donald-trump-go-unchecked.html.

19 http://www.huffingtonpost.com/entry/democrats-latino-turnout_us_5826579ee4b060adb56e8fbd.

20 For Latino voter turnout figures, see http://www.latinodecisions.com/blog/2016/11/10/lies-damn-lies-and-exit-polls/. For more on Latino motivation to vote against Trump, see http://www.latinodecisions.com/blog/2016/04/27/latino-voters-eager-turnout-against-trump-and-the-gop-in-2016/

21 See Latino Decision "2016 Latino Election Analysis" http://www
.latinodecisions.com/files/6514/7880/5462/PostElection2016.pdf.
22 https://www.americanprogress.org/issues/democracy/news/2016/09/30/
145120/protecting-the-right-to-vote-in-the-2016-elections/
23 http://www.latinovote2016.com/app/
24 For Latino millennials' support for Bernie Sanders over Hilary Clinton see
O'Reilly 2016 and Alvarez 2016.
25 https://www.americanprogress.org/issues/immigration/news/2015/09/17/
121325/top-6-facts-on-the-latino-vote/

Appendix A

1 There are multiple ways that social scientists define and use the terms "case"
and "case study" (see Levy 2008, 2; Ragin 1992, 217; Feagin et al. 1991;
Gerring 2004, 342).
2 2000 City of Fort Myers, Florida, "US Census 2000 Demographic Profile
Highlights."

References

Abrajano, Marisa and Zoltan Hajnal. *White Backlash: Immigration, Race, and American Politics*. Princeton University Press, 2015.

Abrajano, Marisa and Simran Singh. "Examining the Link Between Issue Attitudes and News Source: The Case of Latinos and Immigration Reform." *Political Behavior*. Vol. 31, Iss. 1, pp. 1–30, 2009.

Abrajano, Marisa and Costas Panagopoulos. "Does Language Matter? The Impact of Spanish Versus English-Langauge GOTV Efforts on Latino Turnout." *Political Behavior*. Vol. 39, Iss. 4, 2011.

Abrajano, Marisa and Lydia Lundgren. "How Watershed Immigration Policies Affect American Public Opinion Over a Lifetime." *International Migration Review*. Vol. 49, No. 1, pp. 70–105, 2015.

Abrego, Leisy. *Sacrificing Families: Navigating Laws, Labor, and Love Across Borders*. Stanford University Press, 2014.

Abu-Jamal, Mumia. *Live from Death Row*. New York: Harper Perennial Press, 1996.

Acuna, Rodolfo. *Occupied America: A History of Chicanos*. 4th Edition. Boston: Longman, 2000.

Acuna, Rodolfo. *Occupied America: A History of Chicanos*. 7th Edition. Boston: Longman, 2011.

Acuna, Rodolfo. *Sometimes There Is No Other Side: Chicanos and the Myth of Equality*. South Bend: University of Notre Dame Press, 1998.

Alexander, Michelle. *The New Jim Crow: Mass Incarceration in the Age of Colorblindness*. New York: New Press, 2011.

Alim, Samy, John Rickford, and Arnetha Ball. *Raciolinguistics: How Language Shapes Our Ideas About Race*. New York: Oxford University Press, 2016.

Alinksy, Saul. *Rules for Radicals: A Pragmatic Primer for Realistic Radicals*. New York: Vintage, 1989.

Allegro, Linda. "Latino Migrations to the U.S. Heartland: 'Illegality,' State Controls, and Implications for Transborder Labor Rights." *Latin American Perspectives*. Iss. 170, Vol. 37, No. 1, 172–184, 2010.

Almada, Jorge Morales. "Marcha por los inmigrantes." *La Opinion*. March 3, 2006.

Almaguer, Tomás. 1994. *Racial Fault Lines: The Historical Origins of White Supremacy in California*. Berkeley: University of California Press.

Almeida, Paul. "Opportunity Organizations and Threat-Induced Contention: Protest Waves in Authoritarian Settings." *American Journal of Sociology*. Vol. 109, No. 2, pp. 345–400, 2012.

Alvarez, Priscilla. "Will Hispanic Millennials Vote?" *The Atlantic*. April 21, 2016. http://www.theatlantic.com/politics/archive/2016/04/youth-hispanics-vote-bernie-sanders/479328/

Amenta, Edwin and Neal Caren. "The Legislative, Organizational, and Beneficiary Consequences of State-Oriented Challengers." *Blackwell Companion to Social Movements*. Eds. David Snow, Sarah Soule, and Hanspeter Kriesi. Malden: Blackwell Press, 2004.

Amenta, Edwin and Michael Young. "Making an Impact: Conceptual and Methodological Implications of the Collective Goods Criterion." *How Social Movements Matter*. Minneapolis: University of Minnesota Press, 1999.

Anderson, Benedict. *Imagined Communities*. New York: Verso, 1991.

Andreas, Peter. *Border Games: Policing the U.S.–Mexico Divide*. Ithaca: Cornell University Press, 2000.

Aparicio, Ana. *Dominican-Americans and the Politics of Empowerment*. Gainesville: University of Florida Press, 2006.

Aparicio, Frances. "Competing Narratives on the March: The Challenges of News Media Representation in Chicago." *Marcha!: Latino Chicago and the Immigrant Rights Movement*. Champaign: University of Illinois, 2010.

Apocada, Gene. "Disturbing flyers distributed in Pasadena." *ABC Eyewitness News*. KTRK/PASADENA, TX. April 9, 2006.

Armenta, Amanda. "Between Public Service and Social Control: Policing Dilemmas in the Era of Immigration Enforcement." *Social Problems*. December 2015. DOI: 10.1093/socpro/spv024

Armenta, Amanda. "Racializing Crimmigration: Structural Racism, Colorblindness, and the Institutional Production of Immigrant Criminality." *Sociology of Race and Ethnicity*. Vol. 3, Iss. 1, 2017.

Atton, Chris. *Alternative Media*. New York: Sage, 2001.

Ayon, David. "Spanish-Language Media and Mexican Migrant Civic Participation." *Invisible No More: Mexican Migrant Civic Participation in the United States*. Eds. Xochitl Bada, Jonathan Fox, and Andrew Selee. Woodrow Wilson Center for Scholars. 2006.

Ayoub, Phillip. *When States Come Out: Europe's Sexual Minorities and the Politics of Visibility*. Cambridge University Press, 2016.

Bada, Xochitl. "State and local Governments Influence Integration Outcomes." *Context Matters: Latino Immigrant Civic Engagement in Nine U.S. Cities*. Eds. Xochitl Bada, Jonathan Fox, Robert Donnelly, and Andrew Selee. Washington D.C.: Woodrow Wilson International Center for Scholars, 2010.

Bada, Xochitl, Jonathan Fox, and Andrew Selee. *Invisible No More: Mexican Migrant Civic Participation in the United Staes*. Woodrow Wilson International Center for Scholars, 2006.

Bakalian, Anny and Medhi Bozorgmehr. *Backlash 9/11: Middle Eastern and Muslim Americans Respond*. Berkeley: University of California Press, 2009.

Barbassa, Juliana. "Unable to vote but eager to be part of political process, non-citizen immigrants volunteer." *The Associated Press*, October 30, 2008.

Barbassa, Juliana. "Massive elections push aims to register Latino voters." *The Associated Press*. September 26, 2008. http://www.mercedsunstar.com/news/local/central-valley/article3238188.html

Barreto, Matt. "Latino Immigrants at the Polls: Foreign-born Voter Turnout in the 2002 Election." *Political Research Quarterly*, Vol. 58, No.1, March 2005.

Barreto, Matt, Gary Segura, and Nathan Woods. "The Mobilizing Effects of Majority-Minority Districts on Latino Turnout." *APSR*. Vol. 98, No.1, Feb. 2004.

Barreto, Matt and Nathan Woods. "Latino Voting Behavior in an Anti-Latino Political Context: The Case of Los Angeles County." *Diversity in Democracy: Minority Representation in the United States*. Eds. Gary M. Segura and Shaun Bowler. Charlottesville: University of Virginia Press, 2005.

Barreto, Matt, Sylvia Manzano, Ricardo Ramirez, and Kathy Rim. "Mobilization, Participation, and *Solidaridad*: Latino Participation in the 2006 Immigration Protest Rallies." *Urban Affairs Review*. Vol. 44, No. 5, 2009.

Barreto, Matt and Stephen Nuno. "The Effectiveness of Coethnic Contact on Latino Political Recruitment." *Political Research Quarterly*. Vol. 64, No. 2, 448–459, 2009.

Barreto, Matt, Loren Collingwood, and Sylvia Manzano. "A New Measure of Group Influence in Presidential Elections: Assessing Latino Influence in 2008." *Political Research Quarterly*. Vol. 62. No. 2. 2010.

Barvosa-Carter, Edwina. "Multiple Identity and Coalition Building: How Identity Differences within Us Enable Radical Alliances Among Us." *Forging Radical Alliances Across Difference: Coalition Politics for the New Millennium*. Eds. Jill Bystydzienski and Steven Schacht. Lanham: Rowman and Littlefield, 2001.

Baum, Dan. "Arriba! A Latino radio scold gets out the vote." *The New Yorker*. October 23, 2006.

Baum, Mathew. "Sex, Lies, and War: How Soft News Brings Foreign Policy to the Inattentive Public." *American Political Science Review*. Vol. 96, No. 1. March 2002.

Baumgartner, Frank and Bryan Jones. *Agendas and Instability in American Politics*. University of Chicago Press, 1993.

Baumgartner, Frank and Beth Leech. *Basic Interests: The Importance of Groups in Politics and Political Science*. Princeton University Press, 1998.

Beach, Derek, and Rasmus Brun Pedersen. *Process-Tracing Methods: Foundations and Guidelines*. University of Michigan Press, 2013.

Becerra, Hector and Andrew Blankstein. "L.A. Authorities Brace for Huge Immigration Marches." *Los Angeles Times*. April 28, 2006.

Beifuss, Joan. *At the River I Stand*. Memphis: B & W Books, 1985.

Beirich, Heidi, Susy Buchanan, David Holthouse, Brentin Mocks, and Casey Sanchez. "Profiles of 20 Anti-Immigrant Leaders." *The Nativist*. Intelligence Report, Spring 2008.

Bell, Sandra and Mary Delaney. "Collaborating Across Difference: From Theory and Rhetoric to the Hard Reality of Building Coalitions." *Forging Radical Alliances Across Difference: Coalition Politics for the New Millennium."* Eds. Jill Bystydzienski and Steven Schacht. New York: Roman & Littlefield, 2001.

Beltran, Cristina. *The Trouble With Unity: Latino Politics and the Creation of Identity.* New York: Oxford University Press, 2010.

Benford, Robert. "Frame Disputes within the Nuclear Disarmament Movement". *Social Forces.*, Vol. 71, Iss. 3, March 1993.

Bennett, Lance and Alexandra Segerberg. "Digital Media and the Personalization of Collective Action: Social Technology and the Organization of Protest Against the Glboal Economic Crisis." *Information, Communication, & Society.* Vol. 14, Iss. 6, 2011.

Bennett, Andrew and Colin Elman. "Qualitative Research: Recent Developments in Case Study Methods." *American Review of Political Science.* Vol. 9, pp. 455–476, 2006.

Berg, Bruce. *Qualitative Research Methods for the Social Science.* 5th Edition. Boston: Allyn & Bacon, 2004.

Bernstein, Mary. "The Strategic Use of Identity by the Lesbian and Gay Movement" (from "Celebration to Suppression"). *The Social Movement Reader: Cases and Concepts.* Eds. Jeff Goodwin and James Jasper. Malden: Blackwell Publishing, 2003.

Bernstein, Nina. "Record Immigration is Changing the Face of New York's Neighborhoods." *New York Times.* January 24, 2005.

Bernstein, Nina. "Eclectic Crowd Joins a Call for the Rights of Immigrants." *New York Times,* April 11, 2006.

Bernstein, Nina. "Immigrants Panicked by Rumors of Raids." *New York Times.* April 29, 2006.

Blackwell, Maylei. *¡Chicana Power!: Contested Histories of Feminism in the Chicano Movement.* Austin: University of Texas Press, 2011.

Bloch, Katrina. 2013. "'Anyone Can Be Illegal': Color-Blind Ideology and Maintaining Latino/Citizen Borders." *Critical Sociology.* Vol. 40, No. 1, pp. 47–65, 2014.

Bloemraad, Irene. *Becoming A Citizen: Incorporating Immigrants and Refugees in the United States and Canada.* Berkeley: University of California Press, 2006.

Bloemraad, Irene, Kim Voss, and Taeku Lee. ""The Protests of 2006: What Were They, How Do We Understand Them, Where Do We Go?"" *Rallying for Immigrant Rights: The Fight for Inclusion in 21st Century America.* Eds. Bloemraad, Irene and Kim Voss. Berkeley: University of California Press, 2011.

Bloemraad, Irene and Christine Trost. "It's a Family Affair: Intergenerational Mobilization in the Spring 2006 Protests." *Rallying for Immigrant Rights: The Fight for Inclusion in 21st Century America.* Eds. Bloemraad, Irene and Kim Voss. Berkeley: University of California Press, 2011.

Blood, Michael and Peter Prengaman. "Immigration Protests May Not Spur Votes." *Washington Post.* September 4, 2006. http://www.washingtonpost.com/wp-dyn/content/article/2006/09/04/AR2006090400432_pf.html.

Bobo, Kim, Jackie Kendall, and Steve Max. *Organizing for Social Change: Midwest Academy Manual for Social Change*. Santa Ana: Seven Locks Press, 2001.

Bowler, Shuan and Gary Segura. *The Future is Ours: Minority Politics, Political Behavior, and the Multiracial Era of American Politics*. Thousand Oaks: CQ Press, 2011.

Bonilla-Silva, Eduardo. *White Supremacy and Racism in the Post-Civil Rights Era*. Boulder: Lynne Rienner Pub, 2001.

Borland, Elizabeth. "Crisis as Catalyst for Cooperation? Women's Organizing in Buenos Aires." *Strategic Alliances: Coalition Building and Social Movements*. Eds. Nella Van Dyke and Holly McCammon. Minneapolis: University of Minnesota Press, 2010.

Bowe, John. *Nobodies: Modern American Slave Labor and the Dark Side of the New Global Economy*. New York: Random House, 2007.

Boykoff, Jules. *Beyond Bullets: The Suppression of Dissent in the United States*. Oakland: AK Press, 2007.

Broadway, Michael. "From City to Countryside: Recent Changes in the Structure and Location of Meat- and Fish-Processing Industries." *Any Way You Cut It: Meat Processing and Small-Town America*. Eds. Donald Stull, Michael Broadway, and David Griffith. Lawrence, KS: University Press of Kansas, 1995.

Brodkin, Karen. *Making Democracy Matter: Identity and Activism in Los Angeles*. New Jersey: Rutgers University Press, 2007.

Brown, David. "Migration and Community: Social Networks in a Multilevel World." *Rural Sociology*. Vol. 67, No. 1, March 2007.

Browning, Rufus, Dale Marshall, and David Tabb. *Protest is Not Enough: The Struggle of Blacks and Hispanics for Equality in Urban Politics*. Los Angeles: University of California Press, 1984.

Buchanan, Susy and Tom Kim. "2005 Winter Issue." *The Nativists*. November 02, 2006. https://www.splcenter.org/fighting-hate/intelligence-report/2006/nativists-0

Buchanan, Susy and David Holthouse. "Extremist advocate murder of immigrants, politicians: National pro-immigrant marches inspire calls for carnage from radical right." *Intelligence Report*. Southern Poverty Law Center. March 30, 2006. http://www.splcenter.org/get-informed/news/extremists-advocate-murder-of-immigrants-politicians

Buechler, Steven. *Social Movements in Advanced Capitalism: The Political Economy and Cultural Construction of Social Activism*. New York: Oxford University Press, 2000.

Buechler, Steven. "The Strange Career of Strain and Breakdown Theories of Collective Action." *The Blackwell Companion to Social Movements. Blackwell Companion to Social Movements*. Eds. David Snow, Sarah Soule, and Hanspeter Kriesi. Malden: Blackwell Press, 2004.

Building Democracy Initiate (BDI). "Nativism in the House: A Report on the House Immigration Reform Caucus." Center for New Community, September 2007.

Business Wire. "PIOLIN on Univision Radio KSCA is now #1 on the morning FM drive in Los Angeles!!!" *Business Wire*. October 20, 2003.

Bystydzienski, Jill and Steven Schacht. Eds. *Forging Radical Alliances Across Difference: Coalition Politics for the New Millennium*. New York: Roman & Littlefield, 2001.

Cacho, Lisa. *Social Death: Racialized Rightlessness and the Criminalization of the Unprotected*. New York UniversityPress, 2012.

Cameron, Ardis. *Radicals of the Worst Sort*. Urbana: University of Illinois Press, 1993.

Camp, Jordan. *Incarcerating the Crisis: Freedom Struggles and the Rise of the Neoliberal State*. Berkeley: University of California Press, 2016.

Carpenter, David. "Immigrants Demonstrate Economic Clout." *AP Business Wire*. Monday, May 1, 2006.

Castañeda, Jorge. *Ex Mex: From Migrants to Immigrants*. New York: New Press, 2007.

Catholic Legal Immigration Network, Inc. (CLINIC). "The 287(g) Program: Enforcement of Civil Immigration Law by State & Local Law Enforcement Agencies." *CLINIC*, 2009.

Chavez, Ernesto. "Mi Raza Primero!": *Nationalism, Identity, and Insurgency in the Chicano Movement in Los Angeles, 1966–1978*. Berkeley: University of California Press, 2002.

Chavez, Karma. *Queer Migration Politics: Activists Rhetoric and Coalitional Possibilities*. Champaign: University of Illinois, 2013.

Chavez, Leo. *The Latino Threat*. Stanford University Press, 2008.

Chernoff, Allan. "Rallies across U.S. call for illegal immigrant rights." CNN. April 10, 2006. http://www.cnn.com/2006/POLITICS/04/10/immigration/index.html?_s=PM:POLITICS.

Clemens, Elisabeth and Debra Minkoff. "Beyond the Iron Law: Rethinking the Place of Organizations in Social Movement Research." *Blackwell Companion to Social Movements*. Eds. David Snow, Sarah Soule, and Hanspeter Kriesi, Blackwell, 2004.

CNN. "Thousands march for immigrant rights." May 1, 2006. http://articles.cnn.com/2006–05–01/us/immigrant.day_1_thousands-march-largest-protests-immigration-laws?_s=PM:US.

Cohen, Cathy. "Punks, Bulldaggers, and Welfare Queens: The Radical Potential of Queer Politics?" *GLQ*. Vol. 3, pp. 437–465, 1997.

Cohen, Cathy. *The Boundaries of Blackness: AIDS and the Breakdown of Black Politics*. University of Chicago Press, 1999.

Coleman, Mathew. "The 'Local' Migration State: The Site-Specific Devolution of Immigration Enforcement in the U.S. South." *Law & Policy*. Vol. 34, No. 2, April 2012.

Confessore, Nicholas. "Immigration Debates Mirror Concerns in Washington." *The New York Times*. March 26, 2006.

Cook, Maria, Kevin Middlebrook, and Juan Molinar Horcasitas. "The Politics of Economic Restructuring in Mexico: Actors, Sequencing, and Coalition Change." *The Politics of Economic Restructuring: State-Society Relations and Regime Change in Mexico*. Eds. Maria Cook, Kevin Middlebrook, and Juan Molinar Horcasitas. La Jolla: Center for U.S.-Mexican Studies, 1994.

Cordero-Guzman, Hector, Nina Martin, Victoria Quiroz-Becerra, and Nik Theodore. "Voting With Their Feet: Nonprofit Organizations and Immigrant Mobilization." *American Behavioral Scientist*. Vol. 52, 2008.

Cornelisse, Galina. "Immigration Detention and the Territoriality of Universal Rights." *The Deportation Regime: Sovereignty, Space, and the Freedom of Movement*. Eds. Nicholas De Genova and Nathalie Peutz. Durham: Duke University Press, 2010.

Cornelius, Wayne. "Designing Social Policy for Mexico's Liberalized Economy: From Social Services and Infrastructure to Job Creation." Ed. Riordan Roett. *The Challenge of Institutional Reform in Mexico*. London: Lynne Rienner, 1995.

Cornelius, Wayne and Julio Labastida Martin del Campo. "Forward." *The Politics of Economic Restructuring: State-Society Relations and Regime Change in Mexico*. Eds. Maria Cook, Kevin Middlebrook, and Juan Molinar Horcasitas. La Jolla: Center for U.S.-Mexican Studies, 1994.

Cornfield, Daniel and Holly McCammon. "Approaching Merger: The Converging Public Policy Agenda of the AFL and CIO, 1938–1955." *Strategic Alliances: Coalition Building and Social Movements*. Eds. Nella Van Dyke and Holly McCammon. Minneapolis: University of Minnesota Press, 2010.

Corrigall-Brown, Catherine and David Meyer. "The Prehistory of a Coalition: The Role of Social Ties in Win Without War." *Strategic Alliances: Coalition Building and Social Movements*. Eds. Nella Van Dyke and Holly McCammon. Minneapolis: University of Minnesota Press, 2010.

Costanza-Cook, Sasha. *Out of the Shadows, Into the Streets: Transmedia Organizing and the Immigrant Rights Movement*. Cambridge: MIT Press, 2014.

Coutin, Susan Bibler. *Legalizing Moves: Salvadoran Immigrants' Struggle for U.S. Residency*. Ann Arbor: University of Michigan Press, 2000.

Coyer, Kate, Tony Dowmunt, and Alan Fountain. *The Alternative Media Handbook*. New York: Routledge, 2008.

Creswell, John. *Research Design: Qualitative, Quantitative, and Mixed-Methods Approaches*. 2nd Edition. Thousand Oaks: Sage, 2003.

Crummett, M and Schmidt, E. "Spheres of influence and area studies: The Hidalgo-Clearwater connection." Paper delivered at 2003 meeting of Latin American Studies Association. Dallas, Texas, March 27, 2003.

Das Gupta, Monisha. *Unruly Immigrants: Rights, Activism, and Transnational South Asian Politics in the United States*. Durham: Duke University Press, 2006.

Davenport, Christian. *Media Bias, Perspective, and State Repression: The Black Panther Party*. Cambridge University Press, 2010.

Davey, Monica. "For Immigrants and Business, Rift on Protests." *New York Times*. April 15, 2006.

Davila, Arlene. *Latinos, Inc.: The Marketing and Making of a People*. Berkeley: University of California Press, 2001.

Davis, Angela. *Angela Davis: An Autobiography*. New York: Bantam Books, 1989.

Davis, Mike. *Magical Urbanism: Latinos Reinvent the U.S. City*. New York: Verso, 2001.

Dawson, Michael. *Behind the Mule: Race and Class in African-American Politics.* Princeton University Press, 1994.

De Genova, Nicholas. "Migrant 'Illegality' and Deportability in Everyday Life." *Annual Review of Anthropology.* Vol. 31, 2002.

De Genova, Nicholas. "The Legal Production of Mexican/Migrant 'Illegality'." *Latino Studies.* Vol. 2, 2004.

De Genova, Nicholas. "Introduction: Latino and Asian Racial Formations at the Frontiers of U.S. Nationalism." *Racial Transformations: Latinos and Asians Remaking the United States.* Ed. Nicholas De Genova. Durham: Duke University Press, 2006.

De Genova, Nicholas. "The Deportation Regime: Sovereignty, Space, and the Freedom of Movement." *Deportation Regime: Sovereignty, Space, and the Freedom of Movement.* Eds. Nicholas De Genova and Nathalie Peutz. Durham: Duke University Press, 2010.

De Graauw, Els. *Making Immigrant Rights Real: Nonprofits and the Politics of Integration in San Francisco.* Ithaca: Cornell University Press, 2016.

De la Garza, Rodolfo, and Louis DeSipio. "Save the Baby, Change the Bathwater, and Scrub the Tub: Latino Electoral Participation after Twenty Years of Voting Rights Act Coverage." *Pursing Power: Latinos and the Political System.* Ed. F. Chris Garcia. University of Notre Dame Press, 1997.

De Tocqueville, Alexis. [1840] *Democracy in America.* University of Chicago Press, 2011.

Della Porta, Donatella and Mario Diani. *Social Movements: An Introduction.* Malden: Blackwell Publishing, 1999.

Della Porta, Donatella and Oliver Fillieule. "Policing Social Protest." *Blackwell Companion to Social Movements.* Eds. David Snow, Sarah Soule, and Hanspeter Kriesi. Malden: Blackwell Press, 2004.

Delli Carpini, Michael and Scott Keeter. *What Americans Know About Politics and Why It Matters.* New Haven: Yale University Press, 1996.

De Ment, Terri, Raymond Buriel, and Christina Villanueva. "Children As Language Brokers: A Narrative of the Recollections of College Students." *Language in Multicultural Education.* Eds. Farideh Salili and Rumjahn Hoosain. Information Age: Scottsdale, 2005.

DeSipio, Louis. *Counting on the Latino Voice: Latinos as a New Electorate.* Charlottesville: University Press of Virginia, 1996.

Democracy Now! May 2, 2006. Radio program transcripts. http://www.democracynow.org/2006/5/2/over_1_5_million_march_for.

Dionne, Kim Yi, Darin DeWitt, Michael Stone, Michael Suk-Young Chwe. "The May 1 Marchers in Los Angeles: Overcoming Conflicting Frames, Bilingual Women Connectors, English-Language Radio, and Newly Politicized Spanish Speakers." *Urban Affairs.* Vol. 51, Iss. 4, 2014.

Dobbs, Lou. "Radical Groups Taking Control of Immigrant Movement." *CNN.* May 1, 2006. http://www.cnn.com/2006/US/05/01/dobbs.immigrantprotests/

Duchon, Deborah and Arthur Murphy. "Introduction: From Patrones and Caciques to Good Ole Boys." *Latino Workers in the Contemporary South.*

Eds. Arthur D. Murphy, Colleen Blanchard, and Jennifer A. Hill. Athens: University of Georgia Press, 2001.

Durand, Jorge, Douglas Massey, and Chiara Capoferro. "The New Geography of Mexican Immigration." *New Destinations*. Eds. Victor Zuniga and Ruben Hernandez-Leon, Los Angeles: University of California Press, 2005.

Earl, Jennifer. "Tanks, Tear Gas, and Taxes: Toward a Theory of Movement Repression." *Sociological Theory*. Vol. 21, No. 1, March 2003.

Eckstein, Harry "Case Studies and Theory in Political Science." In F. I. Greenstein and N. W. Polsby (Eds.). *Handbook of Political Science*. Vol. 7, 79–137. Reading, MA: Addison-Wesley, 1975.

Edwards, Bob and John D. McCarthy. "Resources and Social Movements." *The Blackwell Companion to Social Movements*. Eds. David Snow, Sarah Soule, and Hanspeter Kriesi. Malden: Blackwell, 2004.

Efrat, Rafael. "Immigrant Entrepreneurs in Bankruptcy." *American Bankruptcy Law Journal*. Vol. 82, 2008.

El Diario (NY). "Latinos no reportan crimenes de odio." February 28, 2011.

Engler, Mark and Paul Engler. "The Massive Immigrant-Rights Protests of 2006 Are Still Changing Politics." *Los Angeles Times*. March 4, 2016.

Epstein, Steven. "Gay and Lesbian Movements in the United States: Dilemmas of Identity, Diversity, and Political Strategy." *The Global Emergence of Gay and Lesbian Politics*. Philadelphia: Temple University Press, 1999.

Escobar, Martha. *Captivity Beyond Prisons: Criminalization Experiences of Latina (Im)migrants*. Austin: University of Texas Press, 2016.

Evans, Sara and Harry Boyte. *Free Space*. New York: Harper and Row, 1986.

Fantasia, Rick. *Cultures of Solidarity: Consciousness, Action, and Contemporary American Workers*. Los Angeles: University of California Press, 1988.

Fantasia, Rick and Kim Voss. *Hard Work: Remaking The American Labor Movement*. Los Angeles: University of California Press, 2004.

Feagin, Joe R., Anthony M. Orum, and Gideon Sjoberg. *A Case for the Case Study*. Chapel Hill: University of North Carolina Press, 1991.

Fearon, James and David Laitin. "Explaining Interethnic Cooperation." *APSR*. Vol. 90, No. 4, 1996.

Fears, Darryl. "An Immigrant DJ's Morning in America." *Washington Post*. April 30, 2006.

Felix, Adrian, Carmen Gonzalez, and Ricardo Ramirez. "Political Protest, Ethnic Media, and Latino Naturalization." *American Behavioral Scientist*. Vol. 52. 2008.

Fennelly, Katherine. "Prejudice Toward Immigrants in the Midwest." *New Faces in New Places: The Changing Geography of American Immigration*. Massey, Douglas. Ed. New York: Russell Sage, 2008.

Ferree, Myra Marx. "Soft Repression: Ridicule, Stigma, and Silencing in Gender-Based Movements." *Repression and Mobilization*. Eds. Christian Davenport, Hank Johnston, and Carol Mueller. Minneapolis: University of Minnesota Press, 2005.

Ferree, Myra Marx, William Gamson, Jurgen Gerhards, and Dieter Rucht. *Shaping Abortion Discourse*. New York: Cambridge University Press, 2002.

Figueroa, Laura. "May 1 Focus of Migrant Work Stoppage." *Bradenton Herald*. April 22, 2006.

Fine, Janice. *Worker Centers: Organizing Communities at the Edge of the Dream*. Ithaca: Cornell University Press, 2006.

Flaccus, Gillian. "Spanish-language media play key role in promoting pro-immigrant rallies in U.S." *AP Wire*. March 3, 2006. http://english.ohmynews .com/articleview/article_view.asp?menu=c10400&no=282396&rel_ no=1&isMail=mail.

Flaccus, Gillian. "Immigrants Try to Extend Boycott Momentum." *The Associated Press*. Tuesday, May, 2, 2006. http://www.washingtonpost.com/wp-dyn/ content/article/2006/05/02/AR2006050200150_pf.html

Flacks, Richard. "Knowledge For What? Thoughts on the State of Social Movement Studies." J. Goodwin and J. Jasper (Eds.) *Rethinking Social Movements: Structure, Culture, and Emotion*. Lanham: Rowman & Littlefield, 2004.

Flick, Uwe. *An Introduction to Qualitative Research*. 4th Edition. Thousand Oaks: Sage, 2009.

Flores-Gonzalez and Gutierrez. "Taking the Public Square: The National Struggle for Immigrant Rights." *Marcha!: Latino Chicago and the Immigrant Rights Movement*. Champaign: University of Illinois, 2010.

Flyvberg, Bent. "Case Study." *The Sage Handbook of Qualitative Research*. Eds. Norman K. Denzin and Yvonna S. Lincoln. 4th Edition. Thousand Oaks: Sage, 2011.

Foner, Nancy. Ed. *New Immigrants in New York*. New York: Columbia University Press, 1987.

Foner, Nancy and Roger Waldinger. "New York and Los Angeles as Immigrant Destinations: Contrasts and Convergences." *New York-Los Angeles: The Uncertain Future*. Eds. David Halle and Andrew Beveridge. 2013.

Fong, Timothy. *Ethnic Studies Research: Approaches and Perspectives*. Lanham: AltaMira Press, 2008.

Fortuny, Karina, Randy Capps, and Jeffrey Passel. "The Characterisitcs of Unauthorized Immigrants in California, Los Angeles County, and the United States." Urban Institute Report. Washington, D.C., 2007.

Fraga, Luis, John Garcia, Rodney Hero, Michael Jones-Correa, Valerie Martinez-Ebers, and Gary Segura. *Latino Lives in America: Making It Home*. Philadelphia: Temple University Press, 2010.

Fraga, Luis, John Garcia, Rodney Hero, Michael Jones-Correa, Valerie Martinez-Ebers, and Gary Segura. *Latinos in the New Millennium: An Almanac of Opinion, Behavior, and Policy Preferences*. Cambridge University Press, 2011.

Frazier, John and Mark Reisinger. "The New South in Perspective: Observations and Commentary." *Latinos in the New South*. Eds. Heather Smith and Owen Furuseth. Burlington: Ashgate, 2006.

Friedman, Debra and Doug McAdam. "Collective Identity and Activism: Networks, Choices, and the Life of a Social Movement." *Frontiers in Social Movement Theory*. Eds. Aldon Morris and Carol McClurg Mueller. New Haven: Yale University Press, 1992.

Gamboa, Suzanne. "Fee increase triggers immigration applications deluge." *Associated Press*. November 20, 2007.

Gamson, William. "A Theory of Coalition Formation." *ASR*. Vol. 26, No. 3, 1961.

Gamson, William. "Bystanders, Public Opinion, and the Media." *Blackwell Companion to Social Movements*. Eds. David Snow, Sarah Soule, and Hanspeter Kriesi. Malden: Blackwell Press, 2004.

Gamson, William and David Meyer. "The Framing of Political Opportunity." Eds. Doug McAdam, John D. McCarthy, and Mayer N. Zald. *Comparative Perspectives on Social Movements: Political Opportunities, Mobilizing Structures, and Cultural Framings*. Cambridge University Press, 1996.

Gamson, William and Gadi Wolfsfeld. "Movements and Media as Interacting Systems." *American Academy of Political and Social Sciences*. Vol. 528. July 1993.

Ganz, Marshall, Kim Voss, Teresa Sharpe, Carl Somers, and George Strauss. "Against the Tide: Projects and Pathways of the new Generation of Union Leaders, 1984–2001." *Rebuilding Labor: Organizing and Organizers in the New Union Movement*. Ithaca: IRL Press, 2004.

Gaouette, Nicole. "Nationwide Raids Intensify Focus on the Employment of Illegal Immigrants." *Los Angeles Times*. April 21, 2006.

Garcia, Arnoldo. "Toward a Left Without Borders: The story of the Center for Autonomous Social Action-General Brotherhood of Workers." *Monthly Review*. July-August, 2002.

Garcia, Dawn. "Spanish Language Media, Text Messaging and MySpace: The Creation of a New Counterpublic Sphere in California." Master's Thesis. Stanford University. June 2008.

Garcia, John. *Latino Politics in America: Community, Culture, and Interests*. New York: Rowman & Littlefield, 2003.

Garcia, Mario. *Memories of Chicano History: The Life and Narrative of Bert Corona*. Berkeley: University of California Press, 1994.

Garcia Bedolla, Lisa. *Fluid Borders: Latino Power, Identity, and Politics in Los Angeles*. Berkeley: University of California Press, 2005.

Garcia Hernandez, Cesar Cuauhtemoc. "Immigration Detention as Punishment." *UCLA Law Review*. Vol. 61, No. 1346, 2014.

Garcia-Rios, Sergio and Matt Barreto. "Politicized Immigrant Identity, Spanish-Language Media, and Political Mobilization in 2012." *RSF: The Russell Sage Foundation Journal of Social Sciences*. Vol. 2, Iss. 3, 2016.

Gardner, Trevor and Aarti Kohli. "The C.A.P. Effect: Racial Profiling in the ICE Criminal Alien Program." Berkeley, CA: Chief Justice Earl Warren Institute on Race, Ethnicity, and Diversity, 2009.

Gencer, Arin. "Parishioners Fast to Protest Migrant Bill." *Los Angeles Times*. February 2, 2006.

George, Alexander, and Andrew Bennett. *Case Studies and Theory Development*. Cambridge: MIT Press, 2005.

Gerring, John. *Case Study Research: Principles and Practices*. Cambridge University Press, 2007.

Gerson, Daniela. "Clinton: Immigration Bill Would Make Jesus a Criminal." *The New York Sun*. March 23, 2006.

Gilmore, Stephanie. *Feminist Coalitions: Historical Perspectives on Second-Wave Feminism in the United States.* Chicago: University of Illinois Press, 2008.

Gilmore, Ruth Wilson. *Golden Gulag: Prisons, Surplus, Crisis, and Opposition in Globalizing California.* Berkeley: University of California Press, 2007.

Gimpel, James and James Edwards. *The Congressional Politics of Immigration Reform.* Boston: Allyn and Bacon, 1999.

Gitlin, Todd. *The Whole World Is Watching: Mass Media in the Making and Unmaking of the New Left.* Berkeley: University of California Press, 2003.

Gitlin, Todd. "The Media in the Unmaking of the New Left." *The Social Movement Reader: Cases and Concepts.* Eds. Jeff Goodwin and James Jasper. Malden: Blackwell, 2003.

Giugni, Marco. *Social Protest and Policy Change.* New York: Rowman and Littlefield, 2004a.

Golash-Boza, Tanya Maria. *Immigration Nation: Raids, Detentions, and Deportations in Post-9/11 America.* Bolder: Paradigm, 2012.

Golash-Boza, Tanya Maria. "The Parallels between Mass Incarceration and Mass Deportation: An Intersectional Analysis of State Repression." *Journal of World-System Research.* Vol. 22, Iss. 2, pp. 484–509, 2016.

Golden, Renny and Michael McConnell. *Sanctuary: The New Underground Railroad.* Maryknoll: Orbis, 1986.

Goldstone, Jack and Charles Tilly. "Threat (and Opportunity): Popular Action and State Response in the Dynamics of Contentious Action." *Silence and Voice in the Study of Contentious Politics.* New York: Cambridge University Press, 2001.

Gonzales, Alfonso. *Reform Without Justice: Latino Migrant Politics and the Homeland Security State.* New York: Oxford University Press, 2013.

Gonzales, Roberto. "Challenging the Transition to New Illegalities: Undocumented Young Adults and the Shifting Boundaries of Inclusion." *Constructing Immigrant 'Illegality.'* Eds. Menjivar, Cecilia and Daniel Kanstroom. Cambridge University Press, 2014.

Goodwin, Jeff and James Jasper. *The Social Movements Reader: Cases and Concepts.* Malden: Blackwell Press, 2003.

Goodwin, Jeff and James Jasper. *Rethinking Social Movements.* New York: Rowman & Littlefield, 2004.

Gordon, Jennifer. *Suburban Sweatshops: The Fight for Immigrant Rights.* Cambridge: Harvard University Press, 2005.

Gorman, Anna and Jessica Garrison. "Sweep Rumors Raise Worries for Immigrants." *Los Angeles Times.* April 29, 2006.

Gorman, Anna, Majorie Miller, and Mitchell Landsberg. "Immigrants Demonstrate Peaceful Power." *Los Angeles Times.* May 2, 2006.

Gottlieb, Robert, Mark Vallianatos, Regina M. Freer, and Peter Dreier. *The Next Los Angeles: The Struggle for a Livable City.* Los Angeles: University of California Press, 2005.

Government Accountability Office (GAO). "Immigration Enforcement: Better Controls Needed over Program Authorizing State and Local Enforcement of Federal Immigration Laws." *United States Government Accountability Office.* 2009.

Grandin, Greg. *Empire's Workshop: Latin America, the United States, and the Rise of the New Imperialism.* New York: Holt, 2007.

Greene, Ronnie. "A Crop of Abuse." *The Miami Herald.* September 1, 2003a.

Greene, Ronnie. "Florida Tops U.S. in Number of Problem Farm Labor Bosses." *The Miami Herald.* September 1, 2003b.

Greene, Ronnie. "Some State Farmers Agree that Changes Are Needed." *The Miami Herald.* September 2, 2003c.

Greene, Ronnie. "The Ties That Bind." *The Miami Herald.* Tuesday, September 2, 2003d.

Greene, Ronnie. "Fields of Despair." *The Miami Herald.* Sunday, August 31, 2003e.

Gregory, Todd. "'Burn the Mexican flag!': A look back at the hateful anti-immigration rhetoric from 2006." *Media Matters.* March 18, 2010. http://mediamatters.org/research/2010/03/18/burn-the-mexican-flag-a-look-back-at-the-hatefu/161857

Grey, Mark and Anne Woodrick. "'Latinos Have Revitalized Our Community': Mexican Migration and Anglo Responses in Marshalltown, Iowa." *New Destinations: Mexican Immigration in the United States.* Eds. Victor Zuniga and Ruben Hernandez-Leon. New York: Russell Sage Foundation, 2005.

Griffith, David. ""Hay Trabajo: Poultry Processing, Rural Industrialization, and the Latininization of Low-Wage Labor." *Any Way You Cut It: Meat Processing and Small-Town America.* Eds. Donald Stull, Michael Broadway, and David Griffith. Lawrence, KS: University Press of Kansas, 1995.

Griffith, David, Alex Stepick, Karen Richman, Guillermo Grenier, Ed Kissam, Allan Burns, and Jeronimo Camposeco. "Another Day in the Diaspora: Changing Ethnic Landscapes in South Florida." *Latino Workers in the Contemporary South.* Eds. Arthur Murphy, Colleen Blanchard, and Jennifer Hill. Athens: University of Georgia Press, 2001.

Guba, Egon. "Criteria for Assessing the Trustworthiness of Naturalistic Inquires." *ECTJ Annual Review Paper.* Vol. 29, No. 2, pp. 75–91, 1981.

Gulasekaram, Pratheepan and Karthick Ramakrishnan. *The New Immigration Federalism.* Cambridge University Press, 2015.

Gutierrez, David. "CASA in the Chicano Movement: Ideology and Organizational Politics in the Chicano Community, 1968–78." Stanford Center for Chicano Research. Working Paper Series, No. 5. 1984.

Gutierrez, David. *Walls and Mirrors: Mexican Americans, Mexican Immigrants, and the Politics of Ethnicity.* Berkeley: University of California Press, 1996.

Hadden, Jennifer and Sidney Tarrow. "Spillover or Spillout? The Global Justice Movement in the United States After 9/11." *Mobilization.* Vol. 12, No. 4, 2007.

Hamilton, Nora and Norma S. Chinchilla. *Seeking Community in a Global City: Guatemalans and Salvadorans in Los Angeles.* Philadelphia: Temple University Press, 2001.

Haraway, Donna. "Situated Knowledge: The Science Question in Feminism and the Privilege of Partial Perspective." *Feminist Studies.* Vol. 14, No. 3, pp. 575–599, Autumn 1988.

Harvey, David. *A Brief History of Neoliberalism*. New York: Oxford University Press, 2005.

Hayduk, Ronald. *Democracy for All: Restoring Immigrant Voting Rights in the United States*. New York: Routledge, 2006.

Hazan, Miryam. *Incorporating in the United States and Mexico: Mexican Immigrant Mobilization and Organization in Four American Cities*. Ph.D. Dissertation, University of Texas at Austin. August 2006.

Hazan, Miryam and Ron Hayduk. "The Democratic Majority and Latino Incorporation: Has the Structure of Political Opportunities Really Changed?" Paper presented at Annual Meeting of the American Political Science Association. September 3–6, Toronto, Canada, 2009.

Heaney, Michael and Fabio Rojas. "The Partisan Dynamics of Contention: Demobilization of the Antiwar Movement in the United States, 2007–2009." *Mobilization: An International Journal*. Vol. 16, No. 1. 2011.

Heredia, Luisa. "From Prayer to Protest: The Immigrant Rights Movement and the Catholic Church." *Rallying for Immigrant Rights*. Bloemraad, Irene and Kim Voss. 2010. Berkeley: University of California Press, 2011.

Hernandez, Daniel. "Stirring the Other L.A.: How the Media and Immigrant Advocates Got 500,000 People To Protest." *LA Weekly*. March 27, 2006a.

Hernandez, Daniel. "A Day of Power." *L.A. Weekly*. May 4, 2006b.

Hernandez, David. "Undue Process: Racial Genealogies of Immigrant Detention." *Constructing Borders/Crossing Boundaries: Race, Ethnicity, and Immigration*. Ed. Caroline Brettell. Lanham: Lexington Books, 2007.

Hesse-Biber, Sharlene Nagy. *Feminist Research Practice: A Primer*. Thousand Oaks: Sage, 2013.

Higgins, Sean. "Why immigration reform didn't happen in 2007." *Washington Examiner*. November 20, 2012. http://www.washingtonexaminer.com/why-immigration-reform-didnt-happen-in-2007/article/2513987

Highton, Benjamin and Arthur Burris. "New Perspectives on Latino Voter Turnout in the United States." *American Politics Research*. Vol. 30, No. 3, pp. 285–306, 2002.

Hill Collins, Patricia. *Black Feminist Thought: Knowledge, Consciousness, and the Politics of Empowerment*. 2nd Edition. New York: Routledge, 1999.

Hoefer, Michael, Nancy Rytina, and Christopher Campbell. "Estimates of the Unauthorized Immigrant Population Residing in the United States: January 2006." *Department of Homeland Security. Office of Immigration Statistics*. August 2007.

Hondageu-Sotelo, Pierrette and Angelica Salas. *Immigrant Rights in the Shadows of Citizenship*. Ed. Rachel Ida Buff. New York University Press, 2008.

Hunt, Scott and Robert Benford. "Collective Identity, Solidarity, and Commitment." *The Blackwell Companion to Social Movements*. David A. Snow, Sarah A. Soule, and Hanspeter Kriesi. eds. 2004 Malden: Blackwell Publishing, 2004.

Immigration Policy Center (IPC). "The New American Electorate: The Growing Political Power of Immigrants and Their Children." October 2008.

Itkowitz, Colby. "She helped bring down Sheriff Arpaio. Now she's ready to take on hate nationally." November 22, 2016. https://www.washingtonpost.com/news/inspired-life/wp/2016/11/22/she-helped-bring-down-sheriff-arpaio-now-shes-ready-to-take-on-hate-nationally/?utm_term=.8eb3c3126244

Iyengar, Shanto. *Is Anyone Responsible? How Television Frames Political Issues.* University of Chicago Press, 1991.

Iyengar, Shanto and Donald Kinder. *News That Matters.* University of Chicago Press, 1987.

Jasper, James. *Protest: A Cultural Introduction to Social Movements.* Cambridge: Polity, 2014.

Jayaraman, Sarumathi and Immanuel Ness. *The New Urban Immigrant Workforce: Innovative Models for Labor Organizing.* New York: M.E. Sharpe, 2005.

Jensen, Devon. "Transferability." *The Sage Encyclopedia of Qualitative Research Methods.* Vol. 2. Thousand Oaks: Sage, 2008.

Jimenez, Tomas. *Replenished Ethnicity: Mexican Americans, Immigration, and Identity.* Los Angeles: University of California Press, 2010.

Johnson, Anna. "Skipping School, Work For Protest On Immigration Has Consequences." *Charleston Gazette* (WV). April 14, 2006.

Johnson, Kevin R. *The "Huddled Masses" Myth: Immigration and Civil Rights.* Philadelphia: Temple University Press, 2004.

Jones-Correa, Michael. *Between Two Nations: The Political Predicament of Latinos in New York City.* Ithaca: Cornell University Press, 1998.

Jones-Correa, Michael. Ed. *Governing American Cities: Interethnic Coalitions, Competition, and Conflict.* New York: Russell Sage Foundation, 2001.

Jones-Correa, Michael, Sophia Wallace, and Chris Zepeda-Millán. "The Impact of Large-Scale Collective Action on Latino Perceptions of Commonality and Competition with African Americans." *Social Science Quarterly.* Vol. 97, Iss. 2, pp. 458–475, 2016.

Jordan, Miriam. "Univision Gives Citizenship Drive An Unusual Lift: Broadcaster Uses Clout to Mobilize Latino Vote." *The Wall Street Journal.* May 10, 2007.

Junn, Jane and Natalie Masuoka. "Asian American Identity: Shared Racial Status and Political Context." *Perspectives on Politics.* Vol. 6, No. 4, 2008.

Kanstroom, Daniel. *Deportation Nation: Outsiders in American History.* Cambridge: Harvard University Press, 2007.

Kateel, Subhash and Aarti Shahani. "Families For Freedom: Against Deportation and Delegalization." *Keeping Out the Other: A Critical Introduction to Immigration Enforcement Today.* New York: Columbia University Press, 2008.

Kerevel, Yann. "The Influence of Spanish-Language Media on Latino Public Opinion and Group Consciousness." *Social Science Quarterly.* Vol. 92, No. 2, 2011.

Kinder, Donald. "Communication and Politics in the Age of Information." Eds. David Sears, Leonie Huddy, and Robert Jervis. *Oxford Handbook of Political Psychology.* New York: Oxford University Press, 2003.

Klandermans, Bert. "Collective Political Action." *Oxford Handbook of Political Psychology.* Eds. David O. Sears, Leonie Huddy, and Robert Jarvis. Oxford University Press, 2003.

Klandermans, Bert. "The Demand and Supply of Participation: Social-Psychological Correlates of Participation in Social Movements." *Blackwell Companion to Social Movements*. Eds. David Snow, Sarah Soule, and Hanspeter Kriesi. Malden: Blackwell Press, 2004.

Klandermans, Bert and Marga de Weerd. "Group Identification and Political Protest." *Self, Identity, and Social Movements*. Eds. Sheldon Stryker, Timothy Owens, and Robert White. Minneapolis: University of Minnesota Press, 2000.

Klandermans, Bert and Sjoerd Goslinga. "Media Discourse, Movement Publicity, and the Generation of Collective Action Frames: Theoretical and Empirical Exercises in Meaning Construction." Eds. Doug McAdam, John D. McCarthy, and Mayer N. Zald. *Comparative Perspectives on Social Movements: Political Opportunities, Mobilizing Structures, and Cultural Framings*. Cambridge University Press, 1996.

Klandermans, Bert and Conny Roggeband. Eds. *Handbook of Social Movements Across Disciplines*. New York: Springer, 2010.

Koopmans, Ruud. "Protest in Time and Space: The Evolution of Waves of Contention." *The Blackwell Companion to Social Movements*. Eds. David Snow, Sarah Soule, and Hanspeter Kriesi. Malden: Blackwell Publishing, 2004.

Koopmans, Ruud. "Repression and the Public Sphere: Discursive Opportunities for Repression against the Extreme Right in Germany in the 1990s." *Repression and Mobilization*. Eds. Christian Davenport, Hank Johnston, and Carol Mueller. Minneapolis: University of Minnesota Press, 2005.

Kretsedemas, Philip. "What Does an Undocumented Immigrant Look Like? Local Enforcement and the New Immigrant Profiling." *Keeping Out The Other: A Critical Introduction to Immigration Enforcement Today*. New York: Columbia University Press, 2008.

Kriesi, Hanspeter. "Political Context and Opportunity." *Blackwell Companion to Social Movements*. Eds. David Snow, Sarah Soule, and Hanspeter Kriesi. Malden: Blackwell Press, 2004.

Krogstad, Jens Manuel, Mark Hugo Lopez, Gustavo López, Jeffrey S. Passel and Eileen Patten. "Millennials Make Up Almost Half of Latino Eligible Voters in 2016; Youth, Naturalizations Drive Number of Hispanic Eligible Voters to Record 27.3 Million." Washington, D.C.: Pew Research Center, January, 2016.

Krueger, Anne. "Sheriff's Officials Describing Incident As Arson, Hate Crime." *Union-Tribune*. April 12, 2006.

Kuper, Ayelet, Lorelei Lingard, and Wendy Levinson. "Critically Appraising Qualitative Research." *BMJ*. DOI: http://dx.doi.org/10.1136/bmj.a1035, 2008.

Kwong, Peter. "Ethnic Subcontracting as an Impediment to Interethnic Coalitions: The Chinese Experience." *Governing American Cities*. Ed. Michael Jones-Correa. New York: Russell Sage Foundation, 2001.

Lafayette, Jon. "Hispanic Media Remains Area of Growth." 2008. www.tvweek .com/news/2008/02/hispanic_media_remains_area_of.php. 2008.

Lattanzi Shutika, Debra. "The Ambivalent Welcome: Cinco de Mayo and the Symbolic Expression of Local Identity and Ethnic Relations." *New Faces In New*

Places: The Changing Geography of American Immigration. Massey, Douglas. Ed. New York: Russell Sage, 2008.

Lazare, Sarah. "Lessons from the Successful Campaign to Defeat the Trump-Style Hate of Sheriff Joe Arpaio." *AlterNet.* November 10, 2016. http://www.alternet.org/activism/lessons-successful-campaign-defeat-trump-style-hate-sheriff-joe-arpaio

Leal, David. "Political Participation by Latino Non-Citizens in the United States." *British Journal of Political Science.* Vol. 32, 2002.

Leal, David, Stephen Nuño, Jongho Lee, and Rodolfo de la Garza. "Latinos, Immigration, and the 2006 Midterm Elections." *Political Science and Politics.* Vol. 41, No. 2, pp. 309–317, 2008.

Lee, Taeku. "Race, Immigration, and the Identity-to-Politics Link." *Annual Review of Political Science.* Vol. 11, pp. 457–478, 2008.

Lee, Tiane and Susan Fiske. "Not an Outgroup, Not Yet an Ingroup: Immigrants in the Stereotype Content Model." *International Journal of Intercultural Relations.* Vol. 30, pp. 751–768, 2006.

Leighley, Jan. *Strength in Numbers? The Political Mobilization of Racial and Ethnic Minorities.* Princeton University Press, 2001.

Leighley, Jan and Jonathan Nagle. *Who Votes Now? Demographics, Issues, Inequality, and Turnout in the United States.* Princeton University Press, 2013.

Lerman, Amy and Vesla Weaver. *Arresting Citizenship: The Democratic Consequences of American Crime Control.* University of Chicago Press, 2014.

Lievrouw, Leah. *Alternative and Activist New Media.* Malden: Polity, 2011.

Light, Ivan. "How Los Angeles Deflected Mexican Immigrants to the American Heartland." Migration Policy Institute. Feature Story. October 2007. http://www.migrationinformation.org/Feature/display.cfm?id=645.

Light, Ivan, Parminder Bhachu, and Stavros Karageorgis. "Migration Networks and Immigrant Entrepreneurship." *Immigration and Entrepreneurship: Culture, Capital and Ethnic Networks.* Eds. Ivan Light and Parminder Bhachu. New Brunswick: Transaction, 1993.

Light, Ivan and Stavros Karageorgis. "Economic Saturation and Immigrant Entrepreneurship." *Immigrant Entrepreneurship and Immigrant Absorption in the United States and Israel.* Brookfield: Ashgate, 1997.

Lincoln, Yvonna and Egon Guba. *Naturalistic Inquiry.* Newbury Park: Sage, 1985.

Logan, John and John Mollenkopf. "People & Politics in America's Big Cities." DRUM Major Institute for Public Policy, 2001.

Lovato, Roberto. "Voices of a New Movimiento." The Nation. June 19, 2006. https://www.thenation.com/article/voices-new-movimiento/

Macia-Rojas, Patrisia. *From Deportation to Prison: The Politics of Immigration Enforcement in Post-Civil Rights America.* New York: NYU Press, 2016.

Marable, Manning. "Building Coalitions among Communities of Color: Beyond Racial Identity Politics."*Blacks, Latinos, and Asians in Urban America.* Ed. James Jennings. Westport: Praeger, 1994.

Marrow, Helen. "Hispanic Immigration, Black Population Size, and Intergroup Relations in the Rural and Small-Town South." *New Faces In New Places:*

The Changing Geography of American Immigration. Massey, Douglas. Ed. New York: Russell Sage, 2008.

Martin, Philip. *NAFTA and US-Mexico Migration*. Gianni Foundation, Berkeley, California, 2005. http://giannini.ucop.edu/Mex_USMigration.pdf.

Marquez, Benjamin and James Jennings. "Representation by Other Means: Mexican American and Puerto Rican Social Movement Organizations." *PS*. Sept. 2000.

Marucci, Michele and Ryan Sholin. *Alameda Times-Star*. "Hundreds March for Amnesty." September 5, 2006.

Martinez, Lisa. "Yes We Can: Latino Participation in Unconventional Politics." *Social Forces*. Vol. 84, No. 1, Sept. 2005.

Martinez, Lisa. "The Individual and Contextual Determinants of Protest among Latinos." *Mobilization*, Vol. 13, No. 2, pp. 180–204, 2008.

Marx, Gary. "External Efforts to Damage or Facilitate Social Movements: Some Patterns, Explanations, Outcomes, and Complications." *The Dynamics of Social Movements*. Eds. Mayer Zald and John McCarthy. Cambridge: Winthrop Publishers, 1979.

Massey, Douglas. *Categorically Unequal: The American Stratification System*. New York: Russell Sage Foundation, 2007.

Massey, Douglas. Ed. *New Faces In New Places: The Changing Geography of American Immigration*. New York: Russell Sage, 2008.

Massey, Douglas S., and Chiara Capoferro. "The Geographic Diversification of American Immigration." *New Faces in New Places*, Ed. Douglas S. Massey. New York: Russell Sage Foundation, 2008.

Massey, Douglass, Jorge Durand, and Nolan Malone. *Beyond Smoke and Mirrors: Mexican Immigration in an Era of Economic Integration*. New York: Russell Sage Foundation, 2002.

Massey, Douglas and Magaly Sanchez. *Broken Boundaries: Creating Immigrant Identity in Anti-Immigrant Times*. New York: Russell Sage Foundation, 2010.

Masuoka, Natalie and Jane Junn. *The Politics of Belonging: Race, Public Opinoin, and Immigration*. University of Chicago Press, 2013.

Mathew, Biju. *Taxi! Cabs and Capitalism in New York City*. New York: The New Press, 2005.

Mayer, Brian. *Blue-Green Coalitions: Fighting for Safe Workplaces and Healthy Communities*. Ithaca: Cornell University Press, 2009.

Mayhew, David. *Congress: The Electoral Connection*. New Haven: Yale University Press, 1975.

McAdam, Doug. *Political Process and the Development of Black Insurgency, 1930–1970*. University of Chicago Press, 1982.

McAdam, Doug, John McCarthy, and Mayer Zald. "Introduction". *Comparative Perspectives on Social Movements*. Cambridge University Press, 1996.

McAdam, Doug and Ronnelle Paulsen. "Specifying the Relationship Between Social Ties and Activism." *American Journal of Sociology*. Vol. 99, No. 3, pp. 640–667, 1993.

McAdam, Doug and Dieter Rucht. "The Cross-National Diffusion of Movement Ideas." *Annals of the American Academy of Political and Social Science*. Vol. 528. Jul. 1993.

McAdam, Doug, Sidney Tarrow, and Charles Tilly. *Dynamics of Contention*. Cambridge University Press, 2001.

McAdam, Doug and Karina Kloos. *Deeply Divided: Racial Politics and Social Movements in Postwar America*. New York: Oxford University Press, 2014.

McCammon, Holly and Karen Campbell. "Allies on the Road to Victory: Coalition Formation Between the Suffragists and the Women's Christian Temperance Union." *Mobilization*. Vol. 7, No. 3, 2002.

McCarthy, John, and Mayer Zald. "Resource Mobilization and Social Movements: A Partial Theory." *AJS*. Vol. 82, No. 6., 1977.

McCarthy, John D., Clark McPhail, and Jackie Smith. "Images of Protest: Dimensions of Selection Bias in Media Coverage of Washington Demonstrations, 1982 and 1991." *American Sociological Review*, 1996.

McCarthy, John, Jackie Smith, and Mayer Zald. "Accessing Public Media, Electoral, and Governmental Agendas." *Comparative Perspectives on Social Movements*. Eds. Doug McAdam, John McCarthy, and Mayer Zald. New York: Cambridge University Press, 1996.

McClain, Paula and Steven Tauber. "Racial Minority Group Relations in Multiracial Society." *Governing American Cities*. Ed. Michael Jones-Correa. New York: Russell Sage Foundation, 2001.

McClain, Paula, Jessica Johnson Carew, Eugene Walton, and Candis Watts. "Group Membership, Group Identity, and Group Consciousness: Measures of Racial Identity in American Politics?" *Annual Review of Political Science*. Vol. 12, pp. 471–485, 2009.

McClain, Paula D., Niambi M. Carter, Victoria M. DeFrancesco Soto, Monique L. Lyle, Jeffrey D. Grynaviski, Shayla C. Nunnally, Thomas J. Scotto, J. Alan Kendrick, Gerald F. Lackey, and Kendra Davenport Cotton. "Racial Distancing in a Southern City: Latino Immigrants' Views of Black Americans." *Journal of Politics*. Vol. 68, No. 3, pp. 571–584, 2006.

McDuff, Jordan. "Invisible Immigration." *Hemisphere*. Vol. 13., Spring 2004.

McFadden, Robert. "Across the U.S., Growing Rallies for Immigration." *New York Times*. April 10, 2006.

Medina Vidal, Xavier. "Immigration politics and group consciousness for newcomers to Southern US politics." *Politics, Groups, and Identities*, DOI: 10.1080/21565503.2016.1169933, 2016.

Mendelson, Margot, Shayan Strom, and Michael Wishnie. "Collateral Damage: An Examination of ICE's Fugitive Operations Program." *Migration Policy Institute*. February 2009.

Menjivar, Cecilia. "Immigrants, Immigration, and Sociology: Reflections on the State of the Discipline." *Sociological Inquiry*. Vol. 80, No. 1, 3–27, 2010.

Menjivar, Cecilia and Daniel Kanstroom (Eds). *Constructing Immigrant 'Illegality.'* Cambridge University Press, 2014.

Merolla, Jennifer, S. Karthick Ramakrishnan, and Chris Haynes. "'Illegal.' 'Undocumented,' or 'Unauthorized': Equivalency Frames, Issue Frames, and Public Opinion on Immigration." *Perspectives on Politics*. Vol. 1, No. 3, pp. 789–807, 2013.

Meyer, David. "Peace Protest and Policy: Explaining the Rise and Decline of Antinuclear Movements in Postwar America." *Policy Studies Journal*. Vol. 21, No. 1, 1993.

Meyer, David. "Social Movements and Public Policy: Eggs, Chickens, and Theory." *Routing the Opposition: Social Movements, Public Policy, and Democracy*. Eds. David Meyer, Valerie Jenness, and Helen Ingram. Minneapolis: University of Minnesota Press, 2005.

Meyer, David. *The Politics of Protest: Social Movements in America*. New York: Oxford University Press, 2007.

Meyer, David and Catherine Corrigall-Brown. "Coalitions and Political Context: U.S. Movements Against Wars in Iraq." *Mobilization*. Vol. 10, No. 3, 2005.

Meyer, David and Debra Minkoff. "Conceptualizing Political Opportunity." *Social Forces*. June, Vol. 82. No. 4, 2004.

Michelson, Melissa. "Meeting the Challenge of Latino Voter Mobilization." *The Annals of the American Academy*. Vol. 601, Sept. 2005.

Michelson, Melissa. "Mobilization by Different Means: Nativity and GOTV in the United States." *International Migration Review*. Vol. 48, No. 3, pp. 710–727, 2014.

Milkman, Ruth. *L.A. Story: Immigrant Workers and the Future of the U.S. Labor Movement*. New York: Russell Sage Foundation, 2006.

Milkman, Ruth and Kent Wong. *Voices from the Front Lines: Organizing Immigrant Workers in Los Angeles*. UCLA Center for Labor Research and Education, 2000.

Milkman, Ruth and Veronica Terriquez. "'We Are the Ones Who Are Out in Front': Women's Leadership in the Immigrant Rights Movement." *Feminist Studies*. Vol. 38, No. 3, pp. 723–752, 2012.

Millard, Ann, and Jorge Chapa. Eds. *Apple Pie and Enchiladas: Latino Newcomers in the Rural Midwest*. Austin: University of Texas Press, 2004.

Miller, Lia. "To Marshal Immigrant Forces, Start at Ethnic Radio Stations." *New York Times*. April 10, 2006.

Miller, Marjorie. "Economic Strife Drives Latino Vote." *Los Angeles Times*. October 26, 2008.

Mock, Brentin. "Immigration Backlash: Hate Crimes Against Latinos Flourish." *Intelligence Report*. Southern Poverty Law Center. 2007.

Mohl, Raymond and George Pozzetta. "From Migration to Multiculturalism: A History of Florida Immigration." *The New History of Florida*. Ed. Michael Gannon. Gainesville: University of Florida Press, 1996.

Mollenkopf, John. "Urban Political Conflicts and Alliances: New York and Los Angeles Compared." *Handbook of International Migration*. Eds. Charles Hirschman, Philip Kasinitz, and Josh DeWind. New York: Russell Sage Foundation, 1999.

Mollenkopf, John, David Olson, and Timothy Ross. "Immigrant Political Participation in New York and Los Angeles." *Governing American Cities*. Ed. Michael Jones-Correa. New York: Russell Sage Foundation, 2001.

Mongelli, Lorena, John Mazor, and Jana Winter. "Alien Nation's United Front – Sickout, Massive Rallies Try to Kick U.S. in the Asset$. *New York Post*. May 2, 2006.

Montero, Douglas and Lorena Mongelli. "10,000+ On the March: Immigrants Hit B'Klyn Bridge in Rights Rally." *New York Post*. April 2, 2006.

Mormino, Gary. *Land of Sunshine, State of Dreams*. Gainesville: University of Florida Press, 2005.

Morris, Aldon. *The Origins of the Civil Rights Movement*. New York: Free Press, 1984.

Morris, Aldon and Naomi Braine. "Social Movements and Oppositional Consciousness." *Oppositional Consciousness: The Subjective Roots of Social Protest*. University of Chicago Press, 2001.

Muñoz, Carlos. *Youth, Identity, and Power*. New York: Verso Press, 1989.

Muskal, Michael and Carol Williams. "Immigrants Take Economic Impact to the Streets." *Los Angeles Times*. May 1, 2006.

Myers, Daniel. "The Diffusion of Collective Violence: Infectiousness, Susceptibility, and Mass Media Networks." *The American Journal of Sociology*. Vol. 106, No. 1, Jul. 2000.

National Associate of Latino Elected and Appointed Officials (NALEO) Education Fund. "Latino Voters in the 2008 Presidential Election: Post-Election Survey of Latino Voters." 2008.

Navarro, Armando. *The Immigration Crisis: Nativism, Armed Vigilantism, and the Rise of a Countervailing Movement*. New York: AltaMira Press, 2008.

Nevins, Joseph. *Operation Gatekeeper: The Rise of the "Illegal Alien" and the Making of the U.S.-Mexico Boundary*. New York: Routledge, 2001.

New York City Department of City Planning. "The Newest New Yorkers 2000: Immigrant New York in the New Millennium." *Population Division*, 2000.

Ngai, Mae. *Impossible Subjects: Illegal Aliens and the Making of Modern America*. Princeton University Press, 2005.

Nguyen, Tram. *We Are All Suspects Now: Untold Stories from Immigrant Communities after 9/11."* Boston: Beacon Press, 2005.

Nichols, John and Robert McChesney. *It's the Media, Stupid*. New York: Seven Stories Press,

Nicholls, Walter. *The DREAMers: How the Undocumented Youth Movement Transformed the Immigrant Rights Debate*. Palo Alto: Stanford University Press, 2013.

Nicholls, Walter and Justus Uiterkark. *Cities and Social Movements: Immigrant Rights Activism in the United States, France, and the Netherlands, 1970–2015*. Malden: Wiley Blackwell, 2017.

Northern Manhattan Coalition for Immigrant Rights. "*Deportado, Dominiano, y Humano*: The Realities of Dominican Deportation and Related Policy Recommendations." http://www.nmcir.org/Deportado%20Dominicano%20y%20Humano.pdf

Nuño, Stephen. "Latino Mobilization and Vote Choice in the 2000 Presidential Election." *American Politics Research*, Vol. 35, No. 2, pp. 273–293, 2007.

O'Donnel, Michelle. "Thousands Turn Out, But Support is Mixed Among New York's Immigrants." *New York Times*. May 2, 2006. http://www.nytimes.com/2006/05/02/us/02protest.html.

O'Reilly, Andrew. "Bernie Sander's Young Latino Supporters Still Skeptical of Hilary Clinton." *Fox News*. June 9, 2016. http://www.foxnews.com/politics/2016/06/09/bernie-sanders-young-latino-supporters-still-skeptical-hillary-clinton.html.

Okamato, Dina. "Organizing Across Ethnic Boundaries in the Post-Civil Rights Era: Asian American Panethnic Coalition." *Strategic Alliances: Coalition Building and Social Movements*. Eds. Nella Van Dyke and Holly McCammon. Minneapolis: University of Minnesota Press, 2010.

Okamoto, Dina and Kim Ebert. "Beyond the Ballot: Immigrant Collective Action in Gateways and New Destinations in the United States." *Social Problems*. Vol. 57, Iss. 4, pp. 529–558, 2010.

Oliver, Pamela. "Repression and Crime Control: Why Social Movement Scholars Should Pay Attention to Mass Incarceration as a Form of Repression." *Mobilization: The International Quarterly*. Vol. 13, No. 1, 2008.

Oliver, Pamela E. and Daniel J. Myers. "Networks, Diffusion, and Cycles of Collective Action." *Social Movements and Networks: Relational Approaches to Collective Action*. Eds. Mario Diani and Doug McAdam. Oxford University Press, 2003.

Omi, Michael and Howard Winant. *Racial Formation in the United States: From the 1960s to the 1990s*. New York: Routlege, 1994.

Orum, Anthony, Joe Feagin, and Gildeon Sjoberg. "The Nature of the Case Study." *A Case for the Case Study*. Eds. Joe R. Feagin, Anthony M. Orum, and Gildeon Sjoberg. Chapel Hill: University of North Carolina Press, 1991.

Pallares, Amalia and Nilda Flores-Gonzalez. *Marcha!: Latino Chicago and the Immigrant Rights Movement*. Champaign: University of Illinois Press, 2010.

Panagopoulos, Costas and Donald Green. "Spanish-Language Radio Advertisements and Latino Voter Turnout in the 2006 Congressional Elections." *Political Research Quarterly*. Vol. 63, Iss. 3, 588–599, 2011.

Pantoja, Adrian and Gary Segura. "Fear and Loathing in California: Contextual Threat and Political Sophistication Among Latino Voters." *Political Behavior*. Vol. 25, No. 3, Sept. 2003.

Pantoja, Adrian, Ricardo Ramirez and Gary M. Segura. "Citizens by Choice, Voters by Necessity: Patterns in Political Mobilization by Naturalized Latinos." *Political Research Quarterly*, Vol. 54, No. 4, Dec. 2001.

Papademetrious, Demetrios. "The Shifting Expections of Free Trade and Migration." *NAFTA's Promise and Reality*. Washington, D.C.: Carnegie Endowment for International Peace, 2004.

Park, Edward and John Park. "Korean Americans and the Crisis of Liberal Coalition: Immigrants and Politics in Los Angeles." *Governing American Cities*. Ed. Michael Jones-Correa. New York: Russell Sage Foundation, 2001.

Parke, Ross and Raymond Buriel. "Socialization in the Family: Ethnic and Ecological Perspectives." *Handbook of Child Psychology: Social, Emotional, and Personality Development*. 6th Edition. Editors William Damon, Richard M. Lerner, Nancy Eisenberg. John Wiley & Sons: Hoboken, 2006.

Patler, Caitlin and Roberto Gonzales. "Framing Citizenship: Media Coverage of Anti-Deportation Cases Led by Undocumented Immigrant Youth Organizations." *Journal of Ethnic and Migration Studies*. Vol. 41, No. 9, pp. 1453–1474, 2015.

Payne, Charles. *I've Got the Light of Freedom: The Organizing Tradition and the Mississippi Freedom Struggle*. Berkeley: University of Califorina Press, 2007.

Pedraza, Francisco, Gary Segura, and Shaun Bowler. "The Efficacy and Alienation of Juan Q. Public: The Immigration Marches and Orientation toward American Political Institutions." *Rallying for Immigrant Rights: The Fight for Inclusion in 21st Century America*. Bloemraad, Irene and Kim Voss. Berkeley: University of California Press, 2011.

Peltier, Leonard. *Prison Writings: My Life Is My Sun Dance*. New York: St. Martin's Griffin, 2000.

Perla, Hector. "Grassroots Mobilization Against US Military Intervention in El Salvador." *Socialism and Democracy*. Vol. 22, No. 3, 2008.

Perla, Hector. *Sandinista Nicaragua's Resistance to US Coercion: Revolutionary Deterrence in Asymmetric Conflict*. Cambridge University Press, 2017.

Perla, Hector and Susan Bibler Coutin. "Legacies and Origins of the 1980s US-Central American Sanctuary Movement." *Refuge*. Vol. 26, No. 1, 2009.

Peutz, Nathalie and Nicholas De Genova. "Introduction." *Deportation Regime: Sovereignty, Space, and the Freedom of Movement*. Eds. Nicholas De Genova and Nathalie Peutz. Durham: Duke University Press, 2010.

Pew Hispanic Center. "Latinos in California, Texas, New York, Florida, and New Jersey. March 2004.

Pew Hispanic Center. "The Hispanic Voter in the 2008 Election." November 5, 2008.

Pirani, Zahida. "New York City Immigration Organizing and the National Call for Immigrant Rights." *Lines*. Vol. 5, Iss. 1 &2, May 2006/August 2006.

Piven, Frances Fox and Richard Cloward. *Poor People's Movements: Why They Succeed, How They Fail*. New York: Vintage Press, 1977.

Polopolus, Leo and Robert Emerson. "The Latinization of the Florida Farm Labor Market." Institute of Food and Agricultural Sciences. University of Florida. Staff Paper 94–9, August 1994.

Pomfret, John. "Cardinal Puts Church in Fight for Immigrant Rights." *Los Angeles Times*. April 2, 2006.

Ponce, Albert. "Racialization, Resistance and the Migrant Rights Movement: A Historical Analysis." *Critical Sociology*, Vol. 40, No. 1, pp. 9–17, 2014.

Poole, Shelia. "Immigration Rallies: Radio Stations Lead the Charge for Hispanics." *The Atlantic Journal-Constitution*. April 12, 2006.

Portes, Alejandro and Ruben Rumbaut. *Immigrant American: A Portrait*. Berkeley: University of California Press, 2014.

Prince, Marie and Courtney Whitworth. "Soccer and Latino Cultural Space: Metropolitan Washington Futbol Leagues." *Hispanic Spaces, Latino Places*. Eds. Daniel Arreola. Austin: University of Texas Press, 2004.

Pulido, Laura. "The Roots of Political Consciousness Among Militant Unionist and Worker Activists in Los Angeles." Los Angeles: Southern California Studies Center, USC, 1998.

Pulido, Laura. *Black, Brown, Yellow, & Left: Radical Activism in Los Angeles*. Berkeley: University of California Press, 2006.

Quesada, Uriel, Letitia Gomez, and Salvador Vidal-Ortiz. *Queer Brown Voices: Personal Narratives of Latina/o LGBT Activism.* Austin: University of Texas Press, 2015.

Quijano, Anibal. "Coloniality of Power, Eurocentrism and Latin America." *Nepantla: Views from the South.* Vol. 1, No. 3, pp. 533–580, 2000.

Ragin, Charles. "'Casing' and the Process of Social Inquiry." *What Is a Case? Exploring the Foundations of Social Inquiry.* Eds. Charles Ragin and Howard Becker. Cambridge University Press, 1992.

Ragin, Charles. *Constructing Social Research.* Thousand Oaks: Pine Forge Press, 1994.

Ragin, Charles. "Turning the Tables: How Case-Oriented Research Challenges Variable-Oriented Research." *Rethinking Social Inquiry: Diverse Tools, Shared Standards.* Lanham: Rowan & Littlefield, 2004.

Ramakrishnan, S. Karthick and Thomas J. Espenshade. "Immigrant Incorporation and Political Participation in the United States." *International Migration Review.* Vol. 35. No 3. Fall 2001.

Ramakrishnan, Karthick and Tom Wong. "Partisanship, Not Spanish: Explaining Municipal Ordinances Affecting Undocumented Immigrants." *Taking Local Control: Immigration Policy Activism in U.S. Cities and States.* Stanford University Press, 2010.

Ramírez, Ricardo. "Giving Voice to Latino Voters: A Field Experiment on the Effectiveness of a National Nonpartisan Mobilization Effort." *The ANNALS of the American Academy of Political and Social Science.* Vol. 602, No. 1, 2005.

Ramírez, Ricardo. "Political Mobilization en Espanol: Spanish Language Radio and the Activation of Political Identities." *Rallying for Immigrant Rights: The Fight for Inclusion in 21ˢᵗ Century America.* Bloemraad, Irene and Kim Voss. Berkeley: University of California Press, 2011.

Ramírez, Ricardo. *Mobilizing Opportunities: The Evolving Latino Electorate and the Future of American Politics.* Charlottesville: University of Virginia Press, 2013.

Ramírez, Ricardo and Janelle Wong. "Non-Partisan Latino and Asian American Contactability and Voter Mobilization." In Taeku Lee, Karthick Ramakrishnan and Ricardo Ramírez, eds., *Transforming Politics, Transforming America: The Political and Civic Incorporation of Immigrants in the United States.* University of Virginia Press, pp. 151–171, 2006.

Rapp, David. "Editor's Notebook: Border Lines." *CQ Weekly Online.* March 27, 2006.

Rector R. "Important poverty: immigration and poverty in the United States." *Heritage Special Report.* The Heritage Foundation. Oct. 25, 2006.

Reese, Ellen, Christian Petit, and David Meyer. "Sudden Mobilization: Movement Crossovers, Threats, and the Surprising Rise of the U.S. Antiwar Movement." *Strategic Alliances: Coalition Building and Social Movements.* Eds. Nella Van Dyke and Holly McCammon. Minneapolis: University of Minnesota Press, 2010.

Reilly, Katie. "Here Are All the Times Donald Trump Insulted Mexico." *Time.* August 31, 2016. http://time.com/4473972/donald-trump-mexico-meeting-insult/

Rios, Victor. *Punished: Policing the Lives of Black and Latino Boys*. New York University Press, 2011.

Rivera-Salgado, Gaspar. "Mexican Migrant Organizations." *Invisible No More: Mexican Migrant Civic Participation in the United States*. Eds. Xochitl Bada, Jonathan Fox, and Andrew Selee. Woodrow Wilson Center for Scholars. 2006.

Roberts, Sam. "Listening to (and Saving) the World's Languages." *New York Times*. April 28, 2010.

Robinson, William. "Undocumented in America." *New Left Review*. Vol. 47. Sept–Oct. 2007.

Rocco, Raymond. *Transforming Citizenship: Democracy, Membership, and Belonging in Latino Communities*. Lansing: Michigan State University Press, 2014.

Rodriguez, America. *Making Latino News: Race, Language, Class*. Thousand Oaks: Sage, 1999.

Rodriguez, Dylan. *Forced Passages: Imprisoned Radical Intellectuals and the U.S. Prison Regime*. Minneapolis: University of Minnesota Press, 2006.

Rodriguez, Javier. "La historia esta de nuestro lado." *La Opinion*. February 2, 2006.

Rodriguez, Juana. *Queer Latinidad: Identity Practices, Discursive Spaces*. New York University Press, 2003.

Roka, Fritz and Dorothy Cook. "Farmworkers in Southwest Florida: Final Report." Southwest Florida Research and Education Center. http://swfrec.ifas .ufl.edu/docs/pdf/economics/extension/econ_final98.pdf.

Rose, Derek. "May Day on Streets. Marches, Boycott as Illegal Immigrants Seek New Laws." *New York Daily News*. May 1, 2006.

Rose, Fred. *Coalitions Across the Class Divide: Lessons from the Labor, Peace, and Environmental Movements*. Ithaca: Cornell University Press, 2000.

Rosenstone, Steven J. and John Hansen. *Mobilization, Participation and Democracy in America*. New York: Longman, 2003.

Rouse, Stella. *Latinos in the Legislative Process: Interests and Influence*. Cambridge: Cambridge University Press, 2016.

Roth, Benita. "'Organizing One's Own' as Good Politics: Second Wave Feminist and the Meaning of Coalition." *Strategic Alliances: Coalition Building and Social Movements*. Eds. Nella Van Dyke and Holly McCammon. Minneapolis: University of Minnesota Press, 2010.

Rucht, Dieter. "Movement Allies, Adversaries, and Third Parties." *Blackwell Companion to Social Movements*. Eds. David Snow, Sarah Soule, and Hanspeter Kriesi, Blackwell, 2004.

Ruiz, Vicki and Virginia Sanchez Korrol. Eds. *Latina Legacies: Identity, Biography, and Community*. New York: Oxford University Press, 2005.

Ryan, Charlotte. *Prime Time Activism*. Boston: South End Press, 1991.

Sabato, Larry. *Feeding Frenzy: How Attack Journalism Has Transformed American Politics*. New York: Free Press, 1991.

Salles, Andrea. "Small, But Spirited – Immigration-Rights Contingent Passes Through Aurora." *The Beacon News*. September 4, 2006.

Sampaio, Anna. *Terrorizing Latina/o Immigrants: Race, Gender, and Immigration Politics in the Age of Security*. Philadelphia: Temple University Press, 2015.

San Diego Union-Tribune. "Answering the Bell: Marching at the Expense of Education." March 28, 2006.

Sanchez, Gabriel. "The Role of Group Consciousness in Political Participation Among Latinos in the United States." *American Politics Research*, Vol. 34, No. 4, pp. 427–450, 2006a.

Sanchez, Gabriel. "The Role of Group Consciousness in Latino Public Opinion." *Political Research Quarterly*. Vol. 59, No. 3, pp. 435–446, 2006b.

Sanchez, Gabriel and Natalie Masuoka. "Brown-Utility Heuristic? The Presence and Contributing Factors of Latino Linked Fate." *Hispanic Journal of Behavioral Sciences*. Vol. 32, 2010.

Sanchez, George. "Face the Nation: Race, Immigration, and the Rise of Nativism in Late-Twentieth-Century America." *The Handbook of International Migration*. Charles Hirschman, Philip Kasinitz, and Josh DeWind, eds. Russell Sage Foundation: New York, 1999.

Sandler, Michael. "A Parting of Ways at the Border." *CQ Weekly Online*. March 27, 2006a.

Sandler, Michael. "2006 Legislative Summary: Immigration Policy Overhaul." *CQ Weekly Online*. December 18, 2006b.

Sandler, Michael and Elizabeth Crowley. "Senate Splits on Guest Workers." *CQ Weekly Online*. April 3, 2006.

Sandoval, Claudia. "A New Realignment?: Using Citizenship Status to Affect the Political Landscape and Black-Latino Relations." Ph.D. Dissertation, University of Chicago, 2014.

Sassen, Saskia. *The Mobility of Labor and Capital: A Study of International Investment and Labor Flow*. New York: Cambridge University Press, 1988.

Sassen, Saskia. *Globalization and its Discontents*. New York: New Press, 1999.

Sawyers, Traci and David Meyer. "Missed Opportunities: Social Movement Abeyance and Public Policy." *Social Problems*. Vol. 46, No. 2, 1999.

Schmidt, Ella. "Whose Culture? Globalism, Localism, and the Expansion of Tradition: The Case of the Hnahnu of Hidalgo, Mexico and Clearwater, Florida." *Globalizations*. Vol. 4, No. 1, March 2007.

Schmitt, Eric. "Bush Aides Weigh Legalizing Status of Mexicans in U.S." *New York Times*. July 15, 2001. http://www.nytimes.com/2001/07/15/us/bush-aides-weigh-legalizing-status-of-mexicans-in-us.html

Schofield, Janet. "Increasing the generalizability of qualitative research." *Qualitative Inquiry in Education: The Continuing Debate*. Eds. Elliot W. Eisner and Alan Peshkin. New York: Teachers College Press, 1990.

Schussman, Alan and Sarah Soule. "Process and Protest: Accounting for Individual Protest Participation." *Social Forces*. Vol. 84, No. 2, December 2005.

Schutt, Russell. *Investigating the Social World: The Process and Practice of Research*. 7th Edition. Thousand Oaks: Sage, 2012.

Scott, James C. *Domination and the Arts of Resistance: Hidden Transcripts*. New Haven: Yale University Press, 1990.

Seawright, Jason. "Case Selection Techniques in Case Study Research: A Menu of Qualitative and Quantitative Options." *Political Research Quarterly*. Vol. 61, No. 2, 2008.

Sen, Rinku. *Stir It Up: Lessons in Community Organizing and Advocacy.* San Francisco: Jossey-Bass, 2003.

Shahani, Aarti and Judith Greene. "Local Democracy on ICE: Why State and Local Governments Have No Business in Federal Immigration Law Enforcement." A Justice Strategies Report, February 2009.

Shanahan, Suzanne and Susan Olzak. "The Effects of Immigrant Diversity and Ethnic Competition on Collective Conflict in Urban America: An Assessment of Two Movements of Mass Migration, 1869–1924 and 1965–1993," *Journal of American Ethnic History.* Vol. 18, No. 3, pp. 40–64, 1999.

Shaw, Randy. *The Activist's Handbook.* Los Angeles: University of California Press, 2001.

Shenton, Andrew K. "Strategies for Ensuring Trustworthiness in Qualitative Research Projects." *Education for Information.* Vol. 22, pp. 63–75, 2004.

Shinnar, Rachel and Cheri Young. "Hispanic Immigrant Entrepreneurs in the Las Vegas Metropolitan Area: Motivations for Entry into and Outcomes of Self-Employment." *Journal of Small Business Management.* Vol. 46, No. 2, 2008.

Sjoberg, Gideon, Norma Williams, Ted Vaugham, and Andree Sjoberg. "The Case Study Approach in Social Research: Basic Methodological Issues." *A Case for the Case Study.* Eds. Joe R. Feagin, Anthony M. Orum, and Gildeon Sjoberg. Chapel Hill: University of North Carolina Press, 1991.

Shore, Herb. "Birth of a Movement." San Diego Democratic Socialist of America. March 27, 2006. http://www.dsausa.org/LatestNews/2006/Los%20Angeles%20protest/mass%20march.html.

Siemaszko, Corky. "N.Y. Immigrants Rally for Rights." *New York Daily News.* May 2, 2006.

Sierra, Christine Marie Sierra. "In Search of National Power: Chicanos Working the System on Immigration Reform, 1976–1986." *Chicano Politics and Society in the Late Twentieth Century.* Austin: University of Texas Press, 1999.

Small, Mario. "'How Many Cases Do I Need?' On Science and the Logic of Case Selection in Field-Based Research." *Ethnography.* Vol. 10, No. 1, 2009.

Smith, Jackie and Joe Bandy. "Introduction: Cooperation and Conflict in Transnational Protest." *Coalitions across Borders: Transnational Protest and the Neoliberal Order.* Eds. Joe Bandy and Jackie Smith. New York: Rowman & Littlefield, 2005.

Smith, Jackie and Dawn Wiest. *Social Movements in the World-System: The Politics of Crisis and Transformation.* New York: Russell Sage Foundation, 2012.

Smith, Jackie, John D. McCarthy, Clark McPhail, and Boguslaw Augustyn. "From Protest to Agenda Building: Description Bias in Media Coverage of Protest Events in Washington, D.C." *Social Forces.* Vol. 79, No. 4. 2001.

Smith, Linda Tuhiwai. *Decolonizing Methodologies.* 2nd Edition. London: Zed Books, 2012.

Snow, David. "Framing, Processes, Ideology, and Discursive Fields." *Blackwell Companion to Social Movements.* Eds. David Snow, Sarah Soule, and Hanspeter Kriesi. Malden: Blackwell Press, 2004.

Snow, David. "Framing and Social Movements." *The Wiley Blackwell Encyclopedia of Social & Political Movements.* Hoboken: Wiley-Blackwell, 2013.

Snow, David and Robert Benford. "Master Frames and Cycles of Protest." *Frontiers in Social Movement Theory*. Aldon D. Morris and Carol McClurg Mueller. eds. New Haven: Yale University Press, 1992.

Snow, David, Daniel Cress, Liam Downey, and Andrew Jones. "Disrupting the "Quotidian": Reconceptualizing the Relationship Between Breakdown and the Emergence of Collective Action." *Mobilization*. Vol. 3, No. 1, 1998.

Snow, David and Sarah Soule. *A Primer on Social Movements*. New York: Norton & Company, 2010.

Snow, David and Danny Trom. "The Case Study and the Study of Social Movements." *Methods of Social Movement Research*. Eds. Bert Klandermans and Suzanne Staggenborg. Minneapolis: University of Minnesota Press, 2002.

Sonenshein, Raphael. "The Dynamics of Biracial Coalitions: Crossover Politics in Los Angeles." *Western Political Quarterly*. Vol. 42, No. 2, 1989.

Soss, Joe, Richard Fording, and Sanford Schram. *Disciplining the Poor: Neoliberal Paternalism and the Persistent Power of Race*. University of Chicago Press, 2011.

Soule, Sarah. "Diffusion Processes Within and Across Movements." *Blackwell Companion to Social Movements*. Eds. David Snow, Sarah Soule, and Hanspeter Kriesi. Malden: Blackwell Press, 2004.

Soule, Sarah and Susan Olzak. "When Do Movements Matter? The Politics of Contingency and the Equal Rights Amendment." *American Sociological Review*. Vol. 69, No. 4, 2004.

Souza Alves and Jose Claudio. "Immigrant Regime of Production: The State, Political Mobilization, and Religious and Business Networks among Brazilians in South Florida." *A Place to Be*. Eds. Philip Williams, Timothy Steigenga, and Manuel Vasquez. New Brunswick: Rutgers University Press, 2009.

Spilerman, Seymour. "Structural Characteristics of Cities and the Severity of Racial Disorders." *ASR*, Vol. 41, No. 5, Oct. 1976.

Staggenborg, Suzanne. "Coalition Work in the Pro-Choice Movement: Organizational and Environmental Opportunities and Obstacles." *Social Problems*. Vol. 33, No. 5, 1986.

Steigenga, Timothy and Philip Williams. "Transnationalism and Collective Action Among Guatemalan and Mexican Immigrants in Two Florida Communities." *A Place to Be*. Eds. Philip Williams, Timothy Steigenga, and Manuel Vasquez. New Brunswick: Rutgers University Press, 2009.

Stokes, Atiya Kai. "Latino Group Consciousness and Political Participation." *American Politics Research*. Vol. 31, 2003.

Suro, Roberto and Gabriel Escobar. "2006 National Survey of Latinos: The Immigration Debate." *Pew Hispanic Center*, 2006.

Suro, Roberto, Jill Wilson, and Audrey Singer. "Immigration and Poverty in America's Suburbs." Metropolitan Policy Program at Brookings. Brookings Institute, August 2011.

Takaki, Ronald. *A Different Mirror: A History of Multicultural America*. Boston: Little, Brown & Co., 1994.

Tarrow, Sydney. *Power in Movement: Social Movements and Contentious Politics*. 2nd Edition. Cambridge University Press, 1998.

Tarrow, Sydney. *Power in Movement: Social Movements and Contentious Politics.* 3rd Edition. Cambridge University Press, 2011.

Tattersall, Amanda. *Power in Coalition: Strategies for Strong Unions and Social Change.* Ithaca: Cornell University Press, 2010.

Teixeira, Carlos. "Community Resources and Opportunities in Ethnic Economies: A Case Study of Portuguese and Black Entrepreneurs in Toronto." *Urban Studies.* Vol. 38, No. 11, 2001.

Telles, Edward and Vilma Ortiz. *Generation of Exclusion: Mexican Americans, Assimilation, and Race.* New York: Russell Sage, 2009.

Terriquez, Veronica. "Intersectional Mobilization, Social Movement Spillover, and Queer Youth Leadership in the Immigrant Rights Movement." *Social Problems.* Vol. 62, No. 3, pp. 343–362, 2015.

Tichenor, Daniel. *Dividing Lines: The Politics of Immigration Control in America.* Princeton University Press, 2002.

Tilly, Charles. "From Interactions to Outcomes in Social Movements." *How Social Movements Matter.* Minneapolis: University of Minnesota Press, 1999.

Tilly, Charles and Sidney Tarrow. *Contentious Politics.* London: Paradigm, 2006.

Tilly, Charles and Sidney Tarrow. *Contentious Politics.* Second Edition. London: Paradigm, 2015.

Torres, Andres and Jose E. Velazquez. *The Puerto Rican Movement: Voices from the Diaspora.* Philadelphia: Temple University Press, 1998.

Torres, Rodolfo and George Katsiaficas. Eds. *Latino Social Movements: Historical and Theoretical Perspectives.* New York: Routledge, 1999.

Tracy, Sarah. *Qualitative Research Methods: Collective Evidence, Crafting Analysis, and Communicating Impact.* Malden: Wiley-Blackwell, 2013.

Tsao, Fred. "Building Coalitions for Immigrant Power." *Immigrant Rights in the Shadows of Citizenship.* Ed. Rachel Ida Buff. New York University Press, 2008.

Turner, Lowell and Richard Hurd. "Building Social Movement Unionism: The Transformation of the American Labor Movement." *Rekindling the Movement: Labor's Quest for Relevance in the 21st Century.* Ed. Lowell Turner, Harry C. Katz, and Richard W. Hurd. Ithaca: ILR Press, 2001.

Twine, France Winddance and Jonathan Warren. Eds. *Racing Research, Researching Race: Methodological Dilemmas in Critical Race Studies.* New York University Press, 2000.

United States Conference of Catholic Bishops (USCCB). "Cardinal Mahoney Launches Immigrant Justice Campaign in Los Angeles." http://www.nccbuscc.org/mrs/cardinalmahony.shtml. 2006.

Vaca, Nicolas. *The Presumed Alliance: The Unspoken Conflict Between Latinos and Blacks and What it Means for America.* New York: HarperCollins, 2004.

Valdez, Zulema. "Political Participation Among Latinos in the United States: The Effect of Group Identity and Consciousness." *Social Science Quarterly.* Vol. 92, No. 2, pp. 466–482, 2011.

Valentino, Nicholas, Vincent Hutchings, and Ismail White. "Cues that Matter: How Political Ads Prime Racial Attitudes During Campaigns." *APSR.* Vol. 96, No. 1. March 2002.

Valenzuela, Ali A. and Michelson, Melissa R.: Turnout, Status, and Identity: Mobilizing Latinos to Vote with Group Appeals (August 2, 2016). American Political Science Review, Forthcoming. Available at SSRN: https://ssrn.com/abstract=2818475.

Van Dyke, Nella. "Cross Movement Boundaries: Factors that Facilitate Coalition Protest by American College Students, 1930–1990." *Social Problems.* Vol. 50, No. 2, 2003.

Van Dyke, Nelle and Holly McCammon. Eds. *Strategic Alliances: Coalition Building and Social Movements.* Minneapolis: University of Minnesota Press, 2010.

Van Evera, Stephen. *Guide to Methods for Students of Political Science.* Ithaca: Cornell University Press, 1997.

Vargas, Edward, Gabriel Sanchez, and Juan Valdez. "Immigration Policies and Group Identity: How Immigrant Laws Affect Linked Fate among U.S. Latino Populations." *Journal of Race, Ethnicity, and Politics.* Vol. 2, Iss. 1, pp. 35–62, 2017.

Varsanyi, Monica. "City Ordinances as 'Immigration Policing by Proxy': Local Governments and the Regulation of Undocumented Day Laborers." *Taking Local Control Immigration Policy Activism in U.S. Cities and States.* Stanford University Press, 2010.

Vennesson, Pascal. "Case Studies and Process Tracing: Theories and Practices." *Approaches and Methodologies in the Social Sciences: A Pluralist Perspective.* Eds. Donatella Della Porta and Michael Keating. Cambridge University Press, 2008.

Verba, Sidney, Key Lehman Schlozman, and Henry E. Brady. *Voice and Equality: Civic Voluntarism in American Politics.* Cambridge: Harvard University Press, 1995.

Voss, Kim and Irene Bloemraad. Eds. *Rallying for Immigrant Rights.* Berkeley: University of California Press, 2011.

Wacquant, Loic. *Punishing the Poor: The Neoliberal Government of Social Insecurity.* Durham: Duke University Press, 2009.

Walker, Jack. *Mobilizing Interest Groups in America: Patrons, Professions, and Social Movements.* Ann Arbor: University of Michigan Press, 1991.

Wallace, Sophia. *Beyond Roll Call Voters: Latino Representation in the 108th-110th Sessions in the U.S. House of Representatives."* Cornell University, Government Department. Ph.D. dissertation, 2010.

Wallace, Sophia. "Papers Please: State-Level Anti-Immigrant Legislation in the Wake of Arizona's SB 1070." *Political Science Quarterly.* Vol. 129, Iss. 2, pp. 261–291, 2014.

Wallace, Sophia, Chris Zepeda-Millán, and Michael Jones-Correa. "Spatial and Temporal Proximity: Examining the Effects of Protests on Political Attitudes." *American Journal of Political Science.* Vol. 58, No. 2, pp. 433–448, April 2014.

Walters, William. "Deportation, Expulsion, and the International Police of Aliens." *Deportation Regime: Sovereignty, Space, and the Freedom of Movement.* Eds. Nicholas De Genova and Nathalie Peutz. Durham: Duke University Press, 2010.

Warikoo, Niraj. "Immigrants' Firing Leads to Protest." *Detroit Free Press*. April 11, 2006.

Warren, Carol and Tracy Xavia Karner. *Discovering Qualitative Methods: Field Research, Interviews, and Analysis*. 2nd Edition. New York: Oxford University Press, 2010.

Watanabe, Teresa. "Immigrants Gain the Pulpit." *Los Angeles Times*. March 1, 2006.

Watanabe, Teresa. "Latino Groups Unite to Launch $5-Million Voter Registration Drive." *Los Angeles Times*. July 19, 2008.

Watanabe, Teresa and Hector Becerra. "500,000 Pack L.A. Streets to Protest Immigration Bills." *Los Angeles Times*. March 26, 2006a.

Watanabe, Teresa and Hector Becerra. "How DJs Put 500,000 Marchers in Motion." *Los Angeles Times*. March 28, 2006b.

Wayne, Alex. "House Panel Approves Legislation Aimed at Illegal Immigration." *CQ Weekly Online*. December 12, 2005.

Wayne, Alex. "2005 Legislative Summary: Immigration/Border Security Overhaul." *CQ Weekly Online*. January 2, 2006.

Wei, William. *The Asian American Movement*. Philadelphia: Temple University Press, 1993.

Weiss, Robert. *Learning From Strangers: The Art and Method of Qualitative Interview Studies*. New York: Free Press, 1994.

Welch, Michael. *Detained: Immigration Laws and the Expanding I.N.S. Jail Complex*. Philadelphia: Temple University Press, 1996.

Wessler, Seth. "How Immigration Reform Got Caught in the Deportation Dragnet." *Colorlines*. Thursday, October 7, 2010. http://colorlines.com/archives/2010/10/how_immigration_reform_got_caught_in_the_deportation_dragnet.html

Williams, Juliet. "Schwarzenegger Says Immigration Debate Has Prompted Threats." *Los Angeles Times*. April 24, 2006.

Wisler, Dominique and Marco Giugni. "Under the Spotlight: The Impact of Media Attention on Protest Policing." *Mobilization*. Vol. 4, No. 2, 1999.

Wong, Carolyn. *Lobbying for Inclusion: Rights Politics and the Making of Immigration Policy*. Stanford University Press, 2006.

Wong, Janelle. *Democracy's Promise: Immigrants & American Civic Institutions*. Ann Arbor: University of Michigan Press, 2006.

Wong, Tom. *Rights, Deportation, and Detention in the Age of Immigration Control*. Stanford University Press, 2015.

Wong, Tom. *The Politics of Immigration: Partisanship, Demographic Change, and American National Identity*. New York: Oxford University Press, 2017.

Woods, Casey. "Opposing an 'Invasion': Membership in Anti-Illegal Immigration Groups Grows in Florida as Debate on U.S. Policy Continues to Simmer." *Miami Herald*. March 31, 2008.

Ybarra, Vickie, Melina Juarez, and Gabriel Sanchez. "Do Perceptions Match Reality? Analysis of Latinos' Perceived Views of State Immigration Policy Environment Compared to Enacted Policies." Paper presented at the Western Political Science Association 2016 Annual Meeting. San Diego, CA, March 23–27, 2016.

Young, Deborah, Rob Hart, and Glenn Nyback. "Immigrants Fill The Streets in Massive Show of Clout." *Staten Island Advance*. May 2, 2006.

Yin, Robert. *Case Study Research: Design and Methods*. 5th Edition. Thousand Oaks: Sage, 2014.

Zald, Mayer. "Culture, Ideology, and Strategic Framing." *Comparative Perspectives on Social Movements*. Eds. Doug McAdam, John McCarthy, and Mayer Zald. New York: Cambridge University Press, 1996.

Zald, Mayer and John McCarthy. *Social Movements in an Organizational Society*. New Brunswick: Transaction Books, 1987.

Zaller, John. *The Nature and Origins of Mass Opinion*. New York: Cambridge University Press, 1992.

Zepeda-Millán, Chris. "Perceptions of Threat, Demographic Diversity, and the Framing of Illegal-ity: Explaining (Non) Participation in New York's 2006 Immigrant Protests." *Political Research Quarterly*, Vol. 67, No. 4, pp. 880–888, 2014.

Zepeda-Millán, Chris. "Weapons of the (Not So) Weak: Immigrant Mass Mobilization in the U.S. South." *Critical Sociology*. Vol. 42, Iss. 2, 2016.

Zepeda-Millán, Chris and Sophia Wallace. "Racialization in Times of Contention: How Social Movements Influence Latino Racial Identity." *Politics, Groups, Identities*. Vol. 1, No. 3, pp. 510–527, 2013.

Zepeda-Millán, Chris, Alex Street, and Michael Jones-Correa. "Latino Racialization: Illegality, Linked Fate, and American Identity." Paper presented at the annual meeting of the American Political Science Association, San Francisco, CA, September 3–6, 2015.

Zimmerman, Arely. "Transmedia Testimonio: Examining Undocumented Youth's Political Activism in the Digital Age." *International Journal of Communication*. Vol. 10, 2016.

Zolberg, Aristide. *A Nation by Design: Immigration Policy in the Fashioning of America*. Cambridge: Harvard University Press, 2006.

Zuniga, Victor and Ruben Hernandez-Leon. Eds. *New Destinations: Mexican Immigration in the United States*. New York: Russell Sage Foundation, 2005.

Index